$14 -

780.92
CHI

EVERYBODY DANCE

Chic and The Politics of Disco

D1150952

First edition published in 2004 by Helter Skelter Publishing
South Bank House, Black Prince Road, London SE1 7SJ

Copyright 2004 © Daryl Easlea

All rights reserved
Cover design by Chris Wilson
Typesetting by Caroline Walker
Printed in Great Britain by CPI, Bath

This book is sold subject to the condition that it shall not, by way of trade or
otherwise, be lent, resold, hired out or otherwise circulated without the
publisher's prior consent in any form of binding or cover other than that in
which it is published and without a similar condition including this condition
being imposed on the subsequent purchase.

A CIP record for this book is available from the British Library

ISBN 1-900924-56-0

CITY AND ISLINGTON
SIXTH FORM COLLEGE
283 - 309 GOSWELL ROAD
LONDON
EC1
TEL 020 7520 0652

£14.00

SFC12977
780.92 CHI

EVERYBODY DANCE

Chic and The Politics of Disco

by Daryl Easlea

Helter Skelter Publishing

ABOUT THE AUTHOR

Daryl Easlea was in music retail between 1979 and 1997. He left to belatedly take his degree in American History and International History at Keele, where he also ran the student radio station. After graduating in 2000, he became the deputy editor at *Record Collector* Magazine, where he remains a regular contributor. His work has also appeared in *Mojo, Mojo Collections*, various *Q* and *Mojo* specials, *The Guardian, Uncut, Socialism, The Encyclopaedia of Popular Music* and *BBCi*. He also compiles and annotates CDs, DJs, broadcasts and was born to dance.

He lives with his darling Jules in London Town.

He could have sat under a Bodhi tree
But Bernard played the bass,
And you don't get piles from dancing
Your way to a higher state of grace

Siôn Hamilton 2003

CONTENTS

AUTHOR'S NOTE AND ACKNOWLEDGMENTS

ALERT: Yet another upper-working class white boy from Britain writes about a group and phenomena that occurred in another country when he was only 12.

I always believed for many years that the story of Chic needed to be chronicled in more than simply a chapter or a paragraph in a wider work. I knew from growing up in the 70s that there was simply something different about them; as I sprang around in Southend-On-Sea, possibly the only place where you could grow musically with prog, pop, punk, pub, rockabilly and jazz-funk living moderately harmoniously, Chic's look, manner and their remarkable music just marked them out as an enigmatic cut-above.

The book contextualises Chic in their time, while also assessing the power, subsequent collapse and rebirth of the disco movement. *However, it is not a history of disco.* There are countless books that explore this topic from Bill Brewster and Frank Broughton's exemplary *Last Night A DJ Saved My Life* to Tim Lawrence's well-written and thorough *Love Saves The Day: A History of American Dance Music Culture, 1970-1979.* The disco movement is secondary to the story of the group, who, through Nile Rodgers and Bernard Edwards, synthesised their influences into a discrete body of music that has subsequently influenced generations. For their production work alone, the duo need to be remembered.

Everybody Dance: Chic and the Politics of Disco grew out of an article I wrote pseudonymously for the now-defunct *Mojo Collections* in October 2001. I then made every attempt to contact everybody associated with the Chic circle. I have been very fortunate that in almost every instance, the ex-members of the group agreed to speak with me. Johnny Mathis remains the only person who declined my overture; certain people I decided early on that I would not contact, as their tale is on the record elsewhere. I was about to make arrangements to speak with Luther Vandross on the day the news of his stroke came through.

A SINCERE THANK YOU TO

Everybody who has been so giving of their time to agree to be interviewed for this project, especially Nile Rodgers, who gave as much as he could from his rather packed schedule, and once over his bemusement at me wanting to write a book on him and his group, was charming and supportive.

To the memory of Tony Thompson, who spoke with me three times in the months before his tragic death in November 2003. Although weak, his sense of fun and pride in what he had achieved was palpable. A big thank you to his widow, Patrice Jennings-Thompson, for her support and help at her most difficult time.

The help and address book of Nile Rodgers' unflappable and ever-droll personal assistant, Sooze Plunkett-Green (and her team) and both of the websites – nilerodgers.com and wearefamilyfoundation.org

I would like to thank everyone who agreed to be interviewed: especially, Karen Milne, who came to the project late and, through her dairies and pocket books provided an accurate and detailed record of Chic on the road; Raymond Jones for his wit and leads; Alfa Anderson for sharing her tremendous inner calm; Luci Martin for her humour; Fonzi Thornton for being the only person in the story who *everybody* had a kind word about; Robbie Dupree for his lovely line in self-depreciation; Bernard Edwards Jr; Rob Sabino and Eddie Martinez.

The British gentlemen: David Bowie, Bryan Ferry, Martin Fry, John Taylor.

Thanks, also, to Patric Nilsson a.k.a. Pocat (Stockholm/Sweden), webmaster of the superlative Chic tribute website. A committed fan's eye view without ever going too far over the top, *www.chic-tribute.com* is the only place you can easily see moving images of the group. His associate and contributor, Glen Russell, for his memorabilia and being the only other person apart from myself who uses the word 'dude' quite so much. Also, sincere thanks for the resource their site provided in terms of gathering together some of the more obscure production chronologies. And also, the help I received from the French website, Frenchy, So Chic: *www.c-chic.com*

There for me before and there for me long after: JC, Spoffy and the Millers, Serena Abbott, Graham James Brown, Wendy Brown, Nathan and Katy; Johnny 'Jazz-Mags' Suckling, Kevin Simpson, Siôn Hamilton, Nancy Wallace, Phillip D.H. Short, Lorcan Devine, Bernice Owen, Alan Taylor, Chrissie Absalom, The Norfolk Absalom massive, Ian Burfield and Paul Hart Wilden – sweet re-emergence; Andrew and Ronnie Branch – good luck for their upcoming twig; Pavling, Matt Cobb, Quendreda Geuter; Robine Laureston, Bod and Mary; Mark Wood; Phil Savill, Mark, Leona and smalls; Sheena and Bob MacDonald; Val Jennings; Simon Dornan, Saskia Kitchen, Lillie and Maisie; Katrina Codman, Val Cutts, the Kube massive (to Pete Cunnane, Selvy Emmanuel, Ben Harrington, Larry Mann, Geoff Jein and Richard Stanley especially) and, last but not least, the greatest living English people: the ever-loving Wolstanton Cultural Quarter: Barry Pitts, Lisa Walmsley-Pitts, Mick Maslen, Fiona Dutton, Rob Ebrey, Jake Boyce, Audrey Ebrey, Megan, Perry, Laura, Patrick.

Patricia and Alan Byford for love and endless computer use.

Sylvia, Howard, Glenn, Craig, Justin, Natalie and all their respectives; Win, Gwyn, Liz, Ian, Kate and the memory of the wonderful Tom Clarke and Eryl

Batcock.

Dr Mary Ellison, Dr Oliver Harris, Dr Bobby Garson and Dr Patricia Clavin.

The support from my friends at Universal: Andy Street, Silvia Montello, Joe Black, Lisa McErlain, Clare 'GK' Skinner, Jayne Homer, Caroline Fisher, Caroline Allen-Coyle, Pete Hill, Ed Ruffett, Greg Turner and Paul 'Veitchy' Veitch, Alex MacNutt, Simon Marks, Deb Saunders, Mark Crossingham, James Bass, Jenita Rahman, Jo Cavanagh, Sue Stebbings, Jerome Ramsey, Jackie Joseph, Martin Nelson, Ali Webb, Bekkie Sunley, Simon King, Kevin Phelan, Sara Verrall and her squirrels, Liz Clarke, Tony Staniland, Emma Parrott, Zein Jalih, Sheenagh Seymour, Giancarlo Sciama, Simon Edwards, Mel Crowe, Karen Hayle, Sarah Phillips, Nick Hayward, Lex, Nick Smith, Sharon Johnston, Dave B and his lovely, chocolate providing wife.

Sarah Watson and Liam Vincent for help and laughs.

Grown-ups and friends at the business end: Rick Conrad, John De Mairo, Paul Lester, David Nathan, Brian Chin, Ahmet Ertegun, Johnny Chandler, David Hemingway, Tara Prayag, Steve Hammonds, Barney Hoskyns, Harry Weinger and Rob Owen, Phil Alexander, Sylvie Simmons, Peter Doggett, Mark Blake, Geoff Brown, the ever-lovely Lois Wilson, Penny Brignall, Colin Larkin, Roy Carr, Dez Parkes, Dave Henderson and Jacqui Pinto, John and Kate Aizlewood and all my friends at *Q*, *Mojo* and *Uncut*. The longest-serving record retailer in Britain (!?), Dave Lewis (www.tblweb.com) at Tight But Loose for his excellent Led Zeppelin input.

To my friends at *Record Collector*, past and present: Jack Kane, Jake Kennedy, Joel McIver, Alan Lewis, Andy Neill, Andy Davis, Sean O'Mahony, Pat Gilbert, John Reed, Val Coughlan, Brenda Cobb, Carol Czyher, Ian Gray, Janice Mayne and even Tim Jones.

Sincere thanks to Adam White and his amazing address book; Mark Hagen for *Top Of The Pops* information; Jessica Connor, Alan Edwards, Sarah Bedford, Nigel Reeve; to everybody who gave me an 'in', thank you so very much.

If I have forgotten anybody, in 98% of cases it's a genuine mistake and I'm really sorry. Let me buy you a drink and give you a hug.

Sean Body at Helter Skelter for being so very understanding.

And finally:
Alan Hodgson – because fundamentally, if you hadn't asked me that question in 1998, I wouldn't be doing this now.
Mark Paytress – for commissioning that initial Chic piece, unswerving support and that ever amusing take on things
If dedications are all I have and words are never enough – to my mum, dad, half-brother and nephew, Hazel, Edgar, Rodney and Deane Easlea – you'll never come back but you'll never go away.
Beyond everything,
Jules Patricia Easlea,
my darling girl.

A percentage of the profits from this book will be shared by The Tony Thompson Fund and the We Are Family Foundation

'We must adjust to changing times and still hold to unchanging principles.'

Jimmy Carter, Thursday 20th January 1977

'I don't know if I was in heaven or hell ... but it was WONDERFUL!'

Lillian Carter, after visiting Studio 54, 1977

'I always thought the world would love me for me dazzling them with my intellectualism – he thought the world would love us for making something that the world would hum along with.'

Nile Rodgers on working with Bernard Edwards
August 2001

'We'd laugh all day long then pick up our instruments and create some wonderful stuff, go back in, listen to it and then go – *holy fuck – did we just do that*!!'

Tony Thompson, October 2003

PREFACE
HAPPY MAN WITH A STYLE OF HIS OWN

THE BUDOKAN, TOKYO, JAPAN is a venue that has more than its fair share of popular music mythology. In August 1966, a frazzled and fading Beatles played a concert in this fabled Sumo wrestling arena, opening up the venue to the West like Admiral Matthew Perry had done 115 years previously to its parent country.

As a concert hall, it became enshrined in the world's consciousness with two albums from the late 70s – Bob Dylan and Cheap Trick both released records within months of each other in 1979 with the title *At The Budokan* – and these LPs, with their washed-out images of men in baseball caps and mascara meant an awful lot at the time and are still known to spark particularly fond memories for that period of western cultural imperialism. Given the unquestioning love Japanese audiences would bestow on their western heroes, if you were a popular group or artist of any standing, the Budokan simply had to be on your touring itinerary.

That Chic should have received the accolade of playing in this legendary hall to celebrate Nile Rodgers' career as a producer in April 1996 demonstrates that, 15 years after their creative peak, Chic were at last being welcomed on to the same stages as the fabled rock acts that had preceded them, and whose fans, at the time, had reacted so sniffily toward them.

The event in question was for a season called the Japan Tobacco Super Producers, and Chic, although by now only containing two of the original players from the classic 1977-1983 line-up, were the star guests. Those two players were guitarist and vocalist Nile Rodgers and bass player extraordinaire Bernard Edwards. Between them they had been responsible for over 50 hit records as artists and producers as well as countless gold and platinum discs. One of their songs, 'Le Freak', became the biggest selling single in the history of Atlantic Records.

Chic performed three concerts in Japan, one in Osaka and two at the Budokan, with the final show taped for a television special and what was to become Chic's *Live at the Budokan* CD. To commemorate Rodgers' production record, they had brought along a coterie of famous friends and guest players for the evening, including Guns N'Roses' guitarist, Saul Hudson, better known as Slash, Simon Le Bon and Stevie Winwood. Three quarters of their old production charges Sister Sledge – Joni, Debbie and Kim Sledge – were also on hand to provide a dose of sororial magic with their rendition of Rodgers and Edwards' greatest anthem, 'We Are Family'.

There was, however, one serious cloud on the horizon: Bernard Edwards was not well. Clearly not well. Edwards had always been a notorious limelight-shunner, preferring to be behind the scenes or at home with his family rather than indulging in the obvious high-life activities of his musical partner. Not that he hadn't in the past, but those days were over. He had been getting fit and had lost a considerable amount of weight. So, his subdued and distant behaviour in Tokyo that April didn't cause any immediate cause for alarm. On one night, Rodgers and Edwards were out in a nightclub doing a meet-and-greet for the great and the good from Japan Tobacco, the people who'd spent all this money bringing Chic all this way across the Pacific.

At the function, Edwards was passing out and falling asleep – but to Rodgers, this was simply the behaviour of the 'regular old 'Nard', bored to tears with all the trappings and commitments that his position brought. Edwards had been known to fall asleep at social occasions before, to the point where Rodgers had always believed that his dearest friend suffered from mild narcolepsy.

By the time of the final concert engagement, Edwards was really ill. It was increasingly apparent that he was suffering from pneumonia, but, true to his professional roots, he refused to cancel the performance. At the side of the Budokan stage, on the final night of the three Japanese concerts, Edwards reached for Rodgers and held his lifelong friend close and, fighting back tears said, 'man, we did it. This music is bigger than us'. Rodgers replied, ''what are you doing, coming up with this philosophical stuff for, Sophocles?' Edwards whispered back, 'the music has a life beyond us – it almost has nothing to do with you and me at all now'.

The gig itself absolutely smouldered. Playing as Chic in concert for the first time in six years, the hits-and-career-highlights-performance rocked. With extended intros, Slash wailing his once-so-prevalent axe throughout 'Le Freak'; Steve Winwood doing his best Jimi Hendrix on 'Stone Free' as a tribute to Rodgers' all-time hero and the Sledge trio once again injecting some gospel glamour into the angular veneers of Chic's groove. Rodgers' and Edwards' in-turns interlocking, supporting and duelling styles were present throughout, with Edwards still in his ever-present suit, while Rodgers now favoured his true Bohemian rock star dreads'n'threads approach.

Although the evening was a celebration of Rodgers as a producer, it was more about the friendship of the pair of them, at that point approaching its 25th year. In the extended work-out of 'Chic Cheer', conceived so many years previously as their rallying call, Rodgers introduces Edwards by saying, 'Now, this is my partner; not only my partner in music, but my partner in life. If it wasn't for him I would not be here in Tokyo tonight; on funky bass, Bernard Edwards'. Edwards returns the compliment 'Now, that young man over there …' After a brief pause, he continues, 'I'm a little sick tonight; I've got the Tokyo flu … But we're still here. This is my dearest friend in the world, we've been together since we were about seventeen years old and we're well into our 40s now. And we've been here a long time and I love him dearly … on guitar, Mr Nile Rodgers.'

After an emotionally charged show, the group returned to the Hotel New Otani. The rest of the touring party departed for America the following day. Edwards was too ill to travel and spent the day recuperating. Rodgers stayed behind as well.

Rodgers checked on his partner that night as he went out to eat. He asked him if he needed anything. Edwards assured his friend that everything would be fine.

'It's alright. I just need to sleep', Edwards whispered.

They were to be his final words. At 1:30 am on the morning of 18th April 1996, bassist, composer, producer, husband, friend and father, Bernard Edwards was officially pronounced dead.

And, as many would argue, with him, died the golden age of Chic.

INTRODUCTION
DANCING HELPS RELIEVE THE PAIN

chic /fi;k /> adj said of clothes, people, etc: appealingly elegant or fashionable. noun > stylishness; elegance• chicly adverb. 19c: French.

disco / 'dískou/ > noun (discos) 1 a DISCOTHEQUE. 2 a party with dancing to recorded music. 3 the mobile hi-fi and lighting equipment used for such a party. > suitable for, or designed for, discotheques. 1960s.

'If you think about it, the whole movement was run by women, gays and ethnics: Donna Summer, Gloria Gaynor, Grace Jones
... I mean, The Village People were revolutionary! People who would never even stand in a room with a gay person were dancing to "San Francisco", and that's what was so subversive about disco. It rewrote the book.'

Nile Rodgers, 1999

CHIC ARE ARGUABLY ONE of the most important groups of the late 20th century. Formed in 1977 and splitting initially in 1983, the New York-based dance act, were of their moment yet strangely timeless. They combined two of black America's classic musical traditions – close vocal harmonies and a watertight rhythm section – together with a huge sweep of the musical past. They then melded this fusion with white rock sensibilities. When you listen to other records of the same era, with their reliance on special effects and overproduction, Chic's music stands out. It's a very blank, repetitive sound, fastidiously but not fussily made. And, for little short of three years, they were one of Atlantic Records' biggest selling acts of all time.

Think Chic; think chic – an inextricable link to the stylish New York disco scene in the late 70s; Studio 54; hedonism; good times. Although now often reduced to two or three records played amid the glitterball-twirling on a suburban disco-retro night, Chic, musically and culturally, were clearly blocks ahead of everything else that was on offer. Even their choice of name was apposite: an African-American band modelled on two white bands (Roxy Music and Kiss), calling themselves 'Chic', located blackness as glamorous and sophisticated. Whereas in the 50s and 60s, it was the black and white of the Civil Rights movement and in the late 60s and early 70s, it was the threat of the Black Panthers; by 1977, blackness had become 'Chic' – colour as a statement that African-Americans are beautiful people. In their tuxedos and evening wear, Chic sent a clear declaration that they as African-Americans were not prepared to either dress or dumb down.

Chic presented a snapshot of American – and, indeed, global – culture at the close of the 70s, a period when economic and social hedonism was giving way to recessionary gloom. But critic Peter Shapiro hits several nails on the head when he suggests that 'art-rockers-at-heart', Chic were never simply about escape. While they undoubtedly enjoyed shaking their groove thing as much as any Peaches & Herb, they also recognised hedonism's limitations and foresaw its dangers, and more saliently, as 'The second best band of the 70s (after Parliament/Funkadelic)' knew how to present them to the widest audience cloaked fully in masking and irony.

Chic can now be viewed as The Beatles or Kraftwerk of the disco movement. Central to it, yet entirely removed from it, they led and they innovated and their influence pervades musical culture to the present day. Unlike other disco acts, they bore similarities to rock groups of the day. The casual white observer would see a recognisable line-up; albums were released on a major label and, in the era of the rising prominence of the synthesiser, the group produced a fantastically organic, functional sound. And there was more to this than met the ear: not only did their music sound magnificent on the dance floor, in the car or on the radio, but their lyrics coursed with deeper, often political meanings.

Chic were a prime influence on later British art-rock-new romanticism. New Romanticism held up the excesses of Studio 54 and sought to reproduce them and their fashions. The rough-hewn, scratchy guitar styling of Nile Rodgers and the economic, metronomic bass style of Bernard Edwards were slavishly copied by bands such as Spandau Ballet and Duran Duran, often without the original flair. Hip-hop may never have caught on so spectacularly had it not been for The Sugar Hill Gang's rerecording of 'Good Times' as 'Rapper's Delight'. Sure, the street-corner phenomenon would have gone overground at some point, but the fact it was on the back of one of the best known breaks in the world propelled it further, faster.

It's not that this innovation hasn't been noted: it simply hasn't been noted enough. Plaudits were not thick on the ground at the time, although critics have subsequently rushed to praise Chic. Alex Ogg argued in 1999 that Chic songs 'expanded rather than conformed to disco's musical agenda'; Dave Marsh states that 'rewriting Chic became almost as great a pastime of the late 70s as rewriting the Beatles was in the late 60s'; Nick Coleman stated in 1992, 'With their singular geometry of sound and sensibility, Chic redefined what was to be expected of dance music.' But *Rolling Stone* encapsulated onomatopoetically the very essence of their groove: 'back in the disco era, when most records went thump-thump-thump, the music produced by

Edwards and Rodgers went bumpity-bip-bop, bing-bang-boom', lifting it out of the ordinary to be something more enduring. But in mainstream opinion, there is still little difference between the sophistication of Chic and the tat'n'tinsel of Boney M.

At the core of Chic were Nile Rodgers and Bernard Edwards. The relationship between them, although musically short-lived, produced some of the greatest tunes in popular dance music. It was one of pop's great partnerships – Rodgers' hippie radicalism often jarring with Edwards' old-fashioned, straight-laced R&B style, but like John Lennon and Paul McCartney before them, that creative friction produced an incredibly exciting body of work. Robert Drake, the New York based engineer and DJ who gave them, as the Big Apple Band, an enormous early break, has little doubt: 'Chic truly are the Rodgers and Hammerstein of the 70s. Their music is classic and has staying power.'

Although it was not obvious, there were different agendas at work within the group at the time. Bernard Edwards, as someone schooled in the groove, was content not to mention social or political issues, while ex-Black Panther Nile Rodgers wanted to talk about a revolution. 'And these were two guys working on the exact same song!' recalls Rodgers. 'Our philosophies defined our personalities. I had my bohemian lifestyle and Bernard was the family man. Everything that was systematic about Bernard was exactly what my anarchy needed.' This systematic anarchy was reflected in a punishing schedule for the duo and an incredible work-rate that saw the band release seven albums and produce a further eight for other artists in the years 1977 – 1983.

Everybody Dance: Chic and the Politics Of Disco puts the rise and fall of Rodgers and Edwards, the emblematic disco duo and leaders of Chic at the heart of a changing landscape, taking in socio-political and cultural events such as the end of the Civil Rights struggle, the Black Panthers and the US oil crisis. There is dancing, up-tight artists, drugs and Muppets but, most importantly, an in-depth appraisal of a group whose legacy remains hugely underrated.

Dr Mary Ellison, Professor of African-American Studies at Keele University, recognises the power of the group: 'Chic have always produced music that gives evidence of communal joy in the face of adversity. The link with the Panthers references freedom and equality that are found in disco and that are quite specific to its polyrhythms, offsetting the sheer speed of the disco beat and reflecting the complex layering of life.'

The speed and complexity will be two recurring themes throughout the tale – the speed with which they worked and the complexity of the characters involved.

The story is set in a period of great musical and social change … and unbelievable possibilities. At the starting point, we find ourselves back at the creative hotbed of Greenwich Village at the tail end of the 60s. Where we finish, we find a music business changed beyond all recognition. The capitalism alluded to as Chic adopted business uniform for their stage and promotional outfits in 1977, has become dominant. Sales are in permanent decline and the business is marketing rather than product-led.

✰ ✰ ✰

While Rodgers and Edwards were constructing and living out their disco dream, the central period covered by the book (1969-1996) signifies the full stop to the innocence and optimism of post-Cold War America. It was a period of almost daily change: in the way lives were lived, how people consumed, even how wars were fought. Bastions of the establishment and the status quo were questioned, and the hopes and aspirations of millions of people who had never previously had a voice were now heard – though a great many of these voices were ignored. The post-war idyll of a safe and prosperous America, espoused by Dwight Eisenhower, was, by the end of this period, a distant memory. The 50s and 60s had been very clearly defined: in the 50s, everyone knew their place, but were beginning to question it; in the 60s, freedoms were being celebrated, liberation was being enjoyed and people's positions were being challenged. The 70s were not as easy a decade to define as industrial strife, political upheaval and a general discontent blurred all the boundaries.

As the 70s progressed, a sense of loss of direction crept in. Discontent towards Richard Nixon's presidency simmered in 1970 with student protests turning violent. Rioting was no longer something Middle America could portray solely as a race issue. Spiro Agnew responded by calling students 'parasites of passion', and intellectuals, 'an effete corps of impudent snobs'.

The American government were doing their utmost to control the voices that had begun to speak out in the 60s. The Black Panther movement, so momentarily terrifying to the white mainstream in the late 60s, had been contained with the FBI's Counter Intelligence (COINTELPRO) Operation. The inner-city rioting of the late 60s had also abated; but the scars of this period ran deep.

The war in Vietnam entered its final stages and then fizzled out in 1973. No substantial victory had been won and America's war debts were amassing. Suddenly America began to doubt itself. It was clear that no matter how much firepower and money the US possessed, they could not conquer a people with such dedicated resistance and hatred of imperialism. Even mass escapist, diversionary tactics such as the space race, and especially the series of moon landings, were over by the end of 1972. When Apollo 17 landed in December, the shutters finally came down on a three-year window of dreams.

Few things could be taken for granted. The OPEC oil embargo in 1973 flexed the Arab nation's muscles against American imperialism. Images of lines of cars forming to fill up with rationed petrol abounded. The hike in the price of oil would have huge ramifications on trade. Big questions started to be asked. In a world where the status quo had been maintained (in the US's favour, of course) for so long, how could America thus be brought to its knees?

But all of this was merely a trailer for the main feature: Watergate. The scandal that followed the cover-up of the burglary at the Democratic National Committee headquarters in Washington in June 1972 was exposed in full televised glory. It demonstrated the lies that the incumbent of the country's highest office was prepared to tell. Leadership at the highest level was exposed as corrupt, which in a famously patriarchal society, set a shameful example to the people. It has been argued that it was simply a case of a President only doing what Presidents had always done, but the sense of disbelief shared by the nation was palpable. And there was now a hungry, baying media ready to exploit, instead of shield, their fallibility. Yet, displaying the acute double standards of American political society, it was also a time when corrupt Presidents could receive 'full, free and absolute' pardons from their successors. On 8th September 1974, less than a month after his resignation, Richard Nixon was pardoned by his former Vice President, Gerald Ford. Ford was the first and only US President not to have been elected by the people. It was, to many observers, an America in disarray. With faith in the system failing, personal politics became more important. Self-betterment, material acquisition, and their ultimate bi-product, greed, were slowly but surely to permeate first American, then the whole of Western, society.

On a social level, the 60s and 70s were a period of unparalleled, often insidious change. The American 70s – like the British 80s – were, on many levels, the end of innocence: a series of small, unconnected events meant that daily lives, moving forward, would be different forever. It is often the routine and mundane that slip through any larger net, but then suddenly, huge, wholesale change has arrived. For example, quietly in 1972, the Universal Product Code, better known as the barcode, the first step towards product homogenisation on the path to corporate globalisation, was introduced. What had seemed so spontaneous, so ad hoc, and almost accidental before, was beginning to be defined, categorised, regulated, industrialised, commodified and exploited.

As popular culture is universally accepted as distraction, these grim and challenging times needed some form of counterweight. As a result, the theme of escape was prevalent in everyday entertainment. White morés took pop back two decades to the rock'n'roll days when there were certainties in life to cling to. Inspired initially by George Lucas' 1973 movie *American Graffiti*, the award-winning *Happy Days* TV series and the 1978 blockbuster *Grease*, the strong visual imagery of the era of the first mass teenage rebellion could now be replayed to the widest popular audience. It was all reproduced in bright colours with any residual edges of danger smoothed out. But there was also another overlooked significance: rock'n'roll was actually old enough to have a revival. This was one of the first times that this had happened in popular culture. Nostalgia was being mined by 40-year-olds reliving their teens.

African-American pop went back even further in the 70s. The string concerto washes, so typical of Kenny Gamble and Leon Huff's Philadelphia International Records or Gene Page and Barry White's love symphonies, sated the African-American appetite. Rather than plundering the 50s, these records evoked the era of the big orchestras favoured by Duke Ellington or Count Basie from several decades previously, which demonstrated an elegance and sophistication not synonymous with rock and roll.

So, a man had supposedly landed on the moon and significant advances had been made in the fields of feminism, sexual equality and, most importantly, Civil Rights. For every dead leader or redundant figurehead, power had supposedly been passed to the people. However, just as Gamble and Huff asked, 'Now That We've Found Love (What Are We Going To With It?)', so it would seem that people were confused and at a loss to know what to do with their new found freedoms.

Momentarily, disco seemed to be the answer.

Dancing has long been seen as the ultimate expression of freedom. When you think of the many references to dancing, and show, within Chic's music – 'Everybody Dance', 'Dance Dance Dance (Yowsah, Yowsah, Yowsah)', 'My Feet Keep Dancing', 'He's The Greatest Dancer', 'Strike Up The Band' – it is geared to a popular view of dancing, as an expression of liberation. And dancing is still one of the most subversive and uncontrolled urges. When the first black-focussed movies came out, such as 20th Century Fox's first black talkie, *Hearts In Dixie*, in 1929, people dismissed them, saying that they were just full of singing and dancing – to which one of the country's most celebrated Afro-American novelists, Ralph Ellison, responded, '*yes, but did you see them sing, did you see them dance*" African-American dance rituals had long been seen as an area where supremacy over whites was assured. Although pop stars had been copying black movements for years, it was only during the explosion of disco that *everybody* started doing it.

Disco was the music that paraded the personal. It was about what you wore, how you wore it, how you danced it. It was all about you. For two, maybe three years, it was a phenomenon. There were no two ways about it. It rose from the gay bars on the seaboards of America, the factory towns of northern America, the French capital ('Chic' and 'discothèque' are two key words appropriated from the French language), and eventually, a London still trying to recover from the hedonistic spotlit-dappled days of the 60s. Disco was for many the musical equivalent of the smiley face and rainbow patches – a place where street-level escapism and optimism were being preached. It was initially emblematic of the freedoms granted and, in its earliest forms, a truly egalitarian, intoxicating force that united blacks, Hispanics, Jews and homosexuals. Because the main themes were about love and dancing, its potency and meanings were often lost. The late, venerated music writer, Lester Bangs, stated in his essay on Barry White, that disco's audience looked like 'Africa in a sportin' hat with a sprinkle seasoning of gays and white folk who were just plain weird – nut and bolt joiners off the factory line, lonely pubescent girls'. It was this very audience that was claiming a music as their own; to dance and to enjoy.

> *Dancing helps relieve the pain,*
> *Soothes your mind,*
> *Makes you happy again.*

What disco was to become was another matter entirely. By the time it had gone overground in the late 70s, everybody had a take on it – it was unlike other musical trends that had come and gone. There was something about disco that penetrated deep into the public psyche. And this was almost entirely down to one film: *Saturday Night Fever*. The misappropriation of the image of John Travolta strutting along as Tony Manero in *Saturday Night Fever* – itself a bleak, downbeat motion picture – served to reduce five years of musical growth into a mass-marketing cliché overnight. And so, in 1977, the year Elvis Presley died, the world got another smouldering, snake-hipped dancer in the shape of Travolta. Where Elvis had stultified under his declining health and full complement of chins, here he was on the *Louisiana Hayride* again, doing dances that could be seen in full, close-up glory. The king is dead, long live the king.

The Anglo-Australian former beat group, The Bee Gees, now sporting medallions, falsettoes and chest hair were featured heavily on the film's soundtrack and became the palatable vanilla figureheads for the music's passage into the mainstream. And made disco the butt of many jokes. In films like *Love At First Bite* and *Airplane!*, the disco floor, that ultimate space for joyful expressions of proletarian freedom, became simply an arena for parody. In rock music journalism, especially, it became common practice to reduce five whole years of a vibrant, enlightening dance movement into one beige suit.

There was money to be made by 'going disco'. The economic climate meant that acts like Kool & the Gang, once a greasy, sassy New Jersey street funk ensemble had been rendered neutral by the smooth grooves and production veneer of Eumir Deodato; Earth Wind And Fire, practically a Black Panther house band at the start of the decade – and soundtrackers of Melvin Van Peebles' groundbreaking proto-Blaxploitation flick, *Sweet Sweetback's Badasssss Song* – left the decade singing about a 'Boogie Wonderland'.

Disco music became reductive shorthand for all that encapsulated the other within music; black, gay, Hispanic, Jewish. And so, it became an easy target for Middle American prejudice. It would be easy to think of the anti-disco record burning activities led by DJ Steve Dahl at Chicago's Comiskey Park on July 1979 as the lightning finale to disco, but in reality it was only the start of a long, protracted passing. Like most cultural events, its ramifications are hard to calculate statistically. Disco carried on for at least a year, but times were changing. Chic's worldwide popularity peaked soon after disco officially sucked. They were seen as completely disco. They blazed onto the scene with 'Dance Dance Dance (Yowsah, Yowsah, Yowsah)' and appeared to espouse the life completely. In the public perception, there was no reference point for them outside disco. Thus, when disco passed, Chic were apparently over.

Like many trends and fads that have wide appeal, where disco ended was a long way away from where it began. By the start of the 80s the music was derided, discredited and broken. It was put to one side by the white rock establishment, as were Rodgers and Edwards as the band's main protagonists. However, the duo were determined to display their credentials and ran headlong into the arms of rock, producing every artist who wanted a splash of dance sensibility. In return, Rodgers and Edwards began to receive a degree of rock credibility.

Disco was the vehicle that Chic crashed in on, and no matter what it was meant to be, many understood it only as the caricature it became in the mainstream. Rodgers and Edwards' rise could be viewed – and let's not be too grand about this – as a Faustian pact with the mirrorball. All those riches came in for sure, realising what Rodgers stated to *Melody Maker* in 1979; 'When disco came in, it was like a gift from heaven. Discos gave us the perfect opportunity to realize our concept, because it wasn't about being black, white, male or female. Further, it would give us a chance to get into the mainstream. We wanted millions of dollars, Ferraris and planes – and this seemed the way to get them'. But what did not come alongside it for the players in Chic was the recognition and wide scale respect that Rodgers, however nonchalant, has always craved.

It was only much later that the smart inferences in the group's material was recognised and that the true significance of Rodgers' Black Panther past surfaced. *The Penguin Encyclopaedia of Popular Music* stated grandly, yet accurately, in 1989 that 'Chic's influence on both black and white music may be as great as that of Chuck Berry on the Rolling Stones'.

Chic really were that important. It couldn't be seen at the time because although everybody knew their records, no-one actually listened to them.

Everyone still knows their records.

Now it is time to *listen* to them.

1.
CAN'T KICK THIS FEELING WHEN IT HITS

'From these beginnings, it is natural that Nile would be the one to bridge
the gap between rock/funk and wistful ballroom romanticism.'
CHIC BIOGRAPHY 1979

THE AMERICA the future members of Chic were born into in the 1950s had both an outer and inner face. It was a cauldron of uncertainty and change, yet outwardly, it was almost impossible to notice. The world image of the country was one of a happy, smiling white suburbia.

In 1945, America had stood victorious. It had just successfully fought a war on two fronts and, by ending its period of isolationism, took its place as a superpower in world hegemony. Less than five years later, the United States had seen the advance of Communism in Eastern Europe and China, the Soviets develop their own atomic weaponry, and faced very real concerns regarding internal security. Wisconsin Senator Joseph McCarthy had sprung up to exploit the prevailing mood of fear and uncertainty with his activities with the House Unamerican Activities Committee. Yet in black inner cities, concerns were still more primal – concerns about basic rights and often, where the next meal was coming from, were paramount. For African-Americans, there had been little change; despite their central role in America's campaign in the Second World War, they were still marginalized and segregated, living in once prosperous areas that had become, simply put, ghettos. The South Bronx was one such area.

In 1950, social workers reported enduring poverty in a section of the southern Bronx. Systematic rent control had been introduced during the Second World War to prevent rents from skyrocketing as, due to the influx of residents, empty apartments became scarce; it soon prevented conscientious landlords from paying for repairs to their ageing buildings.

The South Bronx was where Beverly Goodman, Nile Rodgers' mother was to grow up. And on 19th September 1952, her son, 'Baby Boy Goodman' was born in neighbouring borough Queens' General Hospital.

In 1979, the official Chic biography opened up with the following statement: 'It has long been relegated to his subconscious, but the first music Nile Rodgers ever heard was in the rhythm of rubber thumping against the iron grating of the Triboro Bridge. The car was careening across the East River en route to Queens General Hospital, where Nile Rodgers' mother had an appointment to give birth. As usual, Nile was in a hurry, and before the car had touched dry land, the world had one more guitar player.'

This story was the creation of Rodgers' fertile imagination. 'In the early days of Chic, Bernard and I didn't have any money, we didn't have any team, it was just he and I thinking of stuff,' Rodgers stated. 'We knew we needed to have stories to tell.' Rodgers was the product of Goodman and a nomadic father, Nile Rodgers Senior. 'My mother was only 14 years old when she had me', Rodgers recalls. 'She had a whole plan of handing me over for adoption.' Although rarely discussed, it was commonplace in the black communities in the 50s for pregnant women simply to disappear, immediately before their pregnancy began to show. 'She'd come back and she'd be not pregnant – and no baby. It was a programme where I was going to be handed over right away. You cannot find a birth certificate for Nile Rodgers in New York City. There's just "Baby Boy Goodman".'

The Triboro Bridge story grew because Rodgers recalled tales told by his mother. Beverly Goodman fell pregnant at 13, after she had sex with Rodgers' father as a Christmas present. 'She was a virgin and got pregnant the first time,' Rodgers explains. 'She didn't tell her parents until March, when she was 14. The police arrested her and she became a Ward of Court. They put my mom in a home for wayward girls in mid-town Manhattan. Her most horrible memory of the whole experience was that she remembers one day winding up being the only passenger on a bus, going across the 59th Street Bridge, being treated like a criminal. It took her to Hollis, Queens, to another home for young women and that's where they kept her until she had me. When I was a young kid, I remember her telling me this story that she was going across this bridge and next thing, I was born. That's how it morphed into the 'born on the bridge' story – it was something I heard when I was young. My mom then told me that I wasn't actually born on the bridge. I said, "fuck it, let's stick with it – it looks good in print."'

'My mom didn't want me from day one. When New York City later toured Europe, I had to get a passport. I knew I was born in New York City, but there was no evidence of a Nile Rodgers. My mom didn't even put my dad's name on the birth certificate as father, because she didn't want my new family to trace me back to him.' The baby Nile' s mother duly handed him over for adoption.

'There was just supposed to be this thing that happened,' he says philosophically. 'And I would just become their kid, and that's it.' However, this situation was not to last long.

Given the contradictory phase adolescents pass through in their early teens, there was little wonder Rodgers' mother was confused, having the very real and significant issue of a dependent to consider. However, it became too much to bear. After a few weeks, her maternal instincts got the better of her. 'She went and collected me from this poor woman – she was an albino who couldn't have any children,' Rodgers remembers. It was a story that was to be oft-repeated in the Goodman household. 'I can picture the scene, because my mother has told me a thousand times, that this woman got on her hands and knees and held my mother's legs to keep her from taking her baby back. In those days, biological parents had ultimate rights. In that brief window of time, I had bonded with this woman as well. As a result, for my whole life, I've always felt disconnected from my family.' This dislocation has been present throughout his career: In 1986, Rodgers and his then-girlfriend and business partner, Nancy Huang, gave an interview to *New York Magazine*. 'Everybody adores Nile,' Huang stated. 'Apart from those relations of his. People are always springing up saying they were the first person to buy Nile a guitar'. Rodgers continued, 'People think your relationships change dramatically after you become popular. Mine haven't changed at all. I tell my family "I don't hear you guys complaining that my brother never calls." I didn't get that many calls from them before'.

Although Rodgers barely saw his father, the few times he did meet Nile Rodgers Senior, he realised that he was a deeply charismatic man who looked exactly like his son. 'My father was a professional musician. Which is what my mom says really attracted her to him; he was this cool young guy who was working with all these famous musicians. It sounded sexy to me as a young kid. Whatever he told me it was certainly an easy pill to swallow. He would say he used to play with the big Latin bands, just like on *I Love Lucy*. And so I grew up listening to artists such as Cal Tjader and Mongo Santamaria. It was part of the culture in New York City. I grew up fancying those guys.'

Meetings with his father, who was an alcoholic, were intermittent: 'I physically saw my father the amount of times you could count on your fingers, but they were all very important. I loved him and wanted to reach out to him and be something special.'

One of the final times Rodgers saw his father, later in the 60s, would continue to haunt him: 'I was out with my really cute girlfriend, Alannah, and we'd just come from the movies. We made a great couple. I was in the Black Panthers and my girlfriend's father is the head of the Jewish Zionist organisation, B'Nai Brith, which in those days was its exact polar opposite. We were totally in love – it was the absolute Romeo and Juliet situation. I could see this crowd gathering round a man in the gutter on Broadway and 94th Street. As I was this young activist who believed that he had to go and save the people, I went over. I realised it was my father, suffering from the DTs. It was the penultimate time I saw him alive. It was not a great time, but I didn't internalise it.' Nile Rodgers Sr was to die of sclerosis of the liver brought on by his alcoholism in his 30s, while Rodgers was still a teenager.

With his itinerant, alcoholic father and his young, inexperienced mother, Nile Rodgers was to have a traumatic and nomadic childhood, living from time to time with his mother and various other family members. It is fairly unusual for a son to remember most things about his mother's 21st birthday party. Beverly Goodman was to later find stability by marrying Robert Glanzrock, a Jewish New Yorker who worked in a clothing store. There was another factor that linked his birth parents and his step father: heroin. 'I believed that only children slept lying down and adults only slept standing up,' Rodgers recalls. 'When I would come home from school, all my mom and stepfather's friends were all nodding around the living room. They were all standing up asleep, with cigarettes dangling. I didn't realise they were all on heroin.'

But Glanzrock and Goodman were very much in love. 'My mother found spiritual stability with my step-father,' Rodgers continues. 'I didn't have a steady life but she did; tumult was the norm for them – they lived a beatnik Bonnie and Clyde-like existence. They lived to support their habit – everything else was secondary – including kids and jobs – anything you could do to get drugs. She just adored him. It took a very long time for them to get divorced.'

Although Rodgers spent some time in California from the age of six with his maternal grandmother, the majority of his childhood was spent in and around New York; various neighbourhoods from the 14th Street and below and in the Bronx. From the notorious south – where the young John 'Jellybean' Benitez was also to grow up, all the way up to the semi-affluent Italian section, Pelham Parkway. 'All of this was the Nile Rodgers' neighbourhood', he laughs. Moving to Greenwich Village, his family fell in with a beatnik crowd.

'I never went to the same school for more than a couple of months until I could control my own destiny. When my grandmother passed away – who was one of my primary caretakers – I was 15 or 16, which was pretty much the first time I could say I'm going to stay at this school, regardless of where we move. It was tough. I was always the new kid in class; usually the only black kid in an all-white school, so music became my salvation.'

Music was indeed to become Rodgers' main interest. 'I was raised Roman Catholic, so I had that influence from my grandmother's side, but the real interesting thing about black culture was that although my grandmother was a devout Roman Catholic, the music she listened to was all southern Baptist – James Brown, the Original Five Blind Boys, all that hardcore southern groove. She didn't live in that world, but her family came from the West Indies and moved to New York; there was always that spiritual, voodoo-esque thing going on.' The rich variety of music Rodgers was exposed to was to shape his entire life. 'Occasionally you'd see Elvis – the first record I got was "Blue Suede Shoes" and my grandma gave me the shoes to go along with it. I was really little. I remember what I looked like and how small I was, so I have to assume it was pre-school.'

The phenomenon Elvis Presley caused was to mould and shape popular music as we know it. When he broke through in 1956, it was soon apparent that his was to be so much more than previous popular successes as radio, film and the nascent television service were all being brought together in tandem to market an artist. And, of course, he made real the marketing man's dream: taking black music and making it white. But it was to be The Godfather Of Soul, the incomparable James Brown, who was to leave the most indelible mark on the young Rodgers' psyche.

'James Brown changed my life. I was a kid who went to church and our services were in Latin; very peaceful and restrained and reserved at best. The first concert I ever saw was James Brown, with the cape and the spirit and all that – it was powerful stuff. I should have known even then that my path was chosen. I saw that TV programme *28Up*, which looked at these people every seven years of their life. If a person interviewing me now had seen me at seven, it would have been so clear that I would be the guy I am now. I just didn't know you could make a career out of music. I had heard music all my life, but I had never seen it, there was no visual image for it; so seeing James Brown, it really was like "Holy Cow".'

Bernard Edwards, entered the world a month and a half after Rodgers on 31st October 1952, in North Carolina, out in the sleepy suburb of Beaver Dam, part of Greenville, Pitt County. Greenville was named after General Nathanael Greene, the Revolutionary War hero. The town had begun to make its mark around the 1860s when there were several established riverboat lines on the Tar river, transporting passengers and goods. Cotton was the leading agricultural crop, and Greenville became a major cotton export centre. Before the turn of the century, however, tobacco surpassed cotton and became the leading money crop. Greenville became one of North Carolina's leading tobacco marketing and warehouse centres.

His father, Wilson, like many African-Americans of the era gained employment as a handyman. He was exceptionally good with his hands, an all-round Mr Fixit, while his mother, Mamie, was a homemaker. The family relocated to New York for work when Edwards was 10 years old. Turning their back on the small town life, the Edwards stayed in a building owned by the family in Manhattan.

There is still not a great deal of information regarding Bernard Edwards' childhood, as he simply would not talk about it. His eldest son, Bernard Jr, recalls: 'it seemed to be something he tried to avoid. I wish I knew why. My dad was just like everybody saw him in the world, a very private person, and if it was anything that was going to make him emotional, he would rather be quiet about it than to deal with it.' However, it seemed to be a far more peaceful, settled childhood than Rodgers.

Edwards had an enormous interest in music from the very beginning. He played reeds at his school, P.S. 164, on 77th Ave. in Flushing. He took up tenor sax in junior high and electric bass at the High School of Performing Arts. Edwards Jr has a theory about why his father took up the bass. 'My dad's first instrument was saxophone. He then taught himself how to play the bass on a broomstick. That was amazing – he was like a Prince, ahead of his time. The bass is part of the foundation, the driver in the band – and my dad was definitely a natural born leader. Any chance to be a part of the foundation, my dad would be all for that.' There was a more straightforward equation though, as Edwards himself explained to *Blues & Soul* in 1992: 'I actually started off as a sax player and the only reason I started playing the bass was because at the time I was playing the sax the Vietnam War was on and the bass player who was in the band got drafted.'

In 1954, the year the U.S. Supreme Court ruled unanimously that racial segregation in public schools violated the Fourteenth Amendment to the Constitution (*Brown v. Board of Education of Topeka*), the third component of the last great rhythm section was born. Tony Thompson was born on 15th November in Queens, New York, to a Trinidadian mother and an Antiguan father. He had a sister named Cookie and an adopted brother and sister, Alan and Lisa. 'My dad was a chef at Kennedy airport. That's what he wanted me to do,' Thompson recalled. 'He didn't understand why I would want to become a musician, because there were no other musicians in my family'. However, it was his maternal grandfather that slyly encouraged the rhythm in Thompson. He would bring out his guitar, bongos and congas in the school holidays. 'All the kids could participate. I used to be fascinated by that, which is how I began to get into the drums.'

However, Thompson could easily have become a priest. 'I went to Catholic School all my life and enjoyed it immensely, even though the nuns would hit me. I'd go home to my parents and complain. They would side with them!' Although he was an altar boy, his holy ambitions were to be short-lived.

'When I was in eighth grade, a Priest, Father Gallo befriended me. He took me to a monastery in Staten Island – I really enjoyed the whole thing. The only problem was that when we were supposed to be taking meditation walks in the beautiful grassy knolls behind the monastery, I brought my BB Daisy gun and I was killing birds. And I started to sneak into girls' rooms. It was really whack. I'm glad I went through that phase.'

Thompson, Rodgers and Edwards were of the generation that saw Malcolm X and Martin Luther King's activities writ large, but being so young, they were then more influenced by pop music. The real turning point for Thompson, like an entire generation of Americans, came on 9th February 1964 when The Beatles played on *The Ed Sullivan Show*. Twenty-one years later, *Newsweek* were to ponder the cultural significance of this momentous event. Assessing the manner in which the group had affected the lives of many and have an unrivalled place in the collective psyche; it stated, '*Where were you when Kennedy was shot?* is an interesting question. *Where were you when The Beatles played Ed Sullivan?* is not. Everybody was in the same place: in front of a TV.' Thompson was one of the 73,700,000 viewers rooted to the spot, watching in open-mouthed wonder at the show. 'We were having dinner in our apartment, and I saw The Beatles. It was the turning point for me. They affected me like you have no idea – I knew then and there that I wanted to become a musician. I was so into The Beatles – they were my gods.'

Appropriating the traditional business suit and tie, and with their collar length hair, The Beatles' image appeared to be either parodying the traditional British and American city gent, or an early reflection of how popular musicians would become the new generation of big business – an approach Chic themselves would later employ so dramatically. The Beatles' mixture of humour, sarcasm and humility signified a new beginning, especially when viewed against the creaky, establishment American, Ed Sullivan, all greasedback hair and stiff formality. The irony of the New World appearing as the old authority figure and the Old World invigorated as youthful and exuberant is there for all to see.

For a nine-year-old, these intricacies were all but lost. In the grim months following President Kennedy's November 1963 assassination, here was something funny, joyous, accessible and most importantly, copyable. 'I remember later going to see *A Hard Day's Night* in my neighbourhood theatre in Queens. I don't think I heard any dialogue because of all the screaming that was going on! I knew it was something I just had to be involved in, watching the impact musicians could have on the masses and the influence they could wield. From that moment on, I started banging away while listening to The Beatles and playing on the side of my mum's sofa.' And so, a drummer was in the making. As Thompson rushed home from school to play The Beatles on the radio on his father's big console stereo, even without drumsticks, the house would reverberate to his tapping. 'Anything I could grab, I used,' Thompson laughed.

The first record that Bernard Edwards' was to buy was 'She Loves You'.

Rodgers too, realised that playing an instrument would be a very good step forward. He moved back to New York after a spell in California in the early 60s. 'After my paternal grandmother passed away, I moved to New York City with her son, my uncle Demetrius.' Music started playing a role almost immediately. Even though his nomadic bi-coastal existence may not have been conducive to laying down real roots, at least his musical education was standardised. 'We had a uniform curriculum throughout the United States; New York and Los Angeles were intellectually on the same par – music, art, physical education, all of that sweet sexy stuff was the same, whatever school I went to, so I participated fully in the music classes. They would choose your position in the orchestra on what was lacking – so if I went to one school and they didn't have a tuba player, even though I had asthma, that would be my instrument. As all the kids were novices, you could fit in as it was all cacophonous anyway.'

It was at this point, Nile Rodgers, spending increasing amounts of time in Greenwich Village, really got involved in music. He briefly considered science as a way forward. He told Geoff Brown in 1979 that 'I was into thermonuclear hydrodynamics and stuff like that, physics, the whole thing. Then I got involved with the politics and started checking out the wars and how they were making the atom bombs and that sort of thing turned me off. I got this crazy attitude, I hated technology. A complete rebel. But all that became superfluous. When you get the musical thing inside you, it's amazing, everything else just goes away.' Although he could turn his hand to clarinet and flute, Rodgers, like so many before and after him, realised that if you really wanted to make an impact on the ladies, you needed to be able to play the guitar. It has been said that he took up guitar to impress the girl who lived next door, who was in a group.

'Demetrius' girlfriend had a son, who was a drummer,' Rodgers recalls. 'And he had a band. And in that band was this really cute girl.' The girl wanted neither a clarinettist nor a flautist. She was looking for a guitar player. In an attempt to impress her, and considering he had a basic musical knowledge, he picked up the guitar and played a horrible, discordant noise. She was less than thrilled that Rodgers couldn't play. Within eight weeks, he could. As with Thompson and Edwards, The Beatles were to have a key influence on Rodgers as well. He bought a Beatles songbook and learned how to play 'A Day In The Life'. He told Marc Taylor that 'Within two months of practising, I went back to audition for the band and I could play better than they did.'

As the decade progressed, Thompson's tastes got heavier. 'There was a lot of R&B in our house, but I was always into rock. Cream were my favourite band in the world. So were The Jimi Hendrix Experience. It was the best time ever. For 20 bucks, I could buy four or five albums and each one was a freaking masterpiece! I wish half of these musicians now could have witnessed the era of growing up and turning on the radio and hearing Cream's first albums, or The Who albums – masterpieces!'

As the end of the 60s approached, it was time for Rodgers, Edwards and Thompson to make a career for themselves. Thompson was the youngest of the three and in 1968, he got his first set of drums. 'It was a Telstar – I beat it up and played it for a week straight. I had this battle with my father, about playing music, which made me a kind of a loner. He didn't understand. I was so angry with him. But then, I finally got my first proper kit. It was a large bass drum, with big floor toms. I saw Carmine Appice play with Vanilla Fudge at Randall's Island. He had that kit …' Inspired by his heroes, Thompson began to practise relentlessly.

There was Edwards with his bass midtown, Thompson with his drums in the Bronx and Rodgers with his guitar in the Village. Elsewhere, characters that would all have a significant part to play in Chic's story were growing up across New York. Luther Vandross in the Johnson Projects in Harlem, who lived opposite Alfonso Thornton, nicknamed Fonzi by his mother. Robert Sabino, born in Columbia Presbyterian Hospital in Upper Manhattan, 7th April 1953, over in the Bronx; Luci Martin in Queens; Raymond Jones in Jamaica, Queens; Robert Drake in Manhattan.

The America they were growing up in may have been a troubled country, an uncertain giant, but it was about to witness the blossoming of youth and years of rebellion. And for a group of fourteen to sixteen-year-olds at this point in the Century, anything could have been possible.

2.
THE VILLAGE PEOPLE

'It was a heavy time with seminal, groovy people. There was no press kit; we were doing it by whatever we could get together. It was about having enough money to get to the next gig.'
ROBBIE DUPREE, August 2003

THE RAINBOW COLOURS of the late 60s were undoubtedly muted with deep sadness. The post 1968 Tet Offensive horror of the war in Vietnam, the failure of the promises of President Lyndon Baines Johnson's Great Society programme, the assassinations of Martin Luther King and Robert Kennedy, and the inner-city rioting ensured that it would be only the bohemian minority who could escape and agitate for change. It was in this tumultuous era that the young Nile Rodgers, with his head full of revolution and heart full of harmony, seriously embarked upon music.

And there was no place better in the late 1960s than New York's Greenwich Village to make his dreams happen. At this point, it was a musical wonderland, full of opportunity. The spontaneous way that music happened was about as far away as possible from the packaged, homogenised music industry of today. As Rodgers and Robbie Dupree, a singer from East New York, Brooklyn were to find out.

The Village had become the centre of American bohemian life from the turn of the 20th Century, housing those who sought escape from the conventional. Originally the setting of large country estates, by the 1790s, the estates were sold and divided into smaller lots. Row upon row of houses were built for a new class of tradesman and shop owners. Establishing itself along old estate boundaries, when Manhattan established its grid system, Greenwich Village was already marked out as outside and different. By the 1860s, the area was solidly middle class. During the period of mass immigration from Europe, in the 1880s and 1890s, Irish, Italians and Chinese immigrants moved into the district.

Several generations of American writers and artists have all gravitated to the Village. In the 19th century, it was Mark Twain, Edgar Allan Poe, Walt

Whitman and Henry James and, by the 1920s and 30s, it was Norman Rockwell and John Dos Passos. By the 1960s, it had become a magnet for beatniks and then hippies, to live and work among residents such as Bob Dylan, Peter, Paul and Mary, Dustin Hoffman and Mel Brooks.

Although there were those who believed that the scene had already peaked with the folk boom of the early 60s, with its myriad bars and clubs, it became the premier district in New York City to enjoy music: 'The streets were filled with possibilities,' Dupree recalls. 'You saw The Nazz, with a young Todd Rundgren, playing in Bleeker and MacDougall, The Flying Machine with James Taylor, The Lovin' Spoonful; Jake & The Magicians, Lothar & The Hand People; all these amazing people. Frank Zappa & The Mothers Of Invention had a steady gig at the tiny Garrick Theatre, where they had block-booked it for ages. Everywhere you walked, the people you saw on stage at the Fillmore were just hanging out, and I felt a lot like it must have been to rock'n'roll what Paris was in the 30s to jazz and art.'

Dupree, born Robert Dupuis in 1947, initially inspired by the street-corner doo-wop that he heard as a kid, had been in various bands when he hooked up with bass player John Acerno – who, later, under the name, Johnny Ace, would play for years with John Lee Hooker and Elvin Bishop. 'In those days, we were playing in all of the Mafia bars and places in Brooklyn. I came from where John Gotti's crew came from and the whole mob scene.' Dupree recalls. 'Our band, The Thompson Ferry Blues Band, wasn't doing well and we refused to play cover music. We only played what we wanted to play. Most of the places in those areas were unsophisticated and they only wanted Top 40 – we were fighting the grain. It was really tough.'

Dupree moved to the Village in 1969. 'It was just a lucky time to be there. I was in no way a mainstay – I was just a young guy, a tourist, coming through, trying to make my way. Being able to get our very first jobs in the Village made us feel closer to being a part of that time, not just a witness. John and I moved into the Albert Hotel on University Place. The first day I walked downstairs, Mike Bloomfield and Buddy Miles were in the lobby. I don't want to sound like I was star struck, but I was *extremely* star struck. There was a cool thing happening, not like it became in the 70s, where everything changed. In these days, it was psychedelics and pot-smoking, it wasn't a dangerous place. That's where you went to be somebody; there was Nashville, Los Angeles, Memphis and the corners of Bleeker and MacDougal.'

The musically precocious Rodgers was also delighted to be hanging out in the Village. 'All my life there have been these incredible incidents that happened and I didn't realise history was being made at the time. I was a hippy – I ran away from home and was involved in the whole downtown scene. I wasn't a star, I was a regular kid. I was there when Electric Lady Studios came together – I was there before when it was a nightclub called Generation.'

One character was to shape Rodgers musically throughout this period: James Marshall Hendrix. Hendrix, who spent most of his final year in New

York, had an apartment on 59 West 12th Street, in the Village. 'One night we were playing at this place called The Bitter End,' Rodgers remembers. 'There was this horrible snowstorm and we couldn't get home. I was living in the Bronx at the time. We were all stuck down town, the subways and trains weren't running. We pushed our gear through the snow and got it either to Ornette Coleman's, George Braith's or Calvin Hill's loft. In those days, drugs, fusion, jazz and rock all meshed. I met this guy called Lenny White and a drummer called Jimmy Molinari. Larry Young, the organist with the Tony Williams' Lifetime was there, as was Dave Holland, Chip White, Calvin Hill, me and my guitar player, Tom Murray, Jimi Hendrix and some other cats. This was a very spiritually cool, connected crowd – they were the pulse of 14th Street. We dropped acid and started jamming. It went on for hours and hours, and remember, acid hours were like years.' The freeform composition went unrecorded. 'The only thing I remember was someone saying at the end "did you record that?" and the answer was no! I can remember all of these people – when you think of that one day and now all of those people are dead – Jimi, Molinari, Larry Young. These people were from out of space.'

Rodgers was ready to form a band and he and close friend – close enough that he called him his cousin – Murray, known as 'Blast', responded to an advert in the *Village Voice*, placed by a drummer, a rich kid known only to the group's collective memory as 'Peter', to get together and jam. John Acerno saw the advert and also went to investigate. 'He went over to this rich kid who had a townhouse on Charles Street in the west Village,' Dupree says. 'Nile and Tom were at this jam. Johnny Ace went there to play bass with them and they all seemed to click. Johnny mentioned me to Nile, and he said, "well, bring him, along … and let's do it."'

The band, sometimes known as The Tom Murray Blues Band and later, New World Rising, played acid-fuelled folk-blues-rock around the village, gigging regularly at The Bitter End – Rodgers, Murray, Acerno, and their soon-to-be-famous lead singer, Dupree. Rodgers recalled that they were 'A very political, fusion-rock band. We wanted to be a more sophisticated version of Country Joe and the Fish – we jammed a lot of jazzy stuff.' When New World Rising got their new drummer, Gabriel DeSilva, things began to perk up.

The Village was a cornucopia of incident and surprise: Nile Rodgers was caught up in it all. 'I remember when Jeff Beck came into Generation and Jethro Tull were playing in the park and someone stole their amplifiers. I saw it all happen – I was there when Johnny Winter came to New York. I was hanging out, partying, dropping acid and all that sort of stuff.'

Every bar had its discrete clientele, Dupree enthused; 'The Tin Angel was where all the groupies like Cynthia Plastercaster hung out; The Kettle Of Fish, Café FeenJon; every one of these clubs had incredible art, music and people. I went to see Cream at The Café A Go Go in March 1968, a club on Bleeker Street that had maybe no more than 140 seats in it. They cancelled – instead they had Jimi Hendrix to play, who was brought over because Chas Chandler had something to do with them. You could see anything. Nile used to come with us to a place called Ungano's up on the west side. We were in there nights when Jack Bruce, Janis Joplin, partook in the most amazing jam sessions, after two in the morning. We had a photographer that used to cover us, a guy called John Bellisimo, he had a standard press pass, and we snuck under the wire with him, to all these incredible events.'

Rodgers also was not slow in embracing all the experiences the Village had to offer, and considering he began hanging there when he was only fifteen, he was precocious with it. The night of 3rd June 1968 was one such evening that went wrong. 'I went out one day with this girl, April, and met these military guys, who were on leave or had come back from Vietnam. We had all seen *Hair*. They had slipped hallucinogenic drugs in our drinks. If we'd known, we would have been fine, but we didn't and we freaked out, thinking we were having flashbacks or a very bad trip. I ran out of the house we were in, suffering from some kind of panic attack. They subsequently raped April, which I found out about later. In those days, we would have call boxes that would go directly to the police. I called them and they took me to a hospital. I'm there in the waiting room and I now believe I'm a lizard. I see lizards everywhere; and my skin begins changing into a reptilian pattern.'

To add to this karmic confusion, the ward doors flung open and a new patient was wheeled past at high speed. 'All of a sudden, everything changed and they wheel in Andy Warhol, who had just been shot by Valerie Solanas.' As all medical attention was shifted to the Pop Art guru's pressing needs, Rodgers felt somewhat hard done by. 'All I could think was power to the people, because I had been there first – I know he was famous, but first come, first served!'

But the radical was still a kid himself: 'I was really young – I kept thinking I was independent, but, like on that night, I used to call my mom and my aunt to come and pick me up. At that point I was living in Greenwich Village in a crash pad on Avenue C, but my mom was living in the Bronx. I was enrolled at the William Howard Taft High School up there; she came down and picked me up. I didn't think of myself as a high school student, I thought of myself as a person – I would run away and live on the streets.'

The young Rodgers was swept along by the tide of Black Nationalism that was flowing in the wake of events since 1965: Martin Luther King's assassination in April 1968; the inner-city strife that had been spilling out since the Watts riots and the fashionably defiant statement of athletes Tommie Smith and John Carlos, who gave the black power salute while on the winners' podium at the Mexico Olympics in October 1968. The dichotomy of blacks being contained in the streets of their own country compared to the sacrifices they were forced to make in Vietnam was being played out for all to see in the riots which swept through inner city America in the late 60s. Eldridge Cleaver's quotation: 'They are being asked to die for the system in Vietnam.

In Watts, they are killed by it' could not help but incite interest in the movement which sought to rectify the unjust balance within the inner cities.

The fuel that was added to the fire by King's assassination politicised the young Nile Rodgers. In 1968, at 16 years old, Rodgers became a Black Panther. Few groups within American History have been in turn romanticised and then vilified as were the Panthers. Founded in California in 1966 by Huey Newton and Bobby Seale, they began training as paramilitaries in Oakland for a Civil War against the institutionalised, racist police. However, the violent aspect of their programme was only ever a retaliatory measure and their remit was based on their ten-point plan, which drew countless thousands to it for its social aspects, which were as follows:

1: To determine the destiny of the Black community
2: To ensure full employment of the Black community
3: An end to the Capitalist robbery of the Black community
4: Decent Housing for the Black community
5: True education to be given to the Black community
6: All black men to be exempt from military service
7: An end to police brutality
8: Freedom for all black men held in jail
9: Black Juries
10: National destiny of African-American defined.

On a national level, the Panthers were widely seen as over by the late 60s. Huey Newton had been sentenced to a maximum of 15 years in prison for alleged involvement in a police shoot-out, which had happened in October 1967. He was kept in a cell measuring four-and-a-half feet wide by six feet long at Alameda County Jail in Oakland. As Tariq Ali was to note, 'A blitzkrieg of state repression was to decimate the new Black American leadership over the next few years: beatings, shootings, imprisonment – many of the best people will disappear in a hail of bullets.' But what this oppression, led by California governor Ronald Reagan, did was force the black communities together and awake the personal politics and galvanise young radicals like Nile Rodgers. The 'Free Huey' campaign became a key issue. Although The FBI COINTELPRO operation would ultimately discredit their leaders and the mainstream portrayal of them was as terrorists, the inner-city reality of the movement was frequently that of a helpful, supportive, community-focussed organisation. In white communities, the Panthers were demonised. The press portrayal of them was often no different in the wider black communities. 'The Black Panthers had this bad connotation,' Joni Sledge of Sister Sledge recalls. 'They were warmongers and into fighting – but we realised this wasn't true; they were really trying to stand up for equality.'

For Rodgers, the grass-roots support that the Panthers were to provide to the same oppressed areas of the inner city that he had grown up in, provided irresistible. 'I was a subsection leader of the lower Manhattan branch of the

New York Black Panther Party. I always thought that politics was going to be my life and career, and music was my hobby. I thought I was going to be a serious revolutionary à la Che Guevara.' Although he was a Panther leader, 'there was no big black community there,' Rodgers informed Antony Haden Guest in 1986. 'So ours was the most integrated section. Our section leader was an Indian. We had a guy who was Chinese, a guy who was Puerto Rican. The most interesting thing we did was to found a breakfast programme for grade-school children that actually worked. Everything the Black Panther party did was totally legal – which is why the cops couldn't shoot them. It was a contradiction – how could they let the NRA and the Ku Klux Klan walk around with guns, but not the Panthers. The KKK would go to courthouses with firearms all the time – it was normal protest in America. If you tried to take it away from them, the NRA and Charlton Heston would fuckin' bust yo' ass.'

Other acts in New York could not fail to be touched by the movement. 'Coming up out of Jersey City, we had the Panthers,' Robert Bell of Kool & The Gang, recalls. 'There would be different protests going on and the Nation of Islam was around, too. We would play for various different events – charities, fund-raisers, things of that nature – the Nation of Islam would have bazaars, a festival where you would have food and music and then you'd have teachings of the religion and that sort of thing. There were different other events that were around – the Martin Luther King movement. All these different movements that came out of the late 60s into the 70s.'

This period led to some of the greatest and most militant protest songs that popular music has ever seen. From Curtis Mayfield rocking the sweet soul edge with tunes like 'We Are A Winner', Sly & The Family Stone conflating the personal and the political with 'Thank You (Falettinme Be Mice Elf Agin)' and Charles Wright & The Watts 103rd Rhythm Band's 'Express Yourself'. Rodgers was gathering ideas by the minute.

Rodgers has stated that egos got in the way of making the sub-section a true success. The idealism of the mixed race Panthers jarred with his superiors. A run-in with his lieutenant meant that Rodgers hard associations with the Panthers were over by the turn of the decade.

However, this politicisation of Rodgers did not spread to all members of his band, a pattern that exists to this day. 'I was last on board,' Dupree recalls. 'It was real different for me. Coming from this street gang background, and then walking into a scene with Nile and Tom who were like radical black activist types on the verge of becoming Black Panthers and stuff – it was very eye-opening.'

Guitar player Eddie Martinez, Rodgers' oldest friend, came on to the scene at the tail end of the Panther days. The two met in the first year of junior high at the William Howard Taft School in the Bronx. 'We used to walk to school together,' Martinez recalls. 'We would listen to everybody from Albert King, to Hendrix to Led Zeppelin – the whole gamut from stone blues to heavy rock to fusion.'

The actual affiliation with the Panthers did not last long for Nile, but the spirit continued. Martinez really got friendly with him just afterwards. 'When I was hanging out with Nile, it was just after that phase for him. He was still political, though. I shared the politics of the day, but with us, it was more the politics of fashion. I think it was in vogue at the time.'

For Rodgers, the music scene was to prove the most potent in the late 60s and early 70s. 'I hung out at a little sandwich shop called Blimpy's on 11th St and 6th Avenue. All the big basketball courts were near there. The Waverly Theatre was there. We would see our best buddy, Velvert Turner, who was Jimi's friend. He was the superstar in our world. Everything he wore was a Jimi hand-me-down. When Velvert would walk in, the whole place lit up – he would talk like a cat, a little Jimi clone. It was wonderful for an eighteen-year-old to be one degree separated from Hendrix's world.'

People would later remember Rodgers as a permanent fixture at Blimpy's. Robert Plant and Jeff Beck both later recalled the eager, young afro'd musician who would be there whenever they passed through. 'It was a fantastic time,' Rodgers asserts. 'Back then we could do what we wanted – it wasn't news because everyone was doing it. And we were in such close proximity to history-making musicians and history-making events.'

Meanwhile, back in the band, after years in doo-wop and bar-room bands, Robbie Dupree felt that something magical was happening with New World Rising. 'When we finally joined together and started playing, I could feel the difference, I could feel that it was really happening. Tom Murray was probably one of the most outstanding guitar players that I ever heard in my entire life. He was a showman and a burning lead guitar player, with Nile supporting on rhythm. They had a thing together that was just amazing. To plug into that, as a singer and a blues harpist, with my good friend John, we felt that we were really unstoppable. We spent a great year, 69 into 70. Because we were from diverse areas – they were from the Bronx, which was a million miles away from Brooklyn in a lot of ways, I had never even been there. The gigs we had were quite wild. We played the P and R Bar in the Bronx, a really weird place with a transvestite that worked there who came up on the stage and danced. I think a lot of people at those gigs didn't know what to make of us. It was pretty deep for the time.'

New World Rising were a word-of-mouth, organic band. There was no marketing or publicity. It just sort of happened. Although they had a manager, Rodgers' half-brother, Gram Benskin, (*Benskin is closest to Rodgers in age. He has four half-brothers*), 'there was never a poster, flyer or a name on the drum head – everybody just got together and played,' Dupree remembers. 'It was a strange thing because it didn't follow any business pattern. The band went through a number of incarnations. The nucleus of the band was similar, but the focus changed. 'We were blues first,' Rodgers explained. 'Robbie was such a blues guy. When Gabriel came in, he lifted the quality of our whole band to the next level. A little white guy named Larry came through as well – he was an amazing musician. He had a Farfisa organ and a grey Volvo that matched. He was a real hippie. He looked so much older than us because he had a bald head and a huge beard. Yes, Gabe, Larry, John, Tom, Nile and Robbie – that sounds right – sounds like The Monkees. There was nothing properly recorded – I wouldn't even know where to find it.'

The young group were eager to play anywhere that would have them across New York City. This often took them to some less than salubrious establishments, a pattern that Rodgers, with his future cohorts Bernard Edwards and Tony Thompson would follow for the next seven years. 'One of the very first nights we went out to gig as a blues band, we went to the Gold Lounge on 124th Street in Harlem, exactly one block away from the Apollo,' Rodgers laughs. 'The night we auditioned for the job, we won the gig because of our sheer determination. There was a triple homicide and someone died on John's bass amp – and when the cops showed up they saw the three white guys in our band.'

White faces in Harlem at this point had become almost unthinkable as the rich white suburb had become an exclusively African-American area since an influx of southern blacks migrated north to find work after the First World War. The police looked surprised enough to see a band of teenagers in the middle of this milieu, but to spot Dupree, Acerno and DeSilva, they were simply aghast. The bravado of youth kicked in. 'It was the hardcore Harlem criminal type of club,' Rodgers continues. 'We went, "we're the band and we are performing here". It was amazing – we got the gig and played. We were thrilled to get paid, however small and dangerous it was.' This determination led to them being one of the most sought-after bands in the Village.

JOIN US AT

A Q U A R I U S

PRIVATE CLUB & DISCOTHEQUE
16 DELANCEY ST. (Bet. Bowery & Chrystie St.)
Open 9 p. m. till ? Every Thur. - Fri. - Sat - Sun. Nite
Phone 674-0417   (Dir.: Ind. 'F' Train to Delancey St.)

A Unique Club for people who like people, parties and privacy.

'We had a really cool gig at Aquarius, this pretty funky place in the Bowery,' Dupree recalls. 'This African dude, Armand, had opened up an after-hours club where the décor consisted of 10,000 automobile hubcaps. When the lights were on the whole thing was like stars, reflecting. Originally people came simply to hang out, smoke weed and have a drink – and then musicians who'd worked at clubs in the Village came to check the band out. You walked in and there were these hubcaps, some party lights and a linoleum dance floor, with a jukebox on the left. People would really get off on it. It was illegal as hell, but that's where we could really throw down. After all the years of playing, at that venue with that group of guys, I had decided that that was what I wanted to do for the rest of my life; it was that kind of an inspiration to me.'

Although nothing was properly recorded, the material was a mixture ranging from blues through to folk, with liberal doses of psychedelia: 'I remember we did a lot of shuffles and the standard blues repertoire, initially,' says Dupree. 'I know we did some instrumentals, but I don't recall a song list. We did "Just Drifting", by The Butterfield Blues Band.' They also were the first electric band to play Max's Kansas City, which had opened in December 1965 at 213 Park Avenue South between 17th and 18th, off Union Square. The club now has a fabled reputation as being, with CBGBs, the cradle of American punk rock. 'Before that, it was a folk place – it had no cabaret licence, which meant you couldn't have drums,' Rodgers recalls. 'We were the ones that gave *(owner)* Mickey Ruskin the idea that it was cool to have rock. It only happened because they wouldn't allow us to play at Unganos.' Initial concerns about the electric instruments were soon assuaged when it became obvious that New World Rising could bring at least 300 beer-buying fans with them.

Considering the heavy politics going on, Dupree experienced little racism. 'Nile and Tom were always preaching heavy anti-government shit. They had their Panther buttons on their wild clothes and Tom used to wear African dashikis. To support our gigs, I took a job in the daytime as a telephone installer for the New York Telephone Company. Because I looked like a freak at that time, they put me in Harlem as a telephone installer – they didn't want me in a respectable neighbourhood. And all the people on the street all suspected me of being a cop. Later, they used to call me *Serpico*. I was cool with the people because I was more concerned and I did a better job for them. I could see the poverty first hand, the way they were being dissed by the phone company and the way their phones were getting shut off. So slowly, after coming from a really racist neighbourhood, I was here and I was noticing things like all the babies had cotton in their ears. I never understood it, but it was so roaches didn't get in and give them infections. It really was the poorest of times. I was set straight by working in it in the daytime. When I went back at night to play, music had really given me a lot more understanding about people in a big way.'

Rodgers was as poor as he could be at this period. 'Nile comes from dirt poor life. When I hung out with him, his outfit was like bib-front overalls and sneakers and nappy hair and two different colour socks,' Dupree recalls. 'The guy was as poor as a church mouse. Although he wasn't schooled, he had this incredible intelligence. We also loved Nile and Tom's sense of humour together, they were always really cool with us. It was a beautiful time because music had brought together classes and races, it was a special thing – it wasn't segregated like it is again today. We really felt a brotherhood in that scene. John and I were as close as Tom and Nile; this fusion of people coming together – we had a good, common sense of humour; we knew where we were at business wise – we knew we weren't making it financially, but we were making it musically, which I attribute to the dynamic that Nile and Tom brought to the group.'

Amid all this, in August 1969, Nile Rodgers, by his own admission a 'really sickly, asthmatic, skinny kid,' hitchhiked his way to Max Yasgur's farm in upstate New York for the Woodstock festival. Woodstock, like only a handful of historical events, has become part of the cultural lexicon. It has been said that as Watergate is the codeword for a national crisis of confidence and Waterloo stands for ignominious defeat, Woodstock has become symbolic of late 60s youthful hedonism and excess.

It was here that Rodgers logged something for future reference.

'I wrote "We Are Family" at Woodstock. I heard this band called The Children Of God, and they were playing this song called "Do What You Want To Do". That riff stayed in my head my whole life, how cool those nine chords sounded going up chromatically. Martha Velez in that group was so gorgeous to me; she was an absolute knock-out. Martha's brother, Gerardo, who played in Woodstock that day with Hendrix, is now the percussionist in Chic – and even he didn't recognise that riff.' A decade later, Rodgers would incorporate that riff into one of his and Edwards' most enduring and durable songs.

The commerce and scale of Woodstock, (as Live Aid was later to replicate with a conscience in the mid-80s) was to ultimately change forever the way that music was marketed. The causal effect wouldn't be felt for a considerable time, but Woodstock signified the end of the golden era. 'Much later, I was up at this jazz joint, Mickell's, in Harlem,' Robbie Dupree recalls. 'And one night Bill Graham was there. We got talking and he said 'you know what happened? The Woodstock festival was the end of the Fillmore. Before that, I could call up anybody, any act big or small and they would play the Fillmore. After that event, everybody was afraid to play a small place in case they wouldn't get invited again to the big party. It was a real change. There was no such thing as a festival act before then.' Woodstock in all its peace and love glory was the start of the commoditisation of the hippie ethos.

By the turn of the 70s, the incarnation of New World Rising that could take on any club in New York was coming to a close. 'Shortly thereafter it broke up. John and I went to the Bronx and met Nile at his Aunt's house, on 224th Street. All the windows in the place were broken out and there was cardboard taped into the window-panes. I remember seeing it and thinking that this was hardcore poor – Nile was coming from a really rough place. Tom left the group to go on some radical thing in Harlem and changed his name to Muata.'

For Dupree, this signalled a change in direction. 'The whole scene precipitated me leaving New York City. When that band was over, it felt like a big defeat and eventually, I moved out of New York and went upstate to Woodstock and started over again. I hung out in the city a little bit longer to about '71 and then I travelled a bit and then I came back and moved out completely.'

Bernard Edwards, too, was ploughing his own furrow at this point, playing

Alto sax at Brooklyn's Erasmus High School. 'I was the black kid in the middle of a Jewish neighbourhood,' he recalled in 1985. 'So I heard different things, The Beatles, The Yardbirds, James Brown, Motown.' But it was James Jamerson, the cornerstone of The Funk Brothers, the house band at Motown that gave him his direction. 'I learned how to play by sitting home and listening to tunes like "How Sweet It Is" and trying to figure out every note he played. Then, I'd go onstage and throw those licks into other songs.'

Rodgers was happy to be around the Village, playing in bands, on the look out for opportunities. One such break came on the scorching hot day of 17th July 1970, when, through Rodgers' Panther connections, he and his friend Eddie Martinez went crewing for Hendrix. 'There was a festival at Downing Stadium on Randall's Island,' Martinez laughs. 'Somehow Nile and I managed to get on the stage crew – the sole purpose of which was to see Jimi. We slaved away all day just so we could stand on the side and see him. I was 10 or 15 feet away. It was amazing.' Rodgers continued to hang around and jam where possible with Hendrix.

Jimi Hendrix died in London the day before Nile Rodgers' 18th birthday. It's still the way Rodgers recalls the era, 'My cut-off is before Hendrix died or after Hendrix died.'

Hendrix's death in London on 18th September 1970 can be viewed as the moment that the 60s, and all it stood for, was finally over.

3.
FROM PANTHERS ... TO MUPPETS

"In walks this skinny guy with this big, big afro – it was Nile!"
FONZI THORNTON

NILE RODGERS was already a precocious talent, sitting in on classes at Juilliard and receiving guitar tuition from renowned jazz guitarist Ted Dunbar at the Manhattan School Of Music. He studied classical guitar, and was later to suggest that for a year and a half, he played only classical music. Although New World Rising was fizzling out, he was still jamming at any given moment. His next regular gig was even more cutting edge, yet few knew it at the time: in the touring version of the incredibly popular and radical children's television series, *Sesame Street*.

Founded by young television documentary maker Joan Ganz Cooney, *Sesame Street* acted as a perfect antidote to the troubled times of the early American 70s. It presented a fictionalised ghetto where amid the brownstones, all races seemed to co-exist perfectly. *Sesame Street* was revolutionary in its day, presenting a chaotic multiracial urban neighbourhood, comprising of adults, children and Jim Henson's Muppets. In the years since The *Brown Vs. The Board Of Education* ruling in 1954, it had been extensively theorised that putting urban education at the very top of the agenda would help improve race relations. Henson's otherworldly Muppets were a perfect signifier for this; they were often pastel-hued, and as David Serlin has argued, 'racially abstract' .

Serlin, in his essay *From Sesame Street To Schoolhouse Rock* suggests that it was one of the very first programmes to show black characters, via the Muppets, in a positive light. 'Roosevelt Franklin, an early Muppet character whose name played implicitly with the tradition of post-Emancipation black surnames, was clearly delineated as the programme's ghetto Muppet.' The show had an ear to the ground and this portrayal of beat poet Franklin, part Gil Scott-Heron and part Amiri Baraka was as formative for rap as anything. 'Same Sound Brown' ('Same Sound Brown was a rhymin' man/He would rhyme words faster than I bet you can') was one such example of Franklin's craft. To further underline the show's radical credentials, the Reverend Jesse Jackson appeared on the show in 1971 and first delivered his legendary speech/poem that has subsequently rung out at stadiums and political rallies, 'I Am Somebody'.

Sponsored by the letters W, S, E and the numbers two and three, *Sesame Street* was first broadcast on PBS in November 1969. The 60-minute show, quite rightly, adopted the view that the younger you were, the more open you would be to embracing the concept of racial equality. And there were giant birds; a green frog named Kermit who was an ace reporter; a green miserablist, Oscar, who resided in a trash can; a Count who liked to count and two possibly gay men, called Bert and Ernie, who lived together. Originally titled *The Farm and City, Dog and Kitty, Itty-Bitty, Nitty-Gritty, Little Kiddie Show, Sesame Street* had four original educational objectives; to teach children symbolic representation – learning numbers, counting, and shapes; Cognitive processes – to develop basic problem solving skills; Physical environment – discovering cycles that occur in nature and living things; and finally, and most importantly, Social environment – learning about cultural diversity, family, home and neighbourhood.

With psychedelic animation and acute parodies of rock, funk and soul tunes, it was an ideal gig for the young Rodgers. The ethos of the show informed the ostensibly caring and sharing nature of the times. It was through *Sesame Street* that Rodgers became acquainted with Luther Vandross: 'Luther is one of the most important people in my life, ' he says. 'He shared and gave freely; the record will never be as clear as it really should be as to what this guy gave to me early on. He was the star in our little group, clearly the guy most likely to succeed. How do you not hire this guy when he comes in singing like that? His talent was years ahead of us. When I first met him and his guitarist, Carlos Alomar, and their whole clique, these were the people who would win the talent shows and stuff like that. They were the young Turks who became the pros straight away as their talent was extraordinary.'

Vandross was one of the early stars of *Sesame Street*. His group, Listen My Brother, were featured on an early episode of the show, sitting on the stoops of Harlem singing 'Listen, my brother, listen'. This insert was frequently repeated. The group worked out of the Apollo Theater, arguably the most famous popular music venue in the world. There was a very hard connection with the Apollo and *Sesame Street*. Loretta Long, who played Susan was the wife of Peter Long, the manager of both the Apollo and Listen My Brother. So it became commonplace that there would be a free-flow of talent between the two African-American institutions.

Fonzi Thornton was another member of Listen My Brother who would have an enormous role to play in the Chic story. Growing up in East Harlem, he and Vandross were childhood best friends. 'His sister lived across the street from me in the projects, and a girl I knew at church was always saying that I should meet this guy, Luther, who she went to school with,' Thornton recalls. 'Luther and I have been friends forever – we got into the business together. Listen My Brother was myself, Luther, Carlos Alomar, Robyn Clark and Nat Adderely Jr (*who is now Vandross' manager*). We were all in that group together, a workshop at the Apollo – which consisted of ten singers and five musicians. There were five girl singers, five guy singers and a five-piece band. The first year we were invited on *Sesame Street* to sing a whole bunch of songs. During this time, the Civil Rights movement was in full swing. It was a topical revue and all the songs were original songs written by Edgar Kendricks – Eddie Kendricks' brother, like "Count To 20", "ABC".'

'In its way, *Sesame Street* was revolutionary,' Thornton recalls. 'To have Susan and Gordon (Matt Robinson), a black couple living on the street and outside their building was a little monster in the garbage can. Beside him, there was this big yellow bird, down the street there's a white man. Even though it was in a fantasy, it was like it was showing an integration model. It was teaching good values. We had a chance to go on and do these songs. Those performances would be inserted in the show for around three years. I had a big afro, walking on a wall and me and Luther wearing big afros running up the stairs.' And of course, it gave him an opportunity to work with Muppets. 'It was incredible being around the Muppets. Later, Miss Piggy turned up for the 25th anniversary of Chic. It was divine!'

The success of the show's musical interludes meant a touring version of the show was established. The Muppets would have to stay at home, but the songs and the spirit would go on. 'They hired me and two back-up singers to go on tour,' Thornton recalls. 'The first few weeks we did it, Carlos Alomar was with us, but then he quickly left to become the band leader for The Main Ingredient.' A replacement was needed, and fast. 'In walks this skinny guy with this big, big, big afro – and it was Nile.' The two became fast friends and for the summer of 1971, Rodgers, Thornton and bass player John Mooney became roommates. 'Nile and I became really tight. He was an amazing guitar player even then and he was a singer. We toured that entire summer.'

Rodgers recalls the happy times touring with Thornton and the cast: 'People got that live experience of the show. When we would do "Who Are The People In Your Neighbourhood", it was cool. We were doing a more spiritual thing. On TV, I felt it was almost corny when Big Bird and Oscar The Grouch came along. It worked – it was about music and the quality of the things – these were real shows. That's what the experience was before these great corporate shows. We gigged all over the world. Carlos and Luther had been there before and from that, they eventually moved over to work with David Bowie. It was Carlos and Luther first, then Fonzi and I came in. Fonzi stayed at *Sesame Street*, but the opportunity came to move over to the Apollo, which was a little better for me, because I didn't have to tour.'

✫ ✫ ✫

Eddie Martinez remembers hearing the bass being played out of a window for years up in the Bronx. It was only later he realised that it could only have been played by Bernard Edwards, who, by now, was picking up regular gigs around the New York circuit, where he would occasionally encounter Rodgers. However, it was not enough for Edwards to contemplate giving up his day job at the New York City Post Office, or his studies at the New York High School of the Performing Arts. While Nile laboured initially in the hippie scene, Bernard was hanging out on the other side of music's tracks; the R&B supper club end of things: New York was the place to be if funk and R&B were your thing. For the 18-year old Edwards, the city was full of possibilities.

Acts like Kool and the Gang were taking the City by storm. Based out in Jersey City, they would come across to play the clubs. 'At the turn of the 70s, it was very competitive. You still had live bands – dance funk was being played at places like the Cheetah, Leviticus,' Robert 'Kool' Bell remembers. 'Our peers were Willie Feaster and the Mighty Magnificents and Skip Sonny and Pace Brothers, who were two groups in one, singing and dancing and going the whole nine yards. They were the hottest guys around New York. They were tied in with Sylvia Robinson as session musicians, as well – they were the band playing behind Ray Goodman and Brown and the Moments.'

Sylvia and Joe Robinson's All-Platinum label was something of an all-conquering force within the New York soul community. And unlike Rodgers, who was drawn to acid-rock, blues and jazz, Bernard Edwards was much, much happier with this sweet soul. At the same time, the young Tony Thompson was playing around New York in his various group 'I had this whole thing from the local brothers – "Cream?", "Cream, who?", "Who the hell is Ginger Baker and why is his name written in Day-Glo on your pants?" I had this pair of pants – it had John Bonham on one leg, Ginger Baker on the other', Thompson laughed. 'I had some friends, Rory O'Brien and Billy Koehler, a bass player. Billy and I were always in the same band. Billy was bored with rock and roll and got into jazz and fusion – and then he picked up classical and then upright bass. I started to study with a guy called Norman Grossman from the New York Philharmonic and get into classical. I learned my instrument quickly and I tried to master it – I wasn't playing in some garage band. I was trying to keep up with my friend and mentor, Billy. I'd never really heard stuff like Miles Davis. I remember hearing Miles for the first time – and then Tony Williams, Dennis Chambers and Simon Phillips. You could never anticipate where Tony Williams was going to go – he was just on another planet. That's what I tried to emulate.'

The spectre of being drafted to Vietnam hung over all young American males in this era. There was a lottery draw held 5th August, 1971, which determined the order in which men born in 1952 were called to report for induction into the military. Both Rodgers and Edwards were eligible. Thompson, still only 16, was too young to be called. This lottery had been held annually since December 1969 at the Selective Service National

Headquarters in Washington, D.C. to determine the order of call for induction during the following calendar year. The system was a change from the previous 'oldest man first' method. For the first draw, registrants born between 1st January 1944 and 31st December, 1950, there were 366 blue plastic capsules containing birthdates, placed in a large glass container and drawn by hand to assign order-of-call numbers to all men within the 18-26 age range specified in US Selective Service law. The first capsule – drawn by Congressman Alexander Pirnie of the House Armed Services Committee – contained the date 14th September, so all men born on that date between 1944 and 1950 were assigned lottery number 1. The drawing continued until all days of the year had been paired with sequence numbers.

By 1971, the birth years had moved to 1946-1952. Fortunately, for Rodgers and Edwards, the highest lottery number called for this group was 95; all men assigned that lottery number or any lower number, and who were classified available for military service, were called to report for possible induction.

Rodgers' relief was palpable. 'The big black cloud hanging over my head was being drafted to go and fight in Vietnam. My birth date 19th September came up very late in the lottery system. Fortunately, I was number 255. Considering the others, I was very fortunate. I wasn't a draft dodger, my number was in the lottery system, but it just didn't come up. Some of my friends weren't so fortunate – they had to go or they left the country or they had affluent parents who were able to figure out ways to get them out. In my generation, we were all very independent and we didn't rely on anyone but ourselves – most of my friends were clever, they would go dressed up in women's clothing, acting like some kind of fanatic to get out of there.'

One thing is for sure, it made the 18-year-old even more politicised. 'I don't know anyone my age in New York who wasn't political. That's why when I see politicians of my age today, I think I don't know anyone like you – what country were you living in – when there's always someone saying "I went to Vietnam and I flew 30 missions" – really? Where were you from? That's just not what the world was. It aggrieves me when I see people repainting history. I would see one or two friends that we would see go off and join the military. It was terribly sad – these people were crying and they felt victimised. They felt like they were never coming home. People were drafted with a number like "4". It's scary when I hear people say they think we were not patriotic. We were the most patriotic, "in love with America" people that you could ever meet. The difference is that our concept of loving America means loving every American. I believed and still believe totally in freedom of choice and freedom of speech.'

The fear of the draft underscored the whole New York music scene. Kool and The Gang harboured exactly the same concerns. 'We too all worried about being drafted,' Robert Bell recalls. 'We had to sign up coming out of High School, because we had to have a draft card. We were blessed – I guess God had another destiny for us. A few of my friends did go, some didn't make it back, some of them came back crippled.'

With the threat of the draft being eliminated and the *Sesame Street* tour over, Rodgers was to take up residency at the Apollo, Harlem. And he and Edwards were formerly to make contact.

4.
LOSE MY NUMBER

"I actually think he hated me"
Nile Rodgers on Bernard Edwards

1972 WAS RE-ELECTION YEAR, and Richard Nixon was going all out to secure a second term of office. The hippie dream in the Village was cresting and a nascent, soulful, string-washed music, aiming straight for the feet, was being played in some of the hipper, underground establishments across America.

New York seemed full of opportunity. People flocked from across America and Europe to be there, but it was still a dangerous place. 'New York at the time was just coming out of the 60s mentality and it also seemed kind of divided,' Robert Drake, then a maintenance engineer for Atlantic Studios at 1690 Broadway, who was later to play a significant part in the Chic story, recalled. 'Many blacks and Latinos seemed angry because they were not getting a fair shake with anything. You couldn't get a cab to go to Harlem if you were black and didn't want to if you were white. The ghettos all seemed to be very hostile.'

Of course, if you had money, you were most welcome. One such incomer was Vicki Wickham, who after years of producing *Ready Steady Go* and looking after Dusty Springfield in the UK, came to New York. To her, it was the start of an enormous adventure. 'It seemed wonderful, fun, exciting and limitless in every way to me. Coming from London in the 60s, it was a continuation of the buzz I felt there. It especially appealed to me because the music scene was thriving. Nancy Lewis and I were running Kit Lambert & Chris Stamp's Track Records office. I had lunch every day with Kit at the very posh Russian Tea Room on 57th Street which just happened to be very near the office! By 4.30p.m., we would leave the telephone the restaurant had provided on the table behind and head back to the office, many vodkas and blinis later! They had signed Jimi Hendrix, Arthur Brown and in 1970, Patti LaBelle and the Bluebelles at my insistence.' From then on, Wickham became immersed in Labelle, which is what the group became known as. 'I wanted to cut all ties with their past. There would be no more singing old standards like "Over The Rainbow". This was a new decade, a new day and a new outlook. They morphed into three really strong, opinionated, trail blazing, feminist women. Three lead singers in one group with Patti as their captain.' Between the songs – The Who's 'Won't Get Fooled Again', Gil Scott-Heron's 'The Revolution Will Not Be Televised', Nina Simone's 'Four Women' and Nona Hendryx's 'Can I Speak to You Before You Go to Hollywood?', the clothes – the silver, the feathers and the chains – and the performance, they became larger than life and attracted a diverse audience.

Labelle were to be adopted as Edwards' and Rodgers' favourite band of the era. Tony Thompson would play briefly with them, as would guitarist Eddie Martinez.

After success with *Sesame Street* and an ever increasing book of contacts and catalogue of reminiscence, Nile Rodgers graduated to playing at The Apollo Theater. But firstly, he was to make contact with Bernard Edwards. So how did the main protagonists in our tale come together? How did the two men who, as Peter Shapiro has suggested, 'Distilled and updated Motown, James Brown, Stax and Miles Davis into the most lethal rhythmic attack of the last quarter century' meet and begin to share their incredible vision?

Although they had encountered each other several times on the New York circuit, the first real contact between Nile Rodgers and Bernard Edwards was, to put it mildly, hostile. Edwards had taken up a job at the New York City Post Office, on 33rd and 8th Streets, to support his music and his course at the New York High School of the Performing Arts. Working right next to him on the counter was Rodgers' then-girlfriend's mother. 'She knew what I played and knew I had something special – she was this cool, white chick who knew all the jazz musicians. Although she hadn't heard her new neighbour play, she could tell from his vibe that he was a monster', Rodgers recalls. She discussed the radical prodigy from the Bronx with Edwards. Being a player himself, he showed a modicum of interest. Enough, certainly, to pass on his telephone number to Rodgers. However, the meeting was not exactly written in the stars. Not yet. 'I think he actually hated me,' laughs Rodgers.

Edwards was already a man of few words. As Eddie Martinez, who was to know him well as the decade progressed, remembered, 'He was kind of economical. He could say so much with a single phrase.' Edwards was to become known for his straight talk – and he would leave people in little doubt that he wholeheartedly meant what he said.

Rodgers, the just-out-of-his teens hippie, was explaining to Edwards on the call about the band idea he had, with orchestration – and *everything*. 'I was like, here's what we're going to do, we're going to have oboe, and dulcimer and I'm going to sitar school now, so maybe every third song, we'll have some sitar,' Rodgers recalls. 'I can just imagine him looking at the telephone thinking, "who the fuck is this whacko?".'

After a little more of Rodgers' monologue, Edwards brought the conversation to a swift and brutal conclusion: 'Yo Brother, do you want to do me a favour?', he spat. Rodgers waited with some trepidation. 'Lose my number.' It was clear from his response, that Edwards, 'that arrogant son of a bitch', never wanted to talk to Rodgers again.

Rodgers was not short of people to play with, so his number was duly lost. By using his *Sesame Street* contacts, Rodgers graduated to playing at The Apollo. It was to be a wild and educational time. 'I was working in a bar one night for $15, and the next night I'm on stage at the Apollo with George Clinton and the whole band saying we're going to build a wall of amps, with roadies riveting this construction together. It really felt like we were in control of our community, making up the rules as we went along.'

The Apollo is forever enshrined, mentally and physically, as the premier stage of African-American music. The venue had been operational since the 30s – and had seen every major black showbusiness talent pass through. The 1963 release, *James Brown Live At The Apollo* is still seen as one of the most important popular music recordings of the 20th Century.

Robert 'Kool' Bell, too, remembers the Apollo with huge affection: 'The Apollo was simply the place to play. To get a chance to do amateur hour at the Apollo was a great accomplishment. If your act wasn't happening, you'd be highly embarrassed, because, boy, they would let you know. We played there with Willie & the Mighty Magnificents. They blew us away and sent us back to Jersey!!! We hadn't really established our show – Willie Feaster had choreography and uniforms.' You had to be on the top of your game to play the venue.

Fonzi Thornton, who was in the process of forming his own vocal trio, Fonzi, with Michelle Cobbs and Carol Sylvan, used to rehearse at the Apollo everyday after school. 'Peter Long used to allow us to come and see the shows – so we grew up watching James Brown, Aretha Franklin, Patti Labelle and The Bluebells. We were really truly kids.'

Bernard Edwards, too, was undeniably drawn by the pull of the place: he used to hang around the theatre in his spare time, he reminisced to Nick Coleman: 'The way these guys'd laugh and talk and play cards, and one guy'd walk in and he'd say *this* and another guy'd say *that,* and then they'd start playing. And that was another band formed. Man, you just *had to* be funky.'

Rodgers, the unconventional hippie from the Bronx was funky enough for the joint – but he needed discipline. If there had been any doubt that music was his future, Rodgers was now committed. He would play nightly with acts such as Screaming Jay Hawkins, Aretha Franklin, The Cadillacs, George Clinton's Funkadelic. Whatever the revue was, Rodgers was there to make sure either he could support the artist, who were often singers without bands, singers with a bandleader with charts or bigger bands that needed their recorded sound replicated.

'Almost every record had two or three guitar players on it. It was me, Eric Gale and several others. That's what the Apollo was about – helping achieve the levels of excellence that people who knew the records would expect.' It can easily be seen that Rodgers' later versatility was simply down to the variety of styles he would be expected to play there. 'When you're in the

Apollo house band, you run the gamut. They were the cool days.' And for the previously nomadic late-teenager, the Apollo family, which obviously, when combined with the *Sesame Street* crowd as well, meant that Rodgers now had a new family, was very reassuring for him.

It was understandable that Rodgers would develop professional friendships with the performers. 'Most acts were really nice. I didn't get knowledge and advice *per se*, as I was already in a professional unit, but the bandleaders and musicians proved an invaluable education. I wonder how musicians nowadays learn stuff like that, if you don't have the influence and loving environment.'

The fabled amateur nights became a staple of the performances for Rodgers. 'Boy, did they teach me a lot – and those old-school guys helped me. They could see I was this young hippie with a natural talent but they knew I wanted to be Jimi Hendrix. They were very much "you've got to support the band, you can't come out here and be the star". Aretha Franklin would come out and say, "Oh Me O My' – two flats". You had to play as part of a section. They taught me all I needed to know about section playing, because prior to that, I was into jazz. But really, I just wanted to be a star, even back at *Sesame Street,* there was a lot of solos.'

To supplement his Apollo gig, Rodgers was spending his time in a number of transient day jobs; working at the Sam Goody record chain, picking records for the Columbia Record Club ('the worst job in your life'), messenger ('that lasted one day'), a phone solicitor ('but was so guilty trying to talk people into something they didn't want, it killed me'). Any menial job to Rodgers felt like he was exploiting people. He was fired from a music shop that expected him to recondition old guitars and make them playable. The care and attention he would lovingly administer on tired machine heads and weary fret boards was not appreciated by the store owner. Music was the only thing at which he could stay employed. He would regularly busk in Central Park, opening his guitar case and playing for money. During the Vietnam War, his repertoire would consist largely of protest songs.

Around this time, Rodgers invited Fonzi Thornton to be the lead singer in a fusion band he was putting together. Thornton went and rehearsed. 'That band never really turned out to do anything. We didn't even have a name,' Thornton recalls. 'We were just trying out a whole bunch of songs. I would go up and rehearse all the time up there. This was my first real experience of working closely with Nile.'

Given that by the mid-70s, lots of bands were becoming self-contained – acts such as Isaac Hayes and Barry White came in with their own musicians – work at the Apollo was becoming sporadic. Rodgers had to supplement his income with the jobbing musician's great standby, the pick-up gig. Even if he was playing the Apollo, which in this period was a strict union house, he would be home by 10 o'clock and then go out and commence regular nightclub gigs. It was still in the period where people would rather hear a band play than a record. New York had hundreds of venues on the outskirts of the city that needed a constant supply of low-cost, high-energy entertainment.

On one of these pick-ups, the band seemed to truly suck, but the bass player was fantastic. Rodgers and the bass player were able to work out all the cover versions thrown at them, complementing and supplementing each other's knowledge gaps. 'If they would "say we're gonna do 'Cissy Strut' – in C no flats, no sharps," whoever knew the changes would count in,' Rodgers remembers. 'We had it down to a science; you would have thought that we had been playing together for years.'

Neither Rodgers nor bass player Bernard Edwards knew that they were the same people who had spoken on the phone some months prior. Because of a different pronunciation of Edwards' first name – Rodgers called him *Ber-*Nard, while Edwards was being called his preference, Ber-*Nard*, Rodgers hadn't made the connection that this bass playing genius was the same man who'd advised him to lose his details several months previously. Suddenly there they were, interlocking at rehearsals like life-long friends.

After a short while, Edwards and Rodgers became inseparable. 'If he got a job that needed a guitar player or even if they had one, Bernard would say "fire them, you got to get my boy, because he knows all the songs". I didn't really, but we knew them between us. I would do the same thing. We seemed to be doing this forever.'

Edwards lived on 168th and Anthony Avenue with his wife Alexis and recently born son Bernard Jr while Rodgers lived with his mother on 167th and Clay Avenue, one block away. 'These two people were meant to be together. So this guy who told me to lose his number was destined to be tied to me for the rest of his life – and he lived one block away! This was ordained by the powers of the universe.' Guitarist Eddie Martinez lived around the block also. The connection between them meant that Chic would eventually fall into place easily. From now on, Rodgers and Edwards looked out for each other while playing on the New York circuit.

By April 1972, the major offensive mounted by the North Vietnamese and the Viet Cong on South Vietnam gave the clearest indication yet that the war was not going to develop in the manner the US wished. Events at the Munich Olympics in September 1972 suggested that the threat of terrorism had established itself as a fact of daily life in the 70s. In the early morning of 5 September, eight Palestinian terrorists broke into the Olympic Village, killed two members of the Israeli team and took nine more hostage. In an ensuing battle, all nine Israeli hostages were killed, as were five of the terrorists and one policeman. The Olympics were suspended and a memorial service was held in the main stadium.

The mood within New York was edgy. Panther support was dissipating, and the victory of Nixon at the Presidential election was seen as the final collapse of the liberal left. But, in the pick-up bars of New York and New Jersey, a constant supply of up-to-the moment tunes was required.

Tony Thompson was at large helping supply these tunes, but was harbouring loftier ambitions. 'I used to go to the Village Vanguard with Billy Koehler and a place owned by the Brecker Brothers called Seventh Avenue South. They used to feature fusion band after fusion band. It was the freakin' bomb. They used to have Return To Forever followed by Al Di Meola, The Mahivishnu Orchestra. At this time you would have characters like Billy Cobham, Steve Gadd and Lenny White. It was a great time, musically. And Nile was a good jazz player too. I'd seen him around at clubs. My drum teacher at the time was Narada Michael Walden – he used to pick me up every morning at 6 o'clock. We used to live in an area called Jamaica Estates. He was a guru, a disciple of Sri Chinmoy. I used to be into all these new bands. I went to a restaurant where disciples of Chinmoy would go. I went there and McLaughlin was playing. Mahivishnu was opening for John Lee Hooker. I swear I saw God when Billy Cobham played "The Inner Mountain Flame". I didn't want to touch the drums after seeing him play. Musically, it was intense. This is one of those bands that are just imprinted on my soul. It was an amazing thing.'

It was at these very clubs that disco began to break. Discothèques had long been out of fashion since the days of Arthur and Regines in the 60s. They had become either a playground for the super-rich, or the lowly poor. But slowly, across the decade, people began to return to them. There is much debate about what the first disco record was; the consensus tends to be 'Soul Makossa' by Manu Dibango, an expatriate from the Cameroon, which quietly slipped above ground in 1973. It was a record that was revolutionary in many ways, creating a global groove. As Dibango stated to Gene Santoro, 'Americans said I was doing African music, and Africans said I was doing Western music, and Europeans said I was doing American music.' The record's obscurity and amazing rhythm allowed the people who played these records in public to thrive, picking up rare B-sides, album tracks and creating something that was truly their own. These obscurities complemented the fact that the people who were dancing to the music had so long been in obscurity themselves; gays, African-Americans, Italians, Puerto Ricans. Since the Stonewall Inn riot of June 1969, homosexuality had become more explicit and a subversive society was being forged. It was so far away from the mainstream that it would be at least another couple of years before disco would be able to be quantified and commodified.

American Professor Mary Ellison is quick to point out that these early days of disco were about, 'The essence of black life – that's what disco means to me, the energy, the way it's done, the vitality and a speed which is underscored with an intensity.' The intensity of the music, if not yet the exact form was picked up on by Rodgers and Edwards.

It has been said that the New York disco scene from 1971 to 1974 was a true underground society and art form. An 'odd and tenuous alliance' was formed between two of the most repressed inner-city minorities, African-Americans and homosexuals. As Mark Jacobsen stated in his 1975 *Crawdaddy* essay, *Disco Dreams,* 'It was the complete opposite of the white-hippie sun-drenched spectacle form of entertainment that culminated with mass events like Woodstock. This was entertainment for the shadows: it was urban, rock hard and very primal – the only way to really have a party was behind closed doors, away from prying and disapproving eyes.' This containment provided a flourishing and exciting backdrop to the next five years. And ironically, when *Saturday Night Fever* fictionalised the genre into a blockbuster, more people would know disco around the world than any other form of music, ever.

But the need for live music was still a vital part of these clubs – the DJ had yet to become the sole king. Bernard Edwards began to have a regular gig, supporting old-school vocal group, New York City around the clubs. He felt it would be a marvellous idea if his new, slightly unconventional friend, Rodgers, was to join them also.

5.
DOING FINE NOW?

'We played other people's music as if it belonged to us.
As Bernard used to say, "we attack their shit."'
NILE RODGERS

AS THE WATERGATE SCANDAL unfolded in Washington, Nixon declared the Vietnam War over in January 1973. When the bombing in Cambodia ended in August, it was the final involvement for the US in South East Asia in a war which had been both costly, heavy on civilian and military casualties, and in the main, viewed as pointless.

'A particularly unpleasant surprise in a year of particularly unpleasant surprises,' was the reckoning as the Arab Nations began an oil embargo against the US, a country which imported a third of its oil, in an attempt to raise prices and alter US support for Israel. The seeds of the discontent which ultimately manifested in 9/11 were being sown at this time. Although the embargo was to end in March 1974, the ramifications would be felt throughout the remainder of the decade. Price rises continued for the next two years. The soaring costs of petrol and home heating oil contributed to already worsening inflation. As summer 1974 grew ever longer, the Watergate saga, America's 'long national nightmare' drew to a close with Richard Nixon's resignation and Gerald Ford's assumption of power on 9th August. Although Ford introduced his WIN (Whip Inflation Now) programme, cutting federal spending, consumer prices rose by 12% in 1974 and 11% in 1975. Images of queues of cars waiting for gas seemed to undermine the very essence of the American dream, especially as it hit the Detroit motor industry – General Motors, Ford and Chrysler laid off a quarter of a million workers. Smaller cheaper imported cars flourished. The economy was in meltdown by 1975. Unemployment reached 11%. Tax receipts dropped and the federal deficit rose to unprecedented levels

Musically, these issues were addressed. Although the golden age of agit-soul seemed to be passing, groups such as James Brown's fiery JBs released 'You Can Have Your Watergate, But Gimme Some Bucks And I'll Get Straight', but in the main, concerns musically appeared to be moving away from the socio-political and out ever further, on to the dance floor.

Rodgers, however, was not for dropping the political baton. 'Absolutely not. You can't make a teenage rebel conform to anything,' he recalled. 'Even in the Apollo Theater House band I wouldn't conform. They used to say, "hey man, no jeans." I reply, '"to a hippie, man, jeans are like your uniform! There's no way I'm wearing regular trousers."' If Rodgers wouldn't toe the line in this most regimented of institutions, there was little chance he was ever going to change.

New York City were truly members of the old school. Coming up through the vocal group tradition, singers Tim McQueen and Eddie Schell, had been joined by veterans John Brown (ex-The Five Satins and The Cadillacs) and Claude Johnson (ex-The Genies). Their producer and Chelsea label owner, Wes Farrell, had convinced legendary Philadelphia producer, Thom Bell, to oversee some of their songs. Originally know as Tri-Boro Exchange, the group changed their name and recorded the Sherman Marshall-Thom Bell written hit, 'I'm Doin' Fine Now'. Signed to Chelsea, with its ever-engaging promise of 'a constant new beginning', New York City made No .17 in the US pop charts in summer 1973, and reached the UK Top 20 the same year. Although their follow-up records did not match the timeless appeal of their breakthrough hit, the Stylistics-flavoured 'Make Me Twice The Man' and 'Quick, Fast, In A Hurry' both scraped the US Top 100. Their two albums, *I'm Doing Fine Now* and *Soulful Road* are sweet, competent examples of mid-70s Philly-lite. Buoyed up by the success of the hit single, they needed a live band to go on the road and capitalise on this success. Bernard Edwards, with his snowballing reputation as one of the most electric live players on the New York scene was drafted in to play in the Big Apple Band, New York City's backing group.

'People knew me and Bernard separately. We had two different lineages,' Rodgers recalls. 'The people attached to me came along the Luther Vandross-*Sesame Street*-Apollo Theater pathway; while the pathway to Bernard Edwards was the Willie Feaster & The Mighty Magnificents-BT Express-New Jersey thing. His thing was NJ, while mine was Manhattan and Harlem. His people were attached to a certain sort of gig and my people were attached to certain other sort of gigs.' Rodgers and Edwards had formed a fast friendship. It was only a matter of time before Edwards told the bandleader for New York City that his firebrand friend would be an excellent, if slightly unconventional choice for the gig. 'We were *very* different,' Rodgers laughs. 'I'm an independent hippie guy, wearing hippie clothes and here's this second generation Motown-R&B thing. It was perfect, slick, soul stuff; their suits, their hats, the choreography by Cholly Atkins.' Rodgers still wanted to be his hero, Jimi Hendrix. 'I didn't want to be the background guy to The Temptations –

and it wasn't even The Temptations. I didn't belong there. But my musicality was pretty impressive to them. It was hard for them to fire me – they'd try other guitar players, but it just wouldn't work. Plus Bernard just had to have me. He was becoming used to my sound.'

In 1975, two events were to change Nile Rodgers' life. His role as the New York City's resident upstart guitar player, a cross between Hendrix and Wes Montgomery, meant that Edwards had to fight a permanent battle to keep his friend in employment. The group looked for any and every opportunity to cast him asunder from the Big Apple Band. To compound matters, Rodgers, still playing in pick-up bands and jamming with his huge network of musicians in New York, to put it in his own words, couldn't have 'given a shit'.

The touring with New York City was relentless. On one show, Rodgers returned to the Apollo Theater. Most doors would be open to the act as their manager, Bob Bonanno, had a lot of links, being the son of famous Mafia crime figure, 'Big' Joe Bonanno. The group were treated like returning heroes. When the tour took in Florida, Rodgers recalls: 'We were playing with an early version of KC and the Sunshine Band. This kid, Jerome Smith, plugs into my amp with a Fender Stratocaster, and the sound was unbelievable to me. It was like when I first heard Albert King. I was sitting in the audience and I thought "holy shit, is this what my amplifier is supposed to sound like?" Previously I'd been playing it in a jazz style, all with warm and mellow notes. Bernard looks at me and says, "motherfucker – that's how I've been telling you to play for all these years." I took my guitar to a pawnshop that day, got a Fender Stratocaster and $300 back in cash. That's how expensive the guitars were I'd been playing.'

A quick reappraisal of his sound meant that finally he fell into favour with his old school paymasters; 'I went back and played that show, the same show I'd been playing everyday and suddenly, the sound was crisp, bright and cutting through. The New York City guys were out there doing their thing – and they're looking back and now they love me, they don't care what I have to say!'

With the sound improved, Edwards gave Rodgers a quick lesson in technique that was to shape one of the most recognisable styles in popular music. Edwards had been attempting to show his partner a playing manner for some time, but he simply couldn't get his hands around the neck of the big fat guitar Rodgers had been toting for some time. 'Bernard said to me, "let me show you something" and he starts chugging. He played the same song in a certain style. It sounded like that kid, Jerome, who'd been playing before me.' Rodgers listened and wondered how he could adapt that style, given his knowledge of harmony; if he could blend a choppy rhythm style with all of his McCoy Tyner influences, he would be on to something. It would need practice, but it could be a fantastic update on the sound Jimmy 'Chank' Nolen had achieved with James Brown.

'In those days, I shared rooms with the drummer, and I didn't want to disturb him,' says Rodgers. 'I would go into the bathroom, put towels on the threshold to try and deaden the sound, so I didn't keep the poor guy awake. I'd just started practicing with my right hand. I would finger a chord and not move, attempting to make music in one position like those great one-position guitar players of the past, like Bo Diddley or Muddy Waters, to have all of these sounds coming out of one place. I thought that if I could do this with R&B or dance music or whatever it was we were trying to invent, it would be something unique. So I took my left hand off the guitar and tried to make music without touching it. I needed to make this sound musical. I spent two days just doing that. I went back and played exactly the same show and it was completely different.'

Nile Rodgers never looked back. From that point, any tune he played, on whatever guitar, would sound unmistakably like nobody else but Nile Rodgers. 'That weekend taught me my style. When you listen to a record, you know it's John Coltrane playing. It doesn't matter what tape recorder he recorded it on, it sounds like John Coltrane. When I play guitar, I play like Nile Rodgers. I sound like me. Bernard helped me see me.'

As Edwards and Rodgers were learning their craft around America with New York City, meanwhile, some of their old circle were doing well, too. Luther Vandross had become something of a name on the New York session scene. Another key player on the scene was David Lasley, whose voice would so shape the first two Chic albums. He had arrived in New York from Detroit in the early 70s, as part of the cast of *Hair*. After appearing in the rather less successful spin-off, *Dude*, he began to get lucrative work as a session vocalist. He formed a group, with other *Hair* talents, such as Lana Morrano, called Valentine. Valentine would record sessions and also gig at places like Max's Kansas City, while taking demos around New York.

'Little by little, I became aware of Luther's work,' Lasley recalls. 'I met him at Alee Willis' birthday party in January 1974. I knew about Fonzi as well, but I'd never met him. Luther and I talked about sessions – we were both aware of each other. Everyone had their groups, but we were all doing background work. Everyone was trying to keep their units, but it was clear Luther would succeed.'

And so, Rodgers' *Sesame Street* friend, Luther Vandross, and his old Listen My Brother sparring partner, guitarist Carlos Alomar, appeared to be the first to really go global: they had somehow found themselves in the touring band of pop's greatest journeyman, David Bowie.

London-born Bowie was enjoying only his second year of superstardom after a decade floundering on the art-margins of British pop. His post-apocalyptic rock and roller, Ziggy Stardust, had hit a nerve in 1972, and he quickly became an enormous British star, with a ready-made back catalogue to exploit. Two years later, by the time his American *Diamond Dogs* tour reached its second phase, it had become known as the 'soul tour' or the Philly Dogs tour. As a direct reaction to the excesses of his stardom and the elegant redundancy of the country he had momentarily adopted as his home, Bowie began to immerse himself in the music of his youth, R&B. 'My heart had been stolen by soul and R&B in the early seventies,' Bowie recalls. 'I'd been big on the great little disco scene that was flourishing in Manhattan in the early days around 73-74. Places like The Loft, a black gay disco that had the best records. It was in some guy's (*David Mancusco*) apartment, I think he was also the DJ and he was one of the first in the world to develop the extended mix by segueing records together seamlessly so that there was no noticeable space between cuts.'

Bowie wanted to go to the most authentic studio possible to capture this new direction on vinyl, which happened to be New York's Sigma Sound. His recorded manifestation of this current craze, *Young Americans,* was enlivened by the presence of 22-year-old Vandross on vocals. 'The original idea had been to use the MFSB people,' recalled producer Tony Visconti. MFSB – Mother, Father, Sister, Brother or Motherfuckin' Son of A Bitch, depending on which acronym suited – were the house orchestra and rhythm section of Kenny Gamble and Leon Huff's Philadelphia International Records, arguably the most influential black music of the first half of the 70s. 'But, when I walked in the room there was old regular Mike Garson, Willie Weeks, Andy Newmark – they were not what I was expecting. David didn't want to go 100% authentic and thought there was a safety net by having old faces like me and Mike Garson on board.'

'David said he was going to try this kid out – Carlos had his Gibson in one hand and amp in the other. David received a demo from Robin, Luther and Carlos – and he liked it – he thought he was getting three fabulous singers in one go. I remember Luther looking round wide-eyed at the studio, saying phrases like 'gosh' and 'wow'. Sigma was legendary; that was about the only thing that was authentic about that recording. It was originally intended to be a pure R&B album, but already we were doing our hybrid attack on it. We sort of expected the sound to be there in the walls, but it wasn't. In fact, we could have done that album anywhere in the world, given the musicians we were using.'

Bowie was impressed by the young Vandross. He loved the demo of his 'Funky Music', which, with Bowie's input became 'Fascination'. When Bowie asked him if he could change the lyrics, Vandross amusingly replied, 'You're David Bowie. I live with my mother. Of course you can change the lyrics.' The introduction to his group of former Apollo house band guitarist Carlos Alomar, and his wife, vocalist Robin Wright, with Vandross in the mix, added the authenticity Bowie craved. 'David has got a fantastic ability to do his homework,' states long term producer and associate, Visconti. 'Before we start albums, he would already be listening to a lot of recordings for months, soaking up the vibes and understanding it thoroughly. So by the time we had done *Young Americans*, he must have had about 500 R&B songs in his consciousness and he could break out into any one of them if the band knew the chord changes. I don't think he ever pretended to be black. I think David was affected a little bit – he was definitely an Englishman in that situation. He was trying to find a setting for his latest songs and this time it was a quasi-R&B setting.'

Bowie would put in a great deal of extra hours into his 'homework'. 'Carlos, Jagger and I would go to these all night things,' Bowie remembers. 'Carlos also introduced me to the NY Latin scene, specifically El Corso club and a place called the Leopard. I was buying a lot of stuff on the Fania label around this time, skinny white limey boy doing the Latin hustle and mambo. It was really music for people who stayed up late, you wouldn't hear it on radio and you had to go find a club for it. This whole stew made an obscure but super-important appearance on my album *Young Americans* in 1975'.

The album – a white man struggling with his demons over the sweetest black music – provided Bowie with his biggest US success to date, and the John Lennon-assisted single, 'Fame', became a bona fide US No. 1. Even James Brown himself copied 'Fame' wholesale for 'Hot (I Need To Be Loved, Loved, Loved)'. With Bowie's appearance on *Soul Train* singing his next hit, 'Golden Years', this provided a validation, if it were needed, that this was not simply plastic soul. 'It's just emotional drive ... There's not a concept in sight', he told *The LA Times* in September 1974. One of the fledgling Chic circle had assisted with this. With each subsequent release, the pressure from RCA executives had piled on to provide another *Young Americans*. It would be eight years before he returned to those pastures. And when he did, he would be produced by Nile Rodgers. Many things were to happen before that point, however.

Thanks to Bowie grappling with his soul persona, he provided Vandross with the fillip his career needed. Nile Rodgers was delighted. 'It was fantastic! Not only was it a great piece of work, but also just as a native New Yorker, it was amazing to see what Bowie did for Luther and Carlos, all these cats that I've grown up with from high school, to watch them become involved with a man who I think is one of the greatest in music.' As a result of his involvement with Bowie, Vandross and his vocalists Anthony Hinton and Diane Sumler were signed to the Atlantic subsidiary, Cotillion as 'Luther'. Vandross' success provided Rodgers and Edwards with inspiration they needed.

✩✩✩

It mustn't be forgotten that this tale is played out against a recession. The 70s had not been a particularly affluent decade. The oil crisis had sent domestic prices in America rocketing, and the knocks to the national confidence had led to a period of inflation. Discos suddenly became a more affordable alternative to going out to a gig. You could go somewhere and hear all of your favourite records in one night for half the price of hearing a band whack out an hour of turgid fillers before they reluctantly trotted out a hit at some enormodome miles from downtown. And you could return the following week.

Craig Werner suggests that the Black Power movement called for an art that exposed the enemy, praised the people, and supported the revolution. Did this continue through disco? Disco can be seen as a synthesis of the funk of Brown or Clinton with the sweetness of Philly strings; it certainly praised the people, as virtually every record was a celebration of the self, and the revolution was there for all to see on the dancefloor.

Disco started to move forward and break overground. Along with Gamble and Huff's Philly International, records like Van McCoy's 'The Hustle', George McRae's 'Rock Your Baby' and KC & The Sunshine Band's 'Boogie Shoes' all helped define the genre. Tony Bongiovi set up a small record company, DCA Productions and began to release records such as Gloria Gaynor's 'Never Can Say Goodbye'. Although disco's successes in the mainstream until this point had been, to use Atlantic Records' Jerry Wexler's famous remark, 'accidental and peripheral,' by late 1975, the whole movement began to solidify from a commercial perspective, with Giorgio Moroder and Donna Summer bringing their European space-age sounds to the US charts alongside slick productions like Silver Convention's 'Fly Robin Fly', Johnnie Taylor's 'Disco Lady' and, er, Rick Dees and his Cast Of Idiots singing 'Disco Duck' .

The early days of disco have been described as dirty, spiritual, thrilling, powerful, secret, underground, dangerous, non-blond, queer, hungry. 'The last days of disco might have recalled the decadent fall of Rome, but the first days were filled with hope,' dance site b7b suggests. Disco was as diverse a selection of music as you could care to mention, taking from Gamble and Huff's big Philly productions, Norman Whitfield's Temptation sides, with even funky rock thrown in. The uniting of Philadelphia and Motown came together in the New York clubs. Although 'Soul Makossa' had been underground, Barry White's 'Love's Theme' by Love Unlimited Orchestra can be seen as the start of the form as it became internationally known. Its lushness of strings and horns built on Isaac Hayes' *Shaft* soundtrack, but here was a film score without a movie. It suggested love, romance, opulence, freedom and escape, all underpinned by the funkiest wah wah guitar. It was certainly a concise distillation of the Philadelphia sound, rendered palatable for the widest possible audience.

DJ and *Billboard* columnist Tom Moulton compiled the first mix after a visit to Fire Island; he was asked to put together a side for a Gloria Gaynor album, mixing the three tracks into one continuous piece of music. The disco mix was born. DJs like Francis Grasso, Nicky Siano and David Mancusco emerged, people who actually had the power to put on a show and break records. New York was full of clubs such as The Loft, The Gallery, Soho Place, The Flamingo. Vincent Aletti wrote that, 'the typical New York DJ is young, Italian and gay.'

David Bowie, too, noted the otherness of the music at this juncture: 'The music was black/Hispanic and completely indifferent to what was going down with white kids at the time. It became more inclusive by the mid-to late seventies, of course, but in the beginning it was definitely a new volatile vocabulary for black America'.

The strange, celebratory, volatile music seemed complementary to the altered mood gathering pace as the 70s progressed. If the start of the decade was serious minded, when the funk was dirty and everyone seemed to have a purpose, by the mid-70s, it appeared that everyone was simply partying. 'I think things were changing,' Robert Bell, whose group, Kool and The Gang, had been such stalwarts of the Nation Of Islam Bazaars. 'By the mid 70s, the whole Vietnam thing was phasing out. You still had the political problems within the community, but it wasn't as radical as it was in the 60s. People seemed to be more into having a good time than focusing on their problems. I remember in around 1975, being impressed with Barry White and Love Unlimited, Van McCoy's "The Hustle" – and then Donna Summer began making the waves. Then you had that disco thing with MFSB, along with the Trammps, and then, finally, along came Chic.'

However, it would be at least another year before Chic would join the milieu. Although disco was breaking out, rock was to be more the music of choice for the Big Apple Band, now ending their stint performing behind New York City.

'At that time, we didn't think disco would be so tremendous, so we decided to go with rock instead,' Rodgers told James Farber of *Rolling Stone* in April 1979. 'We were more into those types of dollars. The Trammps did well then, but David Bowie, who was my favourite, was making eight million times more. Our rock ideas had the same concept as Chic. We wanted high-fashion girls in the band. It had to be semi-decadent because we thought that would open us up commercially. Roxy Music did that in England, but they're more receptive to the glitter thing than Americans. Americans would rather get into Donny and Marie than Bryan Ferry.'

The second significant event of the year occurred for Rodgers when he saw Roxy Music in concert. At the end of the UK tour, which was also to spell the end of New York City, The Big Apple Band went out to party. When Rodgers got back to his hotel in Nottingham, his belongings, money from the tour and his passport had been stolen. Rodgers had to make his way down to the American Embassy in London to get a new passport. 'I was just a working musician and would send all my money back to my girlfriend, who unbeknownst to me was spending it all going out with the percussionist from Al Green's band', Rodgers told Geoff Brown in 2003. This girlfriend did more than that. She sold all of Rodgers furniture from the beautiful penthouse that they had been living in and then left him for the other man.

It would not be long, however, before Rodgers would be back on his feet. In London, Rodgers not only got a new passport, but found a lady, who happened to be the girlfriend of General Johnson, from Chairman of the Board. 'I was in love with this girl. I was doing anything she said. She introduced me to General Johnson and Hot Chocolate. Her name was Carrie … the world revolved around her. She was going out with those guys – I was the new black guy to add to her collection.'

'The rest of the group and Bernard went back to the States, 'cos he's married, he's got a family (*as well as Bernard Jr., Portia was born in 1974 and Michael was on the way*). I did the whole club scene in London at the time; which was fabulously exciting to me.' Rodgers recounted what he had heard and danced to in *Smash Hits* in 1979. 'When we'd been in London, we had hung around in places like Gullivers and the Q Club. There were certain songs from that period which influenced our sound. Things like The Joneses' "Sugar Pie Guy", MFSB's "Love Is The Message" and The Jackson Five's "Dancin' Machine".'

'They had great dance music, and jazzy fusion stuff was coming through – this was the time that Jeff Beck started doing those groundbreaking records with Richard Tee. I started jamming around and a few people got a bee in their bonnets, thinking that this guitar player with this new style could be turned into a guitar star.' These people were club people, people hanging around, R&B fans. 'Everybody in England was saying, boy, you could be the next Hendrix.' Clearly for Nile Rodgers, that was music to his ears.

However, all of this was to change when Rodgers was taken out to the Empire Pool Wembley, never the most salubrious of venues, in October 1975 to see Roxy Music, then almost entirely unknown in America. Founded in 1971, their 1972 debut album, *Roxy Music*, was a triumph of both style and substance.

Too ironic for the US mainstream, leader Bryan Ferry, like many pop stars before him, had pastiched American popular music, especially soul, rock and roll and R&B. However Ferry mixed this with a high-European artiness and a level of grandeur that was dismissed as pretence by the British rock press. His effortless cool was viewed jealously by the papers, who dubbed him titles such as Byron Ferrari and Biryani Fury. By the *Siren* album, it was possible Roxy Music had become somewhat formulaic, but it is only with hindsight one can fully appreciate just how out there they were. Ferry had been submerged in black music since he was 10: 'Black music has been very important to me,' he recalls. 'Through Lonnie Donegan covering records like "Rock Island Line" on specialist BBC shows like Jazz Club, they'd play the blues and I got completely hooked. From that, I got into all manner of black music. I started to go to concerts in Newcastle-Upon-Tyne. I saw people like Count Basie, Modern Jazz Quartet, Dizzy Gillespie, Norman Granz's *Jazz At The Philharmonic* Tours. I would be sitting at the Newcastle City Hall, spellbound. I saw Hendrix there also. The big moment for me was in 1967 seeing the Stax Roadshow in London – Otis Redding, Sam and Dave, Steve Cropper, Eddie Floyd, Booker T – all of them; that Memphis/Stax thing was incredible.'

By 1975, leader Ferry had honed his vision of glamour and ennui into a perfect blend of jarring, surreal pop. Surviving the departure of co-founder, electronics pioneer, Brian Eno in 1973, Roxy Music had fashioned itself into an otherworldly commercial juggernaut.

'We see this group called Roxy Music – and I'm like "holy shit, this is happening."' Rodgers remembers. 'If we could take this sophisticated, high-fashion, aristocratic, interesting, cerebral stuff, put a beat to it, make it black and our own thing, we could really be happening too. So I'm thinking Chairman Of The Board, Hot Chocolate and then Roxy Music.'

Bryan Ferry, who was later to work with Rodgers on his albums, *Boys And Girls* and *Mamouna* as well as *The Fly* soundtrack, remembers his relative surprise at hearing this news. 'Nile said that he was living in Shepherd's Bush with a girlfriend. *He was always with women – he was a ladies' man – I don't think he would deny it.* He said he switched on the TV one night and we were on there doing "Love Is The Drug" – and I had my kind of GI outfit with eye patch and the girls were in uniform with tight pencil skirts. He called Bernard and told him – I've got an idea – I've just seen what we are going to do. It was great. I was very flattered.'

Rodgers takes up the story: 'I called Bernard up, and went "man! I've got it! I got what we should be doing. You should see this whole Roxy Music thing. It's so elegant and cool and fashionable – hip and hairdos and clothes and girls around – I don't know what's going on, but it looks cool!"'

'Love Is The Drug' found Ferry dabbling in the dance floor. Ice-cool, it married rumba and beats, passion and dispassion. It was partly influenced by the bourgeoning disco scene: 'I thought disco was really good,' Ferry said. 'I always liked music that had a kind of groove. I liked it very much.'

Thus began a long association for Rodgers and Edwards with the English rock aristocracy. 'I adore Bryan – a wonderful, introspective musician,' Rodgers states. 'These English gentleman kind of guys, Ferry, Bowie; always had a cigarette dangling from their fingers – cigarette in the left, a snifter in the right.'

Rodgers was now really up for doing something new musically. 'But Bernard liked the suits, he liked New York City,' Rodgers laughs. 'To him, when I say fashion, he thought it meant The Temptations.' But this idea of taking white rock and making it black – reverse traffic, if you will, was key and could easily be developed. 'Because at that time in America, everything was just funk. I thought how can we put an interesting spin on R&B. A lot of bands were coming up like Rufus and Chaka Khan, Mother's Finest, P-Funk, self-contained, spiritually rock based R&B bands, stadium R&B if you will. Rock was influencing Black music a lot more.'

Was Bryan Ferry ever aware of the conscious importing of the image at the time? 'I thought there was a kind of sympathetic thing going on; but that was it.'

If this hybrid of rock and funk and glamour were to work, Rodgers and Edwards would need the right team of people.

6.
THE BOYS ARE BACK IN TOWN

*'We also idolised Kiss. When they were on stage, they had a certain vibe
and image, and once they left that stage, you had absolutely no idea
who they were.'*
NILE RODGERS

RETURNING TO NEW YORK, with a plan, Rodgers and Edwards started to
audition musicians to join the Big Apple Band. But before then, there would
be more lucrative and skill-forming support work to do. One such gig was
supporting Brooklyn-born vocalist Carol Douglas. Douglas had just been
riding high in the charts with the perennial pre-disco classic 'Doctor's Orders'.
Although it became the sort of hit that ultimately constrains an artist to being
billed forever with its title inserted in inverted commas between their fore and
surname, Douglas had a fine pedigree. She was actually the daughter of jazz
singer Minnie Newsome, who was immortalised in song by Cab Calloway, as
'Minnie The Moocher'. 'Doctor's Orders' had risen to No. 11 on the pop charts
in February 1975. Although future material was not going to hit as big, she
became a touchstone for the early disco movement.

It was with Douglas that they really built on the work they had done with
New York City. With just a small band, they had to replicate her dense,
overproduced sound on stage – and found themselves filling in all the parts.
'Our sound came long before the Chic recordings. We made Carol's music
sound like what was to become Chic,' Rodgers recalls. 'We had to turn these
big orchestral dance records into something live that audiences would
appreciate. I would superimpose my whole rhythmical concept on it and
rewrite parts so they could have more of a groove. When I played my style
in someone else's song, they always liked it better. I played the rhythm and
the line at the same time; it grooved in a different way. Bernard and I made
the rhythm section sound like the record. If it was just me, Bernard and the
drummer – instead of sounding like the Band of Gypsies, we sounded like
the record. It wasn't just a random thing. He would take the bass line from
the record and play it as well as the embellishments of the other instruments.'

1976 was the year things began to get serious for the Big Apple Band. America celebrated its bicentennial to a deafening sound of whistles. President Ford lost to Georgian peanut farmer Jimmy Carter in the November elections. There was hope that this outsider would bring some simple values back to a Presidency that had become so tainted.

In America especially, the vogue for listening to records and dressing up was back. *Newsweek* commented in 1976 that there were some 10,000 discos in the US compared with 1500 two years previously. Le Jardin had been in operation since the mid-70s and Regines had opened in 1976 on Park Avenue. At the cool underground end, The Loft, David Mancuso's home, was a particularly fantastic place to hang out.

A new hedonism and opulence rang out. Americans, buoyed up by the country's bicentennial, emerging from Vietnam and, as writer Anthony Haden Guest suggests 'the clinical depression of Watergate', were ready to party. Add to that the influx of well-to-do Europeans and Latin Americans migrating toward Manhattan to avoid terrorism, communism and taxes. Gays and women, too, had new, hard-earned money to spend. Disco and AOR dominated the American charts. Nostalgia had become huge business in the 70s. Partially informed by the popular success of *The Great Gatsby*, the look of the past became mined and exploited. With disco's references to Fred Astaire, Ginger Rodgers and Duke Ellington, it captured the backwards-looking mood of the day.

Also, and most saliently for the market Rodgers and Edwards were to aim for, there was a new black middle class – products, as Nelson George has stated, of 'tokenism, affirmative action and hard work', and corporations realised that having black divisions would cater directly for the black masses.

Yet Nile Rodgers and Bernard Edwards were perturbed. Both knew they never wanted to back musicians like New York City or Carol Douglas again. They had had enough of that. But finding a niche appeared to be increasingly difficult. Their sound was becoming instantly recognisable. It was time to get some committed players in. Rodgers and Edwards saw a keyboard player at Max's Kansas City, playing with the R&B band St. James Infirmary, whose style struck a chord with them. Robert Sabino had lived in the Bronx most of his life. His father worked in a luncheonette and as a chauffeur while his mother was a housewife who then worked as a bank clerk. Although his father hailed from an aristocratic family in Columbia, those days were passed.

Sabino grew up as one of nine people living in two rooms; six kids, his grandmother and parents. His father could play almost every instrument, and Sabino grew up with drums, vibes, guitar, banjo, piano, trumpet, clarinet and cornet. Although Sabino had played guitar and piano and brass in high school, he hadn't been particularly bothered until he hit 7th grade.

'I had about six months of lessons at piano when I was ten, and considering I was so awful on guitar, I figured I could be the keyboard player,' Sabino states. 'It was in a garage band, which was where I learned how to do the "Light My Fire" solo. Felix Cavaliere from the Young Rascals became my hero. Because I was R&B and rock and they filled that gap – and they were Bronx people too. I started playing functions when I was 18, in 1970/71. I played around and went from band to band; I was always looking for musicianship.'

While Sabino was studying at Fordham College, Mickey Leonard heard him playing the piano and asked him to join his progressive rock band, Howard, who were based in Connecticut. After a productive spell with them, Sabino returned to New York and began playing local sessions and gigging with groups such as The James Apollo Soul Band and St. James Infirmary. 'St James Infirmary became the house band at Max's Kansas City – that's when I met Nile and Bernard. They heard me play, and took my number – they were looking specifically for a guy that came from a rock background that understood R&B. I gave them my number but I never heard from them.'

Sabino went back to The Bronx, living in a house where he would frequently hear his neighbour across the street blast his guitar out, with all the windows open. It was none other than Rodgers' old school buddy, Eddie Martinez. 'Eddie heard me play and said that his friends, Nile and Bernard, were looking for a keyboard player,' Sabino laughs. 'They had told him that they had got the right guy, but they lost his number. I didn't remember their names, so I had no idea who Nile and Bernard were. I went down for an audition and they both said "that's the guy whose number we lost!"'

Eddie Martinez, who had, by now, begun playing with Labelle, takes up the story: 'Nile was telling me how he's seen this group at Max's, and that their keyboard player was amazing and that he would love to have him in the band. I said, you mean Rob Sabino? I can see him from my window. He was strumming his guitar on the front porch. I wrote down Nile's number and went and gave it to him.'

The Big Apple Band, now with added Sabino, began to take shape. The name, however, would become flexible according to the gig. When they played more rock-oriented shows, they would take the name, The Boys, as their intro song was Thin Lizzy's 'The Boys Are Back In Town'.

'We auditioned for lead singers, and we found this guy called Bobby Cotter, who had just finished from *Jesus Christ Superstar*,' Rodgers recalls. 'So, now it's these five guys and we're now also doing this power rock thing.' Their drummer, Clyde, was not to last the distance. 'He had an incident with this girlfriend, who was the most oversexed woman on the planet. Everybody wanted her and everybody got her. She knew how to deep throat. It was horrible because we loved Clyde and his girl was going through everybody in the band. He came home one night, found her with somebody and punched through the window. He cut his tendons which was the end of his drumming career.' According to Sabino, this wasn't the end of the world, as he believed that Clyde was limited in style and scope. Woody Cunningham, who went on to form Kleeer, who with Chic and Change, would be another part of Atlantic's future R&B nucleus – sat in for a while, but a full-time replacement would be needed.

Omar Hakim, who had been something of a child prodigy, was Rodgers' and Edwards' first choice. Rodgers knew him from the jazz scene, but, at only 15, Hakim would be far too young to perform the evening gigs the group needed to play. 'In the daytime, I was playing at an amusement park in Jersey called Great Adventures and because it was a family-orientated place, Omar could play,' Rodgers states. 'But, most of our gigs were at night in bars – and although the New York City scene was quite liberal, we played a lot of bars that were out of New York, where the liquor thing was quite strict. Although Omar didn't drink, club owners were afraid they'd get busted.'

'Nile was looking for a drummer, someone who could really hit,' Eddie Martinez recalled. 'I gave him Tony Thompson's number and that's how they hooked up.' Martinez and Thompson had first met while auditioning in spring 1976 to be a part of Stevie Wonder's *Songs In The Key Of Life* project. Martinez, who had played with Jerry Mason, who'd recorded on Buddah, had been successful in getting a Labelle gig. They were looking for a second drummer. Martinez gave them Thompson's number, and, briefly, he took the second drummer's position. But it was not to last.

Thompson, who had gigged with The Hues Corporation, Ecstasy, Passion and Pain and The Universal Robot Band, recalled his brief tenure with Labelle. 'I was the last in the line. I had this attitude that I wasn't going to get the gig anyway, so I played my butt off. It was lovely to meet Eddie again, as well as Carmine Rojas. I got the gig. It was the first time I toured, first time I'd been on a plane. The problem was that Patti already had a drummer, Jeffery Pugh – and he was a schmuck. He simply didn't like me. He had been with Patti longer and he was jealous. He set up his drums like a pimp.' Thompson was fired and was duly devastated. The moment Thompson arrived home, he received a phone call from Rodgers asking him to audition for The Big Apple Band. He immediately set off for Brandice High School, in Upper Manhattan, where the group had set up rehearsal camp. Brandice was chosen as Bernard Edwards' uncle was the janitor, and would let the group in on a Saturday. The school was used also as their equipment store. When Thompson arrived, he recognised Rodgers immediately; they had played gigs together backing Jamshied Al Morad, who among the Persian Community in New York, was viewed as their Tom Jones.

When Thompson arrived for audition, none of the band had ever seen anybody who had road cases for their drums before. Thompson played the most 'cacophonous shit', but his technique was truly extraordinary. 'Tony came in and blew us away. I'll never forget it,' Rodgers laughs, 'Bernard said to him "so, brother, let me ask you something. I guess your concept was that you're just going to play all the shit you know and when I hear something I like, stop you and say that's what I want you to play." Tony was like the star and he wanted to make sure we knew how great he was. Bernard had to stress that we were merely asking him to join our band, that this wasn't the Tony Thompson show.'

'I was into fusion, polyrhythms, Billy Cobham, Steve Gadd, all those really great players,' Thompson recalls. 'When I rehearsed with Nile and Bernard, they didn't like my playing too much. Nile thought I overplayed. I came in with a whole bunch of drums and cymbals. Bernard went to Nile and said "If I can take away half the crap that that guy brought down here, he will be a monster player" – and they did!' 'It took a little while for Bernard to believe in Tony,' states Rodgers. 'He had big high-falutin plans, while Bernard was much more down to earth. When Bernard began to trust in Tony and work one-on-one, everything changed. Tony didn't have the discipline that Bernard and I had – I mean Tony was a star. He walked into our situation coming from Labelle, out there on stage being flashy. We were like his roadies.'

Rob Sabino was instantly impressed with their new, starry drummer. 'I'd never heard anybody with that studied attack he had. His power came from a very precise physical way of playing. He didn't have his elbows way up, he could get more volume and varied tones out of the use of his wrists and hands than simply being a slam-banger. But he was a rocker, no question! He was more of a rocker than I was. He was very good at heavy music. We loved him.'

After the audition, Rodgers met Thompson frequently on the Persian circuit. 'Tony and I started doing gigs together; there is a whole Arabic population in New York that lived out in Queens,' Rodgers recalls. 'Tony would work with me and we'd also get on gigs for the gypsies, doing fantastic parties. They always wanted to hear what was current, usually Barry White "Never Gonna Give You Up", and we had that shit down!'

While Thompson and Edwards were supplementing The Big Apple Band with their gigs, Edwards would also be playing around New York. Rodgers would still be playing live with Vandross' group, Luther, where Edwards would occasionally join him. It was a busy, skill-learning time. From the small gigs at the weekends, to playing Radio City with Luther, the core of The Big Apple Band were frequently gigging. As professional musicians, they took every engagement that came their way.

The line-up stabilised as Rob Sabino, Bobby Cotter, Nile Rodgers, Bernard Edwards and Tony Thompson. 'We were doing disco covers, R&B covers. We did some of Nile and Bernard's material and a few of my own songs,' Sabino recalls. 'Norma Jean later did one of the songs, "Saturday". The five of us were out there, gigging. I was the guy with the van – myself and my wife in my yellow Chevy, with all this big stage equipment that they had, and Tony's drums all piled in my van with Nile and Bernard lying on top – with me and my wife and Bobby Cotter and Tony all squashed in the front.'

'New York was funny then,' recalls Fonzi Thornton, the ex-Listen My Brother vocalist who was making his own way at this time. 'We would all be aware of each other's work; I would see pictures of them in record stores as the Big Apple Band, and there would be pictures of me as Fonzi – this guy and two girls – Michelle Cobbs, Carol Sylvan and myself. We were doing a lot of nightclub work around the city. We at one point worked with Joe Frasier, the boxer, who fancied himself as a singer. We would open his show with our act, and then we would come on stage and sing with him. We would dress in sequinned boxing robes. I would often go to a club where Nile and Bernard had been the night before. We used to laugh about playing the New York chitlin circuit.'

There was another primary musical influence on The Big Apple Band. 'We also idolised Kiss,' Rodgers says. 'When Kiss were on stage, they had a certain vibe and image, and once they left that stage, you had absolutely no idea who they are.' Because Rob Sabino liked Kiss, The Big Apple Band/The Boys started going more in a rock direction – and most of their gigs were being booked by a promoter who was putting them in biker bars. They thought they were a white band, and when they came in, there was only one white guy in the band. A lot of times, they had to move quickly.

Playing venues all across New Jersey and New York, Rob Sabino recalls going to clubs that were exceptionally seedy just to get a gig. 'We played some wonderful gigs in some marvellous places. There was a particular gig in Metuchen, New Jersey. It was a longer trip for us in our cranky little vehicle. Nile and Bernard were true New Yorkers without cars, while I was out there in the suburbs. We pulled up outside this real, gangster looking place. We were in a hardcore inner-city black area and all these black guys are in the car, apart from me and my wife, and they wouldn't get out into this club. They said "you go in". Tony said "I'm not going in there". It was the best gig we ever had.'

The band became fearless. Rodgers recalls the times and the varied venues with great affection: 'When a band has something really unique and special, you can change the world and the way people think, even if it is just for a moment. We were booked in a biker bar in Queens, the sort where a black person would walk in and have the shit kicked out of them, as routine. The sort of place you know not to go. Our promoter didn't care because he had his money up front and we were left to fend for ourselves. The owner wasn't there when we arrived, and we set up and played a normal show. The place was going crazy! All these hardcore "I'll kill-a-fuckin'-nigger-on-sight" types love us and we have all these people eating out of our hands.'

The owner returned. 'He comes in while we're on our break, sees us and freaks out. He explodes, saying things like, "fuckin' nigger cocksucker – fuckin' promoter sending niggers to my club."' The owner screamed to Rodgers and Edwards that they were fired. However, the owner's girlfriend has seen the band perform twice already and suggested he reconsider his position. She calms him down and suggests that he should at least hear the group. 'He talks to the patrons, these Hell's Angels types,' Rodgers continues. 'They were all going "you're a genius man, we're having so much fun. These guys are great; they know every song". We played other people's music as if it belonged to us, as Bernard used to say "we attack their shit". Now the owner begs us to unpack. I couldn't help it – I raised the price, saying that we had to pay our roadie. The owner reluctantly agreed – and we absolutely slayed them. The funny thing was Bobby Cotter ended up taking the guy's girlfriend home.'

Unfortunately, for ex-*Jesus Christ Superstar* superstar, Cotter, his tenure with The Boys/Big Apple Band was approaching its end. A wild card at the best of times, his behaviour simply got too much. 'Bobby was a little hard to handle, a bit rambunctious,' Rodgers recalls. 'We ended up firing him – he was way too reckless.'

The group began to form into a unit and would also hang out and see their friends, hanging around rehearsal studios in New York. Vicki Wickham, the manager of Labelle at the time, recalls having to throw them out more than once: 'During early Labelle days they would come down to rehearsals and to the gigs. They knew Eddie Martinez, guitarist and Carmine Rojas and other band members, so always seemed to be around. Often I had to ask them to leave. It must have been if we were having "band meetings" or similar or if they were in the dressing room after a show and it was time to go! I knew them so it was friendly and silly, not officious. Everyone was used to me being "bossy boots" when the time came! I think a few Chic "moments" were inspired by the girls! Luckily they never took it personally and we have since always got on really well.'

With the help of long term friend, Rob Drake, and a set of very fortuitous circumstances, the first months of 1977 was to prove crucial to Rodgers, Edwards, Thompson and Sabino. From the time of the Big Apple Band auditions to the time Chic actually got a record deal, there were to be a number of serendipitous events that were to happen in their world.

7.
NIGHT OWLS

'You had the hippy on guitar, the R&B man on bass, the guy who loved Kiss on the keyboards and John Bonham on the drums. We all came from different worlds, but musically it worked – we didn't even have to talk about it. All we needed to do was pick up our instruments and all hell would break loose. We'd laugh all day long and create some wonderful stuff, go back in and listen to it and then go – holy fuck *– did we just do that!!'*
TONY THOMPSON – 2003

THERE WAS TO BE PLENTY of further machinations before Chic were to make it on to record. Edwards and Rodgers were eager to continue playing, and as The Big Apple Band, they honed their funky, freaky little jams into a working order. Now without 'problem' vocalist Bobby Cotter, the four-piece continued to slug it out in the bars, clubs and discotheques of New York City.

Although New York was portrayed as being in the midst of social decline at this point in its history, this was not felt in its music scene. With punk and new wave happening in clubs such as CBGBs on the Bowery, and disco being played in clubs elsewhere, there was a real uptown and downtown movement. Labelle manager Vicki Wickham remembers: 'There was a community feeling. Everyone knew everyone. We would laugh about musicians with a "718" (Queens, NY) area code because they had all played together, probably some went to school together, they were supportive of each other and would suggest each other for gigs. You never had to audition anyone; someone would simply give you a telephone number.' Players like Carmine Rojas, Sammy Figueroa and Eddie Martinez, all friendly with Rodgers, Edwards and Thompson, were key players on this scene, and often acted as this unofficial switchboard service between musicians.

A deep-seated passion for music was common to all of the players. Although notions of a career and getting on were, of course, prevalent, the love of music was always uppermost in the young players' thoughts: 'I was very impressed by their musicianship,' Rob Sabino recalls. 'Nile is a consummate musician, well-versed in all styles of music. That was the hallmark of most of us in what would become Chic – we could talk about Armenian folk music as well as Led Zeppelin. Nile was a studied musician – more into the jazzy side than I was. He was more jazz-R&B and I was more rock-R&B.'

Rehearsing out at Brandice High School, they were honing their jams. And, like many other bands in their situation, they had little money to their name, but what they lacked in hard cash, they more than compensated for in humour: 'We used to laugh. The entire time I was with them, and into the future with Chic, I did nothing but laugh – laugh and play music,' Tony Thompson recalls. 'We didn't have any money, and we'd go down to the street where we were rehearsing and buy one sandwich between the three of us. We bonded.' It was that bond, with the support of Sabino's keyboards that made for such scintillating performances. 'We considered ourselves a band, and we saw ourselves as that when we first started recording,' Sabino recalls. 'We had some friends do sessions and dubs with us, like (*percussionist*) Sammy Figueroa, others would do their things. We played and discussed how the music should go together. It was Nile and Bernard's decision to stay within those confines, to have the energy of a live R&B outfit – not be overly orchestrated or produced. There would be no gimmicks. They stuck to their guns – that's why I was impressed by them.'

Rodgers, Edwards, Sabino and Thompson were now in an established routine of playing as The Big Apple Band when they were doing their R&B gigs, and then as The Boys when they were playing rock gigs. Then a significant alteration had to be made. In late 1976, Madison Avenue jingle writer, the Mount St Michael High School-educated Walter Murphy, hit big with his single, 'A Fifth Of Beethoven'. Riding the first breaking wave of disco, Murphy had taken the drama of Ludwig Von Beethoven's Fifth Symphony, added crazily syncopated beats, and turned it into a floor-filling smash. The record was credited to Walter Murphy and The Big Apple Band, an ironic choice of name as Murphy had played virtually every instrument on the record himself. With its cheesy syncopation, it couldn't have been further away from the pared-down grooving that people had been witnessing courtesy of Rodgers and co. in clubs across New York.

Rodgers recalls that, 'everybody thought it was us, as we had been playing around all the discos. We were just blown away! How can this guy take our name? I'm sure he didn't know that The Big Apple Band already existed – but the record was bigger than big, so we now had to commit to a name.' Also, it was important to select the right name as the group's aspirations were growing. Rodgers was to tell *The Washington Post* in 1978 that, 'we didn't want to be a small band playing bar mitzvahs the rest of our lives. So we got into disco.' And by early 1977, disco was ready to saturate the mainstream in a manner unseen by pop music since The Beatles in the 60s. However, before the name had to be settled on, some records had to be made. It was time properly for the band to enter the studio.

There was a new optimism in America as Jimmy Carter was inaugurated in late January 1977. His down-home credentials meant that he received a remarkable 90% of the black vote and swept the South. His first, symbolic gesture of walking back from the Capitol to the White House with his wife and daughter truly reinforced his status as an 'outsider in the heart of America'. Instead of taking the motorcade, the short walk signified his desire to get closer to his people. His pardon to most Vietnam draft resisters appeared to wave a flag for the liberalism that had been so sadly repressed in the Nixon/Ford years. Although there were detractors who felt he had little firm policy and a false bonhomie, the difference between his predecessors and Carter, who like Franklin Delano Roosevelt 40 years before him, adopted casual clothes to talk directly to the nation from his armchair, was notable.

With this bright start, it was time for Rodgers and Edwards to mobilise. Rodgers has stated that a handful of characters played a critical role in assisting Chic on their path to success. Robert Drake is one of them. He was, at this time, the resident DJ at the prominent New York club, The Night Owl. He had drifted into DJing in 1973 by way of a happy accident, when he had been designing the sound system for the club. When the owners of the club came to visit him in his apartment and saw that he had two turntables side by side, they assumed Drake was a DJ. He was actually a studio engineer, who had worked with Ahmet and Neshui Ertegun, Arif Mardin and Sheldon Vogel at Atlantic.

I dabbled in music programming for myself and close friends for many years but never actually did it for an audience,' Drake recalls. 'They asked me if I would be interested in spinning a few nights at The Night Owl. When I told them that I had never DJ'd professionally, they asked me to come down to the club, which was a very posh penthouse, laid out like a living room. I went one night and discovered that their DJ did not mix records. I liked the music that he played but was unfamiliar with it because I was so absorbed with jazz. Inside of two weeks I was mixing his music, at which point they let him go and hired me for five nights a week. It catered mostly to an upscale black crowd, with me as the token white DJ.'

Drake got to know Rodgers and Edwards through Bobby Cotter, who had been introduced to him by Drake's room-mate, Kenny Lehman. Cotter and Lehman had spent time on the road together in the touring version of *Jesus Christ Superstar*. Drake ended up recording a demo for The Big Apple Band. 'We began to record material with him,' Rob Sabino recalls. 'Nile began trading session playing for studio time in order to make a recording. We used to do things like go into Electric Lady and The Hit Factory at two in the morning.'

Drake was impressed by what he had heard. 'Understanding the calibre of musician that they were, I gave them keys to my studio,' he recalls. 'I told them that they could rehearse whenever I was not recording in exchange for playing on some of the demos that I was doing for BT Express and Brass Construction.' Demo'ing material also gave Rodgers and Edwards the opportunity to call up friends to help them out. So often the core of the band would be augmented by Martinez, percussionist Sammy Figueroa and long-term friend Luther Vandross.

The demos that the band began kicking around were an extrapolation of an idea Rodgers had had of setting classics to a disco beat, in a more sophisticated style than records such as 'A Fifth Of Beethoven'; a disco rendering of 'Bess, You Is My Woman Now' and other George Gershwin tunes were what had been decided on as part of a 'Manhattan Symphony'. Yet one of these fledgling tunes was clearly head and shoulders above the rest; as part of this proposed disco symphony, there was a song called 'Everybody Dance'.

'It was me, Bernard, Rob and Tony; Eddie Martinez was on there, doing a guitar solo,' Rodgers recalls. 'There's a little harmony guitar thing in one of the breaks which I did for them when they were demo'ing it – you can hear that on the finished record,' Martinez was justifiably proud of his contribution to the track. 'We were all starting to come up together,' Rodgers continues. 'We got Luther to come in and sing, as we had been helping him in his band and had his girls – Alfa Anderson and Diva Gray – sing on the track. We had done most of that, but we didn't yet have a full song. The sound was tight and it rocked.'

The Night Owl was considered a buppy club; the clientele would come in and dance in their business clothing. It was here that Rodgers could see how the glittery, gaudy, upscale crowd would come to unwind after a busy day at work. The Night Owl began playing a demo of 'Everybody Dance' in heavy rotation, and it seemed that things were beginning to happen for the group. Their stylised, mannered track made perfect sense in this environment. 'People were freaking out,' Thompson recalls. 'They were going wild over this stuff and they didn't know who the freak it was. We would be in the DJ booth, watching the response and they would put on this demo and people would be going crazy. We knew we had something.' As disco was getting ever more lucrative, 1977 was the time to market that something.

Although 'Everybody Dance' had been recorded more for amusement than hard-nosed commerce, there was a swell of interest in the record; an opportunity presented itself that would help introduce Chic to the wider world. 'Dance Dance Dance (Yowsah, Yowsah, Yowsah)' – the record which was to make this introduction, had its genesis in a request for Edwards to do a record, on behalf of the New York Tourism Office to extol the virtues of the city. The theme song – 'I Love New York, What A Great Vacation' was designed to promote the city as a holiday destination in the post-*Taxi Driver* days when the streets were not thought of as especially traveller-friendly. However, the record's writer, producer and Drake's room-mate, Kenny Lehman needed a B-side.

Lehman was a writer, arranger and alto sax player who had been in the psychedelic band The Last Ritual, before joining Chelsea Beige and playing on their sole album, 1971's *Mama Mama Let Your Sweet Bird Sing*. He had subsequently gone on tour with *Jesus Christ Superstar*, where he had met Bobby Cotter. Lehman was to play a key role in Chic's initial success; he was even briefly considered to be an equal partner with Rodgers and Edwards.

Lehman first encountered the group when, in-between jobs, he established a company that booked bands for high school proms. The Cotter-led Big Apple Band, although musically streets ahead of the majority of their competition, could find little work. 'I had a little business called Prom-otion,' Lehman recalls. 'We were trying to sell bands for all the prom seasons. I put together a bunch of acts and put them on tape. I was able to sell all the bands apart from The Big Apple Band. They were incredible in terms of their skills and their musicianship, but the high schools were looking for something a little different back then. They were scuffling, trying to make it in the city. They were constantly recording little demos over at Robert Drake's studio. That's when I came across them. I thought they sounded great, especially the way that Nile and Bernard could both lock in. At the time Bernard was working a lot more than Nile. Nile's style was a little more unorthodox, and when you're an innovator, you don't get as much work. They were brilliant and worked as a team. They had this really unique thing and they were funny as well. Nobody was making any money, but they were making incredible music.'

Now a respected sessioner and producer, Lehman set to work on this New York B-side with Edwards. However, because Edwards had never written lyrics before, the pair got to a point where they could take the song no further. 'So Kenny calls me up to assist in writing the song, but not tell Bernard,' states Rodgers. 'So I get there and listen to it – and I say to him, *"what the fuck did you do?* I know what Bernard does, and *this is all Bernard."* He was jamming away with a Philly-influenced drummer. I added some bits to it. I told Kenny that I had to call Bernard, as the cut was becoming just him and me. So I called him, played him my part – and he and I wrote the song that became "Dance Dance Dance (Yowsah, Yowsah, Yowsah)."' Rob Sabino simplified the myriad of ideas that the two of them had, and suddenly Edwards began adding a melody out of the blue: 'he's got this whole song with the exception of the "Rumba, el tango' section," Rodgers recalls. 'I added that because I was reflecting the dance scene, wanting to talk about my life too.'

As the song was taking shape, Edwards began to talk about an old movie that he had recently seen on the TV. Released in 1969, *They Shoot Horses, Don't They?* was a perfect example of the changes that were sweeping Hollywood at that time, moving away from the established studio-controlled system. A dark little film, directed by Sydney Pollack and starring Jane Fonda, Michael Sarrazin and Susannah York, it centered on the desperation of those, who post-Depression, were forced to take part in the dance marathons that became popular in 1930s America in a desperate attempt to win a big cash prize. In the film, everybody is trapped by circumstance – the participants in the never-ending dance marathon; the audience, reduced to participating in such a sick spectacle; but most importantly, the endless repetition of the dance bands and the frenzied compère, played by Gig Young (who won an Oscar for his performance), whose relentless chant of 'Yowsah, Yowsah, Yowsah' acts as a clarion call for the proceedings. The only real redemption in the film was through death. Rodgers, too, had also seen the film and the memory had stuck with him; by using the central refrain from the film, it could prove a slyly ironic commentary on the current dance boom, where the ostensible optimism masked a country in doubt and decline.

The way Rodgers was thinking at the time meant that it would have been impossible for him to write a song called 'Dance Dance Dance' and for it not to be laden with meaning. 'We began writing songs that were full of history, culture and the black experience, loaded with people overcoming their situation,' Rodgers recalled. The double meanings, the masking even, that were to surround a handful of big Chic records was as subversive as anything Gil Scott-Heron was releasing. It didn't matter if you didn't get it, the point was that it was simply there. '"Dance Dance Dance", was all about the Great Depression. *They Shoot Horses, Don't They?*, all about how the poorest people in America could use dancing – even though it was almost slave-like – just to make 500 dollars, which was more than they could make in a year. People died during those dance marathons.'

'Human suffering has always been used as a form of entertainment – go back to the Coliseum, marathons, and people going to watch people die in a dance marathon. One couple would be the winner, take the money home and survive. The first time I went to a nightclub and I saw a DJ playing a 12" and it went on forever, a light bulb went on. In the old days the music was live, for however long the band could play – so it was slavery on both levels – people were watching the spectacles.'

✫ ✫ ✫

So, as the fledgling band pieced the tune together, they realised that Lehman had been sidelined. 'Kenny had been knocked out of the picture, even though he started the project,' Rodgers recalls. 'Bernard and I said that we had the right thing for him to do. As it was a white guy in the movie, we asked him to try the refrain.'

'So,' Lehman recalls, 'I held my nose and did the "Yowsah Yowsah Yowsah!"'

Kenny Lehman was a little more than just the voice on the record, however. 'Nile and Bernard started working on the song,' Lehman recalls. 'I started putting all these string and horn parts together. It was created like a creative arrangement – it was very complex – everything flowed from one motif to another. I was listening to Frank Zappa at the time, getting the idea from the strings and the horns.' Lehman received a co-credit for his work on the piece: 'He wrote it with us,' said Rodgers. 'He did the orchestration. We felt bad, we felt it did start with him, so let's bring him back in.'

The cream of New York session players came in to finish the track, including Luther Vandross and his singers. 'Then it was all done,' Lehman continues. 'Luther had a remarkable voice – his technique was impeccable. We got a bunch of the best. It was a real production. We didn't yet have a band called "Chic", just an idea that hadn't been created yet. We all loved the track.'

And still, the name. They toyed with naming themselves after a brand of orange juice called Orange Julius, ('It had all these symbols which were cool to us,' Rodgers laughs. 'A red devil with a pitchfork – damn wouldn't that be cool? We didn't understand trademarks then') and, somewhat unsuccessfully, Allah and The Knife Wielding Punks. 'I thought bands with names like Teenage Jesus and the Jerks were really funny,' Rodgers continues. 'I was working with a lot of Middle Eastern players like Jamshied Al Morad and Go'goush. I thought that Muslims would think we were cool. I didn't realise that you can't say anything negative against God. They just flipped out! They were saying – "I need to talk to you my friend" … we were going, well, isn't Allah just the word for God?'. They were going, "no no – it's the *name* of god." We felt terrible, because these were our friends.'

So, after considerable deliberation, The Boys and The Big Apple Band became Chic. Edwards had mentioned the name well before, when analysing Kiss and Roxy Music. Rodgers states: 'We did this whole mathematical bullshit, numerology – "well, there's two Ss, an I and a K in Kiss, and there are twos Cs, an I and an H – it's only two letters away from K – in Chic". We were in that ball park. It was that kind of rock and roll stupidity, but it made sense to us.' Rodgers and Thompson thought the name sucked at first. But several months later, realising they had to be called something, the name suddenly appealed. 'We thought that this name is genius, it's really cool.' Edwards was quick to remind them that he had mentioned the name the previous year and that they had both hated it. Rodgers replied, 'well, it sucked three months ago – now, it's cool!'

So, Chic was finally chosen. After previous discussions about adopting Roxy Music's style, suits seemed wholly appropriate for Chic. The image was one of proto Yuppy, early Buppies even. As Rodgers explained to Marc Taylor: 'People used to say, man, you guys look like bankers – that's what we wanted to be. We were always talking about getting ahead. That's what Chic was like. Our costumes made us look like bankers and business people. To us, it was just as over-the-top and flamboyant as Kiss.'

In the year when a buzz-phrase was 'dress for success', the appropriation by Chic of the business suit reflected the changes there had been in America since the Civil Rights movement. In 1965, black students accounted for 5% of enrolments in US colleges. By the end of the 80s, this figure had risen to 12%. Epitomised by Bill Cosby's epochal *The Cosby Show*, by 1990, 46% of black workers held white-collar jobs. However, the divide between the haves and the have-nots was growing ever wider. In the lowest strata, around a third of the African-America population, the jobless rate hovered around 60%. Given the widening gap, Chic, who were all from poor origins, captured the buppy spirit. Self-belief was high on Chic's agenda: 'I remember there was an air about the three of us,' Tony Thompson remembers. 'We would walk round New York just as the Chic thing was coming together. We owned that fucking place, man. We owned the city. We were getting free food in restaurants – anything we wanted – people would look at us differently – it was just a weird vibe. We would go to these clubs, and people would know about us. We were like gods to these people. It was freakin' nuts.'

Pleased with look, record and name, 'Bernard, Nile and I agreed that we would be Chic', Lehman recalls. 'I would do all the arranging; they would do the arranging in the context of the rhythm section – and then if this all works, we would consider going out on tour.'

A record deal was next on the agenda.

8.
TURNING TURTLE

*'Sometimes, encouragement is all you really need to hang on
in there 'til it happens.'*
VALERIE SIMPSON

KNOWING THAT THEY HAD a great, individual record recorded, the path for
Chic to get their debut single, 'Dance Dance Dance (Yowsah, Yowsah,
Yowsah)', released is both detailed and convoluted. After months of peddling
the demo unsuccessfully around the record companies in New York, Kenny
Lehman, Nile Rodgers and Bernard Edwards were drawing a blank. One
company, Atlantic, had turned the track down twice. But when Lehman went
to buy a new four-track tape recorder from Crazy Eddie's music store in
Manhattan, the story begins in earnest.

'I saw an old friend of mine, who knew me as a player; he used to hang
out at all my old gigs. He also knew Robert Drake,' Lehman recalls. 'He told
me that the guys he worked for – Lenny Fogel and George Kava – had some
money and wanted to do some work in the music business. They had an
electronics store on 46th Street called Sound City and they were looking for
an arranger for a band they had, called Shade. After a while, I started
arranging them.' Fogel and Kava had money and wanted a way to spend it.
Impressed with Lehman's ability in the studio, the entrepreneurs asked him
to join them as a partner in a new creative company, Turtle Productions.
Robert Drake's studio was to become Turtle's office and Fogel and Kava paid
the rent. 'Robert was really struggling and it helped him out a lot,' Lehman
continues. 'It was a good deal for all of us. It also meant that Robert was a
guaranteed guy to work for us when we needed productions doing.' Lehman
told Fogel and Kava that in 'Dance Dance Dance (Yowsah, Yowsah, Yowsah)',
he had an A & B side with which the entrepreneurs could break into the
music business. They went back to 'Dance Dance Dance' and tidied up
another demo that they had been working on, 'Sao Paolo', with sax and flute
arrangements by Lehman.

Another person who believed in what they were hearing was Valerie

Simpson, who knew the group, through her brother, Jimmy, a regular at The Night Owl. 'When Jimmy Simpson heard "Everybody Dance" at The Night Owl, he went *"holy shit, who are these guys?"* Rob goes – that's Chic, my friend Nile', says Rodgers. 'He called Ashford and Simpson, saying that they had to hear us. Ashford & Simpson get this close to signing us – they loved what we did. They said, "you can do more with two chords than anyone we've ever heard". They did something that changed our lives: They didn't sign us, but they hired us to arrange their record. We rehearsed "By Way Of Love (Express)" and "Don't Cost You Nothing". They gave us a big cheque and a sweet wonderful letter saying "thank you for your musicality". That gave us the confidence to continue.'

'We recognised them as being unique as soon as we heard "Dance Dance Dance",' Valerie Simpson remembers. 'They were young, fine and fired up! They definitely had their own space. At that point they had had many rejections, but we said YES! We just didn't have the wherewithal to launch them ourselves. But we knew they were going to be big. And sometimes encouragement is all you really need to hang on in there 'til it happens.'

A record had been made, backing had been provided, they had the support of industry veterans, but the group was still at something of a loss as to how to market it. As Rodgers and Edwards did not have any connection with that side of the business – knowing musicians but not promoters, the task of selling the record fell on Lehman's shoulders. 'The rest of it was the politics of selling the thing. I got to enough people, but I didn't get to any presidents,' Lehman recalls. 'I got to a lot of characters and record labels, but everybody said no. Atlantic turned it down flat. It didn't get anywhere near Jerry Greenberg. I exhausted all my connections. I used my Capitol connections through Last Ritual and Epic with Chelsea Beige. They said it was colourful and unique but it was nothing to do with them.'

Rodger Bell, Lehman's manager, recalls that, 'Lenny Fogel and George Kava didn't know what to do with the record and they were just about to sell the record off as a tax right-off. There was this great loophole in taxes for masters.' However, there was one last chance. 'There was this guy hanging out at Robert Drake's studio, called Everett "Blood" Hollins,' Lehman continues. 'He was a trumpet player, who'd been banging around for years. He was a talented, energetic guy, a real character. And he and his band decided that they are going to do an album.' Hollins was unconventional, and certainly a street player. 'I didn't know if he was a pimp or a musician when I met him. He looked like a real hustler. He was always trying to get money, because he knew that Lenny and George had plenty. He couldn't finish his album and get it done.' Hollins had good connections with one of the record labels, but they needed to hear a finished record. 'He kept on pressuring me to get money from Lenny and George,' Lehman laughs. 'He could really hustle people and I knew he knew people in the record business.'

Rodger Bell told him to go back to Hollins, and inform him that he would get money from Fogel and Kava for him to finish his album, if he would take

'Dance Dance Dance (Yowsah, Yowsah, Yowsah)' and get it sold. 'This is the kind of guy that could make it happen,' Bell states. 'They might not fit the bill, but that's what guys like this can do.' Lehman returned to Hollins and proposed the deal. He heard 'Dance Dance Dance (Yowsah, Yowsah, Yowsah)' and believed that he could easily sell it. 'Next thing you know, he goes to Tom Cossie. Cossie had been working over at Buddah – he had been head of promotions there and had a lot of pull. Blood Hollins was tight with Tom Cossie. Cossie heard it and wanted it.'

'When "Dance Dance Dance (Yowsah, Yowsah, Yowsah)" came across Tom Cossie's desk he realised that it wasn't the average R&B record,' Rodgers recalls. During his tenure as Senior VP of RCA Records the Pittsburgh-born Tom Cossie had helped launch and develop the careers of David Bowie, Lou Reed, Cuba Gooding, The Guess Who, Waylon Jennings and John Denver. He and his partner, Mark Kreiner, heard Chic through DJ Drake. 'He knew the record was special and quickly wanted to meet us,' Rodgers continues. 'He asked us what other material we had recorded. We played him "Everybody Dance" which was already popular downtown. He went "wow! That's better than this." He continued "holy shit; let me give you a singles deal." If "Dance Dance Dance (Yowsah, Yowsah, Yowsah)" hadn't happened, "Everybody Dance" and the rest of our career probably wouldn't have seen the light of day. That was the great thing about real record guys. Tom Cossie was a real record guy – he heard our record, went 'this is a smash. I will give up my job. I will sell the house for these guys – this is a hit! How often does a hit walk into your life?'

After taking the record around a considerable amount of business doors and having it thrown back in his face, Buddah Records showed great interest in Blood Hollins' recommendation. A deal was struck between Turtle Productions and Buddah. 'Dance Dance Dance (Yowsah, Yowsah, Yowsah)' was pressed up and promos began to fly up the dance chart – but Buddah Records had no proper papers for the deal. 'Cossie, who was consulting for Buddah must have just put it through himself. As a result, Turtle signed over only to Tom Cossie, not to Buddah', Lehman recalls.

Buddah had been set up by former Cameo-Parkway executive Neil Bogart in 1967, in partnership with Art Kass and Artie Ripp. After cleaning up with the bubblegum boom, by the mid-70s their fortunes were in decline. Bogart left to start up the Casablanca label, leaving Kass and Ripp as sole owners. Now owned by Viewplex, a slide and projector manufacturer, they were in dire financial straits. These financial issues aside, Buddah pressed up copies of the singles. However, the label was stalling – promos were out, and although proving hugely successful, they had 30 days in which to decide whether to pick up the option or not.

In response, Tom Cossie went up to his old work-mate, Atlantic Records' Jerry Greenberg's office on the Avenue of the Americas. Jerry Greenberg was unlike many other record executives of the time. A boisterous, garrulous, Jewish New Yorker, his Gene Wilder good looks had been seen frequenting many discos, and he had an ear to the ground. After a brief tenure as the drummer/vocalist in the beat band Jerry Green and the Passengers, he joined Atlantic in 1967 as Jerry Wexler's personal assistant. When Warner Communications bought Atlantic in 1969, Wexler spent his time in Florida, leaving Greenberg to work closely with Atlantic's president, the formidable Ahmet Ertegun in New York.

After holding positions such as Vice President of Radio Promotion and Vice President of A&R, in 1974, Greenberg became, at the age of 31, the President of Atlantic, the youngest person to hold such a position within the record industry. He was then signing artists and overseeing the company on a daily basis and he was a major player, having personally signed Abba, Genesis, Foreigner and the Spinners. He was a real eclectic musical visionary, understanding Manhattan Transfer, Roxy Music, Led Zeppelin and R&B. He was also one of the first businessmen to realise the potential of disco. 'One of my close friends was Steve Rubell. I realised people would go to clubs, hear music that they like and six months later it would be on the radio,' Greenberg recalls with affection. 'I would hang out at 54 and other clubs, and hear what was going on. Atlantic was voted the Disco Record Company Of The Year between 1976 and 1978. We were on top of it.'

Cossie had worked for Greenberg in promotion, so hoped he would at least provide a listening ear, although his company had rejected the record twice before. 'Tom Cossie comes up, and plays me the record,' Greenberg recalls. 'I loved it. I remember telling him that it was an absolute smash'.

Cossie made it clear to Greenberg that the option was not being picked up by Buddah. Greenberg knew a winner when he heard it and immediately began talking about cutting a deal: 'I said "let's work it out right away". I called my lawyers downstairs. "Cossie says that he wants to do the fastest record deal ever". He wants white label copies of "Dance Dance Dance (Yowsah, Yowsah, Yowsah)" pressed up for the *Billboard* disco convention that very weekend.'

Within 24 hours, a deal memo was drafted and signed. The deal was split between Lehman and Bell's Turtle Productions and Kreiner and Cossie's MK productions. 'In the meantime, I get a call from Arista boss Clive Davis. He says "Jerry – how can you do this to Art Kass?" Greenberg was astounded. 'What do you mean how can you do it? He had an option for 30 days and he didn't pick it up. Clive said "you're going to put a little guy out of business". I replied "Listen, if I don't sign them, then someone over at Arista's gonna sign them and you're gonna put *me* out of business! This is a hit record – the guy offered it to me and they're free to sign."' With a typical Greenberg flourish, he concluded to Davis, 'Look, Art fucked up – gimme a break. I didn't want to make anybody feel bad, but business is business.' Davis, whether genuinely concerned for his old colleague or speculatively on the poach, acquiesced and Greenberg signed Chic to Atlantic. Rodgers, Edwards and Lehman were elated. So too were Lenny Fogel and George Kava. *This was not just any old record company. This was Atlantic.*

The label was founded in 1947 by Ahmet Ertegun, the son of a Turkish diplomat, and student Herb Abramson, and named as a response to the west coast jazz label, Pacific. Ertegun, still co-chairman of the company, said in 2003, 'I've been, in one way or another, running this company since it began. Whatever has happened at Atlantic Records since it started, I get credit for – and many of the things I'm credited for were done by others: Arif Mardin or Jerry Wexler or my brother, or any one of a number of other people. I'm always asked where I found an artist. You're given credit for all the things that go wrong, so it's not all peaches and cream – but it's been wonderful. I do get involved to a certain extent with everybody that comes through here and Chic were certainly one group I remember fondly.' Atlantic had an incredible soul, R&B, blues, jazz and rock tradition. Although it had the heritage, it was not a disco label – although, as clubbing was his pastime, Jerry Greenberg was looking to introduce as many acts that reflected the current scene to his roster.

'Atlantic was a different place,' Rodgers remembers with awe. 'It wasn't just about Ray Charles or Ruth Brown – it was about the Stones, Yes, or Led Zeppelin. Ahmet Ertegun had become a very social New York person, because he could get you tickets for their gigs. We just couldn't figure out how we were going to survive there, because our music had nothing to do with what was going on at Atlantic. It wasn't a dance label; they didn't have a dance department. When we got there, they scrambled to catch up – they had this record, "Devil's Gun" by CJ and Company, and they put it out on a 12" with a yellow label, a generic jacket which said "disco" on it in pink letters. We thought that that was cool, so we asked for our record to be stuck in a similar bag. We thought we have one thing on our side – it's not just about R&B now – it was either Led Zeppelin, which we knew we were not or the disco guys, but that wasn't a great fit either, so we came up with urban legends about us, to look as if we were really part of the New York dance scene and somehow it stuck. That's the power of the printed word.'

In true escapist fashion, Rodgers sought to mask his itinerant, dirt-poor roots. 'When Bernard and I were putting together this early press stuff, we thought we have to control this machine – or else no one else is going to get it. There was no-one who understood.'

☆☆☆

With a new deal with Atlantic in place, the white labels of 'Dance Dance Dance (Yowsah, Yowsah, Yowsah)' were circulated around the disco convention. Greenberg takes up the story with characteristic aplomb: 'They bring the parts in, we cut masters. I arrange for a helicopter to fly the masters out to our pressing plant in Philadelphia and on Thursday, we have 2000 white labels that say "Chic – 'Dance Dance Dance (Yowsah, Yowsah, Yowsah)" to give out at the disco convention – the rest is fuckin' history. It's one of the great record biz stories. How fuckin' Greenberg did a deal and got it out within three days.'

The buzz that the record created at the disco convention was enormous: 'Other records were rolling off frequencies less than 60 cycles a record. We were boosting that shit. Nobody did that in those days. We cut deeper and wider grooves and have to that bass response, so you could take that record home and it didn't skip. We were pushing the limit,' Rodgers recalls. It was one of the first pop songs where you could feel the speakers rumble in clubs with every bass-beat.

A little extra spin was needed to push the record to the widest audience. The label proudly stated that the record was mixed by Tom Savarese. Savarese was one of the first celebrity DJs in America, having won the *Billboard* Number One Disco DJ title at the convention in both 1976 and 1977. He also had a new gig at the recently-opened Studio 54, the club that championed the record. 'It was all marketing,' Rodgers continues. 'We took him into the studio. He made one edit and it was all off the beat. Poor guy. He didn't really have anything to do with it. It would be like saying "Brain Surgery – Operation by Nile Rodgers'!" But using his name located Chic at the heart of the disco-loving zeitgeist, and Saverese became the first DJ to 'edit' a Top 10 single.

There was delight when 'Dance Dance Dance (Yowsah, Yowsah, Yowsah)' was finally released on Atlantic in October 1977. When Bernard Edwards took his finished copy home, there was much excitement in the household. 'When he came back home, every song to him was a great song – he would play songs and we would love them. But that one was special,' his son, Bernard Jr recalls. 'I remember him and my mother moving round the house dancing and singing. She used to clean to it.' It finally represented a concrete achievement after six years of hard work.

'Dance, Dance, Dance (Yowsah, Yowsah, Yowsah)' was to sell a million copies in its first month and become a huge worldwide hit. 'It went Top Five, just behind all those singles that came out from *Saturday Night Fever*,' Rodger Bell recalls. 'It would have got to No. 1 had that record not been there. It was released in the run up to Christmas, by an unknown act. We still took off anyway. All the people who'd been saying it was overproduced were all now saying how great it was.' The record was nominated for a Grammy in 1978. It penetrated the psyche of recent New York dweller, David Bowie. 'I was aware of Chic from day one,' he recalls. 'I loved the original Chic tracks from 'Dance Dance Dance' onwards'.

Much was made of the 'yowsah' refrain. For some listeners, it seemed as if they were saying 'yowsah', in terms of 'yowsah, master', the subservient cry of slave to owner. With the televised version of Alex Haley's *Roots: The Saga Of An American Family,* more were aware of its significance. *Roots* had been published in the summer of 1976 and had provided a necessary underscore to the pomp and circumstance of the bi-centennial celebrations. By the time it aired on nationwide US TV in January 1977, it was nothing short of a phenomenon.

Rodgers has said that, 'We couldn't believe they were so short-sighted that that's what they'd think we were saying. I was a subsection leader of the lower Manhattan Black Panthers. But no one knew that. I used to keep that a secret because I didn't want to endanger Bernard and his family.' Also, there was the almost entirely overlooked fact that it was actually the white guy, Kenny Lehman, on the record saying it. With the power that disco music was to wield, it could be interpreted that culturally, whites were becoming slaves to the black beat, as millions sought to appropriate black dance steps on dance floors across the world.

It was therefore decided that in future any deeper meanings would be covert, not overt, in Chic's lyrics. 'That was the bargain between Bernard and I – Mr Black Panther was never going to be politicising our music,' Rodgers said. 'That meant that the lyric writing had to be as clever as hell. There's no way I could write a song that could be blatantly "Dance Dance Dance" and that was the end of the story. It doesn't work for my soul. That's how Chic were supposed to work. It pains me that people don't understand the intellectual content of our lyrics after how hard we worked on a song.' This level of double entendre and masking was essential to the next three years of Chic, and can be heard on some of their greatest work. And everybody could dance to it.

African-American poet and commentator Amiri Baraka stated in his article, *The Blues Aesthetic and the Black Aesthetic* that, 'the highest intelligence is dancing. Not the Arthur Murray footsteps advertising! The highest thought is doing, a being not an abstraction.' The music Chic were beginning to produce was all about the now, about doing; about making it happen. 'Dance Dance Dance (Yowsah, Yowsah, Yowsah)' is an extremely intelligent record. It simply didn't matter if 97% of its end users overlooked its history lesson.

Brian Chin has called the record a roll call of 'disco's mythic history', a description of the dancing experience –

> *'Rumba, el tango,*
> *Latin hustle too*
> *Yowsah, yowsah, yowsah –*
> *I want to boogie wit' choo.'*

– on some levels there was little to separate it from Silver Convention's 'Get Up and Boogie' or KC's 'Boogie Shoes'; but that bass, those horns and strings literally leap out at you. The flutes and countermelody; the repetition. 'Best of all is Rodgers' guitar,' Chin continues, 'teetering on the edge of the mix underpinning the whole song. After three and a half minutes, Edwards takes the simplicity-itself bass line to the top of the fretboard and the song enters another dimension. Rob Sabino's off-kilter synth solo sounds as if it's an extra terrestrial trying to communicate with the dance floor.' Already, Chic sounded different. The vocals were detached and striking, having little of the warmth or passion of other R&B acts. Critic Peter Shapiro has gone as far to suggest that the title phrase is intoned by the vocalists like 'deer caught in the headlights.'

The record, although flawed, established the Chic template: strings, subtle horns and the Chic choir. Rodgers and Edwards quickly assembled five stalwart vocalists to aid them in their task: Norma Jean Wright, Alfa Anderson, Diva Gray, David Lasley and, of course, their great, long term supporter, Luther Vandross, who marshalled the team together. The vocals were layered with as many as six to seven singers in the background doing as many as four overdubs. This is what created the very heavy choral sound. The leads were done frequently singing a syncopated rhythm style patterned, often, around Edwards' bass line. Chin believes this special technique – almost the musical equivalent to Colonel Sanders' 11 herbs and spices – should have been kept a secret. 'Nile said that he always had men singing with the women – that would give it vocal dexterity. That to me was a production secret that he shouldn't have shared with anybody – men singing in unison with the women – that was one of his secrets to make that vocal sound unique.'

'Dance Dance Dance (Yowsah, Yowsah, Yowsah)' went to No. 1 in the US disco chart, No. 6 in the pop and R&B chart. In Britain, when released in November 1977, it reached No. 6 and remained on the chart for 12 weeks.

With this success, 'Jerry Greenberg got very excited, and put money up for the album,' Kenny Lehman recalls. As it became obvious that Atlantic were going to put a *lot* of money behind them, relations begin to worsen between all production and management parties. The newly-formed MK productions started to nudge Turtle out of the frame. Kreiner and Cossie suggested that Rodgers and Edwards should set up their own company.

9.
'AN UPTOWN BOOKER T AND THE MGS'

*'At that time, everybody got together; black, white, gay, grey
and just had a good time.'*
ALFA ANDERSON

CHIC'S SELF-TITLED DEBUT ALBUM was released in America on 22 November 1977. The cover artwork continued the Roxy Music theme, featuring two models and a stylized font – very *Country Life*. It was a fine, if anonymous seven-track recording, an outsider's approximation of what sophistication should sound like. The aspirational desires of Chic were made clear from the off – unlike other records of the time which had ideas rooted in the cosmos, this record lived in the real world – albeit it one of opulence and bright, shining hope.

It had a budget of $35,000 and it was recorded between Electric Lady and The Power Station, in less than three weeks, in a freewheeling yet business-like manner. Lehman recalls a happy atmosphere of cooperation, recorded with friends. The vocal dynamics were incredible in the studio, with Vandross playing the unifying force. 'I really respected Luther because he was such an awesome vocalist,' says Norma Jean Wright. 'He was, bar none, one of the best singers that I had ever worked with. Not only that, he kept us all in stitches because he was so gregarious and just really a lot of fun to be around. Luther and I sang a ballad on the first Chic album entitled "Falling In Love With You", and it is still one of my favourite songs.'

Whatever problems may have been looming between MK and Turtle productions, the sessions were joyous and speedy. There was an almost palpable sense of release, that finally, after so much waiting, they were now not only cutting an album, but one that looked as if it would be successful. 'We had a ball cutting that album with Bob Clearmountain and Tony Bongiovi,' Kenny Lehman recalls. 'We had great studio singers headed by Luther. It was still a production, though, as there was no featured vocalist. It had a lot of different colouration, variety and I felt like I was at my peak, writing for strings and horns, I felt as if, I was breaking new ground. Nile and

Bernard would be together at my house constantly, we went over to Brooklyn, doing some at Robert Drake's. We would do pre-production ahead of time to cut back on studio time. We worked our butt off – and, as a result, they loved it at Atlantic.'

Some of the album was simply the demos that they had cut when working with Robert Drake on the Gershwin tunes earlier that year at Sound Ideas. 'We had set a date and went there after midnight to record for 10 hours,' Drake recalls. 'Lo and behold, they surprised me with four originals, "Everybody Dance", "Strike Up the Band", "Sao Paolo" and "Est-ce Que C'est Chic". Most of those tracks were used for the first Chic album.' Although it's a slender album compared to their latter releases, it has a perfect veneer of faux-sophistication.

The final mixes were recorded at the newly opened Power Station, which was to become the group's studio of choice. 'We went to Electric Lady and put the strings on "Dance Dance Dance", mixed both that and "Sao Paolo,"' Rodgers says. 'Then went to what was to become The Power Station. We were the first project at that studio. The first thing they had done there was mix Meco Monardo's "Star Wars", and the first instruments to set up in there to record were Chic's.' Respected session-player Monardo was also to play on several later Chic productions.

'On the first album, we did everything we had to do,' Rodgers recalls. 'We knew what the structure of an album was, but we had to stand for who we are and as we are a rhythm section, you've got to indulge me. It had an instrumental. I took the view that you're going to hear me play music, so hear me play a song without singing. Too bad if you don't like it.'

David Lasley was drafted in to add vocals. 'I was aware of Nile and Bernard, but had never worked with them,' he recalls. 'I had worked with Kenny, however. I'd worked with a guitar player, Jerry Freidman, a legendary session guy. He was the first man I heard talking about Nile Rodgers and that was around 1975. I remember people were talking about their sound. It was disco, but the sound had a life force of its own. I came in after "Dance Dance Dance (Yowsah, Yowsah, Yowsah)" became a hit single and they had to jump in and go straight into album mode. Luther, me, Alfa and Diva. Those tracks were all done in two days at The Power Station, Friday and Saturday.'

Of the other material, 'Sao Paulo' is a text-book jazz-fusion instrumental from the day, and would not, to these ears, sound out of place on a Shakatak album. The track was also a product of Rodgers' fertile imagination. '"Sao Paolo", starts off with all these birds on the shore. We had absolutely no idea at the time that Sao Paolo was a metropolitan city, inland like New York. People from Brazil think it is intellectual genius taking these sounds from Ipanema beach and superimposing them over "Sao Paolo". They thought it was mad and clever: we didn't know any better. It probably should have sounded like the music from *Eraserhead*.' But mad and clever was what it was all about. The quality of ideas and the playing, on what ostensibly appeared to be another random disco album, elevated it from the other releases of the day. The woodwinds, provided by Lehman, give the album a different bite to the rest of Chic's career.

As well as their first anthem, 'Everybody Dance', *Chic* also contained 'Strike Up The Band', (with its nod to Boz Scaggs' 'Lowdown'). Rodgers was passionate about having an anthem with which to introduce the band. 'Part of the Chic template came from a very specific R&B school,' Rodgers states. 'R&B bands would have an intro song – Kool and The Gang would come out to "Kool And The Gang". So we wrote a song that was going to introduce our next shows.' 'You Can Get By' was an uplifting cut, showing the need for self betterment, removing shabby clothes and letting natural beauty show through. Rodgers told Marc Taylor: 'Because of my political history, I couldn't stand to be in a band that wasn't about uplifting the race. So, what we would do was hide it in our songs.' The Norma Jean showcase, 'Falling In Love With You', was, despite blandly blank lyrics, the first great Chic ballad, showcasing David Friedman's vibes.

The album succeeded perfectly in introducing the warmth of Chic's sound to the wider world. This sound came about through a natural jamming process: Edwards told *High Fidelity* Magazine in 1979, 'We'll work out a tune at home and tape it there, ironing out all the different parts.' He harked back to the success of the Big Apple Band in helping with this. 'Years ago Nile and I worked in a three-piece show band, where we had to cover all the different instrumental parts between us. So now, it's natural for us to hear all the parts of a song when we write it. Also, jamming at home first helps us lock into the groove before we take it to the studio. We get the same loose, good-time feeling we used to get as kids jamming in the basement. After we've worked out the tune, we'll go into the Power Station and lay down tracks as soon as possible. Our engineer, Bob Clearmountain, gets our natural sound on tape. He's really a key part of our team.'

The sound surprised and delighted many a critic. Don Waller called the album 'an uptown Booker T and the MGs'. *Billboard* was fulsome in its praise, stating in December 1977 that, 'this is a diverse set from the group which has a major disco hit with "Dance, Dance Dance (Yowsah, Yowsah, Yowsah)." That good-timey cut is included, along with several less gimmicky tracks which could move the group strongly from its disco base into pop, soul and MOR radio formats. These include a super-sexy Diana Ross-styled vocal number, a male vocal cut with good R&B possibilities and a flowing, melodic Brazilian-flavored instrumental. Best cuts: "Dance, Dance, Dance," "Sao Paulo," "You Can Get By," "Falling In Love With You."'

It wasn't just the media who were impressed: Robert 'Kool' Bell, the head Gangman, recalls hearing Chic for the first time on this record: 'I knew they were going to be successful – they had a little bit of class. Times were changing; people were looking to have a good time and Chic just kind of fell right into the slot. They were the classier side of the disco thing; Chic were slick, taking the French word, they were on another level. They had a little funk to it – they were different – they had a little bite to them...' Finally, the public were

impressed: in early 1978, buoyed up by the continuing strong performance of 'Dance Dance Dance (Yowsah Yowsah Yowsah)', the album reached No. 27 on the pop charts and No. 12 on the black charts.

Everyone who came in touch with the group wanted to help as much as possible and the list of thanks on the album sleeve was a summary of the previous year. Among the 16 names receiving special thanks were Kava and Fogel; Jimmy Simpson; Rodger Bell and 'Blood' Hollins. One of the most heartfelt thanks went out to Bernard's first wife, Alexis Edwards. 'Everybody knew my mum,' Bernard Edwards Jr recalls. 'She used to send food down to the studio; not just that, she was literally a supportive wife. He was never at the studio getting nagging calls or things like that. She made herself available to him when he needed it – and that was a rarity. A lot of the women want to get wrapped up in the glitz and the glamour, and the money. She was raising us – she wasn't out there buying Chanel and whatever. Everyone respected her as such – she never disrespected herself.' The credit on the sleeve of their debut album bears out the love and respect that Chic all felt towards her.

By late 1977, The Night Owl, the club which had cemented The Big Apple Band's transformation to Chic, had closed: Rob Drake had continued to play there until the fire department closed the club down for overcrowding. Because he was always DJing, he never saw the line that was permanently around the corner to get in. He went off to DJ in Italy. Alexis Edwards threw him a leaving party. His help had been essential for Chic.

With a nationwide release, the buzz generated demanded some vocalists to take this studio project further and then possibly out on to the road. The time had arrived to put together a touring band.

One of the key architects of the sound, Rob Sabino, was not to join the touring group. Sabino had been leading a double musical life since joining The Big Apple Band. 'I was faced with a decision, because I was primarily a writer and arranger myself. I'd joined The Simms Brothers Band with my old Howard band colleague, Mickey Leonard, and I wanted to start recording with them. I'd written more rock material with them, as I didn't write in the disco style. We used to do some of my material with The Big Apple Band, but since we had become Chic and there was a specific flavour, direction and image, it would not have been right to do my stuff.' Sabino decided to leave. However, Rodgers, Edwards and Thompson were not going to let their old Big Apple Band comrade simply disappear; 'They told me that they still would love to use me on the studio sessions. I'll always be grateful to them for that.' Sabino was able to combine his membership of The Simms Brothers and return to the studio and play with Chic. This long and fruitful relationship meant Sabino played on every single Chic and Chic Organization album apart from 1980's *Real People*.

Norma Jean Wright, who had sung on the studio sessions, was to become their lead vocalist. She had been born in Tennessee, where her mother had been a school teacher, who gave up her job to look after her children, while her father was a supervisor at a steel factory. 'I knew I wanted to become a singer at the age of eight', Wright recalls. 'My sister and I sang duets for my family and we also were in the children's choir at church. So I was motivated and I knew even then that one day I would pursue my dreams to sing.'

She had been singing while living in Toledo, Ohio, including on the rare soul gem, the *Timeless Legend* album by Timeless Legend. She relocated to New York in 1976. 'When I moved to New York, it was so vibrant, and there was so much musical creativity going on throughout the city,' Wright recalls. 'There were some great live bands, there was jazz, blues, funk, r&b, rock, gospel, dance, classical, you name it, it was all right here in this big city. I remember going to this club called Mickells, and I heard Phyllis Hyman sing for the first time. Her voice was as rich and as smooth as butter. I found my niche and made friends pretty quickly, and so I didn't feel so badly about being an out-of-towner however, there were times that I missed my family and friends from Ohio. Nevertheless, I was always optimistic that I was destined to sing, so this kept me going.'

'Initially, when I moved to New York, I auditioned for a local band,' she continues. 'Luci Martin auditioned for the same band. We were both hired and subsequently, we became good friends. So I met Luci before any of the other guys in Chic.' Luci and Norma Jean had been working in Canada, when back at a party in New York they were introduced to Rodgers and Edwards by mutual friend, Lynaa Davis. Wright auditioned for Chic, at the time when they were working on 'Dance Dance Dance (Yowsah, Yowsah, Yowsah)'. When the single was picked up by Atlantic, Norma Jean returned from Canada to be their vocalist.

A touring replacement was needed for Sabino. Tony Thompson introduced Raymond Jones to Rodgers and Edwards. After leaving Labelle, Thompson had played briefly with Jones in the Queens-based disco band Ecstasy, Passion and Pain, which had also featured vocalist Barbara Roy and Connie Harvey. Impressed with Jones, Thompson recommended him to Rodgers and Edwards. 'I was 19. My main background had been Latin music, and I started doing some R&B and disco stuff,' Jones remembers. 'Ecstasy, Passion and Pain had this maniacal manager who got us gigs in Brooklyn – at 2001 Odyssey, the club where they filmed *Saturday Night Fever* and places like Cherry Hill, New Jersey – it wasn't exactly Mafia-related, but it certainly had that kind of overtone. Through that band, I met Tony. I loved what he did and he liked what I did. When he was working with Nile and Bernard, they already had Rob on keyboards – but he couldn't make a gig, so Tony called me and I sat in. I guess they must have liked what they heard, because when they put the touring band together, I got the call.'

A string section needed to be drafted in, to swell the sound: Karen Milne became the section leader. 'I was a classical violinist, a kid barely 20 years old,' she recalls. 'New to New York City from the mid-west, the autumn of 1977. A typical day, collecting mail … I was checking the bulletin board for kittens for sale when I noticed a small handwritten index card, partially hidden by other things. "Up and Coming Disco Band looking for Female Violinist," it said.' Milne was invited to a rehearsal studio on 52nd Street,

where she auditioned in front of Rodgers, Edwards and Thompson, Jones, Wright and Vandross. Within a few months, she became Thompson's partner, as well. Violinists Cheryl Hong and Marianne Carroll joined at the next rehearsal. Several days later, auditions for a horn section took place. Jeanne Fineberg and Ellen Seeling joined. With the strings and horns in place, the group were ready to rehearse in earnest for live work.

So, from their studio collective roots, Chic were on their way to becoming a recognisable pop band. The early press pictures make the group

– Rodgers, Thompson, Edwards and Wright – look like they are off on the yellow brick road. When you look at these pictures, it is Norma Jean alone that fronts the group. 'The public image of Chic at this point was Bernard, Tony, Norma Jean and me. We didn't look like hot stars. The art director Bob Defrin, took two second-string models and put them on the cover of our debut album,' Rodgers states. 'People thought that was who Chic was.'

'Nile and Bernard's choice for the

cover of the first LP they specifically selected models whose ethnicity was questionable,' future member Alfa Anderson recalls. 'It sort of blurred the lines. At that time, everybody got together; black, white, gay, grey and just had a good time.' Norma Jean Wright recalls being frequently asked by radio DJs which one she was on the album cover.

'Bernard and I did our job too well,' Rodgers recalls. 'We wanted to be anonymous, as we were always comfortable behind singers, like New York City or Luther, which is why we made the girls take centre stage.'

Chic's inaugural live performances featured Norma Jean, standing centre, flanked by Rodgers and Edwards, with Vandross and Luci Martin standing all the way over to the right, with the horns and strings upstage left.

Luci Martin was born in Queens on 10th January 1955. She had trained with a former Alvin Ailey dance student and had become a singer-actress in road companies of *Hair* and *Jesus Christ Superstar*. She passed the audition and became second vocalist. She also had a blues-rock background. 'I'd met Norma Jean through a band I called The Never-Ending Rehearsing Band. We never performed, but boy, did we diligently rehearse,' Martin sighs. 'We became very good friends. Through the years we would look out for each other.' Norma Jean got in touch with her when the vacancy for a backing vocalist came along. 'It was raining when I went over to the audition. I listened to the record, and they asked me to sing a couple of things. They said "we need to discuss this" and proceeded to walk down the hallway and then walk straight back up again and say – OK, you're in.'

'Norma was in the middle carrying the show', Rodgers recalls. 'It sounded like the record, but it didn't look as people thought it was going to. So, at our first couple of shows, the audience didn't understand. People were complaining as to where the other girl was. Norma Jean could have been one of these girls on the album cover.'

Rodgers and Edwards decided that the group needed a light-skinned and exotic counterpoint to Norma Jean Wright, and the two girls could be put together to recreate the debut album sleeve on stage: 'We had open auditions,' Rodgers recalls. 'We auditioned Clair Bathe who was to sing "There But For The Grace Of God Go I" for Machine. She was good, but she couldn't dance – and we really needed a dancer. Bernard and I were designing the role of the second girl in Chic, which exists to this day, as a means to get every designer to give us clothes. We needed a girl who was small enough to wear sample sizes. While Norma Jean – and later Alfa – was singing, so the other girl would be doing the fashion show, getting the latest fashions from designers. Luci Martin, Norma's friend, stepped down from backing vocals and came out front. Her dancing made us look balanced.'

To fill the backing vocalist vacancy, Vandross' old sparring partner and session singer from the first album, Alfa Anderson joined. 'It sounded the same, but people went crazy and it balanced the stage,' Rodgers laughs. 'We put together a band from the best of them. Norma just did the first album, then we got Luci as well', Thompson remembers. 'Luci was my favourite singer and person in the world. She's great. It was a whirlwind of things how we all got together.'

One thing would be most important for the expanded group: image. Building on the Roxy Music template, it was absolutely essential that the band looked the part; a high-fashion shop-window. Rodgers and Edwards ensured that they controlled how the group should look. 'They took us shopping,' Karen Milne recalls. 'We went to all these fancy stores and designers – all these outfits and shoes, and make-up people and all those kind of things. They definitely had that look they wanted. It was never anything too revealing or outrageous, ever. It was always respectful, sophisticated and classy. We got a lot of Norma Kamali stuff, all bright colours. I'm a redhead and I always wore either a bright red dress or a black dress. They would put my hair into a ponytail and make me look like a cheerleader.' Luci Martin was delighted at the clothes shopping: 'It was a tremendous perk. It was like playing dressed up, like going through mom's closet!'

The image; the appropriation of business dress, a reflection of the Buppy culture, showed that African-Americans could now dress up and be a part of the establishment. And, with the touring band, they offered a model of racial integration as well. Chic's music and appearance was one of the strongest yet subtlest political statements in popular culture in the late 70s.

And then, the record that they had been playing down at the Night Owl for all those months, 'Everybody Dance', became Chic's next single, released in March 1978. Written as part of Rodgers' mythical dance extravaganza, 'Everybody Dance', by now around a year old and the star track on the Chic album, was a ready-made follow-up, waiting to happen.

Bernard Edwards' place in the rock and roll hall of fame was secure for the opening bass part of 'Everybody Dance' alone. With its relentlessly up message, one of Rodgers simplest, it was as if a manifesto was being laid out for all to hear. Chic were to be practitioners of the good feeling. Intoned with one of Norma Jean Wright's most soulful vocals, the redemptive and healing power of music and dancing is again writ large.

'Music never lets you down puts a smile on your face, any time, any place;
Dancing helps relieve the pain, soothes your mind, makes you happy again.
Listen to those dancing feet, close your eyes and let go:
But, it don't mean a thing if it ain't got that swing
… strutting to our favourite tune, the good times always end too soon.'

Sabino's lilting piano figure, Thompson's close mic'ed drums and Vandross' unmistakable voice on the chorus serve to make the record irresistible, and then, as if to emphasise its rock knowledge, it finishes with a George Harrison-esque slide guitar solo.

When Rodgers said that Edwards sole purpose as a musician was, 'to produce care-free music for those who work hard five days a week and go out at the weekend to dance and have fun,' it could not have been closer to the mark. This single was a perfect example of his maxim. It reached No. 9 in the UK and No. 38 in the US. But this was still nursery slopes stuff compared to the peaks of what was to happen next. But, before that happens, it is important to assess what was happening in the world of music in 1977/78.

10.
FREAK OUT!

'It all happened against the backdrop of one of the heaviest recessions
in the United States. You saw people being really depressed.
That whole dance thing – that's where people went to try and escape.'
KENNY LEHMAN, 2004

WHILE CHIC WERE GETTING their record deal, two events were unfolding
that would ensure their mass popularity: the opening of Studio 54 and the
filming and international release of *Saturday Night Fever*. By the end of 1977,
the first year of Jimmy Carter's presidency, the world and his dog seemed to
be clambering aboard the disco bandwagon, as it was the music of
celebration and escapism. And, with everything in place, it was time for Chic
to ride on the wave of the phenomenon that was about to break world-wide.

It is 2nd May 1977, and a very special birthday party, organised by
designer, Halston, is taking place. With her hair thrown back, the birthday girl,
Bianca Jagger, is sitting astride a white stallion – a gift from Mick, then still
just about her husband. A man sporting a moustache is leading her and the
horse. At first glance, it appears he is wearing some kind of close-fitting body
suit. On closer inspection, you realise he is actually stark bollock naked, with
his entire outfit painted on. Bianca is looking as sultry as is befitting the
legendary socialite and wife of the world's most dandified rock star, in her
off-the-shoulder red dress. The man leading the horse looks like what was to
become the stereotype of the homosexual male – Latino with a thick
moustache and thinning hair. However, this is not on a ranch or a country
estate – this is on the dancefloor at what became the most notorious nightspot
of the 70s – Studio 54.

Later the same evening, Bianca with her stellarbiz buddy Liza Minnelli
would be photographed holding white doves. As the music of choice of the
establishment – disco – had become increasingly opulent and moved away
from its underdog roots, a suitable venue had to found where these
mechanically plump and gaudy tunes could be showcased. In an old CBS
television studio on 254 West 54th Street, New York, the music met its match.

An enormous cut-out of a spoon feeding cocaine to the man in the moon welcomed guests to the cornucopia of discretion and understated opulence that was Studio 54.

Bianca astride her mount is one of thousands of images that have come to symbolise Studio 54: Leonard Bernstein tangoing in wild abandon with his daughter Jamie. Minnelli, again, her hair caught splayed and wild, with an afro'd dude, throwing his arms in the air. John Travolta and Sylvester Stallone ordering drinks. Al Pacino looking startled with retinas the size of rugby balls. A fat Liz Taylor here, a fat Liz Taylor there, here a Liz, there a Liz, everywhere a Liz, Liz. All of this fuelled by their high of choice; drink, laughing gas, amyl nitrate, cocaine, Quaaludes, and for some, music. In a world where George Lucas' *Star Wars*, released to such phenomenal success in May 1977, was storming ahead at the box office, Studio 54 became somewhere you could reach the galaxies yourself.

Every generation gets the musical craze it deserves. The 70s got disco. And at the forefront of the mania were this superannuated nightspot and a film and record called *Saturday Night Fever*. Although progressive rock or punk may affectionately be recalled when discussing the era, disco was the one music that briefly united America and the UK in a manner unseen since The Beatles 13 years previously. If the music's roots were shady; Civil and gay rights-inspired and underground; it didn't matter because now, with some celebrity and pop favourites The Bee Gees in tow, it was safe, sanitized and mass-produced.

Studio 54, the primary symbol of disco, opened on 26th April 1977 with an invite that ordered: 'THE PLEASURE OF YOUR COMPANY IS REQUESTED FOR THE PREMIERE OF STUDIO FIFTY-FOUR TUESDAY EVENING THE TWENTY-SIXTH OF APRIL NINETEEN HUNDRED AND SEVENTY-SEVEN AT NINE O'CLOCK. ATTIRE – SPECTACULAR'. The club, run by fledgling restauranteur Steve Rubell, and his lawyer Ian Schrager, became the world's premier disco venue. Although their first venture, a club in Douglaston, Queens, called The Enchanted Garden, was shut down due to neighbour complaints, this was not going to happen again. Their new venture was not to be a dowdy, eyes-focussed-on-feet club. It was, as, Brewster and Broughton comment in *Last Night A DJ Saved My Life*, the 'last throw of the 70s dice. Blowjobs in the balcony; adultery in the ante-rooms; buggery in the bathroom'. In the pre-AIDS world, Studio 54 was a syncopated Sodom and Gomorrah. The 5,400 square feet of dancefloor had 54 different lighting effects; technology that had first been used on the NASA space program was utilised to illuminate the debauchery.

Studio 54 was far from being the first disco. In the 60s, everybody knew about clubs such as Chez Regine in Paris, the Whiskey A Go Go in London and Arthur in New York. However, the notion of dancing to records had waned in the Age of Aquarius, when live music took precedence. With the advances in Civil, gay and women's rights, dancing, for so long the ultimate form of personal freedom and celebration, had become fashionable again.

Although there were many other clubs, it was Studio 54 that grabbed the popular imagination. From the very building where shows such as *The $64,000 Question* had been filmed, this new hedonism and opulence rang out. Americans were ready to party. One of the beautiful people who viewed this spectacle was Vicki Wickham, manager of Labelle and Dusty Springfield. 'Studio 54 was heaving. Things were new and for the first time just as they had been in London. There was extreme energy. There was nowhere better to relax on huge, comfortable leather banquettes and watch the endless comings and goings of beautiful people, hear great music, dance, pull someone heavenly and the next day, do it all again!,' she recalled.

Also, the prevailing political climate ensured that disco had a different feel to it than other movements: 'It all happened against the backdrop of one of the heaviest recessions in the United States,' Kenny Lehman recalls. 'You saw people being really depressed. That whole dance thing – that's where people went to try and escape.'

Today, disco either gets rubbished or over romanticised; a shorthand for the crimes performed against 'serious' music, or it becomes revered beyond all proportion. It can often be easy to forget that, in the midst of all of this, there was a cavalcade of brilliant, shining records. DJs like Richie Kraczor and Wayne Scott spun the sounds. Although it was mainstream in its selections, anthems such as Frantique's 'In the Bush' were to break big time through the club. And in 'Dance Dance Dance (Yowsah, Yowsah, Yowsah)' and the white labels of 'Everybody Dance', Chic provided a magnificent soundtrack to the early days of the club.

The music was reaching a commercial apogee. With tuned-in people like Jerry Greenberg running record companies, more money was invested into the disco dollar. The music industry woke up to the whole new club audience – bypassing radio, these records could be played, adored and purchased. By 1976, the 12" single (which replaced a 33rpm 7") became the industry standard. Ahmet Ertegun, the man who had introduced Ruth Brown and Ray Charles to the mainstream musical world was completely smitten: 'I loved disco music,' Ertegun recalls. 'Disco music produced some tremendous hit songs, as well as being dance records. "I Will Survive" became like an anthem. Donna Summer had such a great run and she was a wonderful singer. It keeps coming back – you think it's over and the next thing you know, you're somewhere and you hear "YMCA"; it has not, and never will, leave us'. All of these records were to become huge records for Studio 54.

Bryan Ferry, too, was a regular on the scene. He had taken up part-time residence in New York after splitting Roxy Music in 1976.
'It was exciting – it was a lot more exciting than London to me. It was New York at its hottest,' Ferry recalls. 'You would find such an incredible mixture of people, every night of the week. Manhattan's amazing, because you could go to several things in one night and they would all be different scenes. Only a few blocks apart – and you always ended up in 54 or Xenon. It was like art people, with a few music people – Nile was in on all that – although there

weren't that many musicians. You'd see Truman Capote, Holsten, Andy and all his Factory gang. And then in would arrive the socialites, the black tie people – Ahmet Ertegun would come in with some weird kind of Newport people – it was an incredible mixture of all sorts; models; playboys. Nile was very much at home with all of that. And they danced to his groove.' It wasn't to everyone's taste, however. 'I went to Studio about twice; it was too glitzy for me,' David Bowie remembers. 'I became a Mud Clubber around 1978. That was the club for me.'

Studio became the place to test the hits. Ahmet Ertegun sent a copy of the newly-recorded Rolling Stones track, 'Miss You', to Rubell; the crowd went wild. Rubell informed Ertegun that the Stones were about to have one of their biggest hits of all time. By summer 1978, The Stones, too, would 'go disco'. Wayne Scott, the DJ at Studio 54 recalls, 'Studio 54 was such a show – at the gay clubs, you could play things that were different. At Studio, you had to stick to the *Billboard* Disco Top 20. All the *Billboard* people were there and all the people who sung the *Billboard* hits were there. We were also expected to mix in some alternative records like Talking Heads who were very discoized anyway.'

'When Studio 54 was in the middle of its whole "oh my god" phase,' DJ John De Mairo recalls. 'The DJ was Richie Kraczor – playing stuff that was what The Garage turned into, but it was so overwhelmed by the scene that the music was irrelevant. If you know Mick Jagger and Liza Minelli are going to be hanging out, that becomes more important than the music that is being played.'

'I knew Steve Rubell, of course, but I wasn't a druggie so didn't spend long stretches downstairs in the "office," which the white powder brigade did,' Vicki Wickham recalls. 'I just visited and "collected" people and took them back upstairs. There was a balcony with an overhang, great for people-watching and on the main floor plenty of places to sit/lie down! Remember too, like London, I was privileged and could get through "the velvet rope" so never had to wait.'

Getting into the club could, of course, prove a nightmare. Using promoter Carmen D'Alessio's extensive contact list and Marc Benecke on the door, Studio 54 became world famous for its notoriously selective and frequently arbitrary door policy. Rubell himself would often oversee Benecke. Disco historian Brian Chin remembers: 'They wanted some of the picturesque street stuff, the gay stuff, so the glitterati wouldn't think it's all sterile and unhip inside – they wanted some of these people inside as accessories.' Rubell called it 'tossing the salad', making sure that no particular group had precedence in the club.

Other clubs benefited from the erratic and highly individualistic door policy of Studio – Le Jardin, New York New York, Xenon. Chin continues: 'There was no time to be upset by not getting into Studio. How can I be so upset with not getting in there when I could just walk into clubs like Better Days? You could just nip in, there was no attitude – always welcome – some champagne with a little grenadine in it. The Garage was big and imposing. Better Days was always good and vibey. It cut many ways, across race and class.'

Disco was the movement that symbolised helping yourself as opposed to helping each other. 'The whole unity thing started to break down,' Chin recalls. 'People started to want to be successful in their own way. They went out to the whole disco party, and realised that they could make money in their own way, with the whole disco culture, look and style.'

By late 1977, things were changing. Rodgers, speaking in Anthony Haden Guest's *The Last Party*, noted that by this point, the 'Bohemian aspect was all lost. Now you had Frank Sinatra doing disco records, you had Dolly Parton doing disco records. You had anybody doing a disco record, to get a hit.'

The opulence of Studio and the bleak subtext of the dance marathons in 'Dance Dance Dance (Yowsah, Yowsah, Yowsah)' seemed to be coming true, a point that was not lost on Rodgers. 'When I went to a nightclub in the old days, it was like a spectacle. And it was replicating itself all over the world. People in the mid-west started imitating Studio 54. Then you'd go to some den of iniquity in Paris or London and that, too, was imitating Studio 54. It was great. It was interesting to me as a political person and we wrote about it, at first from afar and then it seduced me – and I got into it – it sounds like an over-intellectualisation, but it's not. It's exactly how it happened.'

How had disco travelled from its hip, underground roots, to this position? Easy: money. 'It became very elitist; you had to be able to have the cash to hang in there on the top levels,' Robert 'Kool' Bell recalls. 'To get in to Studio or Xenon, you had to be a player with serious cash. You don't walk up to Monte Carlo unless you got some money.'

But while Studio 54 and its myriad copycats were crystallising disco at the time for effete rich people, a film and album were to be released that were to shake popular culture to its core, and Chic would indirectly benefit. With the release of *Saturday Night Fever*, everyone could join in. Although the highbrows sneered and the originators of the music had long moved on, the film and its music were a phenomenon.

The film was based on Nik Cohn's slender article, *Tribal Rites Of The New Saturday Night*, which was published in the *New York* magazine on 7th June 1976. The story centred on Vincent, who, like countless others, stuck in the grind of the day job, lived for the weekend at the 2001 Odyssey club in the Bay Ridge area of Brooklyn. Although at the time it was taken as reportage, it was actually written using a composite of what Cohn had seen in black clubs such as Othello's on 8th Avenue, mingled with his experiences from his youth in London's Shepherd's Bush. Whatever it was based on, it grasped the timeless nature and universal understanding of living for the hedonism of a Saturday night.

Cohn and Australian-born impresario Robert Stigwood – who had known each other in passing in the UK in the 60s – became friends when they lived five blocks away from each other in New York. Stigwood read the piece, recognised its potential and approached Cohn to buy the rights. The reaction to the story was instant. 'I was stunned,' Cohn laughs. 'I couldn't credit the reaction. It was a pretty fair piece. But that it spawned a global phenomenon, I was the most astonished person you could ever think of.'

Stigwood had enjoyed a varied and frequently successful career in pop from producing John Leyton's 'Johnny Remember Me' in the early 60s to working with The Beatles' manager Brian Epstein, and, of course, managing The Bee Gees. He had diversified into stage and film and had enjoyed a remarkable run of successes, from *Hair* and *Oh! Calcutta*, to *Jesus Christ Superstar* and *Evita*. Stigwood produced the film of *Tommy*, directed by Ken Russell. The newly-formed RSO Films were ready and primed for success. He also had young actor John Travolta – then best known as Vinnie Barbarino on US TV series *Welcome Back, Kotter* and for his supporting role in *Carrie* – under a three-picture contract, in a manner not dissimilar to the classic ownership of stars by studios in Hollywood's golden era.

With a charismatic star and a robust story, the film started shooting in April 1977. John Badham was to direct, replacing original director John G. Avildsen. Aside from TV movies, he had only one picture to his credit, the Motown-funded *The Bingo Long Travelling All-Stars & Motor Kings*, which starred Richard Pryor and James Earl Jones. *Serpico* writer Norman Wexler shaped Cohn's crepuscular vignettes into a script. All that was needed now was some music.

The music of *Saturday Night Fever* was largely a reflection of what could be heard in many mid-town New York clubs at the time, as disco had been around for some three years by this point. Stigwood and music supervisor Bill Oakes were shrewd enough to choose existing hits that paid homage to these roots; the main dance sequence is supported by 'Boogie Shoes' from KC & The Sunshine Band. 2001 Odyssey's house band, The Trammps contributed the huge and era-defining 'Disco Inferno'. The US 1976 No. 1 'A Fifth Of Beethoven' by Walter Murphy, the record that had made The Big Apple Band become Chic, was there too. The soundtrack also resuscitated the career of Kool and the Gang, now in their 13th year. They were looking for a new direction when the president of De-lite records, Gabe Vigerito, cut a deal to add 'Open Sesame' to the *Saturday Night Fever* soundtrack. 'Before that we were trying to cut a track that would fit into the whole disco thing, into the clubs, while at the same time maintaining an integrity and style that was still Kool and The Gang,' Kool recalls. 'That's why you hear the disco beat in "Open Sesame", but the horns are very creative – they go all over the place! We didn't want it to sound *disco* disco; we wanted disco with a little integrity. It went into one of the biggest movies ever relating to dance and disco, so it worked perfectly for us.'

However, Stigwood had no new music for the film, as he had been preoccupied with trying to sign The Rolling Stones from Atlantic. He turned to one of his most long-standing and successful acts: The Bee Gees, who were in the process of recording the follow-up album to *Children Of The*

World at the Chateau D'Herouville in Paris. The film, Stigwood reasoned, would perfectly ride the wave of popularity they had enjoyed since their rebirth as southern soul gentleman in 1975.

More out of loyalty to him than any belief in the viability of the film, they obliged. 'Stayin' Alive', 'How Deep Is Your Love', 'If I Can't Have You' and 'More Than A Woman' were already in the bag and they adapted one they were recording to become 'Night Fever'. The rest, they say, is history.

The Bee Gees have always had a dislocated view of their part in the film's success. Becoming such unwitting figureheads of the movement, they have always maintained a distance from the project. Maurice Gibb commented in 1978 that, 'We wrote the entire musical score of *Saturday Night Fever* in a matter of hours. We spent as much time at the premiere party as we did in composing the music!' and his brother, Robin, was to add in 1997 that, 'we had been down on our luck, and someone said "would you write some songs about a painter who goes out dancing in the evenings?" so we did. If we'd known Travolta would make such a good job of it, we wouldn't have knocked out any old rubbish and sung in those stupid voices!'

Although their Stylistics-inspired falsetto was an obvious target for cynics, rubbish their material was not. 'Stayin' Alive' has possibly one of the greatest codas in popular music, displaying the song's downbeat nature: 'life going nowhere, somebody help me, yeah', and 'How Deep Is Your Love' is one of those copper-bottomed classics to die for, on a par with any high-period Lennon and McCartney.

The movie worked on several levels: it was the truth; DJ John De Mairo recalls: 'The clubs were used as a release; people were planning Saturday night all week. Tony Manero had a bullshit job in a paint store – all he cared about was Saturday. Dancing and living the experience – that was definitely true.' This was also to inspire Rodgers and Edwards to go back to one of their old Big Apple Band numbers and issue 'Saturday' as Norma Jean's solo debut release.

When the X-certificated film was released in December 1977 in America, and March 1978 in the UK, the response was phenomenal. John Travolta with his charisma, Italianate good looks and unusual name, was clearly superstar material. On the multi-coloured floor of 2001 Odyssey, his nine months of dance training paid off with a remarkable set of moves. He strutted, preened and grooved. Dressed in his polyester suit, you simply could not take your eyes off him.

'It's a really iconic performance. You never doubt that Travolta is Tony Manero,' states Cohn. 'To break it down without him, it's probably not that good. The love interest is very sappy; nobody else is particularly good. It's like watching *Jailhouse Rock* and saying, well nobody else is much good in the film – it really doesn't matter. I don't think of it so much as a film, but one of the great star vehicles.'

In an age where everything seemed to be heading into space, this gritty movie kept its message within easy reach of all audiences. The fact it was such a deeply downbeat film, which climaxes with three rapes and a suicide and contains language, that even today, puts it beyond Martin Scorsese, became entirely overshadowed by the set piece dance sequences and Travolta's opening strut.

It showed that on the dance floor, you could be anything you wanted to be, do anything you wanted to do. *Saturday Night Fever* encapsulated the frustration inherent in growing up, mapped out right there in Cohn's words; 'You live with your parents, you hang with your buddies and on Saturday nights you burn it all off at 2001 Odyssey. You're a cliché. You're nowhere, goin' no place'. It was a classic rites of passage movie. Tony Manero could have been Jim Stark in *Rebel Without A Cause* 22 years previously or Jimmy Cooper in *Quadrophenia*, two years later.

Even the ultimate bauble of the excessive whims of the rock aristocracy – the double album – 'went disco'. The two-disc soundtrack album came out before the film, with its iconic image of Travolta and the oft-parodied satin'n'medallion'd Gibb brothers. With their five new songs – 'If I Can't Have You' was sung by ex-Eric Clapton vocalist Yvonne Elliman – and adding in their two previous floor fillers, 'You Should Be Dancing' and 'Jive Talking', the album became a veritable Bee Gees greatest hits. George McManus, the marketing manager for Polydor/RSO in England at the time recalls, 'If you hadn't seen the film or weren't even a Bee Gees fan, you'd heard so many tracks on the radio you thought, oh well, I'll buy it anyway. It's one of Polydor/Universal's biggest selling albums of all-time.' It marked the beginning of albums being milked for singles; at least 11 of the album's 17 tracks were released. With opportunities for marketing like this, why did artists need to spend quite so much time in the studios? 'I was there when The Bee Gees did *This Is Your Life*,' McManus recalls. 'Michael Jackson phoned them up and said that *Thriller* was directly inspired by *Saturday Night Fever*.' *Thriller*, of course, with its six singles from its nine tracks was to cement the-singles-off-albums routine as standard industry practice.

The Bee Gees made disco safe for the white masses and their soundtrack to *Saturday Night Fever* touched more people than the film ever did – its X Certificate kept teenagers away, but everybody could dance to those records or see the promo of the three hirsute brothers on *Top Of The Pops*. *Saturday Night Fever* went to No. 1 in the UK in May 1978 and remained there for an unbroken 18 weeks – the longest spell at No. 1 since *Sgt Pepper* 11 years previously. It stayed on the charts for 65 weeks.

With Studio 54 creating headlines for its clientele in the highest strata and *Saturday Night Fever* allowing the touch of opulence to be introduced even at the Essoldo in Eastleigh, it was as if the marketing campaign was truly universal – you could read in the papers about the champagne lifestyle in New York, hear the singles that endlessly propped up the top end of the chart, see the film, buy the album and then take your own dreams out to your local Odyssey.

With its huge success – $142 million in US takings alone to date – other disco films followed in its wake. The sweet-natured, LA-set *Thank God Its Friday* starring Donna Summer has been cited as the most authentic replication of the Studio 54 experience. The cheap, tacky Camden Town-set, *The Music Machine*, starring Patti Boulaye, clearly was not. Joan and Jackie Collins tilted their caps towards disco glamour with *The Stud* and *The Bitch*. *Roller Boogie, Rollermania, The Disco Godfather* all looked for the disco dollar. Even John Holmes starred in the porno version, *Saturday Night Beaver*.

That Travolta was pastiched not once but twice on film in *Love At First Bite* and *Airplane!* shows how far the film had penetrated the popular psyche. And that's before Tim Brooke-Taylor appeared as John Ravolta in The Goodies' *Saturday Night Grease*.

The whole world got the fever: hundreds of artists got the beat: Rod Stewart welded together Bobby Womack and Jorge Ben and created 'Do You Think I'm Sexy'. The Beach Boys spiced up 'Here Comes The Night' with beats. Frank Sinatra, Dolly Parton and Ethel Merman all 'went disco'. The Stones, of course, cut 'Miss You' in Paris – the home of the discothèque in late 1977 – popping their head above the disco parapet. They too enjoyed a US No. 1 in summer 1978, and this scene is quite discrete from the mechanised Eurodisco espoused by Italian producer Giorgio Moroder, Pete Belotte and Donna Summer. Atlantic released an album of disco cover versions of Led Zeppelin songs. Classical music, used to such great effect by Walter Murphy gave the music the sense of the sophisticated. Mike Oldfield, until recently a tubular bell-clanging philosophical hermit released a blue vinyl 12" single called 'Guilty'. The Muppets, too, had a disco dabble: The Bees Gees granted permission for the *Sesame Street* characters to record the ever-remarkable *Sesame Street Fever* album. It was a long way from Listen My Brother.

Disco was everywhere – it was going overground in an incredible way. Radio realised the fantastic potential of the music. As Brewster and Broughton state in *Last Night A DJ Saved My Life*: 'In July 1978, a largely unlistened to mellow rock station, WKTU "went disco". Within two weeks, "Disco 92" had increased its listeners five fold.' By the end of the year, the station was shaking conventional stations' strongholds. WKTU became a broadcasting sensation, with its reliance on playing music that was breaking in the clubs, long before its release date. Although this is standard dance industry practice now, in 1978 it was radical indeed. By the end of the decade in America, there were over 200,000 nightclubs, with nearly a quarter of a million people frequenting New York nightclubs alone.

It was this high commercial phase of disco that changed everything. As soon as a label is placed on something by music writers and as soon as it is commodified by the powers that be, what was initially a gaggle of unconnected records and styles, became unified and packaged. Rigid tempos became the order of the day, and the synthetic template laid down by Giorgio Moroder and Donna Summer's crooning-in-outer space anthems became seen as something that could easily be emulated.

'There was white exploitation of the form,' Alfa Anderson suggests. 'And the resultant product became weaker and more processed, almost homogenized so that it would have more mass appeal.' And in some respects, Chic were to lose out to both whites and African-Americans. 'In the very beginning die-hard fans of R&B did not like disco because the fear was that the genre would weaken what had always been a very strong African presence in soul music. Chic were not taken seriously by many soul music aficionados. We were considered "cute". I know people who only recognise the power of what Chic did today. We were painted with that same "this-is-just-a-flash-in-the-pan' brush."'

Some old bands smelt a dollar, no matter what they later say: 'When disco culture came in with the fashions, and the clubs, Studio 54, we were still effective in these clubs with their own identity,' Robert 'Kool' Bell believes. 'We just wanted to maintain Kool and The Gang – we wanted to be effective on the dance floor.'

It all seemed giddy and hedonistic. Disco was a flag-waver for all manner of outrageousness and an obvious target for conservatives. The space race may have ended, but aliens were swamping popular culture, be they actual extra terrestrials (*Close Encounters*) or in music, gays (the Village People); blacks subliminally appropriating white symbols of power (Chic in their business suits); women being explicit about having sexual pleasure (Donna Summer). With all this permissiveness played out in such explicit detail, white mainstream America would soon need to hit back.

✫ ✫ ✫

In these giddy times, Chic's initial success did not immediately escalate them to the top of the list; Rodgers and Edwards still had to run the gamut of Studio 54's notorious door policy.

It was snowing in New York when Rodgers and Edwards stepped up to Studio 54's fabled doorway on 31st December 1977. The pair had been asked to join Grace Jones, who was partying inside. Already the pair were sporting clothes commensurate with the fact that their debut single had just sold a million copies within a month. Both dressed in black tie, Rodgers was wearing a Cerutti dinner jacket and Edwards was in Armani. 'Grace Jones ruled the nightclub scene and decided she wanted us to produce her next album. She told us to come and meet her on New Year's Eve at Studio 54, but we weren't on the list,' Rodgers explained to *The Observer* in 2003. Rodgers' then-girlfriend, who knew Marc Benecke, had previously been able to get Rodgers in without any problems.

They went to the club's back door and attempted to get in. Their names weren't down. While the club rocked to their early hits 'Dance Dance Dance' and the still-to-be-released 'Everybody Dance', the two main protagonists were outside being denied admission. 'We said, "We're Chic", and the guy on the door said "Chic? Shit!"' After checking through Grace Jones' personal list, the pair moved to the front door, where at least, Rodgers thought, Marc Benecke would recognise him and let them through. As Rodgers told Anthony Haden Guest in *The Last Party*: 'Marc totally disregarded us. He didn't give us a second look … . Our lives before we had our hit were fun and interesting, but it was tough to make it. Now we had made it and we had the ultimate rejection'.

Thinking that maybe someone else would come out and look for them, Rodgers and Edwards remained on the snowbound 54th street. It finally got too much. After considerable further negotiation, the notoriously fascistic door staff held their position and the duo were cast out into the night.

After picking up some champagne, cocaine and marijuana, the duo decided to have their own private party back at Rodgers' apartment on 52nd Street. Naturally, they started to jam. As Rodgers continued in *The Last Party*: 'We were just yelling obscenities … fuck studio 54 … fuck 'em … fuck off … fuck those scumbags … fuck them! … We were entertaining the hell out of ourselves.' Suddenly, the music began to coalesce. The guitar and bass part locked in and a repeated refrain of 'Aaaaaaaah, fuck off!' became the jam's focal point. Eventually, the fuck became freak. Off became out.

With its reference to the disco scene's more complex and obscure dances, the freak, and Rodgers' acid past, 'Le Freak' was to become Chic's commercial zenith. Within a year, with one single tune, Nile Rodgers and Bernard Edwards were to capture the zeitgeist like two funked-up Samuel Pepys, recording for posterity '54' in the lyrics of one of the best-selling singles of all time:

> *Like the days of stomping at the Savoy,*
> *Now we freak, oh what a joy,*
> *Just come on down to 54,*
> *Find a spot out on the floor …*
> *Freak out, Le Freak, C'est Chic.*

CITY AND ISLINGTON
SIXTH FORM COLLEGE
283 - 309 GOSWELL ROAD
LONDON
EC1
TEL 020 7520 0652

11.
JUST CAN'T WAIT FOR SATURDAY

'Suddenly we moved from a two-star motel to a five-star hotel.'
Luci Martin 2004

IT WOULD BE NEARLY A YEAR before the world got to hear Chic's new material. The group, which by now, swelled to 13 members for live work, still had 'Dance Dance Dance (Yowsah, Yowsah, Yowsah)' and then 'Everybody Dance' to promote. They had to fix their personnel and finally, free themselves of Turtle Productions. 1978 was to be a year both of considerable consolidation and breathless change for Chic.

As the band toured the US, opening for long established acts like The Isley Brothers, Trammps and Rufus, the discontent that had been simmering between Rodgers and Turtle's Lenny Fogel was about to burst forth. Impressed with their no-nonsense techniques and deep connections within the music industry, Rodgers and Edwards were now committed to being with Marc Kreiner and Tom Cossie at MK productions. Fogel and his partner, George Kava, were, after all, two men who ran an electronics shop who wanted to break into music. Cossie had worked in music for years.

On top of personal acrimony between Rodgers and Fogel, Turtle also wanted to produce other groups as well through Kenny Lehman. If there was to be any producing, Rodgers and Edwards wished to be the sole producers. MK also discussed offering Rodgers and Edward their own production company.

'I got caught in the middle of something quite uncomfortable,' Kenny Lehman recalls. 'Lenny Fogel never really handled or treated Nile and Bernard very well. They really had a dislike for him. I was a partner to them both. This conflict was ongoing – I know Nile and Bernard were chomping to get away from them. Lenny did not handle people well and George was more like a silent partner. He was like the guy who only became involved when he had to. Lenny had Brooklyn arrogance.' It was this Brooklyn arrogance that really began to grate with Rodgers.

'Chic really was me and Bernard,' Rodgers says. 'When we started, there were all these other people, but no one ever understood it like we did. The relationship was about Nile and Bernard. We tried to work with people, and so we said "you guys help us market it, *but we are Chic*". In fairness to everybody, in the beginning, Chic was only one of many things we were going to do between us and Turtle.' When 'Dance Dance Dance (Yowsah, Yowsah, Yowsah)' took off, all parties started to claim Chic for themselves – and, unsurprisingly, given the winding road they had already travelled, Edwards and Rodgers were not prepared to share it. 'Suddenly, no one wanted to work on the next thing, they tried to take our thing; it was like all of ours together. Hit records are hard to come by; all of a sudden, we had had one. They thought we could just come up with this stuff all day long. It was like "let's honour the original contract – we are going do this for Chic".'

MK Productions, the company set up by Kreiner and Cossie, now needed to distance themselves from Turtle Productions. Ongoing disputes between Rodgers and Edwards and Fogel and Kava exacerbated matters. Although he hadn't been with them from the start, Lehman had formed a good working relationship with Edwards and Rodgers: 'It was only when things started to get tense we started to have our issues', Lehman recalls. The final split from Turtle was acrimonious.

'Here was me with Turtle Productions and here's me with Nile and Bernard, pretending that we are going to be Chic,' Lehman recalls. 'I'm wearing two hats, as I'm producing as well. We said the three of us would be producers. At the same time, I'm tied in with Lenny Fogel and George Kava. They also wanted to put out more bands, more acts. I knew at some point that I was going to have to make a decision, when one of them took off. I got caught in the middle of something quite uncomfortable.'

'The moment MK Productions came on the scene, things changed. MK wanted everything,' Rodger Bell recalls. 'And at the top of the list, it was to get rid of Turtle Productions. They started to work on Nile and Bernard – and so, Kenny gets put on the bad side of the list.'

Kreiner and Cossie found a loophole in the contract between Rodgers, Edwards and Turtle. A meeting was set up in mid-1978 with lawyers present. 'The option with George and Lenny was about to expire. Because of what had gone on, it was decided not to pick up the option. It was enough for them to fight it. It hurt me big time also, in the final analysis. I remember sitting in a room with a lawyer for Turtle and a lawyer for MK,' Lehman recalls. 'There were these lawyers, Lenny, George, Nile and Bernard, me and Tom and Marc. There was a lot of tension. It wasn't hateful, but it didn't feel good. At that meeting, I was caught in this crossfire as we discovered they wanted to get out of the contract'.

Lehman, however, was offered the option to stay with Chic. 'Nile and Bernard sat me down and offered me the opportunity to stay with them, but they made it clear that they would be the sole producers from thereon in. I could still do all the arranging, if I required, but they wanted to go and do their thing. At that point in time, I was really brainstorming with Rodger and looking at all the possibilities that were open to us, although I wasn't particularly enamoured with Lenny and George either.' But Lehman was not prepared to be demoted after he'd had a hit record and a gold album.

In return for Turtle getting right out of the picture, MK would still pay an ongoing percentage to them. Lehman and Bell received a money settlement and kept Turtle's other act, Shade, who were later to become Roundtree. Lehman and Rodger Bell took the opportunity to set up their own company, Aria Productions.

'With his big hit to his name, he set up in Brooklyn his own production company and made a lot of deals,' Brian Chin recalls. 'He put out some real disco classics, such as "Angel Man" by Loretta Hughes.'

Roundtree released their debut single, 'Get On Up' on Island in 1978, produced and arranged by Lehman and with Bell credited as Executive Producer. 'Manhattan Fever', the B-side of their second single, 'Discocide', was a re-recording of one of the very first tracks that Rodgers and Edwards played on with Lehman.

Lehman went on to score the infamous Broadway disco musical, *Got Tu Go Disco* in 1979, which on paper, bringing together two very theatrical forms, should have been an enormous success. With a budget of $2 million, the play opened at the Minskoff Theater, which, on 45th Street, was merely nine blocks away from the Studio. Marc Benecke was to be the doorman in the play. With Irene Cara in the lead role, this thinly-disguised tribute to Studio 54 lasted nine days. Disco was something you did; not something you went to a theatre to watch.

From now on, Chic would just solely and legally be Nile Rodgers and Bernard Edwards, working in conjunction with Kreiner and Cossie and MK. Chic were not to have a manager per se, Simo Doe, who was the head of black PR at Atlantic, working with Henry Allen, was the group's closest ally at Atlantic, liaising between the suits and the group. 'She took care of us like a mother hen. We loved her', Rodgers recalls.

Rodgers and Edwards would quickly form their own company: The Chic Organization Ltd.

With a million-selling single behind them, a production company that suited their needs and a worldwide phenomenon that they could ride, 1978 was shaping up to be a good year for Rodgers and Edwards.

The iconic line-up of Chic that everyone knows was about to take shape, as Norma Jean – the only member of Chic that wasn't a native New Yorker – left the group: 'Norma gave us some kind of problem,' Rodgers recalls. 'Maybe she felt usurped; she got upset. She wasn't even on the first hit, we just hired her – as you know, that's Luther, Diva and Robyn Clark on that first hit. That's her on "Everybody Dance", though. She was certainly part of that movie but she wanted to be the star, and remember, Chic is an entity. She was only part of the team.' After the first tour dates, where she went from being alone in the spotlight to sharing the stage with Luci Martin, she left the group.

'She never came out with us again,' Rodgers continues. 'We got her her own record deal and we made her own album and told her to go off and be a star. We could deal with that. We were not egotistical guys; but in Chic, we couldn't deal with a star.' As few people actually knew what the group looked like – they'd only seen the album cover – this personnel change was absorbed quickly and quietly by the general public.

'Once Chic's first album became successful, I was offered a solo deal with Bearsville/Warner Brothers,' Norma Jean recounted to chictribute.com. 'Everyone felt this was a good idea because Atlantic and Warner Brothers were both housed under the same umbrella, although they were different labels. The initial plan was that I would continue to be Chic's lead vocalist and also be allowed to do a solo deal, and that Nile & Bernard would produce my material. However, it became legally complicated and I was not allowed to continue on with the group, which was very disheartening to me. I have read several erroneous articles stating that it was my decision to leave Chic. For the record: it was "the powers that be" that made that choice for me.'

'Norma got her butt out of there so quick with her solo album, it was almost like the two albums were recorded simultaneously,' Raymond Jones recalls. 'She did some touring and split. She knew she was going to have her own career.'

'It was a difficult time,' Luci Martin recalls. 'We were still developing ourselves as a group. There wasn't anything secretive about it; they were also working on Norma's stuff. We'd do a publicity shoot, and then they'd do one for Norma, as those wheels were in motion for her solo career. This was expected, as this was what had been told to all of us, that we would all follow in Norma's footsteps, each one would branch off from the group and have the opportunity to do the solo thing. The plans were very big to get different projects going at the same time. Of course, who knew the amount of success that the group were to have. A lot of things wound up getting put on the backburner for the sake of the group itself.'

☆ ☆ ☆

Alfa Anderson, who had sung so perfectly on the first album sessions and provided such sterling vocal supports on tour with Luther Vandross behind Norma and Luci, stepped forward. 'It was because of Luther I got the opportunity to sing with Chic. That then allowed me to move into the position vacated by Norma Jean. Luther and I did the background vocals for the first tour.'

Anderson, born on 7th September 1946, had come to New York from Augusta, Georgia in the early 1970s to get her Masters degree in teaching

English at Columbia University. A gifted student as well as an exceptional singer, she had supplemented her teaching at Hunter College by session work and weekend club dates. 'I grew up in a very sheltered life,' Anderson recalls. 'I'm the person who came to New York, and saw a neon sign in a window saying "the world's best coffee" and I actually believed it. In my universe, no-one could make that claim unless it were true!'

'I had been singing with some friends of mine that I knew from Augusta called Raw Sugar. We used to sing in this club on Columbus Avenue called The Cellar. It just escalated from there. I was singing at the weekends, working with my voice, taking voice lessons, meeting artists. It was never my intent to meet the artists; it was my destiny. I met all of these wonderfully talented people and I was surrounded with music." Through her singing, Anderson would encounter characters such as Nat Adderely Jr, Angie Bofill and Najee. 'I became part of this incredibly supportive, nurturing group of artists. Of course, that circle includes Luther and Fonzi.'

Anderson met Vandross through singer Ednah Holt. 'We happened to be at the same rehearsal studio in Manhattan; I had been working with Lou Courtney and Buffalo Smoke. Luther was very shy; I bounded over and said hello. He had this pair of overalls on. He slowly lifted his head, said "hi" and put his head back down. Then I watched him sing. He opened his mouth and it was the voice from heaven. We hit it off from that point on. My session work started with Luther. At that time, he was the session king. I learned a lot about background singing by working with him. I was a part of his group, Luther, and we had grown to be very good friends.'

She had caused some doubt with Rodgers and Edwards when she came to sing with Chic the preceding year. 'Bernard used to tell the story of our first meeting,' Anderson recalls. 'It was Luther, David Lasley and me at this session. I remember Luther telling me that he wanted to do this session for this friend of his. It was disco – and we were really into R&B at the time. I made the comment that I really did not want to record a disco session. Luther encouraged me and said that it would be fun – and that they played great music.'

'We went and I listened to the music and absolutely fell in love with it. Bernard kept looking at Luther, David and myself and kept questioning Nile as to who I was, because I looked the epitome of a teacher. In the down time when they were booting up the song, I was marking papers. I looked very much the school ma'am with glasses. Bernard kept saying "are you sure that these people can sing?"' Within minutes, there was little doubt that she could. She went on to sing on every Chic recording.

'I thought Norma Jean would work independently and with the group', Martin says. 'It threw me off a little when she left, as she was my security blanket in a world that I was not used to. I didn't know Alfa. It was a little bit difficult, as she knew all of Luther's people – and I didn't know any of them. As a result, I always felt a little outside of the group.' However, there was little time to focus on these issues as the touring schedule and demands on the group were enormous.

Anderson, with her gravitas and poise and well-honed singing voice, and Martin, with her stunning looks and upbeat disposition, complemented the band perfectly. 'Luci and Alfa – they were team players,' Raymond Jones recalls. 'Luci probably wanted more vocals, because she was a good lead singer; she didn't have as much play as she should have had. If you listen to the singing, the style was pretty regimented, but then that was part of the overall concept.' 'Luci and Alfa were real sweet,' Rob Sabino recalls. 'Real nice girls. I have nothing but very fond memories of them.'

Anderson was thrilled with her new position: 'I felt excited, nervous, blessed. I loved the music. Being a part of that group was my heart's desire. From the moment I heard the music in the studio, I became so enraptured with the sound that I decided that I was going to sing those songs to the best of my ability and that I was going to stamp them with my voice, so that my voice could become an integral part of what they were doing. That's how badly I wanted to be a part of that group, so when the call came to go out as one of the background singers, it was wonderful; but when the opportunity came to follow in Norma's footsteps, it was a dream come true.'

However, just to make sure she had some fall-back if the glamorous life was not to prove successful, Anderson kept her options open: 'I was quote-unquote "fresh off the farm" and here I am catapulted into this world of glamour and glitz and fame and I thought that I would be teaching college English!' Anderson took a leave of absence from teaching. 'I grew up in a society that, though we celebrated the arts, you always had to have that "secure job". When I first went with the group, I had no idea if it was going to work for me'.

The *Norma Jean* album was like a rehearsal for what was to come. It was time for Rodgers and Edwards to display their credentials as producers. Part of the deal with Atlantic was that Norma Jean would have the opportunity to record a solo album once Chic hit big. Signing to Albert Grossman's Bearsville label, a subsidiary of Warners, the plan was always that Rodgers and Edwards would produce the record. Bearsville was a strange choice of label for Norma

Jean to record on. Grossman was the founder of and guiding force behind Bearsville. He had come to prominence as a personal manager during the 1960s, when he guided the careers of artists such as Peter, Paul and Mary, Bob

Dylan, The Band, Janis Joplin, Paul Butterfield, and Dr. John. In the early 70s, Grossman shifted his base of operations from New York City to Bearsville, NY. He phased himself out of management and concentrated his energies on the formation of Bearsville Records and studios. Home to Todd Rundgren and Utopia, whatever the label was, it wasn't particularly disco.

'We needed Chic to get Norma Jean her own record deal. She always wanted to be a solo artist and to establish Bernard and myself as viable producers,' Rodgers recalled to Geoff Brown. 'It was our way of saying to the industry that we could produce hit records. We didn't want it to be a mechanical disco production. We wanted to let people know that the producers play the stuff.'

The album was recorded at The Power Station across the spring of 1978. Although not yet bearing The Chic Organization Ltd. stamp, *Norma Jean* contained all of the extended team. Rob Sabino was back, fitting in the sessions between The Simms Brothers schedule, Vandross, Lasley, Gray and Anderson were all present and correct. Industry veteran Gene Orloff was the concert-master for Rodgers' string arrangements.

The album's clear stand-out track was the lead single, 'Saturday'. It was a perfect distillation of the whole *Saturday Night Fever* scene, into one pulsatingly upbeat groove. And it also had a pedigree, as it had been one of the songs, co-written with Bobby Cotter, that The Big Apple Band had taken around their various dives and clubs throughout 1976 and 1977. Featuring some of Rodgers most stunning guitar work and Edwards ever-bubbling bass, Norma Jean's impassioned vocal finds her barely coping with the chagrin of the week before the night itself arrives.

> *'Just like some old jerk all I do is work;*
> *I'm no robot, I just have to party and please my body.*
> *Let's go disco, meet the guys and gals, they're all my pals.'*

The song, surprisingly, failed to be a hit. The strength of the tune means that the remaining six cuts on the album struggle to keep pace. The cover of Sam Cooke's 'Having A Party' is uninspired; The Norman Whitehead-Chris Dawkins written 'I Believe In You' is a fairly perfunctory ballad, whose backing, despite a sterling performance from Norma Jean, noodles on to a dead stop.

The second side opener, 'Sorcerer' was much more like it. Although still second-string Chic, it has a beautiful fluidity to its groove, a haunting piano figure (not dissimilar to Roy Ayers Ubiquity's 'Everybody Loves The Sunshine'), and, unusually for Chic, a little studio trickery in the shape of the explosions – magic spells, no doubt – that arrive in the instrumental passages. 'The sessions for my debut album were exciting for me,' Norma Jean recalls. 'I was encouraged to write my first song, "This Is The Love" and I was much more involved creatively and was allowed to express these ideas.'

The two ballads which follow, 'So I Get Hurt Again' and Norma Jean's debut song, are pleasantly unremarkable. 'This Is The Love' is a Michael Jackson mid-90s power ballad in waiting, rhyming 'bad' and 'sad' as well as 'cry' and 'die'. 'I Like Love', apart from having one of the tritest titles of their entire canon, is a really upbeat, hidden treasure, especially on the wild freakery of Rodgers' rhythm playing towards the fade. All in all, the *Norma Jean* album was good, but it wasn't right. A competent breeze through their abilities, it really felt as if it was a dry run for what they truly had up their sleeve.

Rodgers commented later to Geoff Brown that the album was: 'highly political – Norma is the only artist we don't have control over as far as marketing plans, as far as release dates or anything like that. That situation has been rectified and her new stuff is, I'm pretty sure, gonna be successful because Bernard and I are very in tune to the market.' Rodgers commented that 'you can hear the progression of Bernard and myself's writing style – it's gotten a lot more intellectual but at the same time it seems just as simple as before.'

Although the group were about to break on an unprecedented scale, Norma Jean's second solo album, which was heralded by the 1979 single 'High Society'/ 'Hold Me Lonely Boy', failed to materialise. Norma Jean was later to tell chictribute.com that 'There was a plan for my second album but Nile and Bernard's fee was much more than the label wished to pay.' And, there is no holy grail of left-over material. 'All of my songs recorded were released.'

'High Society' is a great lost single, however. It has the full power and confidence of the high-plateau Chic Organization productions; more mannered and less frantic than the earlier, obvious disco material, with the Chic strings, clipped and bountiful. All key points are there in the song. The rags to riches American Dream story, the observer watching someone climb the rungs of the social ladder, the inspiration provided to others and the aspirational intent;

> *'I'd like to go from poor to rich –*
> *make the switch,*
> *change for the better.'*

A vibe and percussion solo dominates the final two minutes – looking for new ways to convert clichés of the pop record in the way the horns chased the strings on 'I Want Your Love'. Nonetheless, it is a downbeat and sombre experience; arguably the group on cruise control. Raymond Jones' piano and Sammy Figueroa's percussion and piano workout on the flip side 'Hold Me Lonely Boy' is very barrelhouse in its approach – the scything strings have really taken hold by this point as well. This would be the last time that Norma Jean Wright would be produced by Bernard Edwards and Nile Rodgers.

It wasn't the last time that Chic and Norma Jean's paths would cross, however. She would do some session work with the group in the coming years. She would end up working extensively with Raymond Jones in the 90s.

This was, however, the last production that Chic were to perform in anonymity, because, for the next 18 months, as the confused 70s became the money-grabbing 80s, everything was to go into vertical take-off for The Chic Organization Ltd.

'1-2 Awwwwwww ... Freak out! ... Le Freak, C'est Chic.'

And then, Chic created a monster. 'Le Freak' is what Chic did in the war; it is why 25 years later, books are being written about them. It is the epitome of the Chic sound, effortlessly crafted. It is why they are not Ottowan. It is overplayed, over-known and still under-appreciated. From the count in, immediately we hear its irresistible rhythm: it oozes sophistication.

The ultimate irony of turning the hatred that Rodgers and Edwards had felt toward Studio 54's door policy out onto the dance floor and making it positive was fantastic. 'Once we've shared what we both know about a subject, we'll give it a shot. I had never set foot in Studio 54, I just knew there was this dance around called The Freak,' Bernard Edwards said in 1979. 'There's even an underground Freak where people take their clothing off! That's how that happened.'

'"Le Freak" was a fantastic song,' recalls Ahmet Ertegun. 'Simply a great, great record.' The Freak, which had been popular in New York clubs, saw two dancers bend at the knees, spread their legs, and bump their pelvises together, in time to the music. Rodgers told the BBC that the dance in the song was, 'the closest thing to having sex without going all the way.' It was also reported to be sexual slang for cunnilingus.

If there is one moment in Chic time it is this. Although 'Le Freak' owes something musically to the first album's 'Strike Up The Band', with its call of 'feeling the rhythm and catching the vibe'; it just had everything in correct measure; the gnawing guitar figure, the syncopated handclaps, the chorus vocal and then after two and a half minutes, a breakdown featuring one of the simplest bass parts ever; a six note repeat, the very antithesis of complexity, with the Chic choir intoning but three words. David Lasley remembers it with great affection: '"Le Freak" will always be my favourite. The 16-bar breakdown where we just sing "I say freak" – that kills me.' And, this was before the days of looping and sampling. All vocals were cut live, but there was a little trickery to underscore this passage: 'To get the weird-sounding handclaps on "Le Freak,"' engineer Bob Clearmountain recalled in 1979, 'I turned the tape itself upside down and recorded the claps through the echo chamber. Then when I turned the tape right side up for playback, the echo came immediately before the clap.'

UK critic Garry Mulholland suggests that 'calling "Le Freak" a disco record is like calling *Taxi Driver* a film about cabbies. It is the greatest moment of disco's greatest band, and perhaps the greatest pop record ever made out of balancing sublimely joyful and muscular musicianship with chilly, contemptuous cynicism.' Part of the record's spontaneity is due to the fact that it was quite impromptu: 'Luci and Alfa learned the lead vocal for "Le Freak" on the spot,' Lasley recalls. 'It was amazing how fast they learned. They left it for the end of the day – it went pretty quickly.' With the late night rush to complete the vocal, something very special happened. It became so much more than simply a pop record. It was recorded on the fourth complete run through.

The story-telling aspect of 'Le Freak' takes the record right back to the African-American slave-fire tradition. Martin and Anderson lean in conspiratorially and ask, 'Have you heard about the new dance craze? Listen to us; I'm sure you'll be amazed.' The story about to be imparted is of the utmost gravity. Immediately, the band have cast themselves in the dominant, superior position: they already know about this dance; we, the listener, do not. 'It surely can be done,' is a valedictory cry not just for the triumph of dance, but of self-betterment.

It is as if Martin and Anderson, ably supported by Vandross, Lasley and Gray are hawking a remedy around: Dr Rodgers Travelling Show has arrived in town to help you. If all the pressures of commerce are grinding you down – then here, my friends, is the release. And, as if to re-emphasise Chic's complexity, it's not just The Freak – but *Le* Freak, parading Chic's French-inspired sophistication.

By comparing Studio 54 with The Savoy Ballroom, Rodgers and Edwards were making a claim that Chic were spearheading a new renaissance; something that would reach its apogee with their next album, *Risqué*. The Savoy Ballroom, known as 'the home of happy feet' was one of the most legendary clubs in New York. Situated on Lenox Avenue between 140-141 Streets, it was owned by Moe Gale and managed by Charles Buchanan. It opened its doors on March 12, 1926, three years before the Wall Street Crash of 1929 and the ensuing depression. With America in 1978 teetering on the brink of stagflation and a second oil crisis, it was not too much of a leap of faith to see Studio 54 in a similar light.

However, whereas Studio 54 was a palace of hedonism for the rich, The Savoy had far greater cultural significance, as it was one of the first racially integrated public places in America. With its carpeted lounges and mirrored walls, The Savoy was known as the 'world's finest ballroom'. The ballroom had two bandstands, coloured spotlights and a spring-loaded wooden dance floor. Visited annually by around 700,000, as a result, the floor had to be completely replaced every three years. There were also hostesses with whom a guest could dance for a dime or be tutored on the latest steps. The two bandstands allowed continuous live music all night, and provided the stage for the famous battles of bands. The most famous, and one of the most highly publicised, was the battle of Chick Webb vs. Benny Goodman, when both bands were at the peak of their popularity. Dizzy Gillespie, Charlie Parker, Art Blakey and Thelonious Monk all played there.

But it was the dance fads that the venue launched that really made the venue one of legend: The Flying Charleston, The Lindy Hop, The Stomp, The Big Apple, Jitterbug Jive, Peckin', Snakehips, Rhumboogie. With The Freak, Rodgers was adding his own stamp to this list. Although the Savoy had closed in 1958, its cultural significance lived on. And with 'Le Freak', it would be remembered by a whole new generation.

'Le Freak' was to sell a reputed six million copies in America alone. Entering the US charts on 18th November 1978, the record went platinum and became the biggest-selling record in Atlantic's history. It hit No. 1 in America, where it remained for six weeks. It went to the summit of the R&B charts in December 1978 and remained there for five weeks. It went gold in Belgium, Italy, South Africa, Great Britain, France, Brazil, and most of the rest of the world. In Canada, it became the best-selling song in the nation's history.

At Christmas 1978, Chic had the No. 1 single in America. No self-respecting party of the 1978 festive season was without it. And the success of the new track gave an incredible halo effect to its parent album, *C'est Chic*. 'Le Freak' made the news section of *Billboard* on 20th January 1979 for becoming the first single in the history of the US chart to have three separate runs at the summit of the Hot 100 in the chart's 20-year history. Although interrupted by Neil Diamond and Barbra Streisand's 'You Don't Bring Me Flowers' and the again by The Bee Gees' 'Too Much Heaven', it just kept rebounding. With the record's success, Alfa Anderson finally handed her notice in to Hunter College. 'I realised that it was more than just making records and going on tour,' she recalls. 'It was a phenomenon.'

✫✫✫

It was on *C'est Chic* that Rodgers and Edwards married the string washes of Philly with the funk of JBs and P-Funk. The Chic sound here was sparse, nuanced, even bleak. Ken Barnes points out that, like Holland-Dozier-Holland's greatest compositions, Chic's best songs always kick off with a chorus. The lyrics were often a joint effort, yet the more political lines – unsurprisingly – fell to Rodgers. The songs would always evolve from jams. 'Bernard and I would just start to play. If anyone were around us, they would go, "Wow, it sounds like Chic!" I would write something. He would say, "Damn, man! You got five songs in there! Let's cut those shits up and make an entire album"' It was from these jams, that the pair had been crafting all year, that their most commercial album came.

Nile Rodgers had said to writer

chic cheer
le freak
savoir faire
happy man
dance dance dance

i want your love
at last i am free
sometimes you win
everybody dance
(funny) bone

Bob Gallagher in early 1978 that 'the second album is in our sights now. It'll head in the same direction as the first but we'll be pumping up the musicianship to show how the 13 of us work together in the studio. In that way, it'll be an extension of the Chic concept, a concept that means a commercial crossover sound ... and plenty of ladies.'

Housed in an anonymous style-magazine sleeve, *C'est Chic* emphasised all that had become remarkable about the group. It boasted Rodgers' string arrangements, the Chic strings – Cheryl Hong, Marianne Carroll and Karen Milne, the metronomic drumming of Thompson, the guest vocalists Vandross and Lasley, the impassioned/dispassionate lead vocals of Martin and Anderson and the incredible interlocking of Rodgers and Edwards' guitar and bass.

In using industry veteran Gene Orloff as their concertmaster, Chic had a definite link with the musical past as he had worked with artists such as Nat King Cole, Cannonball Adderley, Aretha Franklin, Charlie Parker, Frank Sinatra, all the artists the young Edwards and Rodgers had admired in New York in the 60s. Orloff had to marshal the string section into action. He was naturally suspicious of the three young women who were given the parts to play. 'I remember how absolutely rotten he was to us during the first few recording sessions,' Karen Milne recalls. 'Until he admitted that we were all talented and could play, and, more importantly, were there to stay.'

'Everyone kissed up to Gene....he was, after all, the top string recording contractor in town at the time,' Milne continues. 'Nile was very professional with him and would always ask him for suggestions from the booth, during the sessions. It shows that Nile didn't have an ego when it came down to string arrangements and the technical range of the various instruments. I'm sure there were conversations between Gene and Nile and Bernard that went something like, "So, Nile, *where'd you pick up these three babes.....?"'

Orloff's old-school chauvinism was something of a surprise. He usually worked with an all-male string section, which he had brought along to rehearsals. 'He actually came up to the three of us, whom he had seated in the very back of the studio, and said, "if you girls are having problems with this tune we can go out in the hall and practice." We were so shocked,' says Milne. 'The three of us, all very good players, but so young and new to the "scene" just sat there, not believing what we had just heard. Between him trying to make us feel like we didn't know what we were doing and his hired pals putting the moves on the three of us ... Good God!'

Although there was this collective of performers, Rodgers is in no doubt who was responsible for Chic's success: 'the people who worked on our records had no idea how it was going to turn out. That's how it always was. We painted a picture that we were a collective – we *are* an extended family, but the artistic decisions were always up to two people.'

Settling-in issues aside, with *C'est Chic*, the band got into their stride. In America, *C'est Chic* went to No. 1 on the R&B album chart and reached No. 4 in the pop chart. The basic tracks for *C'est Chic* were recorded in four days and it was recorded concurrently with the sessions for Sister Sledge's 'We Are

Family'. Rodgers and Edwards were now the sole creative forces in the band. They worked quickly at The Power Station: 'The pair played off each other,' Tony Thompson recalls. 'Bernard was very firm – Nile would be cracking jokes, but they would both know how to get what they wanted. Nile had his way, Bernard had his way, but both Nile and Bernard knew how to work everybody to get what they wanted out of them. With singers and musicians that didn't even know they had it in them, Nile and Bernard could get it out of them.'

It was the same for Thompson: 'they would get things out of me that I didn't even know I had in me. All those fills, I'd play a couple of times and screw up. Nile and Bernard would know I was capable of better and they wouldn't build me up.' Edwards, especially, had a special way with Thompson and would goad him into playing better. 'They would talk about my mother. Bernard would say "look you asshole, it's no wonder you can't play – did your momma teach you how to play the drums or something?" They would belittle me to the point that it would piss me off, so when I went back to play it again, I'm going to shove it in their ass, I was so pissed off. You'd think they'd do that once or twice and then I'd learn. I never learned! At the last recording we ever did together, they were still doing that to me!'

Besides 'Le Freak', *C'est Chic* contained three sucker punches: 'Chic Cheer', 'I Want Your Love' and 'At Last I Am Free'. As an anthem, 'Chic Cheer' became the ultimate concert opener and rallying call. Its asymmetric beats and repeated riff, is rap before its time. As the mantra went, 'If you're fans of Chic, consider yourself unique!'. The song's durability was proved well into the 90s and 21st century, with the song being sampled firstly by Faith Evans on 'Love Like This' and then topping the UK charts as 'Be Faithful' by rapper Fatman Scoop in 2003.

'I Want Your Love' became the album's second single. Originally intended for Sister Sledge – Kathy Sledge in fact swears that you can still hear their voices on the chorus – no record more reinforces the concept of Chic's sophisticated simplicity, an understated elegance that reinforces a point. It is probably their most economical recording. Nothing is

left to waste. The despair that underpins the groove is writ large – if ever the shimmering shards of light scattered by a mirrorball was turned into a beautiful yearning pop song, it is this. The showcase for the six vocalists in unison is remarkable. Anderson sings the lead as if her life depended on it. 'Please don't make me beg'. Edwards' bass is little short of beautiful; 'I'll share my dreams and make you see how really bad your love I need'.

The insistent nagging guitar is a metaphor for unrequited need, while the instrumental passage where the horns chase the strings is one of pop's most shining yet over-looked moments. The horns and strings echo Norman Whitfield's arrangements for Rose Royce, (Indeed, the similarity was noticed by UK short-lived TV advertised company Dino who released a single CD compilation of both acts called *Greatest Hits Side By Side* in 1991). The break is a dry run for 'Good Times' – the crispness of Thompson's snare, the re-introduction of strings – it has such a live feel. Jose Rossy's shadowing of the main riff on tubular bells reclaims them out of hippie hands, and adds an iridescent gloss to the tune, and then, just as you feel you could spend the rest of your life listening to it, it disappears. Peter Shapiro suggests that 'Chic's great theme would be the disco lifestyle's inherent fatalism'; the yearning need of 'I Want Your Love' makes for an incredibly elegiac, beatific groove.

But then, the following song goes even further: 'At Last I Am Free' is a stuttering, mesmeric series of repeats over a dreamy, almost dead-stop tempo, with Anderson and Martin intoning the chorus, as Shapiro suggests 'alternately sounding like zombies and angels'. It is seven minutes of slow-burning glory.

The song itself harked back to Rodgers' Village days. 'I wrote that song initially without Bernard. It was long before Chic – that was back when we were New World Rising. It was a power ballad back then, a big epic rock thing,' Rodgers recalls. 'We didn't do anything save for change the feel of it. When I wrote "At last I am free / I can hardly see in front of me", I was in the Panthers. We went to a demonstration in Central Park. I had dropped acid and the cops had gotten the orders to disperse the crowd. It was quite typical of the time; something that had started as a be-in turned violent. After the cops had beaten us up, I remember trying to walk out of the park to the nearest hospital. Every step I took, the buildings took a step as well. I was walking endlessly. When I finally got to the edge of Central Park I was like – at last, I am free! Although back in New World Rising there was no melody in the verse. Bernard later added the love song stuff.'

One could look for deeper meanings about freedom from oppression, but in this instance, there are none. 'Bernard said the woman in the song could hardly see because of tears. I could hardly see in front of me, because I was tripping!' Yet the pleading of the verses, done in Anderson's very best late night drawl gives them gravitas. The song is one of her personal favourites. 'I loved the melody; I loved the words. That song spoke to how I was feeling,' Anderson recalls. 'Because there was I, someone who was groomed to have a regular job, but my talent freed me from that and I found myself in the middle of something that was incredible and slightly intimidating at the same time. Even though I did not write the lyrics, there was a lot that I could relate to. I remember thinking that I wanted to put my heart into that song, so that someone else could hear it and feel what I was feeling.' After all the pathos Anderson invests, the record just falters, collapsing under its own almost unbearable beauty, falling to Andy Schwartz's piano.

Billboard at the time called 'At Last I Am Free,' 'a straightforward soul ballad.' In reality, it was anything but. Arguably the single greatest moment in a catalogue of great moments, the meandering groove has been labelled many things. English art-rocker Robert Wyatt was to cover the song in Britain in February 1980. Pared-down to the point of blankness, there is something sacred in the manner in which he repeats the title phrase. His brittle, cut-glass intonations suit the song perfectly. He released it as a single, backed with his cover of Billie Holiday's 'Strange Fruit'.

The remaining material struggles to match the album's classics: the Edwards-voiced 'Happy Man' with its walking bass figure is bright pop, and an accurate reflection of his straightforward, no-nonsense persona. 'Sometimes You Win' is a charming duet between Anderson and Edwards. It helped to establish musically the template for Italian studio-based disco act Change. The New Orleans horns make this one of the most joyous, if minor, Chic songs. 'Savoir Faire' continues the theme of an instrumental per album, as this slow groove is very much a partner of the debut's 'Sao Paolo'. The desire to test the listeners with more instrumentals was writ even larger here, allowing Rodgers' full expression on the electric. For this alone, it remains one of Rodgers' favourite Chic tracks.

The album closes with the somewhat perfunctory 'Funny Bone', with crowd noises and laughter, funky Rob Sabino clavinet and a great horn/string riff, with a generous nod to Average White Band's 'Pick Up The Pieces'. The track, which was written by Edwards and Rodgers for Thompson, as 'Bone' was one of the many nicknames they had for him, ends the album with Thompson stating, 'Just one more thing – the whole world's a circus, don't you be the clown – Ciao!' There was no questioning who the ringmasters would be in 1979.

'Bone' was one of three names used by the group for Thompson: the others were 'dip' because he had studied with Narada Michael Walden, who was a disciple of Guru Sri Chinmoy who had renamed Carlos Santana 'Devadip'. 'His other nickname was "crash",' Rodgers laughs. 'Because he played the drums so fucking loud.'

Rodgers told *Pulse* magazine in 1985 that 'For our first album, we were in a state of shock just to have a record deal, but for the second one, we thought we were grown up and professional. To me, it's still the perfect record: It had the best mixture of jazzy stuff and real-ultra-pop stuff. And I got the chance to play the guitar solo in "Savoir Faire" which is still one of the best things I played from a compositional point of view.' But for Chic, there were to be better things to come.

There was no stopping the potency of the machine. There had never been a better time for transient celebration on the dancefloor. By the turn of 1979, the disco industry was estimated to be worth $4 billion, as Brewster and Broughton say, more than movies, television or professional sport. And Chic had had the biggest disco No.1; made by African-Americans dressed as bankers. For the Christmas season of 1978, Chic were leading the way. The two partners began to celebrate their success in different ways.

Their bond was confined to the studio and they seldom ever hung out together. 'Our respect and love for each other's musicality couldn't get any stronger,' Rodgers recalls. 'Charlie Parker and Dizzy Gillespie; John Coltrane and McCoy Tyner; Nile Rodgers and Bernard Edwards – we go together. But we didn't hang; because he didn't hang. And when we hung, it wasn't like what I did – I'm a hippy guy, dropping acid, seeing colours. I wanted to go out and dance around in muddy water and think the world is a beautiful place. That is my sense of aesthetic. Bernard was the opposite. His house was modern – he was that *MTV Cribs* dude long before his time.'

Nile Rodgers became something of a regular on the New York club scene, while Edwards remained distant and aloof. Ahmet Ertegun recalls 'I would only know Bernard through seeing him occasionally in the office. He was a very charming and nice man, but I never really got to know him. I used to see Nile at lots and lots of parties – he was very much the man about town.'

When success began to happen, Bernard Edwards, ever the reclusive individual, cleared out of New York. 'When things started popping off we moved to New Jersey. In Fort Lees, there was a condominium called Galaxy,' Bernard Edwards Jr recalls. 'We lived there. Cheryl Lynn was there, Kool from Kool and the Gang was there.' But even that was too starry for the unassuming Edwards. 'It wasn't just us. We lived there for a while and then we moved out to Stamford, Connecticut.'

To promote *C'est Chic*, the group embarked on an enormous tour of stadiums across the Americas, with dates in Rio de Janeiro and Sao Paolo – where they were treated like conquering heroes. However, Chic became something of an enigma in America. A huge band, but no-one really knew what the huge band looked like: 'We were looking at Roxy Music – and it was just like Kiss – you wouldn't be able to tell who the hell we were if you stood next to us at a party. And that's all we cared about; being famous and anonymous,' Rodgers says. 'It's come back to bite us in the butt, because we've done it too well and there is such a huge disconnection between our music and our name and us.'

With their level of anonymity and reputation for hard work, it was time for the disparate duo *really* to flex their muscles.

12.
LOVE IN A FAMILY DOSE

'Nelson Mandela heard the prison guards whistling "We Are Family"
and he knew that four young black women in America sang that song – and
that was one of the things that gave him hope, that he knew
the world was changing.'
KATHY SLEDGE 2004

BY THE END OF 1979, Bernard Edwards and Nile Rodgers' production style
could be likened to a film director being labelled an auteur. They had, as with
their own recordings, a precise vision of how an artist should sound, look and
what the lyrical content should be. They were to make records that were
extensions of themselves, which allowed a select group of outside artists in
on the Chic secret. And for an 18-month period, Rodgers and Edwards were
white hot. Their production style was developing into a sparse, textured
sound; functional, with barely any trappings of convention: few stellar solos,
few emotive vocals; an economy and restraint. Strings and horns were utilised
when really necessary – there were hardly ever any embellishments for the
sake of it. Whereas in 1979, it was simply accepted, a lot more would have
been made of this today. Disco historian Brian Chin states: 'It's symptomatic
of the way the record industry treats black producers. The captains of the
music industry only have room in their head for three things at one time. They
seem only to ask for one of the top three record producers at any one time.
In 2003, it's Timbaland, the Neptunes, and Missy Elliot. Everybody else is like
a non-person. Nile and Bernard have been through the whole arc of it – being
the sought after ones and then no longer being wanted.'

The record that really sealed Chic's reputation in America and Britain was
the Sister Sledge album, *We Are Family*. Jerry Greenberg, then President of
Atlantic, who had maintained close contact with them after pulling out the
stops to sign them to Atlantic recalls, 'Nile and Bernard became family by this
point; they were my act, my babies. We had a wonderful relationship.'
Rodgers was certain of the duo's worth: 'I was like "Jerry, we can make your
secretary a star – all she's got to do is what we tell her to do. Point us to

somebody in this building who is not a star and we will make them a star, no matter who it is, because we're going to make the record and our rhythm section is the star, we'll just put whoever in it.'"

Seeing as there was such a fantastic machine-tooled undercurrent to Chic's work, it was obvious that they would produce other artists with a degree of alacrity. After the relative success of producing the *Norma Jean* album, Rodgers and Edwards were given the choice of the Atlantic roster with whom to hone their production skills. The Rolling Stones, then looking to follow up their *Some Girls* album, were discussed and dismissed, as was Bette Midler. Instead, Rodgers and Edwards chose Sister Sledge. It was the first time that they had produced outside their immediate circle.

'They said that they wanted to produce other acts – I mentioned Sister Sledge,' Greenberg continues. 'They had heard about them, they knew all about them. I sat across from Nile at the desk and said "I love these girls; they're also like family to me".' With Rodgers' artistic magpie-ism and referencing reaching its peak, an idea was hatched. 'That's where he got the lyrical idea for "We Are Family" from,' Greenberg laughs. 'When he told me that a decade later, I asked him "well, why didn't you give me a writer's credit?"'

The Sledge sisters, Kathy (b. 6/1/59), Debra (b. 9/7/54), Joan (b. 13/9/56) and Kim (b. 21/8/57), had been born into a musical family. They were raised by their maternal grandmother Viola Williams, their mother Flo and their older sister Carol. Flo was a dancer who had married Edwin Sledge from the tap-dance team, Fred and Sledge. The four sisters had, by this point, long been in the business; and, through their parents' work, were brought up with an acute political awareness: 'In our homes, Civil Rights were talked about. When we were little just to see someone black on television was quite a big thing,' recalls Debbie Sledge. 'Our parents were entertainers – they would tell us how they had to go through back doors of hotels – they weren't allowed to eat in restaurants,' Joni Sledge adds. 'But, as you know, music is one of the key weapons of Civil Rights – it certainly cuts through barriers.'

Initially known as Mrs Williams' Grandchildren, the four sisters formed into an act in 1971, recording for the Philadelphia label Money Back. They had enjoyed middling success in the R&B charts, and had already released two albums, *Circle Of Love* (1975) and *Together* (1977) on Atco. They even went on to sing as part of the entourage that accompanied the fabled Muhammad Ali-George Foreman 'Rumble in the Jungle' fight in 1975: 'That was just amazing,' Joni Sledge recalls. 'It was all a big, giant dream and we were so excited. We were surrounded by amazing musicians and artists: BB King; The Pointer Sisters; it was all a fantasy. They all took us under their wing; all looking out for us. We were just giddy and excited. It was really cool.' Africa was to leave an impression on the Sledges that would remain with them for the rest of their lives. So, the girls certainly had a musical past.

Although the infectious, Jackson Five-inspired single 'Mama Never Told Me' was a UK Top 20 hit in 1975 and remains one of pop's unsung gems, the rest of their career was somewhat idling. There had even been a persuasive rumour that had the *We Are Family* album not come along, they would have split. As a result, the album was anything but middling.

Kathy Sledge, whose vocals so brightened and enlivened the Chic Organization's sound, states 'It's understandable that people thought we had been created by Chic. We had never had records on that scale before and it was like they were introducing us to the whole music scene. We were actually thinking of stopping by the time we had an offer from the "Yowsah Yowsah Yowsah" people, as we had just done something from the "Fly Robin Fly" (*Silver Convention*) people. We felt we had given our lives, sacrificing many simple things, like cheerleading practice. We would travel overseas on the weekend; then you would come home, get on the bus and go to school. You'd be sitting there with your girlfriends and you'd talk about what you did at the weekend; one had been to the mall, and one had been to the movies and I'd been in Japan. I either felt like I was bragging or lying!'

It was of utmost importance, after the tepid public reaction to the *Norma Jean* album, that the Sister Sledge project was successful. 'They had their early hit records, then Norma Jean had her hit, but it was on Bearsville, not Atlantic,' Kathy Sledge remembers. 'So, Atlantic approached them and said 'why did you give another label a hit? Why not record one of ours? They said we will, but it's got to do well. The world is watching us, we can't flop, and we really need the marketing machine behind us. They had a strong machine behind them and they had the confidence that what was behind them was really going to be heard.'

Sister Sledge, Bernard and Nile in the Studio

So, with both Rodgers and Edwards and Sister Sledge having something to prove, they worked fast. The album was recorded at The Power Station simultaneously in late 1978 with *C'est Chic*. It was the newly-founded Chic Organization Ltd. working at their very best. 'I felt glad that we were with a new team', Joni recalls. 'It was a really refreshing form of freedom. It must have been wonderful for Nile and Bernard to do what they wanted with us. We soon found out that we didn't have that independence!'

'For the *We Are Family* sessions, Nile and Bernard worked incredibly fast and they knew what they wanted, which I thought was so cool,' vocalist David Lasley remembers. 'The fades of those tracks could be up to eight minutes long at times – you would be running out of air, gasping for water, but it would continue on.'

Rob Sabino, who travelled back and forth from his gigs with The Simms Brothers to record, recalls the sessions with affection: 'We would work out songs, write the chords on a napkin and we – Tony, Bernard, Nile and I – would go out in the studio and play. Ideally, they would always try and get you at the start to recreate that Big Apple Band spontaneity. That was what was beautiful.'

'With the Sister Sledge stuff, Kathy was so strong, and she and Bernard seemed to find a way to work,' Raymond Jones recalls. 'It was a case of Kathy showing Bernard "this is what I do."' Kathy also had a profound affect on the vocalists within Chic: 'Luci told me that it was Kathy who allowed Bernard to open up the vocal style of the group,' Jones continues.

Debbie Sledge recalls: 'We were just getting our feet wet. It was all a big adventure to us. Meeting Nile and Bernard was another adventure to us. We were so young.' Norma Jean Wright was still around for the sessions: 'Sister Sledge were all very nice, and very, very talented. I thought Kathy Sledge was a great lead vocalist and I was in love with their songs. When I first heard "He's the Greatest Dancer" and "We Are Family", I just knew they would be

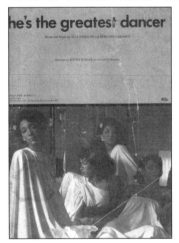

hits!' And hits they would be. Chic was forming perfectly into their working pattern at this point. Coming into the studio with virtually the entire track complete, Edwards and Rodgers would have the vocalists sing the lyrics in the dark with a simple light to illuminate the lyrics. The artist would have little prior knowledge of the words, so the performance would be fresh, creative and spontaneous. Kathy Sledge recalls: 'As I got to know them, I realised how brilliant they were, individually, as a team and as producers. It was certainly interesting working with Nile and Bernard, because we were not allowed to hear the material until the moment that we recorded it. With "He's The Greatest Dancer"; I recorded it, learning it line by line. They would go, "OK, sing 'one night in a disco';" I'd sing it; then they'd go "on the outskirts of Frisco". I wasn't allowed to hear "We Are Family" either, and recorded the song in one take – but that's what they wanted, the spontaneity – that's what made them who they are.'

'A lot of those lines we had to make up because the melodies weren't clear – and a lot of those lines were written as we were singing,' says Joni Sledge. 'Nile or Bernard would be there with lyrics – and we were given them fresh off the press. It was a process of being able to connect with what they were thinking – sometimes it was clear, sometimes it wasn't – you had creative licence to do what you thought.'

But, as a fairly veteran act, Sister Sledge were used to having a little more freedom with their harmonies. The sessions were not, therefore, all sweetness and light. The eldest singing sister, Debbie, in particular, had issues with the production style of Rodgers and Edwards while recording at The Power

Station: 'I clashed with them,' she recalls. 'I guess they played good cop, bad cop. Bernard would always play the hard guy, breaking the news to us that we did not like.' One of the key objections was simply, that as a trained vocal group, they resented the presence of the Chic choir – at this point Diva Gray, Vandross, Lasley, Anderson and Martin. 'I objected to them using any other singers on our records. I would state clearly to them that we are a complete singing group, we're self-contained. Bernard would play the hard nut, where Nile would explain how they were trying to get a sound. I would reply, "well, what is it, we'll get it for you – we can do it all". That was the only clash we had. I couldn't deny that they were doing great work.'

This creative tension led to what is still, arguably, the Chic Organization's greatest outside production. David Lasley recalls that it wasn't a struggle for power between the two outfits, it was simply a case of expediency: 'The real reason – and it certainly wasn't because they couldn't sing – it was a simple question of time and money – they didn't have very big budgets. At that point, Sister Sledge had only had one hit. When everyone is looking at their clocks, they needed to get their session singers on there.' The mysteries and techniques of the recording process were writ large to David Lasley. '"We Are Family" is all unison vocal apart for the words "everybody and sing", which is in harmony. I knew those records were different; they were very long and so much unison. You remember the choruses in a Chic track much more than the solo vocal. It becomes a chant, an anthem, a mantra. It's so infectious.'

'Debbie was always the one who would give us vocal harmonies,' Kathy continues. 'She was really excited about doing the vocal arrangements. From my perspective, it was frustrating not being able to practice a song and not being able to really know it.'

Lasley, one of the key session vocalists in New York at the time recalls: 'There was some exchange. We were in the lobby. I think we had recorded the Chic stuff first. We were doing songs from both the Chic and Sister Sledge album on the same night. We were in the lounge and Luther and I were sitting, waiting. Sister Sledge arrived in a pretty good mood and then they realised that we were the singers. I don't know if they had been told that there were going to be additional singers on their record. They were shocked.

Debbie was really not best pleased. We started doing the track "We Are Family" – Luther told them that it simply didn't matter; that this would be such a big hit record and that when it's in the Top 10, you will be so glad that this is the way it is. The girls looked at him and smiled. Of course, he was to be proved right.'

Kathy Sledge recalls meeting Vandross for the first time. 'I'll never forget the day that I really met

Sister Sledge on stage with Luther Vandross

Luther. We were listening to the playback of the backing track of "We Are Family." He was leaning against the glass. There was something about him that just seemed a little sad. I now understand – what was that man doing singing backgrounds for! His voice was amazing to me – he had so much talent and he was only singing backing vocals. Then he became Luther and the whole world knows who he is. He is one of the most dynamic entertainers – and I think wow – his voice graced our songs.'

The finished album centres on three undeniably fantastic cuts: 'He's The Greatest Dancer', 'Lost In Music' and 'We Are Family'. Craig Werner in *A Change Is Going To Come: Music, Race and the Soul of America* sees the famous trio of songs Rodgers and Edwards produced for the Sisters, as – echoing writer Ken Barnes phrase – 'the ultimate disco manifesto'. 'He's The Greatest Dancer' – a song originally intended for Chic – introduces the dance floor as a kind of ritual ground, while 'Lost In Music' testifies to the transformative power of music. 'We Are Family' reasserts a gospel vision of unity and harmony at a troubled time. Kathy Sledge's impassioned lead vocal on the track is absolutely incredible, arguably bringing for the first time, explicit *joie de vivre* to Chic's work. 'We Are Family' may go down as Rodgers and Edwards' most robust work of art.

Edwards and Rodgers had been writing around the clock to get the songs written. Their old friend, Eddie Martinez recalls dropping in on them at this time. 'I remember vividly, Nile and Bernard had a room set up in a hotel on the west side, and they had their guitars and amps, and some tape recorders,' he says. 'They started playing back a track they had just written – it was "We Are Family" – I recall them thinking it was so good that they were tempted to keep it for themselves.'

When Kathy Sledge first heard 'We Are Family', she knew it was the one: 'I took away a rough mix of it back to the hotel. I was dancing in the mirror to it, thinking that it was kind of nice. They took my ad-libs and moved them around – and put them where they wanted.'

The riff that Rodgers had kept in his head since Woodstock around a decade previously was gradually coming to fruition. After an initial meeting with the Sisters – where they had done their homework and listened to both the Norma Jean single and Chic's debut album, Rodgers began to add lyrics to what was to become the Chic Organization Ltd's most well-known track: 'Nile and Bernard had this mysterious thing about them. We had always worked together – there's that line in "We Are Family", "we flock together like birds of a feather." My sisters and I were so used to singing, working, living together – we would even clump together like cattle. If one went into the green room, we'd all go. I think we freaked them out, we were that close. When I listen to those words, I realised it was about us. But they were very intense. I didn't really understand it at the time.'

'We Are Family' is a gargantuan tune: it is the sort of record that you are so familiar with that if you never heard it again, you could still remember every nuance of it. It has soundtracked, at one time or another in its 25-year history, a whole raft of political and social events. It all hangs around the simplicity of the chorus:

> *'We Are Family*
> *I got all my sisters with me;*
> *We Are Family;*
> *Get up everybody and sing.'*

The record's effortlessness is astounding. As an anthem of unity, it's unassailable, having passion, depth and vision. At a time when the liberal experiments of the American 60s were seen to have finally collapsed and disco music was soon to be rendered redundant, the record penetrated the popular psyche sweetly, succinctly and saliently.

'"We Are Family" is the template,' says Rodgers, proudly. 'Luther Vandross is all over it. Sister Sledge came right in at the end and, thank God, they did. Thank God for Kathy because she took it to a whole new level. But when they walked in, they heard this huge, wonderful thing that we had already recorded. When I wrote the track, I just wrote a cute little pop ditty – it was Kathy who turned it into that magnificent piece of dancing artistry.'

This huge, wonderful thing became a global smash hit, reaching No.1 in the US R&B chart and becoming a No. 2 US pop hit and a No. 8 UK hit. It was adopted as a Civil Rights, gay and feminist anthem, a family reunion soundtrack as well as the rallying cry of the Pittsburgh Pirates, who won the 1979 world series. It is possibly Rodgers and Edwards' finest political statement, arriving at the height of disco, espousing unity, love and betterment. '"We Are Family" is still the best record Nile did,' Bryan Ferry argues. 'Wherever you hear that, wherever you are, whatever age group, people just get up and dance – it crosses across all barriers.'

'I realise how important "We Are Family" is,' Kathy stated. 'I recently sung it for a human rights convention, with the guys from *Queer Eye For The Straight Guy*. You see roomfuls of people just cheering for it – it could be human rights, it could be the girl scouts – it just grabs you that way. People constantly tell us what that record means to them; it's brought so many people back together.' 'We Are Family' was to give hope to Nelson Mandela when he was in prison in South Africa. 'He heard the prison guards whistling it,' Kathy continues, 'and he knew that four young black women in America sang that song – and that was one of the things that gave him hope, that he knew the world was changing.' Nelson Mandela is arguably the most potent world political figurehead of the late 20th Century. His story espouses the struggle for freedom and racial equality, and since his release from prison in 1990, he has met virtually every major world leader. His knowledge of 'We Are Family' serves to indicate the global reach of the disco movement.

'I thought "We Are Family" was one of the greatest songs that I'd ever heard,' Raymond Jones recalls. 'That was before it became used at all of the sporting events.' The real joy of the record can be found in the last minute of the album version; where the jam extends and Kathy is truly caught up in the rapture – you can almost hear everyone snapping with the length of the groove – Kathy's voice begins to give way and she encourages, in turn Rodgers to rejoin the song; Bernard to 'play his funky bass' and for Tony to 'come on'. And that is it. It builds to a rhapsodic, repetitious crescendo.

Although a lesser hit in America, 'Lost In Music' was a record that struck a tremendous chord in the UK. The line 'Lost In Music' was very personal to both Rodgers and Edwards: 'It's about Bernard and me,' states Rodgers. 'It's not about Sister Sledge. It tells the story of how the music had the power to change a very sad life into a somewhat happy optimistic life. When I say that music is my salvation and we are lost in music, that was our own personal joke, long before we turned it into a song. There would be times when Bernard would call me up. When I didn't want to be bothered, I would say, "man, I'm lost in music". That was like the code to stop fucking with me 'cos I was writing a song. It was all good – it was our signal to let me call him back in an hour.'

It encapsulates Rodgers' childhood and youth in the Village perfectly, and how he could never stay with the record shops and guitar repairers that tried to take him away from his first love.

'Responsibility to me is a tragedy, I'll get a job some other time'

and

'Lost in music / feel so alive / I quit my 9 to 5'

and

'some people ask me what are you gonna be – why don't you go get a job.'

It is little short of a freedom manifesto.

Many have connected with the record's sentiments. Duran Duran, who were at this point idolising Chic from afar as they grew up in England, would later sing vocals on the 1984 remix of the single. One of the most unlikely cover versions it received was from English new wave institutions, The Fall, in 1993 on their UK Top 10 album, *The Infotainment Scan*. Although many commented on the unusual choice of cover for Mark E. Smith and his Salfordian stalwarts, it is not too much of a leap of imagination to understand that Smith could not fail to latch on to a tune which achieves a trance-like state through repetition.

And then, the album's opener and debut hit single, 'He's The Greatest Dancer' was possibly the best celebration of the overall ennui of the scene. It was the story of *Saturday Night Fever* set to music. Whereas other songs of the era over-egged the disco pudding; Rodgers' account of the events in the disco 'on the outskirts of Frisco' displayed an eye for detail and acute observational skills. In one of his most celebrated lyrics, we trace Kathy Sledge out to another random night at the sort of club that had burgeoned in the wake of Robert Stigwood's all-conquering film. As all the tired out-of-towners are throwing the similar, weary shapes across the floor, the main protagonist arrives, with the sort of body that would shame Adonis; wearing the finest clothes and delighting the crowd and the young Kathy. One character, one chance – mundanity is lifted. The chances that thousands of young black urban professionals were taking in the late 70s are played out in this song. The dancefloor had become a microcosm of all life, the ritual ground. But it was Kathy's wide-eyed innocence topping it off that made the record work. It is difficult to imagine the same effect being achieved if Anderson or Martin had sung 'oh what, wow!', allowing it to set the scene perfectly for the whole album.

Rolling Stone suggested that with *We Are Family*, Rodgers and Edwards provided the 'fluid propulsion and gave their songs elegance'. The messages of peace and harmony that Rodgers carried with him from his hippie days run throughout the album – although many border on homily, the message is clear; love and unity are the answer, even deep within the 'me' generation. To that end, it is probably the Chic Organization's most relentlessly upbeat album: Whether it be the joyous voyeurism of 'He's The Greatest Dancer' or the 'all that killing each other, you should be loving your brother' in 'Easier To Love'. No mention of the album is complete without 'Thinking Of You', which has the sweetest touch of all Rodgers-Edwards compositions; the fluidity of the guitar figure and the wonderfully expressive bass combine beneath one of the purest expressions of love ever recorded.

'I love "Thinking Of You",' Kathy states. 'We recorded it late at night, about 2 o'clock in the morning. My sister Kim, who has incredible timing, gave me a lot of those ideas, and I would add them in. I enjoyed and still enjoy singing that the most. It's like when you get runner's high. Well, I get vocal high. I go to another level.' 'Thinking Of You', all simplicity and emotional depth, was the album's hidden gem. It was to become a hit in Britain in 1984, where it gave the album a whole new lease of life.

During the recordings, the 19-year-old Kathy Sledge used to be forever haranguing her new producers. 'I used to drive Nile crazy. Here you had this teenager person following behind him, saying "do you think it's going to be a hit?" He would look at me, smile, and say "trust me, baby, this is going to be *huge*." And I used to say to my sisters, "how does he know?" We had had at least nine singles out, and we were used to all these executives telling us our records were going to be hits and then you'd never hear them. When Nile said it, it felt the same way. But I'll never forget the day that "He's The

Greatest Dancer" came out. That was the song that woke me up that morning on the radio.'

The *We Are Family* album is also full of the Chic players coming to maturity in the studio; Sammy Figueroa's congas on the introduction to 'Thinking Of You'; Rodgers' string arrangements; the unison vocal on the title track; the play-out of 'You're A Friend To Me' is one of the best grooves on the album and arguably – with an embarrassment of riches, one of Edwards' very best bass moments.

The packaging of the album again pointed towards the sophistication that was being imported by the Chic Organisation. The cover portrays the Sledge sisters draped all in white in a Very Large Room Indeed. It is as if the white material were dustsheets, suddenly pulled aside to reveal these treasures that have been covered over for a considerable period of time. The Chic Organization revealed the potential within.

The album went to No. 3 on the American charts and reached No. 15 in the UK in 1979 – spending a remarkable 39 weeks on the charts. It was to be the calling card Rodgers and Edwards needed to propel them on to the biggest stages.

When working on the album, Raymond Jones began to realise there was a formula for Rodgers and Edwards success: 'A girlfriend pointed out that everything was in the same key ... and I thought about it and most of the songs were either in A, E, G or D which are really good keys to play guitars in,' Jones recalled. 'I think everything had a sort of harmonic overtone as you were working around those particular keys. There were a few songs away from that – "Everybody Dance" was in Cm, but in the main, all the stuff – "Good Times" in E; "We Are Family" in A; "I Want Your Love" in A. They were easy for them to play and easy for us to understand. It was a distinct sound. It was a deliberate thing with the two of them to keep things in those keys.' It was the simplicity that spelt hits.

13.
THE CHIC ORGANIZATION LTD.

'At one point in pop, there was Abba, Chic and Blondie.'
MARTIN FRY

ALTHOUGH POLITICALLY the city was in turmoil, the late 70s were a time when New York was the cradle of creative activity. At that time, The Power Station, at 441 West 53rd Street, was like a revolving door for Chic; it was as if the Organization had moved in. Sister Sledge recorded one day, Chic the next. The recently-opened studios were owned by respected, old-school producer Tony Bongiovi, and were housed in a former Consolidated Edison plant in the Hell's Kitchen area of Manhattan. It was full of the hottest music makers of the day, soaking up the studio's vibe. Brian Eno came down to The Power Station when Chic were working. Bruce Springsteen was a frequent user of the studio and it was here that he recorded and mixed *The River*.

Tony Thompson recalled The Power Station with a considerable amount of pleasure; 'It became like a second home. We seemed to spend our lives there – ordering food, hanging out in the lounges and creating some wonderful music. It was just like old family – everybody was great. Jon Bon Jovi, who was Tony Bongiovi's cousin, used to sweep up the place, that's how he got studio time; he wouldn't say much, but he was just the sweetest, most determined guy – we would always say "hi" to each other. You never had any idea he had all that going on. Our engineer, Bob Clearmountain – there were so many talented cats in that house, man.'

Bryan Ferry, the inspiration behind Chic, also came to use the studio in the late 70s: 'I was lucky to go to The Power Station,' he recalls. 'The vibe there was great and Nile was a very big part of it. He and Bernard had a room booked all year round. The engineers were great. It was a funny place – it was owned by the Bongiovi family so all the engineers were Italian and white – which is so often the case in black music. They had this black thing and rock thing – Springsteen was there all the time; Bob would do Chic, Springsteen, us – it felt like a really vibrant meeting place for many styles of music at the time.' Raymond Jones flipped when he saw Ferry's old Roxy

Music partner, Eno, one of his idols, at the studio. 'I wanted to go over there and lick his boots and Nile and Bernard were like – "get your ass over here! – you are on this payroll." I was always listening to Bowie records and Eno records – *Before And After Science* – and my ears were wide open to the Britpop stuff like XTC. "Life Begins At The Hop", "Making Plans For Nigel" …'

Chic did the majority of their recording in the wood-panelled and octagonal Studio A, working with engineer Clearmountain. An article in *High Fidelity* magazine gave a flavour of how the group used their studio, telling of how one of the two adjacent, smaller glass-enclosed areas was set up for their rhythm section with bass and guitar amps, keyboards (Fender Rhodes and clavinet) and amps, and a drum kit. Amps and drums were baffled with four-foot dividing walls, which allowed Rodgers, Edwards, Thompson and Andy Schwartz maximum eye contact and communication. This added considerably to the intimacy of the recordings. The article continued to say how Clearmountain close-miked the instruments, with twelve to sixteen mikes on the drums alone to ensure there was absolutely no sound leakage. The tight sound in the small room came from the fact that they were playing live.

'Bernard and Nile work very fast in the studio with rhythm tracks,' Clearmountain explained. 'The basic tracks for both the *C'est Chic* and *We Are Family* albums were cut in four days altogether. "Le Freak" took about two hours – the track we used for that was, I think, the fourth complete run-through. They never use a click-track and rarely have to fix or change any notes in the track they decide to use.'

Raymond Jones recalls the hit-making there: 'The way we worked was to keep the sound but try to contour something exclusive for the next artist with the same basic players and the same concept. Sheila does sound different from Johnny Mathis.' Rob Sabino was a regular at the studios. He would fulfil his commitments with the Simms Brothers when in the US and make it to the studio to record. It was a very mad time: 'Sure, I was flat out,' Sabino laughs. 'The Simms Brothers would be playing up in New England, and I would get back at 3 a.m., have three or four hours sleep and then rehearse and record for Chic projects for years – from the beginning of Chic until David Bowie's *Let's Dance*. When you're young, it's not a big deal. I think now I was a maniac. I didn't know any better.'

The Simms Brothers were momentarily fortunate as well. Through winning a battle of the bands contest, they won the opportunity to open for Peter Frampton at the New Haven Coliseum. Frampton was enamoured with them, booting off his troubled support act, The Climax Blues Band, in favour of them. After signing to Elektra, the group received favourable reviews for their album, *Back To School*. However, due to some questionable financial moves by their manager, Paul Ahern, it was to be all over very quickly for them.

A third keyboard player was present at most of Chic's sessions, Andy Schwartz. Raymond Jones recalls: 'Andy wanted to direct his career along the lines of Billy Joel, but that didn't happen for him. He wanted to be the nice

Jewish boy from Long Island who wrote great songs. There's nothing wrong with that, but the world already had one.' 'I didn't really know Andy Schwartz – he was never one of us,' Rob Sabino adds. 'He was a session player.'

The Chic Organization fascinated people. Based at 110 East 59th Street, New York, NY 10022, and run in conjunction with MK Productions, the company of Mark Kreiner and Tom Cossie, it seemed like a pastiche of Motown. It handled all the production requests that started to flood in and it came to be run as a proper business. 'We were run as a company. It was Bernard and I and these financial people,' Rodgers recalls. 'We had our financial investments. In fact, some were quite pioneering. We did some innovative things for musicians in those days. We also invested in mobile CAT scanners. We started a business in Florida; where there are lots of retirees and the hospitals couldn't afford the scanners because they were a million dollars apiece. We purchased them from General Electric and sent them out in 18-wheelers as mobile diagnostic units. We made great money and made sure we were doing a community service. That was one of the investments of the Chic Organization.' The Organization offices were to relocate twice; firstly to Two Sound View Drive, Greenwich, Connecticut and then to 48 Signal Road, Stamford, Connecticut, where it became the Chic Music Organization.

Speaking in 1979 to James Truman of *Melody Maker*, there was little doubt that, in addition to being the sole spokesmen of the band, Rodgers and Edwards were virtually the sole beneficiaries of their success. Together they controlled the running, finances and music of Chic and its offshoots. Edwards was quick to point this out: 'We'd been ripped off so many times that this seemed like the only way. Chic was evolved to try and fulfil something that we'd never had and we don't intend to let go of it. We have to stay ahead of our business; we have to keep abreast of our situation at all times. To some people that may sound corny and conservative, but this is now the rest of our lives we're working on.' The duo were generous but had no intention of cutting anyone else in on their deal. They were not going to share with anyone. They had worked for it. And the work ethic was very strong.

In fact, their work ethic was remarkable. The pressure of 1978/79 would have finished off lesser groups: 'We loved it, it was fine for us working on four albums at one time,' Rodgers recalls. 'I like to work at that pace. We liked working like that, when the juices are flowing. Maybe it's bad for the health, it's certainly not bad for the art and it's certainly not bad for the record. Half of what made it so exciting was that time was limited and we didn't sit around and nitpick over the ideas. If we did it and it felt great, it was good enough. Having too much time is a bad thing.'

Rolling Stone were able to see behind the glitter. James Farber, writing in May 1979 was right when he suggested that Chic were 'the Boston of the disco world, coming from nowhere just one year ago to share the limelight with such top disco stars as the Village People and Donna Summer. Actually, Chic is not a real band but a two-headed monster, rounded out by a dozen musicians and singers who aren't part of the decision-making process.' The parallel with Boston is accurate. There had to be a degree of suspicion of any group that apparently came out of nowhere to have a run of massive success and yet still be faceless and anonymous. But that is where the similarity ends; there could be little question of them working quite so slowly as that reclusive supergroup.

Chic entered 1979 riding the very top of disco's rollercoaster. As Jimmy Carter's policies began to look stagnant in the US, the Labour government in Britain was about to capitulate to the Conservative Party led by Margaret Thatcher. How disco had been received in America was one thing, but in Britain, it was a very different tale.

1978 had been a bumper year for British pop. Although punk, which had momentarily caused so much horror from the London-centric popular press, was maturing as a musical type, it only accounted for 4% of all single record sales in Britain. The genre defined as 'soul' also accounted for 4%. 'Pop', whatever exactly that was, still enjoyed far and away the highest market share at 24%. Music was seen as a huge recreational pastime, with 79% of all homeowners having equipment on which to play their latest records. The newest trend was the music centre, a Perspex-lidded compendium-sized rectangular slab that gathered the three main musical modes of carriage together – radio, tape and turntable – all inside of a majestic piece of furniture. The cassette was beginning to challenge the supremacy of the LP, and CDs were still four years away.

But what was there to listen to in the post-punk confusion of the British music scene? 1977/1978 marked the resurgence of the single in the UK with confections such as 'Mull Of Kintyre' by Paul McCartney and Wings at their most trite, the Boney M singles and the hits from firstly the *Saturday Night Fever* and then the *Grease* soundtrack making the 7" record a desirable must-have. The UK charts during this period seemed to have temporarily become a clearing house for the strange; with acts like jazz-funk petty criminals, Ian Dury and The Blockheads, doo-wop *pasticheurs* Darts, nursery rhyme soulsters Boney M, Swedish hit machine Abba (who contrary to any retro-fitted public opinion, were, at the time, idolised only by schoolgirls), and middle-of-the-road punks with a pyjama-wearing pianist, The Boomtown Rats. Roxy Music returned with *Manifesto*, an album that had actually been finished at The Power Station. Its airy grooves certainly adopted a disco sensibility. By the time of the third single from the album, 'Angel Eyes', they were temporarily abbreviated to simply 'Roxy'. The sleeve, with the close-up of two female mannequins, Roxy in full serif-ed font glory and the handwritten script of the title bore a striking similarity to recent Chic sleeves.

The Mecca ballrooms and mirrorballed halls of the UK were a million miles away from the opulence of Studio 54. Britain had had a hard time in the 70s which had seen inflation and a widescale strike impact the economy. It was into this climate that Chic were accepted in Britain with a mixture of love and fervent bemusement. They appeared like a black Abba with their songs of life and love, all performed with strange dispassion. Legs and Co. had danced to them on the programme before, but when Chic first appeared live on *Top Of The Pops* on 19th January 1979, they were clearly different. We are not talking David Bowie performing 'Starman' seven years earlier; but we are talking a clear difference marked out by the elegance of the ladies and the smartness of the gentlemen. This was a smartness unseen – it wasn't the exaggerated cummerbund'n'tie creations favoured by the male vocal acts of the 70s, or the sharp-cut mod attire of the Miracles as they whirled around behind Smokey Robinson. Chic sported fashions you'd be more used to seeing on *Racing From Ascot* or at a regatta. Simply put, these looked like black toffs.

But even in England – in a culture where comedy programmes such as *Love Thy Neighbour, Mind Your Language* and *Mixed Blessings* were 70s TV staples – where we'd only just become used to seeing ethnic monorities at all, it was most unusual to see an image of *rich* black people. Images of blacks were confined often to television stereotyping or the hyper-exaggerated Uncle Tom-isms of characters like Bobby from Boney M. The publicity photographs of the five main players in Chic certainly looked the part. Their look, as Shapiro notes, 'laid the ambiguity/distance schtick on thick.' It was simply inscrutable, different.

The music was clearly refined and unusual. For their two singles of the year, 'I Want Your Love' and 'Le Freak', Chic were to rank 16th in the BPI's Top 20 singles artists of 1978/79, ahead of Heatwave, The Brotherhood Of Man and The Commodores and 'Le Freak' was to go gold in 1979. *C'est Chic* was Chic's commercial zenith in Britain. The album was promoted initially as *Tres Chic*, complete with its cover of a scantily-clad model holding a light sabre (*but of course*) with the addition of 'Everybody Dance' and  'Dance, Dance, Dance (Yowsah, Yowsah, Yowsah)'. The album finally hit the charts in the winter of disco-ntent, February 1979. *C'est/Tres Chic* went to No. 2, amid major label disco cash-ins such as EMI's *Don't Walk – Boogie* and Warners' enormous TV-advertised disco album, *The Best Disco Album In The World*, which certainly wasn't the *only* disco album in the world, at that point. Chic and Sister Sledge accounted for a good percentage of the tracks.

The sludge brown scenes of London's Leicester Square full of uncollected rubbish – yards from the doors of The Empire discotheque, where the annual

Disco Dance Championship was held – were alleviated by the marbled finish of the cover of Chic's ice-cool album. Chic's message of dancefloor freakery offered rays of sunshine. Although the left-of-centre clubs were falling in love with jazz-funk, the pop sensibility, detachment and glamour of Chic enabled them to become one of the most high profile acts of 1979.

So, the group was received differently in the UK, where black music was viewed either as a delicacy by the cognoscenti, or simply for mass dancing on a Saturday night. In clubs around the land, a new generation were listening. Martin Fry, who was about to form ABC, and later would have a hard connection with Chic when Edwards produced their work, recalls: 'It's maybe a mod thing or northern soul thing – but these records from America sounded immaculate. We wanted to make something as shiny and as perfect as those records. Our generation was Ian Curtis and Mark Smith. It was all post-punk. We wanted to capture the flavour, the drama and the glamour that was in the music we were hearing in clubs and discos – and also that Saturday night feeling of being indestructible. It didn't matter whatever crap was thrown at you for the other six days of the week, you could be a king for one night, an idea which is right through the middle of *Saturday Night Fever*. That feeling of euphoria and optimism wasn't in the air in 78/79 – especially in Sheffield.'

By 1979, Chic were phenomenally popular – they had not only clocked up more than 50 million dollars worth of sales for Atlantic; but every record they had released has gone at least gold, and the more recent ones had turned multi-platinum. As Fry states: 'At one point in pop, there was Abba, Chic and Blondie.'

Rob Sabino lived in London throughout the Chic and Sister Sledge UK breakthrough. As the records he had recorded on the late shift and on the early mornings at The Power Station were climbing the UK charts, he had been in a flat in Grosvenor Square, London at the expense of Warner Brothers, recording with The Simms Brothers.

Fry was listening in while at university in Sheffield. He felt that 'There was a real dignity in Chic's stuff all the time, combined with the illusion of simplicity. The humour in the lyrics is very attractive as well. On the one hand, they are very complex lyrics and on the other, they are almost banal. If you were learning the English language, you could learn off Chic records. I could imagine French kids singing along to "I Want Your Love." But, at the same time, "He's The Greatest Dancer" is genius – That whole Gucci/Fiorucci – that tongue-in-cheek thing was there all along.'

With Britain, America and Europe falling for their charms, as 1979 progressed, Chic looked ever more unassailable. The leg-work done by Rodgers and Edwards, with their trusted cohort Thompson meant that they could take on any project, any size. It was time to make an album commensurate with their ability. People could differentiate their records from factory-made run-of-the-mill disco, couldn't they?

14.
CHIC CHEER?

*'We were talking to people in a time of financial chaos and putting a
bright face on it. We were entertainers. Our responsibility is not necessarily
to educate first – it's to entertain first. If we can educate at the same time,
then we're clever!'*
NILE RODGERS 2003

IN 1979 A HELPLESS and emasculated Jimmy Carter was portrayed by the
American Right as presiding over the last party before the sharp swing to the
right that lay ahead. Prices rose in America by more than 13%. The second oil
crisis of the decade hit: OPEC boosted prices to more than $30 a barrel –
gasoline rose from 30 cents to $1 a gallon. Energy related costs fed the
runaway inflation. Back interest grew and economic activity remained in the
doldrums, the phrase 'stagflation' was coined. That summer, Carter spoke of
the crisis of confidence of the American electorate, which appeared to deflect
the blame back to the American people. 'Jimmy Who?' was a best selling
bumper sticker of the year.

At a time of general nervousness, common enemies are frequently sought.
It was time for disco, which had initially given a voice to so many
disenfranchised parties, to be cut down to size. Bernard Edwards' closing
statement on Chic's 1979 press release was 'We've been lucky. Add a lot of
hard work on the road and in the studio, and a diversity of musical
backgrounds, and the result is a band that will sustain no matter what fads
come and go. Chic will always be in.' Within two years, Chic would already
be nostalgia.

The backlash against disco had been building throughout the course of
Chic's career; even esteemed cultural historian Simon Frith said in *Time Out*
416 in 1978 that 'Everybody hates it. Hippies hate it, progressives hate it,
punks hate it, teds hate it, *NME* hates it. It isn't art: no auteurs in disco, just
calculated desiccating machines.' So when the Disco Sucks backlash hit across
America, it slowly, yet surely crippled Chic.

And so, the disco movement buckled in the American popular psyche on

12th July 1979 at Comiskey Park, Chicago, overseen by W-LUP DJ Steve Dahl, under the banner 'disco demolition'. In the intermission of a twi-night doubleheader baseball game between the Detroit Tigers and the White Sox, a huge pile of disco records were covered in lighter fluid and then set ablaze. Anyone who brought disco records to the game for burning was allowed in for a mere 98 cents. Dahl was an overweight, bespectacled shock-jock, who had taken to wearing military headwear and had *himself* actually hosted disco parties. But he saw an opportunity and sensed the backlash that was swarming around him. The field ended up completely trashed, and the White Sox were forced to forfeit their second game. The event made the international news.

Bill Gleason, the veteran commentator of the *Chicago Tribune* reported:

'It was the most disgraceful night in the long history of major league baseball in Chicago. It became frightening long before thousands of young people maniacally ran into the playing field at about 8:40 pm. My wife and I were watching the middle innings of the first game from seats behind the screen and above the aisle that divides upper and lower boxes. Across the aisle were seven young men who were getting themselves "up" for the evening. They passed around a bottle of peppermint schnapps. They washed that down with a bottle of brandy. Some of them ordered ice cream from a vendor. And they shouted their anti-disco obscenity.

They were vulgarians who came to Comiskey Park to be ruffians. They were not there to watch the White Sox play Detroit.

'The highlight of the between-games ceremony was to have been the blowing up of all the disco records that had been tossed into a huge box in deep centerfield. Large fireworks were touched off in a row in front of the box. Then a fireworks "bomb" within the box was detonated. That was supposed to be the end of it.

Instead it was the beginning of the horror. When the records exploded, young men and young women left their places in the lower deck.

Dozens ran onto the field. Hundreds. Then thousands.'

The spectacle was played out fully on television. It was the end of an 18-month campaign that had been brewing across Middle America in order to contain the music that had so caught the popular consciousness. That it was picked up by the media with such alacrity demonstrates the latent hatred that had been festering. Two-bit bar bands would decry disco at every opportunity. Disco was diametrically opposite to the macho posturing of white rock. Groups who had flirted with disco moved on and acts that had once been popular couldn't get arrested. As Brewster & Broughton suggest, as there were no bands in disco, no tours, or souvenir t-shirts, it was difficult to quantify and compartmentalise and treat like white rock. Or, of course, sell like white rock. A few journalists wrote passionately about it, like Brian Chin and Tom Moulton, but in the main it was totally ignored or treated with great disdain. Craig Werner suggests in *A Change Is Gonna Come* that, 'the Antidisco movement represented an unholy alliance of funkateers and feminists, progressives and puritans, rockers and reactionaries. Nonetheless, the attacks on disco gave respectable voice to the ugliest kinds of unacknowledged racism, sexism and homophobia.'

'It felt to us like Nazi book-burning,' Rodgers sighs. 'This is America, the home of jazz and rock and people were now even afraid to say the word "disco". I had never seen anything like that. I remember thinking – we're not even a disco group.' Whenever there has been public revolt of this kind, be it Nazi book-burning, or a more recent American example, the burning of Beatles records in the wake of John Lennon's supposed anti-Jesus comments in 1966, it has been prompted by the politics of the Right. The manipulation of popular fears and demonisation of change-threatening minorities are often made explicit in a public moment of anger. Minorities had found ostensibly freedom, success and wealth through this music and the white working-class sought once again to repress through this aggressive and hate-filled action.

For Rodgers and Edwards, the main problem was timing. Because Chic's recording career began simultaneously with the rise of disco, Chic had no past and were seen by the American public as a manufactured act, akin to Silver Convention. Rodgers is still hurt by the memories; 'Kool And The Gang: they were an R&B semi-jazz groove band. All of a sudden, disco became big and they went disco,' he claims, laughing, 'It's almost like when people say – "hey, my man over there turned gay – before that he was hetero – the guy turned gay on me." Kool And The Gang turned disco – but they could turn back. The Rolling Stones turned disco – but they could turn back. Because Chic were there when disco was big, we were big. When disco sucked, we sucked. People couldn't tell the difference between us and Lipps Inc! We wished we'd been in a different era. All the time.'

'It didn't really bother us that much because we never felt we were "disco disco,"' Robert 'Kool' Bell remembers. 'We did dance music – music with a groove that was on the funk side. We weren't a disco group per se – we were just growing musically.'

The disco sucks movement had an enormous, overarching impact – sounds had to be changed and adapted: 'Kool' Bell: 'Then after that the whole anti-disco thing started to happen. We decided to see if we could change our sound and compete with Earth Wind And Fire and The Commodores and that's when we came up with James "JT" Taylor and "Ladies Night." It still related to disco and to clubs, but no one had heard that flavour before, and certainly not heard Kool and The Gang with a lead vocalist. "Ladies Night" was just funky enough and just danceable enough that it slipped straight through and it opened up the door for us into the 80s.' It was a passage to the 80s that Chic, as an outfit, were not to be granted.

'I thought it was all very silly. It was just a publicity thing,' Nik Cohn states. 'Ninety-five percent of pop music has always been absolute shite – you only ever judge 5% and I think the top 5% of disco stands up very well. Anybody getting angry enough to go burning disco records – I mean, Jesus Christ. There was something behind it also. I could see that electronic music, drum machines, brought exciting new possibilities. It was the moment when pop music became very precious. It became like jazz, when people would say it couldn't be played on an electric guitar – it was ugly conservatism.'

Norma Jean Wright, who by now had begun a lucrative session vocalist career, was clear: 'I thought the disco sucks thing was a backlash that was unfair and unwarranted.' 'I was lucky – I was able to separate the cultural monolith of disco, from disco the music,' reckons Rob Sabino. 'Disco the music was just fine – it was R&B, but for this era we were concentrating more on quarters on the bass drum. It was R&B-tinged pop. Some of the music was a little superfluous, but then again, all pop is. "The Leader Of The Pack" is extremely superfluous and trite. I just thought it was great dance music.' Sabino later came particularly to resent being labelled as disco. 'I knew what we were – we could play anything. I also viewed it as a racist statement, because a lot of the anti-disco statements was anti-black also.'

'You see, I really didn't see Chic as a disco band,' states Raymond Jones. 'When we toured opposite Cameo, Atlantic Starr and The Bar-Kays, we were like another funk band that happened to do music that people danced to. We were in Brazil at the same time as The Village People – nice guys, but who had very little in common with us. I understood the connotations of disco, but it was like there weren't many bands in that genre of music that had our level of musical depth. Nile is a jazz player at heart. Bernard's realm was so wide. Tony could play any damn thing they presented to him.'

Fonzi Thornton, who was on the verge of taking over from Luther Vandross as Chic's No.1 backing vocalist felt, too, that the backlash had little to do with them: 'When the whole thing came out, I didn't feel part of it, as there was this whole scene of confections that started with "Disco Duck". I thought our music was apart from that, so the disco sucks thing never bothered me one little bit. I thought we were doing orchestral funk dance music. There was a real attention to the quality of the music we were putting out.' But soon, people would pay scant regard to that.

Ahmet Ertegun, the President of Atlantic during Chic's golden years is still full of hatred for that period: 'I think those are the kind of generalisations that are made that are not really valid. In reality – everybody has a preference for a certain kind of music, but there certainly is not much credence to people who say that they don't like that particular kind of music – that doesn't hold water because there's very good music in all forms. Just because you like Mozart it doesn't mean you can't like Bob Wills and the Texas Playboys. One doesn't make the other one bad.'

Disco sucks was largely a chance for racist as well as homophobic expression. 'My response is "coloured" by my experience as a woman of African descent living in a racist society,' Alfa Anderson states. 'The whole of American society must share responsibility for the disco sucks phenomenon simply because we all (wittingly or unwittingly) contribute to institutionalised racism. It is a fact that the spectre of racism hovers over our country. It is ubiquitous. Not in all individuals but in the systems that make sure that people of African descent are never allowed to forget that our skin colour is how we are judged. After the struggles of the 60s, more and more people became aware of the lies inherent in perpetuating racism and challenged what the founding fathers set up. The 70s made it more difficult for racism to continue as much on a personal level, but it was, and still is, strong systemically. The next tactic then is "divide and conquer". The ability to perpetuate racism in this country is due in part to African peoples' criticism of, and public denunciation of each other. So every time a person of colour denigrated the work, it became that much easier for the larger society to attack it. My premise applies to every facet of American society, not just music.'

And it was an insidious hatred that pervaded – and the ramifications would continue on and dog the next three years of Chic, which, coupled with addictions and personality clashes, would lead to their demise. 'When people started saying "disco sucks",' Rodgers stated to Marc Taylor. 'We started saying "we're proud to be a disco band." We were so angry that people would victimise an entire movement because it felt to us like black people were dominating the charts, the pop charts, the only charts that counted. We were ruling it, so the only way to get the rock guys back at the top of the charts was to say "these guys suck" and "let us have our charts back." That's what it felt like to me. It was scary.' And so, Chic, were frozen slowly out of the party they had helped to start. After their next album, *Risqué*, No. 43 was as high as they got for the remainder of their career.

As it was now 'official' that disco sucked, it was a difficult time for the wave of British artists that were now travelling the US, who felt very differently about the music. British new waver Joe Jackson: 'When I first went to New York, Chic was happening. The one thing I always remember was that I always liked disco; I liked the better stuff, Donna Summer and Chic. When I first started touring the States, there was this war going on between the rock fans who liked the so-called new wave, and disco. So everywhere I went I would be greeted with crowds of people chanting "disco sucks" and I was supposed to be their hero. I was given badges saying "disco sucks" and I didn't know what to do. I didn't have the heart to tell them I actually quite liked disco.'

It wasn't just Chic that felt the cold winds starting to blow. 'Politically, we were classified as a disco act,' Kathy Sledge recalls. 'I never looked at Sister Sledge as a disco act. We had sung all of our lives and had done cabaret and R&B shows. We were entertainers, and our records happened to happen at the time.' 'When you then heard Billy Idol doing "White Wedding" several years later,' Sabino recalls, 'with its guitar, all of a sudden disco is known as dance music, because there is a white guy singing. I was more upset about that.'

So after three remarkable years of success, Chic would soon barely be able to get arrested in their own country. As the social and political advances that had been earned across the decade began to be confined, contained or eroded, so did the public support and love for the disco movement.

However, it is easy and glib to conclude that this was the immediate end of disco. In the same way it is easy to assume that punk swept away all before it on a tide of sputum in Britain in 1976. The slow absorption into the mainstream meant that records such as 'Funky Town' by Lipps Inc. (producer Steve Greenberg and vocalist Cynthia Johnson) weren't even released until 1980. But the 'disco sucks' movement certainly sounded the death knell.

'Looking back, disco was a better thing than people give it credit for,' Rodgers told *The Face* in 1982. 'We were going to places like South Carolina, where normally we'd have been lynched, and these rednecks were dragging us into their homes and giving us drinks. They loved us and we'd never found that before. You have to remember how completely ignorant most Americans are of jazz and R&B. They're our only native culture and still the average

American knows nothing about them. The whole reason why Bernard and I got into music was to try and transcend those barriers. It's that which makes us continue, even more so than wanting to make hit records.'

If Chic were going to ride out all the disco backlash pessimism, it would have to be with something very, very special. They were to have one last, huge, commercial and artistic hurrah with the album they had been working on during the gaps in their schedule since the start of 1979. And the lead single was arguably to be their most influential record of all. The album was called *Risqué* and the single, 'Good Times'.

☆☆☆

Craig Werner writes in *A Change Is Gonna Come* that 'during the Studio 54 years, Chic provided a living heartbeat in a musical scene increasingly threatened by minstrel vultures … . Chic's own "Good Times" delivers an eulogy for the era in the guise of a celebration.' The enormous swing to the right in American politics that culminated in Ronald Reagan's presidency was precipitated by Chic's greatest hit. With its ominous jet airliner take-off, the groove of 'Good Times' smacks somewhat of a distant desperation, a robotic reminder that if you repeat a mantra of happiness long enough you may finally actually believe in it. With this record, Chic could be seen as the house band on disco's Titanic, with popular culture's smiling passengers mistaking the iceberg for a mountain landscape.

For the recording of their third album, there were to be some fundamental changes to the overall sound. Luther Vandross was, by now, starting to break into the mainstream, and no longer had time to fulfil his Chic session duties and David Lasley had moved to California, to return only sporadically to New York, as he hated flying. 'Bernard called me when I was back in LA – the moment I got in almost – and asked me to do a session that was to become "Good Times",' Lasley recalls. 'I would have loved to have done it. There was a dramatic shift; it went from it being me and Diva and Alfa; it abruptly shifted to Fonzi, Alfa and Michelle. There was never any fall-out.'

In came Rodgers' long-term friend and old *Sesame Street* sparring partner, Fonzi Thornton. 'I got a phone call from Bernard, who I had never met. He said we're well aware of who you are, why don't you bring your two girls down and come and sing for us. Carol Sylvan had left the group the week before. So Michelle Cobbs and I learned all the songs and we went down and sang for them. Bernard and Nile loved what we were doing. The following week we went on a small promotional tour with Chic. We were still riding chartered buses to get around. We went down to South Carolina and we sang with them.

'The following week we went to the studio. Bernard said to me, I want you to sing what I'm telling you. The song says:

> *'Good Times,*
> *these are the good times,*
> *leave your cares behind.'*

'He said sing it high, it's there in a key for the girls, but I think we can do it. We put that down. Then on top of that they put me and Ullanda McCulloch singing the hook. And then added Michelle, and then Alfa and then Luci. The sound of Chic was always the sound of three girls singing at an alto range and one guy singing almost too high for his range. I could always negotiate them, but that's where this sound came from, the tension in that sound. For many years I was singing on the records – but the songs with group leads, I sang both leads and background with the girls. And nobody knew there was a guy singing, because my voice blended in so well. I was known in the industry as the secret weapon in Chic.'

Although Vandross in particular would be greatly missed, the shift in personnel was warmly received. 'Fonzi and Michelle came in and brought a new and different energy to the sessions,' Alfa Anderson recalls. 'And "Good Times" was simply the most infectious bass line balanced with the most perfect guitar licks that I had heard. That song still makes me very happy.'

After a long battle with retro-popsters The Knack's 'My Sharona', on 18th August 1979, Chic's finest moment, 'Good Times' finally stood atop the American chart. The single remains their lasting legacy and arguably one of the most significant records of the 20th century. When 'Good Times' came out, it was the very start of the next stage of the groove. Although many attempted it, only Rodgers and Edwards succeeded in introducing both irony into disco and a bass line that was to form the beginning of popular hip-hop.

Rodgers is justifiably proud: 'We were talking to people in a time of financial chaos and putting a bright face on it. We were entertainers. Our responsibility is not necessarily to educate first – it's to entertain first. If we can educate at the same time, then we're clever! During the late 70s we were going through the greatest recession since the Wall Street Crash. We loved how, at the height of the depression, there was some of the happiest music ever. When we did "Good Times" we were really paying homage to the great bands that flourished during the 20s. During the Great Depression they wrote "Happy Days Are Here Again," because they could drink booze again. Every lyric in the song was a throwback to depression-era songs. I even ripped off "Happy Days Are Here Again / The Time Is Right For Making Friends." Then I took an Al Jolson song that said "The stars are going to twinkle and shine this evening, 'bout a quarter to nine" – so I went "let's get together, about a quarter to ten".'

The record was a subtle marriage of past and present; political and apolitical; disco and lindy-hop. 'We thought during disco everybody was just partying. I don't ever remember going out and hearing people talk about recession. In those days you wanted to be original. It's not like today where you just take a loop – you wouldn't directly steal, at least if you were a true artist, and we believed we were true artists. We would re-write. We would never copy. It was blasphemous to us, because I come from a political era and you never did that. The depression was the inspiration. That was, as Lionel Richie would call it, "the code vibe".'

'Then we thought that you couldn't deny the history and place of music in people's lives that basically don't have much of a life in terms of financial reward. So then we got political – there are two worlds, that of the haves and that of the have-nots. In a place like Studio 54, all you needed was a certain sense of style and you could be part of that crowd. So we used "Good Times" to talk about all of these peculiar contradictions in the world. Every lyric in that thing was a throwback to depression era songs.'

However, this seminal record has long been the source of misunderstanding: 'People asked how we could write a song called "Good Times" in the middle of the greatest recession since the 1930s,' Rodgers sighs. 'We looked and said "are you a fucking idiot? Can't you hear the double entendre working here?" Listen to the lyrics, we are comparing it to the Great Depression! If Dylan was standing in front of a tank singing "happy days are here again" – people would say "oh, check Bob". It would be loved and would make all the sense in the world. That's the politics of what we are talking about, people don't understand that the same content coming from me sounds totally different coming from you.'

'Good Times' is economy running riot. 'Bernard made me not overwrite,' says Rodgers. 'His greatest strength was to edit. My natural inclination is to overwrite, his was to make it simple.' This was the zenith of Rodgers and Edwards working together: Tony Thompson recalls: 'Nile and Bernard would hear different things. Nile was a bit more on the fluff side, say like "Rollerskates, rollerskates" that kind of fluffy, corny addition that could make the record special. Bernard was at the serious end of things. He had an image thing going on. He was always hip to the image. He was always hip to what's new – clothing-wise, restaurants, new this, new that – he was always on top of things like that. That's what he brought lyrically and in terms of our image – he would know exactly what clothes we should wear and what shops we should get them from. He used to do all that.'

Listen to this track again. It's one of those records that you are so familiar with that sometimes you may feel that you never need to hear it again. But its striking, repetitive strangeness amid the glory of the beat merits your immediate attention. 'It takes the African idea of repetition emphasising what is important, making you think about the other elements going on beneath it,' Dr Mary Ellison argues. 'There's this dialogue going on between the apparent and the hidden. The complexity reflects real life, which is never simple.' And what was real was becoming increasingly blurred in the giddy bubble of success in the middle of which Chic found themselves.

It attracted the attention of heavyweights: 'Chic were really fantastic,' Gil Scott-Heron recalls. 'I liked to dance, I liked to go out to clubs. "Good Times" was a real favourite of mine. I just thought that was what young people were doing at the time.'

All the component parts of 'Good Times' continually surprise: the four-note string refrain alternating on the verse; the almost claustrophobic tightness of the vocals. And then the break. The break, the space in that break is remarkable. Edwards' 20-note riff drives the record forward over Thompson's crispest snare-crack. It was used on street corners throughout the world as the backing to what disco did next: hip-hop. Raymond Jones' Fender Rhodes gradually reintroduces the melody. 'My part in "Good Times" is so simple. I don't have to ever worry about playing with Steve Reich or Philip Glass, because I played minimalist music with Chic,' Raymond Jones laughs. 'The receptionist who would give us our cheque back then would say "I like your solo" and I would say *"What solo? It's just a bunch of block chords!"'*

The whole piece has a graceful ennui. The occasional string stabs, which were so gleefully appropriated by Joseph Sadler, who, under his better known street name, Grandmaster Flash, used and corrupted the washes on his 12" rumination of the record, 'The Adventures Of Grandmaster Flash On The

Wheels Of Steel'. Rob Sabino's piano drizzling back into the track, all underpinned by the robotic slap of the live handclaps. When Rodgers reintroduces his rhythm, it's simply one of the brightest shining moments in pop.

The highly individual and idiosyncratic string arrangements were Rodgers'. 'I'm not trying to put down any of the arrangements,' Raymond Jones states, 'but you can hear that they were orchestrated through a guitar. It's just the way he voices things – it's very clear and very concise. It's like listening to Todd Rundgren playing a sax solo – it's like a guitar player playing sax.'

The vocal magic was also very special: 'It was very lush, but it was also very soulful,' Fonzi Thornton recalls. 'Singing in unison, with a little harmony thrown in, made the sound very dense. Matching female voices and a male voice to make a sound that still has so much feeling that I'm really proud of. When I hear those records on the radio today, I'm so proud of that work, because it still sounds good. We've been sampled again and again, so the quality has stood up over all these years.'

With 'Good Times' at No. 1, Chic were successful beyond their wildest dreams. In summer 1979, they had achieved the feat of having two No. 1 pop singles, an international career, producing successfully for others and – unlike many other bands of their ilk, they were able to enjoy album success as well. Tony Thompson, 'We had gone from being a band that ate the same sandwich, to become the hit of New York and then the world in terms of people buying our records, and selling out concerts – it was a whirlwind that I will always cherish.'

★★★

Recorded at The Power Station, Kendun Studios, California and Electric Lady in New York over eight weeks in winter/spring 1979, *Risqué*, released in August of that year, is the album that the rock cognoscenti coo over the most. It's a complete album that is as integral to the Atlantic label as any of the great rock albums that had taken it out of Black America and into the world in the late 60s. With a budget of $160,000, it was a widescreen record with widescreen ambitions. With a full design concept that looked like something from the Hipgnosis stable, its sepia sleeve sat well alongside the other major Atlantic release of the summer: Led Zeppelin's *In Through The Out Door*. Atlantic even went back to its silver label, a staple of its jazz and R&B roster, as a one-off for the album. *Risqué* is an album that dwells on relationships; bleak, unrequited ones, ones tinged with sadism and despair; relationships with the past, and, of course, with the dance floor. It is an extremely mature work and several light years away from 'Sao Paolo'.

As a result, *Risqué* remains Chic's most sustained artistic statement, containing some of their most poignant moments. Past and present black culture was sifted into a cauldron and given a liberal stir. 'It was to do with Cab Calloway, Count Basie and Lena Horne,' Rodgers maintains. 'Being

African-Americans, because our skin is black, we've never been able to assimilate into culture the way other races have. During the Harlem Renaissance, people who were second and third descendants of slaves came up with their own class system and royalty to beat this: "Duke" Ellington, "Count" Basie, "King" Pleasure. Now we're Counts and Kings and Dukes. We were paying tribute to people who were oppressed and not having any voice that really could be heard except through their music and their art. Now we're accepted because we can inform and entertain and make people feel good. Everything had to fit the vibe.

The Harlem Renaissance, the literature, music and art force that so defined African-American entertainment from the 20s was freely referenced: 'When I think about the Harlem Renaissance,' Alfa Anderson suggests, 'I think more about the writers during that time – I think about Langston Hughes and Zora Neale Hurston because they dealt with issues of race and gender and sexuality in America. I think that Chic did a similar thing in music; in a different way; our way was not to point the issues out, as they had done, but to blur the lines, to bring everybody together.'

The recording of what was to become the *Risqué* album was fraught with some difficultly, namely a serious falling out between Rodgers and Edwards about what was going to be the lead-off single. Atlantic demanded 'My Feet Keep Dancing', and, although this fantastically taut, claustrophobic swing is up there among their very finest works, it was not a patch on the record that they both wanted to lead the album with. Both parties felt that the other wanted the single out. Both finally realised that together they could overthrow Atlantic's wishes, and 'Good Times' blazed the trail. '*Risqué* felt very special, very fresh and it did feel edgy at the time, as evidenced by the title,' Anderson recalls. 'You could see, feel and hear the group's evolution.'

Crispin Cioe at *High Fidelity* Magazine watched the recording process for *Risqué* at Studio A in Electric Lady: Rodgers was overseeing the eleven violins, four violas and two cellos that comprised the string section, under the auspices of Gene Orloff: 'Unlike much of disco,' Cioe wrote, 'Chic's sound uses strings as rhythmic devices, playing countermelodies with accents that closely follow Edwards' syncopated, punchy bass lines. While Nile conducted the strings, Bernard and Bob Clearmountain sat in the booth, checking the VU meters, commenting on phrasing and intonation, and cracking jokes. Gradually, I began to understand their approach: They merge a loose and funkily precise rhythm section with stately strings and graceful female voices. This is the Chic production concept that has spun gold for all concerned.'

The working methods were instinctive by this point: 'Nile and Bernard would always get together before they came to the studio and map out the song,' Fonzi Thornton recalls. 'But the song happened in the studio once they heard the sound of the group. The sounds would happen there – sometimes they would have a hook idea, some words and a melody, but they would finish writing it right there, and then give out the parts. But it would start with them putting me down first and then layering the other singers on top of me.

As that worked, we would just go and stand in front of the microphone. Bernard was in charge of laying down the vocal tracks. Nile and he would both agree on the sound. They had a different way of working. I was used to being well-rehearsed and going over it again and again, while they favoured a much more organic sound. Once we got the sound and performance, we were ready to go on. That is why there was so much life to it – it wasn't about being perfect, it was about having an edge and that big urban sound. It's also because we were working in The Power Station and those big, cavernous rooms added a whole depth to the sound.'

Much was made of the high-concept murder mystery sleeve. The art direction and design was done by Carin Goldberg, now a member of the American Institute of Graphic Arts. The characters portrayed by Anderson, Edwards, Martin, Rodgers and Thompson on their album sleeve could be seen as humorous exaggerations of their individual roles within Chic. The cover plot revolves around the gigolo (Rodgers), the maid (Martin), lady of the house (Anderson), the unconcerned butler (Thompson) and the man of the house (Edwards). 'That cover was such a political act amid all the other stuff that was going on,' Anderson states. 'It took a lot of guts to do that. It's like this whodunit. Who really could have done it – was it the lady of the manor? Was it the maid? Was it the butler?'

'We got tired of just doing the same old kind of cover so we decided we'd do something with a theme that tied in to some of the tunes on the album,' Edwards told *Blues and Soul* in 1979. 'Like "What About Me," "My Forbidden Lover" and "Can't Stand To Love You." So there's really a whole mini-story linking the songs and the cover. We were thinking about all those old mystery movies – Charlie Chan, the whole 40s thing – the Agatha Christie books. So the essence of what *Risqué* is about is "who done it?" We'll be illustrating that through our stage show more – we may even be putting together a whole mini-movie about it for the stage.' Unfortunately, the mini-movie idea came to nothing.

Risqué was Chic's greatest feel moment. 'It was all about authenticity,' Rodgers says. 'We did the whole Agatha Christie thing. Albums were concepts in those days. We were no less artistic and conceptual than Parliament or the Rolling Stones. This was our version of *Their Satanic Majesties Request*. Everything had to fit that vibe. We even rented expensive magazines and props so nothing was out of place on the album cover.'

Rodgers and Edwards' image management was at its creative peak. 'They allowed us to have a great deal of input into the styles and colours of what we could wear, but the image of the group was very much a part of their vision,' Anderson recalls. 'I bought into that. I remember Luci and I having conversations with them. They talked about the days of Duke Ellington, when people really dressed up to go on stage – and they loved the Motown thing where people were groomed to do the job they wanted to do. They wanted to bring a type of elegance to dance music. During that time people wore costumes on stage. We never wore costumes, we wore designer clothes

All photos Hammersmith Odeon, October 1979, BARRY PLUMMER

© EVERETT COLLECTION / REX

The fictionalised ghetto where amid the brownstones, all races seemed to co-exist perfectly: Sesame Street (L-R) white, black and Hispanic children, Oscar The Grouch, Susan (Loretta Long).

© ANGUS MAYER / REX

Roxy Music pictured in 1975, around the time when Nile Rodgers first encountered them.

THE INVISIBLE LEADERS OF THE CHIC CHOIR:

Luther Vandross

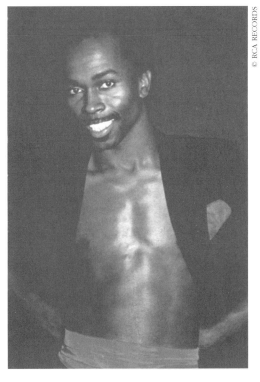

Fonzi Thornton

Marrying the string washes of Philly with the funk of JBs and P-Funk: Chic, 1979: Alfa Anderson, Tony Thompson, Bernard Edwards, Nile Rodgers, Raymond Jones, Luci Martn. (Karen Milne is just out of shot.)

© SIPA PRESS / REX

'Point us to somebody in this building who is not a star and we will make them a star': Sister Sledge 1981 – clockwise from bottom left – Joni, Debbie, Kathy and Kim.

© REX

© PETER MAZEL / SUNSHINE / RETNA LTD

On tour, 1979: Tony, Alfa, Bernard, Luci and Nile.

© JOHN CARVER / REX

Live in London, 1979. 'It was a real shock seeing them on stage, able to do it, perfectly note-for-note, but with a real live excitement, pizzazz and flash that was completely unexpected.' – Geoff Brown.

THE PRODUCTION CHARGES:

© COURTESY OF MICHAEL OCHS ARCHIVES / REDFERNS

Diana Ross, early 80s.

© MICHAEL RUTLAND / RETNA LTD.

*Nile Rodgers and Debbie Harry at
the Koo Koo launch party, New
York, 1981.*

© EBET ROBERTS / REDFERNS

*Rodgers, Edwards and Bowie,
New York, 1983.*

COURTESY OF FAN GLENN RUSSELL'S MEMORABILIA COLLECTION

'Tony played with a sort of recklessness that was very exciting. It worked fantastically with the organisational skills of me and Bernard': Tony Thompson.

© JOHN BELLISSIMO / RETNA

Three and the ragged tiger: John Taylor, Rodgers, Nick Rhodes, Simon Le Bon, mid 1980s.

© GAB ARCHIVES / REDFERNS

The eighties Blind Faith: The Power Station – Robert Palmer, John Taylor, Andy Taylor, Tony Thompson 1985

The Chic Organization Ltd: Nile Rodgers and Bernard Edwards, 1982.

Nile Rodgers and Miss Piggy New York, Jan 2003.

The Chic one: entrepreneur, businessman, producer: Nile Rodgers.

which was novel at the time and helped to shape my aesthetic. And I loved it. They never asked me to wear anything that I felt was demeaning to me as a woman. That was so affirming – being asked to wear something that would elevate me to the level of a woman, not a toy. How political is that?'

There was a considerable amount of talent involved on *Risqué*. The subtext to the album's second single, 'My Forbidden Lover', is ripe for exploration. It viewed the stigma of any sort of relationship away from the norm, whether it be extra-marital, interracial or gay; the irresistible urge of the forbidden. 'What About Me' centred on the selfism predominant in the late 70s. 'Can't Stand To Love You' was a dark vignette about sinister love ('Little punk do it for me, or I'll number your days') and 'Will You Cry (When You Hear This Song)' is a painfully beautiful ballad, one of Anderson's best performances. It makes the familiar unfamiliar. It is very much the companion piece to 'At Last I'm Free'. When she sings 'for years you played hide and seek with my love, you are just that kind of guy' over the swooping string arrangement, it's almost unbearably poignant.

Anderson recalls how Edwards would tease vocal performances out of her; intuitively knowing when the right take had occurred. Often this left her in a state of near rapture. 'I'm a ballad person; I've always loved them. I remember with "Will You Cry (When You Hear This Song)", Fonzi was in the studio; it was close to a take. I had taken a break and come out of the booth. Fonzi wanted to speak but Bernard quickly told him not to say anything so as not to spoil the moment. I had worked really hard, and I felt like I had really found the essence of the song. I got a lot of encouragement from Bernard. He taught us all of the songs; he was the one who got performances out of us; whether he had to make us angry, or whatever; he made sure that he got the performance: he was really good at that.'

'You see, we try to write songs that will relate and the fact is that people – especially in big cities – definitely relate to the concept of a love affair outside the conventional boundaries that society had set up,' Rodgers told David Nathan in 1979. 'The whole disco scene has produced a new culture really. Add to that the general permissive society and the fact that there are more and more single people out there – it's no longer wrong not to get married it seems – and you'll see that we're writing about a whole new development. We're just observing what's going on out there and what's important to us is to stress the love content in personal relationships, whatever they may be. We're not looking at life through rose-coloured glasses – we're just trying to make observations about the nicer aspects of permissive society!'

'My Feet Keep Dancing' demonstrates both Chic's intelligence and sophistication. It underlines how dance is a celebration of life; even with the sound of vaudeville tap dancing as the 'solo'. As dance floors around the world were being appropriated by all manner of lumbering honkies displaying their weary post-Travolta chops, Chic demonstrated exactly how you should dance. The song pays generous tribute to the heroes of vaudeville, The Nicholas Brothers and Our Gang. Getting these old showmen, Fayard Nicholas and Eugene Jackson (with Sammy Warren) out of retirement was an explicit nod to the golden days of dancing. 'We were saying "thank you" to the aristocrats in the ghetto,' Rodgers recalls. 'Their form of dancing was Lindy-hopping and tapping.' The Lindy Hop, purportedly named after Charles Lindbergh's solo trans-Atlantic flight in 1927, signifies the Swing Era, and was the staple dance at The Savoy until it closed its doors in 1958. 'Well, you couldn't see Lindy-hopping, but you could hear tapping,' Rodgers continues. 'We thought no-one would know why we did it, but we didn't care. If you do art properly – the fallout will be good sales. People don't need to know why they like it, they just do.'

Garry Mulholland describes 'My Feet Keep Dancing' as 'the usual funky Chic elasticity … dumped for a monotonous staccato so insistent, it becomes a hypnotic drone. The strings clinch it: an endlessly climbing loop of staccato screeches, trapped in an unending circle. Dancing was never made to sound so much like a nightmare.' Its No. 21 chart position in December 1979 in the UK would be the last time the group were to have a UK Top 75 hit until March 1983.

'We had a ball recording. I can understand now that producers have to do what they do in order to get the product. There were times when I was in tears,' Anderson recalls. 'There were times when I was really pushed outside of my comfort zone to give them something memorable. It is only in retrospect that I can say that. At the time I was just trying to get my vocal. At that time I didn't understand that every day we make history – we don't just study it, we make it. So at the time I was just trying to do the best job I could at that moment.'

Risqué brought out, and continues to bring out, the big critical hitters: Peter Shapiro suggests that 'My Feet Keep Dancing' is, 'as if they were either hypnotised or thought that by repeating the phrase so many times that they'd keep the bogeyman away' and *Rolling Stone* suggested that 'Can't Stand To Love You' was 'ambivalent, since the protagonists appear perpetually addled and adrift in a disco fog. Finally, Chic seems to question the value of fashion itself: this group's music is even chillier and more emotively ambiguous than the high-gloss haute couture photography that inspired it.' Danny Baker at the *NME*, possibly one of the only British writers to 'get' Chic at the time, wrote: 'Chic pulsate with New York drive, they stir admiration for their song-structuring and impress with their playing. It was recently said that Chic sound so satisfied and bourgeois, something I find totally baffling. That description would fit swish like Patrick Juvet or Diana Ross – even rubbish like Amanda Lear – but Chic are too much of a living outfit, they sweat too much and remain raw enough. They sound anything but bored and machine-like.'

Stephen Holden reviewed the overall sound and Chic's place in the disco movement within his review for *Risqué* in *Rolling Stone*, November 1979: 'Chic's signature sound – in which mannequin voices issue cryptic telegrams above a contoured bass, an agitated guitar and unusually light drumming – is one of the most evocative in all of disco, because it dispenses with such stock ingredients as heavy-breathing eroticism and synthesized gimmickry. It's airy and blank, spare and sometimes forbiddingly austere.' The forbidding austerity is none more apparent than on *Risqué*, which is all angular veneers, thrown shapes and dark shadows.

Risqué was released in the UK in August 1979, and while only reaching No. 29, it spent 12 weeks in the chart. In the US, it reached No. 5, four places behind *In Through The Out Door*. Yet in the UK, its sales were cannibalised by the rush release of the greatest hits album, *Les Plus Grandes Succèses Du Chic*, which came out that December and reached No. 30. Perhaps Atlantic were already realising the limited shelf life of their project.

Risqué was an incredible disco noir – glacial cool, dispassion, claustrophobia, it was all there. It was disco as the entertainment of the shadows that Marc Jacobsen had mentioned in *Crawdaddy* four years previously. It hasn't been bettered by any release from anyone in the Chic Organisation since. This was a serious album and it knew it.

However, possibly it was a little too serious and dark for the American mainstream: Earth Wind And Fire trounced Chic at the Grammies for 1979.

15.
DELIGHT

*'We just knew how to find the pocket and
we knew how to rock it.'*
ALFA ANDERSON 2004

AS THE **1980S** BEGAN, a new music form was going overground. Whereas its immediate predecessor, disco, had been all sleek veneers and resolutely uptown, hip-hop was the music of the street and the projects; the sound battles which relocated Chic's effortless beats away from the mirror balls and back to the ghettoes.

'They asked LL Cool J in 2002 what, in his opinion was the most important thing that's ever happened in the history of hip-hop,' Nile Rodgers recalls. 'He said the release of "Good Times". You know when artists are interviewed; there can be this almost political agenda: what's the best last book to have read, because no one wants to come off saying anything too corny. But when they asked LL he said "Good Times" – he said what a lot of hip-hop guys would really believe, but they would come out with a standard answer like "The Breaks" by Kurtis Blow . It's more politically correct not to say the groove that hip-hop was originally taken from. I was flattered. I thought so that's how these guys really think, the best thing to happen to hip-hop was this R&B dance record called "Good Times".'

"Good Times" was the one. It changed everything. It spawned its raft of imitators: the most notable was called "Rapper's Delight", released in October 1979 by The Sugar Hill Gang. Sylvia and Joe Robinson, who had been behind New Jersey label All-Platinum, understood the potency of the music that had been heard on New York street corners. It wasn't the first 'rap' record. 'King Tim III (Personality Jock)' by The Fatback Band is commonly credited with that honour, but this was the one that truly saw the form popularised. Whereas Chic had always travelled down the route of politically acute lyrics which embraced a positive message and equality, The Sugar Hill Gang added macho swagger and bragging to the mix. The fact they were copying Chic was an irony not lost on Edwards and Rodgers: 'Most rock artists are nothing but copycats, not even good technicians, who sit around downing everyone else's music,' Edwards said in 1979. 'We don't do that, we like rock. I mean guys like Led Zeppelin, we love that shit.' But, with "Rapper's Delight", a new form of copycatting was occurring.

Alfa Anderson recalls hearing the record for the first time: 'We felt amazed that somebody could actually do that; just take a track and use it as their own. They dropped the track when we were out of the country, touring England. I thought it was clever, but I thought it was really sneaky. We appreciated the artistry, but the fact it was done the way it was, was a little unscrupulous. But look what it started, look what it started!!!'

The Sugar Hill Gang – 'Big Bank' Hank Jackson, Guy 'Master Gee' O' Brien and 'Wonder' Mike Wright – assimilated, under the aegis of the Robinsons, what had been happening on the street and perfectly distilled it on to record. A great deal of the rhyming styles were appropriated from Grandmaster Caz from The Cold Crush Brothers. The record, aside from a composed introduction, was a straight reworking of "Good Times", played by the formidable Sugar Hill house band: Doug Wimbush, Skip McDonald, Keith LeBlanc, Duke Bootee, Nate Edmunds with the Chops horns. Chic's place in the hip-hop hall of fame is secure because of their recreation of this simple groove.

At first, Rodgers and Edwards were not credited with writing the hit, which caused more than passing consternation to them. Rodgers first heard it when he was at a club called Leviticus on the Westside, owned by upwardly-mobile street African-Americans called The Best Of Friends. He absolutely loved it, and assumed it was something distributed among DJs and not for sale. When he heard it again on the radio, he and Edwards were straight on the phone to the Robinsons. An out-of-court settlement quickly restored their name to the label credits and one of their most lucrative copyrights. 'It took us too long to get that groove together for us to let that go by,' Rodgers told Nelson George in 1980. He then shrewdly added, 'If you combine the sales of the single "Good Times" and "Rapper's Delight", you have the biggest selling single of all time.' As "Rapper's Delight" became the first recognisable record of a new genre, it is has been forever recycled on radio and TV for the past 25 years. The record went platinum with a month, and was selling around 50,000 copies a day. 'When the Sugar Hill Gang appropriated the "Good Times" instrumental for "Rapper's Delight," Carol Cooper wrote in *Village Voice*, 'it was Edwards's percussive, attitudinal bass line they coveted – a bass line that dictated the cadence and timbre of rappers' rhymes for the next three years.'

Bernard Edwards Jr, now a hip-hop producer himself, states, 'everyone is so overwhelmed when they realise who my father was. I attribute that to MCs Star and Buckwild in New York. They called Chic the godparents of hip-hop. All the rappers respect and look at them as such. I work for Dr Dre and Aftermath. A lot of the cats in the genre have got tremendous respect for me when they find out who I am. There's a mutual respect – Dre is my idol right now – he's the modern day Quincy Jones. He rocks the party – it's almost like watching my father work – they are both meticulous and particular. It's all about the hit – let's make it work. I love it.'

'If disco had sucked in such a major way, hip-hop would have not stepped in and appropriated it quite so generously,' Raymond Jones told Nelson George. 'Its extremely aggressive, macho nature has been seen as a counterpoint to disco's overall fruitiness, but then without the legacy of the breaks from the record pools and the mighty "Good Times" breakdown, hip-hop would not have got a look in.' The new genre's marriage of old and new proved an instant hit that quickly rose above novelty.

By 1981, the continual ripping off of the 'Good Times' riff, was beginning to rankle with Edwards. 'In the last year we've been listening to the radio. There's been at least 20 or 30 groups that have actually re-written a tune or something around a tune that we wrote. We're not hassled, we don't go round yellin' or screamin' about it. But for some reason, we're not respected as songwriters and producers in the rock areas, where we've influenced a lot of people.' Apart from Grandmaster Flash's incredible deconstruction of it as 'The Adventures Of Grandmaster Flash On The Wheels Of Steel', records as diverse as The Clash's 'This Is Radio Clash', Level 42's 'Love Games', Blondie's 'Rapture' and Brian Eno and David Byrne's 'Regiment' all used the riff in various ways.

But none took the groove and recycled it quite so obviously as Queen's 'Another One Bites The Dust', which was a note-for-note recreation of the sound, and became a US No. 1. Edwards explained to *New Musical Express* in 1981 that Queen's bass player, John Deacon, had spent time hanging out with Chic at the studio: 'That's OK. What isn't OK is that the press started saying we ripped them off! Can you believe that? "Good Times" came out more than a year before, but it was inconceivable to these people that black musicians could possibly be innovative like that. It was these dumb disco guys ripping off this rock and roll song.' The inherent racism was still very much part of the music industry. Ill-feeling began to fester.

For a group that were received predominately in clubs and on the radio, Chic's live concerts became the prime shop window for displaying the abilities that all the performers had crafted for so long. The years slaving behind New York City and Carol Douglas had not been in vain. As the stages got bigger, the Organization were there ably to fill them. And, as a result, Chic took to the road with a passion and started playing the game seriously.

Their tour arrived in England in late 1979 to a rapturous reception and venues in cities such as Brighton and London shook to Chic's tunes. The shows were planned with a military-like precision, and the pre-publicity was rich and full. Anderson suggested to David Nathan in *Blues and Soul* that she had 'been taking acting lessons and we want to use what I'm learning in our show' while Martin contended that she was 'crazy and we wanna show more of that onstage! It's about showing that we have a good time on stage and that what we're doing may be hard work but it's also fun!' Thompson concluded that 'everyone has hidden talents and they should be brought out.' Chic's shows of this period are now referred to in hushed, almost mythical tones, because they brought a shard of glamour into the post-punk new wave landscape.

The on-stage line-up looked deeply impressive. The recently-joined Fonzi Thornton recalls, 'Alfa and Luci stood in the middle, Michelle Cobbs and I stood to the right, just behind Bernard's shoulder, so you had these three fabulous looking woman and three fabulous looking men. Raymond Jones and Andy Schwartz were off to the left, and behind them were the Chic strings.' With an ever increasing array of hits to choose from, the live shows played to tremendous receptions. And audiences realised that this was no mechanised group relying on tapes, it was all live and dynamite.

'We did a lot of improvising, but we always wanted things to be spontaneous and natural,' Anderson recalls. 'We never wanted it to be so choreographed that there was a move for every word. We often made fun of the over-choreographed acts in rehearsal. We would take a phrase like "I love you baby" – so for the "I" we would point to our eyes; for the "love" we draw a heart; for "you", we'd point; and then we'd hold a baby! We always left room to be natural.'

☆☆☆

Chic were warmly accepted by Britain. James Truman in *Melody Maker* was quick to point out that 'the "innovative" new wave bands from Public Image to Gang Of Four freely borrow from disco (though they might prefer to say

'comment on') while disco acts don't and have no need to, return the compliment.' He continued 'Catching up with them in Bournemouth, musically, from the carefully assembled medley of Sister Sledge hits to the faultless reproduction of their own singles, Chic put on the most immaculate, professional … show I've ever seen. But it's never clinical; simply a logical stage adaptation of the disco soundtrack, allowing rather than enforcing a reaction.'

The Hammersmith Odeon shows in October 1979 are viewed as a high-water mark in Chic's history. 'I fell in love with London,' Luci Martin recalls.

'That gig was awesome for me – the reason why it's so memorable was because you could feel the energy coming off us at that time. You always got what I was feeling on stage. I never quite learned to mask that – I was thrilled and you just knew it.'

Venerated music writer Barney Hoskyns was later to comment on their Hammersmith Odeon show that, although as time passes and details start to fade, 'Any fears that the genius of their records would forsake Chic onstage were banished within seconds of their first song. Do I remember what the song was? No, but I do know that I completely lost myself in the dancefloor mantras of "I Want Your Love", "My Forbidden Lover", "My Feet Keep Dancing" – entrancing, heartbreaking loops to which I could have swayed all night. I know that the way Nile Rodgers and Bernard Edwards locked together on "Le Freak" and "Dance, Dance, Dance", with Nile chipping and chinking over 'Nard's bubbling bass runs and Tony Thompson's tight-as-a-gnat's-bottom drums, was a thing of unearthly groovesomeness. I know that Alfa Anderson and Luci Martin were the epitome of erotic Jazz Age grace, swaying and sashaying as they purred their songs of forlorn love. I know that Jill Furmanovsky took a picture of the four of them at the show that still brings that magic night back to life.'

Geoff Brown, who wrote for *Blues And Soul* at the time, was also blown away by their performance: 'How good they were was confirmed when they came over and played here,' he recalls. 'You thought, you can do it in the studio, as you are studio bodies, but it was a real shock seeing them on stage, able to do it, perfectly note-for-note, but with a real live excitement, pizzazz and flash that was completely unexpected. They did it with a real life and vitality. I saw them, and then about a week after, Sister Sledge were in town. They had a session band with them trying to replicate the Chic hits. The rhythm guitarist struggled manfully, but he did have a terrible, terrible time trying to play with Nile's feel. It showed how much of an extraordinary originator Nile was. It was so far forward in the mix, as a solo – you realised how innovative that had been when in the next couple of years everybody tried to copy it. Chic played the Sister Sledge numbers and did a better job than they did.' Brown recalls interviewing Chic on the tour, also: 'They were very charming and beguiling, witty and amusing. Nile and Bernard were loquacious and erudite, well-read. Music was their driving force, but they knew a great deal outside of that. They had been round the block a lot, but absorbed a lot of information from different areas.'

It was an immaculately delivered, high-octane performance. 'They always understood that music started from the rhythm section upwards,' Thornton recalls. 'I have visions of Bernard on stage shouting at Tony and Alfa "Move yo' ass, move yo' ass". While he was performing, he would listen to everything that was going on.'

Tony Thompson sums it up succinctly: 'We always felt especially important in England.'

☆☆☆

We were in Paris, there was an electrical problem,' Thornton recalls. 'We had to cancel the gig and return later to play it. That first time in Paris, I remember Cheryl Hong was very adventurous; she, Michelle and I went out on the Metro. When we were in other countries, we would always be hanging together. Everybody had a cool disposition, and Bernard and Nile were very careful about the people they brought around us, as we were a family. The thing about being in the business – we always look out for each other – there are always people around, who don't understand what we are doing. We didn't need drama added to any situation. We always learned to hang out with each other and have a good time. Bernard and Nile loved cars – we would pull into a city and they would be trying new cars from the hotel. I remember telling Michelle "I got to learn to drive. I'm sick of sitting in a hotel room, while they are pulling out all over the place." We took driving lessons, 'cos we wanted to drive in foreign cities.'

'We had the best time on the road,' Thornton continues. 'Bernard and Nile treated me like a king. I was the only male on stage that was singing – although Nile and Bernard would provide back up, they were really concentrating on playing their instruments. In order for the sound to work, they needed Alfa, myself, Michelle and Luci to carry all the singing. They featured me, they paid me well, they always made sure all the accommodation was really comfortable. Chic was a very well-appointed band. At the start of every tour, they would let you go to Charivari. It was located at 72nd St and Columbus Avenue in Manhattan, a big fashion store and you could get just the right costume you needed and everybody would be decked out, from the band to the singers. They taught me to be a high fashion guy – as they were from early on. They treated us royally. We laughed the entire time – we would be on the buses, whether we were in Italy or in Hoboken. We did a show in San Diego at a big stadium – we had to get in these go-karts as the backstage area was so huge and the audience were just screaming out for us, as we were all going to the stage. We were on that show with Cameo – we just turned the place out. We did a similar show at the Meadowlands in New Jersey – there was an explosion when I sang.'

'We were activists,' Anderson recalls. 'Chic concerts were among the very first concerts that would draw people of all ethnicities. I recently played myself in a play, telling the story of African-American music. The director of the play said she was the white girl sitting in the corner at my concerts. It just reminded me that we had so many different ethnicities at our shows; but then our band was racially mixed. The group was political to me in that respect. We did not separate people. It was a time where we brought people together. It was designed that way.'

Whatever stresses there may have been within the group, touring, like recording, was an opportunity for harmony. 'There wasn't really tension, because of the way Bernard led the band,' Thornton explains. 'Alfa and Luci were the face of the band, and sang on virtually all of the records. I used to take the girls to one side and rehearse them. And on the road together, we all had an understanding of what our work was.' 'Luci, that's my girl. We had great times together,' Anderson recalls. 'We had some difficult moments, but we always managed to work through what we needed to work through and to talk with each other.'

'There was so much going on on tour and so much focus on being creative and finding one's identity, when we all got together, it was like a family gathering at your mom's house,' Martin laughs. 'There was some bickering, there was some laughing, some joking – there were card games on the bus. Music playing and it was like yelling at your brother "turn that down, I'm trying to sleep!"'

☆☆☆

In Britain, it was like no-one had seen such rare and exotic creatures before. *Smash Hits*, the then-recently established teen bible sent Robin Katz to interview them. His opening gambit was, 'When you think of Chic, you think less of faceless megastars,

but more of strategy. If Gladys Knight and the Pips call themselves "Perfection in Performance", then Chic's clever twosome Nile Rodgers and Bernard Edwards are Perfection in Planning. Yowsah, yowsah yowsah-no angle left unconsidered, no detail overlooked.' The article perfectly encapsulated the machine-tooled aspect of the Chic Organization before fissures started to appear. Everything, just like the records was in the right measure.

'In the past three years, we've changed our thinking on a couple of things,' Rodgers told Katz. 'At first we listened to the radio to hear what everyone else was up to. Now, we don't listen that much. We don't make an effort to keep track. We stay away from other artists because we don't want to be too influenced by others, subconsciously or otherwise. In order to make it to a massive audience, we deliberately didn't take chances. We were careful about how far we went in one direction or another. Now that we have an audience that spans a big age group, we want to expand a bit without alienating anyone. It's being careful in a different kind of way. At first we wanted to avoid being musically controversial. Now we have to keep from being musically stagnant.'

Katz concluded: 'the impression you get from the Chic brothers is that whatever angle the planet Earth slips to, they are ready to slide along with the natural curve of survival. If disco continues to sell, they will keep making disco records. If disco heads towards the slide, they don't mind packing their underrated guitars and moving into something else.' But there was still mileage for their underrated disco guitars on this tour.

Bernard Edwards discussed Chic's writing formula with *Smash Hits* in 1979: 'Nile and I have a way of working that hasn't changed over the years,' said Bernard. 'Call it our formula or whatever. One of us gets a title. Then we kick it around. We think about what we want to say with it. We talk about a possible plot or story or whatever.'

With their formula intact, it was time to enter the new decade. Although disco was routinely being discredited; Chic still appeared to hold all of the ace cards. They had just begun work on four projects simultaneously; the follow-up to *Risqué*, a second Sister Sledge album; a Eurodisco album for French chanteuse, Sheila and a production for one of the most famous and important black stars in the known universe: Diana Ross.

16.
UPSIDE DOWN

'Any musician wants to be successful, no matter what he says. A lot of people destroyed themselves by trying to force a formula on the public which might not become popular until they're dead and gone. It's been like that for thousands of years, man. Cats like Handel were playing for the kings and queens and they were real popular, superstars, right?'
BERNARD EDWARDS, 1979

ON 4TH NOVEMBER 1979, the US Embassy in Tehran was taken over by militant Iranian students under instruction from their religious leaders. 66 Americans including diplomats and their staff were held hostage. Ayatollah Khomeini demanded that the former Shah was extradited from New York. When the US government suspended Iranian oil imports, freezing assets, and threatened military action, 14 female and black hostages were released in the ensuing 14 days, but 52 were held onto. The failure of the US immediately to coerce Iran into submission became a metaphor for the general feeling of weakness and lack of trust the Americans had in president Jimmy Carter. When an abortive rescue attempt failed in April 1980 killing eight servicemen, it looked like America had become powerless.

At Christmas in 1979, the Russians invaded Afghanistan. Fearing that this was a Soviet plan to make a launch for the Persian oilfields, Jimmy Carter let it be known that the US would defend their interests. At his January 1980 State of the Union address, Carter called the Soviet invasion, 'the most serious threat to peace since the Second World War.' Russia dug in further.

Against this backdrop, the 1980s already felt like a very different decade: musically, disco was limping on; while the impact of Chic on popular dance music was plain to see. Nineteen-eighty itself was a time of remarkable productivity for the group with four albums being released that bore their stamp: their own *Real People*; Sister Sledge's second album, *Love Somebody Today*; Sheila And B. Devotion's *Spacer*; and Diana Ross's *diana*. As the group were so busy, it didn't matter that their riffs were being Xeroxed and replicated throughout the US and UK charts. If Chic didn't have the time to make it, there were several other 'Chics' that you could choose from. The most notable and affectionately slavish copy was that of producers Fred Petrus and Mario Malavassi's Italian dance outfit Change. Petrus and Malavassi initially approached Rodgers and Edwards to produce them; Rodgers was too busy and declined.

Change's debut album, *The Glow Of Love* is simply the best album Chic never made. 'A Lover's Holiday' is probably the best of the contemporaneous Chic tributes – with its neat, interlocking guitar and bass figure, gang vocals and none other than Luther Vandross adding his magic to the chorus. It was Chic length, too. Six minutes, thirty seconds, all present and correct; a vivid lyric about a disco, a poor party and making your own fun; with its Sabino-esque piano part, it was a perfect re-creation. Other stand-out tracks, 'Searching' and 'The Glow Of Love' provided a perfect showcase for Vandross and it was indeed, after years of trying and being the mainstay behind so many acts, the record that made him. And in true Apollo style, Fonzi Thornton followed on from Luther and sung on Change's follow-up albums.

'I always felt that if you compared them side by side, Change could be lushly melodic, where Chic had a tendency to be sparser, a bit cold,' Brian Chin notes. 'Part of what made them Chic was that there was a certain angularity – it's a little bit cubist. Change was more about making an extremely melodic record – they also had the kick drum four on the floor, which Chic only occasionally applied. That's the main difference. If you've heard boom-slap, boom-slap, you know it's not going to be R&B but acts like Chic. That's why Chic got sampled; the subliminal thing that was always different.'

Chic even inspired British imitators, the short-lived but momentarily influential Linx. David Grant and Peter 'Sketch' Martin saw themselves as an East London version of Chic. The even had their own version of the Chic Organization; The Solid Foundation. Speaking in December 1981, they told *The Face* magazine 'We wanted Solid (Foundation) to be just like the way Nile and Bernard Edwards work: two men writing songs and generally looking after the whole of their business.'

Rodgers tipped the cap to them musically by playing guitar on 'Tinseltown', the closing track on their second and final album *Go Ahead*. 'Linx were quite leftfield,' Martin Fry recalls. 'They were coming out of an R&B tradition, but it was pop as well – they were quite radical when they first emerged. They were two black guys who wanted to be treated as businessmen, with respect.'

New York disco was also mutating into the No-Wave/Mutant disco scene, which was centred around Ze Records. Acts such as Kid Creole and The Coconuts, led by ex-Dr Buzzard bass-player August Darnell, Cristina and James White and The Blacks, working on the margins, were able to combine punk and funk. Talking Heads, under the tutelage of Brian Eno, were proving that white boys and girls could have the funk, taking Hamilton Bohannon's work almost note for note and recreating it with David Byrne's incredible playing and wordsmithery. Chic, then completely at the eye of this cultural storm, had few options but to recede. Slowly.

☆☆☆

The reunion of Sister Sledge and Chic on *Love Somebody Today,* released in February 1980, was not as joyous as the first record. 'Whereas the first album was trial and error, with everything to prove,' Kathy recalls, 'the second found some of the lustre gone. No-one ever asks that much about it. We knew each other well; we were coming off a big hit together. We believed in each other.'

Sister Sledge had enjoyed whirlwind success since their last album, constantly touring and making public appearances, with a consistent demand for their new-found greatest hit, 'We Are Family'. At 19, Kathy should have been ready to be a party animal. 'My nickname on the road was Killjoy,' she laughs. 'I used to go straight to my room, order room service and kick back. Partying sometimes would remind me too much of work, so I never really partied. I would have an incredible time with music on stage. Too much of anything is not good. When you take anything to the extremes, you lose balance.'

'At the time, Nile and Bernard were very "formula" and that was seen as very important,' Joni Sledge recalls. 'The record company wanted to keep that formula. We were like pawns in a chess game. We totally respected them, but you never know what would have happened if we'd had more input. Especially on the second album, we thought we should show who we were, but again, they just wanted to repeat the formula. Nile and Bernard had their method and technique that worked for them and that they didn't want to stray too far away from. They had a sound, and their sound was their singers. So when you heard a track, you knew that there was another hit coming out from their camp. You can hear their backing singers very strongly in the mix.' After discussion, it was agreed that the second Chic Organization Sister Sledge album would be, apart from the lead single, free from any of the Chic singers. Instead of Luci, Alfa, Fonzi and Michelle, there would just be the four sisters.

'There was not resentment, but possibly a frustration,' Debbie Sledge adds. 'There are aspects of us that aren't tapped into when using a formula. You don't lose your joy in the music, but you had to use up your creative energies.'

Edwards was in full effect at these sessions: directing the band, dictating the musical direction, arranging the vocalists. He was certainly in charge. 'Very much so,' laughs Joni. 'Although all of that changed years later, when he became very humble, became a real sweetheart of a guy. But, in the beginning, it was very much the other way around – Nile was the nice guy. Then it changed, Nile became the dictator!'

'We simply hoped for more of our own expression,' Joni recalls. 'If we'd stuck with them, maybe we would have had more expression – but the record company were always trying to recreate *We Are Family*. It was one of those once-in-a-million type things. It was symbolic of that love and that energy – more about what we thought of each other. You can't recreate it because it is what it is.'

Except for the lead single, the album is a chance to hear Chic unplugged, if you will; it is the only album from the original canon without the Chic choir in evidence. As a result, it acts as proof of what the choir brought to the proceedings. To fill the considerable void, the string section is in their place. '"You Fooled Around" is probably my favourite,' Kathy remembers. 'We did a lot more vocals on it. I think it was a combination of everything. *Love Somebody Today* wasn't as disco as *We Are Family*. Tracks like "Easy Street" and "You Fooled Around" are light and jazzy. It was a case of the record company wanting you to be disco, and keeping your market as you grow.'

Love Somebody Today saw the façade slip, revealing, as so much can in pop, that a great deal is achieved by smoke and mirrors. The sophisticated art deco image of the previous album was replaced by a nice set of sweaters supplied by KnitSnitches.

The album's commercial performance was a shadow of the former record's success. Joni Sledge ascribes the shift in record company mores as being at least partially to blame for this: 'All of our records prior to *We Are Family* went straight to the R&B chart, but they didn't cross over. The difference with *We Are Family* was that Nile and Bernard put a lot of promotion into that album. It was the first real time that R&B artists were being honoured in the across-the-board charts. However, by the time of *Love Somebody Today*, record company emphasis went away from club music, they started to promote heavy metal and things like that. I think it was a political thing – it wasn't that audiences were sick of it – they just wanted to get their power balance back. And were not putting dollars into promoting acts like Chic and Sister Sledge. We could never believe that, after *We Are Family,* we had no promotion dollars. The only thing I could think of was discrimination.'

There were early signs that the album was not to be the runaway success of its predecessor. The lead single, 'Got To Love Somebody' was released in December 1979 and only reached No. 64 on the US pop chart. In Britain, where a sizeable fan base had been established, the record could only muster thirty places higher, a comedown from the Top 10 positions of the first *We Are Family* singles.

Nonetheless, the album was not without its high points. The Kathy Sledge-sung ballad, 'How To Love' is a remarkable, hidden piece of Rodgers and Edwards' artistry. Picking up from the previous album's 'Thinking Of You', Kathy emotes over Andy Schwartz's piano and arguably the last great performance on record (bar *Real People*'s 'Open Up'), of the Chic strings.

Edwards and Rodgers were too busy to produce Sister Sledge's follow-up album. Cotillion enlisted Narada Michael Walden, Thompson's old drum tutor to record an identikit Chic album called *All American Girls*.

Although *Love Somebody Today* represented the law of diminishing returns, the project that Rodgers and Edwards had begun working on during the end of the sessions was to cement their production reputation. In November 1979, the basic tracks for The Chic Organization's next project were being laid down at The Power Station. But this was not to be for an aspiring starlet or a group of down-home singers. This was to be for none other than Diana Ross.

Ross could not be bracketed in with the artists then turning disco – she had done it already, in the high watermark of the first flush of disco – what were 1976's perma-sumptuous US No.1 'Love Hangover', or the July 1979 remix of 'I Ain't Been Licked' from *The Boss*, if not disco stormers? What was the discofied version of *The Wizard Of Oz*, *The Wiz* – which had seen the 32-year-old Ross take the role of Dorothy from the 17-year old Stephanie Mills who had played the role on Broadway – all about? What Ross undeniably was, in terms of commercial popularity, was the first lady of African-American song. Not the best singer, by any means, but as an artist, she represented a great deal of freedom. She had risen from the projects in Detroit to become one of the most recognisable faces and voices in popular music across the globe.

It was Ross' children, Rhonda, Tracee and Chudney, who goaded their mother into the Chic project. Ironically, at this period, Ross was deep in her affair with Gene Simmons from Kiss, the group that Rodgers and Rob Sabino had so idolised in the Big Apple Band days. Ross turned up to see Chic at the Santa Monica auditorium in California. As Rodgers said to Adam White, 'Diana couldn't believe the crowd reaction. She said "I haven't seen this since the Jackson 5." She was backstage, dancing and into it. "My kids made me come and see this show, all they were talking about was Chic, Chic, Chic. That's what I want my record to sound like."' She wanted a record that her children could sing.

News that Chic were about to produce Ms. Ross was the talk of their

autumn 1979 British tour, their last commitment before going into the studio
with her in New York. *Smash Hits* stated 'If Chic have their way, Diana Ross
may win a brand new audience of young fans in time for a new decade.' But
they posted the question that was on everybody's lips: 'What does it feel like
to produce an album for a singer who was your idol when you were a
teenager?'

'I love the lady's voice,' Bernard Edwards replied. 'But at this point in my
career I don't get that impressed by meeting famous names. Nile and I want
to show people that we can really write with this album. We want to bring
her to a new audience. We want to put back the kind of dancing, fun and
variety she used to have without losing the sophistication. As with Sister
Sledge we are going to have complete control on what goes down in the
studio from start to finish.'

Rodgers and Edwards had, by now, established a set pattern of working
with their charges. Their style was to sit down with the artists for a couple of
hours, find out all about them and then go home and write the album for
them. Ross knew it was the last album she was going to record for Motown
and wanted something edgy. Rodgers quickly saw how malleable she was
initially prepared to be: he later explained to *Dick's Diana Ross* website: 'The
Diana record was about liberation on every level. She was willing to change
everything about what she was doing up to that moment in time. She became
a jazzier, more sophisticated version of who she had been previously.'

'We interviewed Diana for the content of the record. It was all about the
fact that she wanted to have a new life. It was all about "new" for her. I just
kept thinking of the words "I'm coming out." But I'm also thinking about
people hiding inside all their lives, and they're showing the world where
they're coming from. I thought "I'm Coming Out" would be the perfect
statement – and I applied that to her life. I never made any reference to her
about people coming out of the closet or anything like that. I just wrote the
song, and I told her that she inspired the words, which is true. The sexual
implications were just there. The song is ultimately about anyone in the prime
of his or her life taking the bull by the horns.' Rodgers recalled to *Billboard's*
Adam White how Ross told him at their initial meeting that 'I don't want this
record to sound like L.A at all. I left California, I'm in New York, I've got a
whole new life here.'

However, whereas Rodgers and Edwards may have been able to suppress
the potential Sledge uprising, it was the complete control aspect that was to
jar with Ms. Ross. It was the first time that the duo had worked with an
established artist, and their speedy and benignly dictatorial working methods
were alien to Ross. To this end, the *diana* album may have been one step
too far for Rodgers and Edwards. It exposed their limitations: All manner of
rumour and sigh flowed out of the gossip grinder.

The recording began with sessions for 'I'm Coming Out', 'Give Up',
'Tenderness', and 'The Work Song' (which was later to be re-titled 'Upside
Down'), and continued into January 1980. 'We had never worked with a

superstar when we worked with Diana,' Rodgers admitted in 2001. 'So we didn't understand about the psychological area of producing, because everybody we had worked with up to that point were all good friends of ours – if we said "Jesus Christ, what are you doing singing that bullshit?" they would shoot back "hey, pal, your guitar part's no picnic either." Nothing was really personal. Bernard would say – "oh, man, you played that part on the last record." And although I might think, that's my buddy – he cares for me, I'd say: "hell, I'm playing it on this record, too."'

The tale behind the making of the *diana* album was a classic saga of the old meeting the new. Recording sessions took place at The Power Station. When Ross' entourage swept through the studio, they demanded everyone leave bar Rodgers and Edwards. Thompson, who was sitting there, made it very clear to her that as the person drumming on her record, he would not be leaving at this instance. Ross was also unhappy with Alfa Anderson's guide vocals for the project: 'When we did the Diana Ross record,' recalls Fonzi Thornton, 'they had Alfa go in and sing reference vocals for Diana for her to listen and learn. When she heard Alfa's voice, she didn't want to be influenced by another woman singing and she asked for a guy to sing the songs. Nile and Bernard called me up and I did all the reference vocals. Diana learned the songs by listening to me.'

'Ah, Diana,' laughs Anderson. 'She would just prefer that someone else did it.' Was it simply a case of you being a better technical singer? 'I would never say that.'

There has been talk of Rodgers and Edwards' intransigence in the studio. 'When Diana walked in, she heard the whole record done,' Rodgers recalls. 'We don't make demos, we only make records.' When Edwards, the 'bad cop' of the Chic producing partnership, suggested that Ross may have been singing 'underneath' one of the tracks, the following dialogue ensued, as recalled by Rodgers:

'We were very tactful with Diana Ross. I'll never forget it, we were trying to say she was singing flat. Bernard's exact words were,

"Um. Excuse me Diana, I think you're singing a little under the track."

"Bernard, I've never heard that before, what does 'under the track' mean?"

"Under the track".

"What do you mean, under the track?"

"Under the track".

"You mean under the pitch of the track?"

"Yes – that's it!"

"You mean FLAT?"

"Yes."

Bang. And that was it – 'she stormed out of the studio, screaming "BERRY GORDY NEVER TOLD ME I SING FLAT!" We never saw her again for 30 days.' Ross allegedly went to the South Of France. 'Diana Ross is one of my dearest and best friends. We get along great. I don't even think she remembers it. But it was pretty over the top.'

However, it was not all doom and gloom. 'Ms. Ross would come in the evening and record a track she had already learned,' Raymond Jones, who played keyboards with Andy Schwartz on the album, recalls. 'She was fun. I enjoyed my time with her. I didn't see any bust-ups – and remember, at this point she was one of the most important women in the world – Suzanne dePasse was her babysitter.'

The album was delivered to Motown by Rodgers and Edwards in March 1980. They were accused of trying to make their sound shine and Motown's first lady look poor by comparison. When Ross arrived in Britain to record *The Muppet Show* in May 1980, she played her fan club secretary Jim Hegarty their mixes of the album. She had previously been to see Frankie Crocker in tears, terribly upset about the project. She returned it to Rodgers and Edwards to remix the album. They were dismissive, as it was surely another example of her legendary temperament. A light remix was offered, which was not to her liking. So it was remixed without Edwards and Rodgers' knowledge at Hitsville in Los Angeles in April 1980 by Ross' long-term engineer, Russ Terrana.

Ross was credited as saying at the time that, 'I proceeded to make the record more Diana Ross and less Chic-ish. They've only been in the business, what, two years? I believed my 20 years' experience in showbusiness would be of great value to the project.'

'The basic problem was that we had two different concepts of what her voice should sound like,' Rodgers countered back then. 'She hears her voice in one way and we hear it in another way. When it got to a point where she wanted her voice to sound a certain way, we couldn't take the responsibility for it because that's just not how we make records.' By the time of its release, it became, as Ross biographer J. Randy Taraborelli notes, 'an unwanted step-child'.

'I was devastated on first hearing Motown's mix. I was in tears over our artistic vision,' Rodgers told Brian Chin. 'It had been a long recording process,

because Diana removed herself at one point. It's not true to say the record company took it away from us. It was their record all along. They recreated our work with a different slant.'

From its sing-song choruses to sweet trombone solos, *diana* is a remarkably bright album, given its troubled birth. It is an artistic portrayal of complete freedom; Rodgers and Edwards' writing symbolises Ross' breaking free of the shackles of Motown on one level, but moreover, the work has a universality; celebrating gayness, blackness, equality; an album of challenging ideas, friendship and freedom. And who better to pilot these themes than the most successful African-American female artist in the world? 'I'm Coming Out', is a celebration of her coming out from her career straightjacket, leaving Motown and dressing down. Adding to that, the wider messages of sexual liberation, even civil rights messages can be found lurking in the subtext.

As Brian Chin notes: 'It's about a moment in which three titanic forces – Chic, Diana Ross and Motown – combined ambition, talent and a deep regard for the history, meaning and potential of music into a culture-defining creation.' The grittiest manifestation of Chic's initial ideas is 'Have Fun (Again)', which demonstrates the knotty structures Rodgers was accustomed to using in his jazz-rock days – and for once, Ross sounds as if she's on the street instead of looking down from a penthouse window. 'Friend To Friend', one of Chic's most poetical slowies, sounds almost like a minuet. 'Now That You're Gone' invents the Madonna ballad three years before she did. 'Give Up', the album's underrated closer, features one of Ross' most liberated performances.

The album was released with no player credits on it whatsoever. 'I have a letter from Diana Ross apologising, saying that on the first 80,000 you are not listed,' Rob Sabino recalls. It was certified platinum and became one of the biggest albums in her career. *Rolling Stone* called the album 'streamlined-designer-funk' and that Rodgers and Edwards 'came to the rescue' for her. It was kept off the No. 1 spot in America only by Barbra Streisand's *Guilty*. In Britain it only made No. 12, but remained on the charts for 32 weeks. Rodgers and Edwards were approached again by Ross the following year to produce her first RCA album, *Why Do Fools Fall In Love?* They respectfully declined the offer. It had been an interesting enterprise, and one that was hugely successful, commercially.

The Chic mix was finally released on a 'deluxe edition' of the album in 2003, which gained fantastic reviews. However, it didn't actually feel that different in the end. 'It's difficult now to see what she got into such a flap about,' Geoff Brown laughs. The flap was simply that they dared to tell her what to do. It is possible that even if they had delivered *What's Going On* for her, she would have asked for it to be redone. When Alfa Anderson heard the mix again it brought memories flooding back. She stated: 'It was wonderful to really have an opportunity to listen to Nile and Bernard again; you can hear them grow and stretch and reach. They would have been even more

powerful had their collaboration been allowed to last a little longer.' And make no mistake, some of their best playing can be found on this album. It also gives a whole new flavour to 'Upside Down' – the extended play-out of Rodgers guitar at its most frenetic is no longer smothered away. However, the original version of 'I'm Coming Out' is a rare moment in that it proves Ross' instinct was right – it's one of those delicious tracks that you have always heard but have hardly ever listened to – the elegant simplicity of Edwards' bass, always in the pocket; Meco Monardo's trombone and the ever-present gang vocals of the Chic choir; Russ Terrana's tightening up made all the difference and frankly, the sloppiness of Meco's trombone solo on the original does seek, somewhat, to undermine Ross.

The album brought back bittersweet memories for Tony Thompson. After being hounded out of the studio by Ross, he remembered the day when Rodgers and Edwards surprised him: 'I was working on *diana* and I walk into the studio to cut some tracks and there was this girl there in the studio. Nile and Bernard, knowing that I was very inquisitive said, "Tony, we want you just to shut up – you are not going to play today, I just want you to follow this lady." I was asking a million questions that no-one was answering; so I jump into this cab, which pulls up outside a Porsche dealership and there's this car that's on the showroom floor and she goes, that's yours. They bought me my first car and I didn't even have a licence! Nile had a Porsche and Bernard had a Ferrari – I was with them all the time and I was the only one who didn't have a car, so they bought me one, right out.'

Even despite the frictions present in the recording of *diana*, the duo were now fantastically in demand as producers, bringing their hand-tooled productions to outside artists. There was, however, one unfinished bit of business before Chic themselves could release their own record. It was, in many respects, a work of science fiction.

✫ ✫ ✫

Not every assignment The Chic Organization undertook was done for high art reasons. A great side project that was done solely with the meter running was the opportunity to produce French pop megastar, Sheila. In a way, this should have been the apex of their productions – an opportunity to work with a genuine chanteuse after three years of folding French into their lyrics. In reality, it wasn't.

Anny Chancel was born on 16th August, 1946 in Paris. As Sheila, she had become a huge pop star/model/actress in France in the 1960s. In the late 70s, she updated her bubblegum pop formula, singing with three African-American singers and dancers, the B (lack) Devotion. She made her first imprint on the UK Top 20 with her showstopping disco-to-go cover of 'Singin' In The Rain' in March 1978. A lesser follow up, 'You Light My Fire', followed in July. Rodgers and Edwards were approached early the following year. The single they cut – which later led to them being offered the album deal –

'Spacer' is arguably among the Organization's very finest silverware.

'The track "Spacer" was throwaway – we'd seen *Star Wars* and *Close Encounters,*' Rodgers laughs. 'We saw Sarah Brightman and Hot Gossip do some silly thing in Britain – "I Lost My Heart To A Starship Trooper" – so we thought we'd use a little Sarah Brightman, a little *Star Wars*, and a little Ziggy Stardust. So we took the character of Harrison Ford as Hans Solo flying around and made it a

romance. It was silly. Nothing is bullshit, but that was the closest to bullshit we'd ever done.' With its crisp metronomic beat, the virtual re-write of 'Good Times' works best, understandably, on 12". Although it failed to ignite in America, it was a huge hit around the Continent and 'Spacer' reached No. 18 in early 1980 in the UK, where it remained on the charts for 14 weeks.

The album Chic wrote to go with the single was a perfect example of them writing to order. 'The only time we ever wrote an album that *was* bullshit, was Sheila and B Devotion's *King Of The World,*' Rodgers recalls. As Sheila could barely speak a word of English, Rodgers and Edwards' initial meeting did not go as smoothly as possible. 'We didn't get it, so we started making up stuff. It's ridiculous, right? No matter how ridiculous this is, they're paying. I mean, *"Papa Zulu X-Ray"*?' 'Mayday', from which that immortal line springs is an interesting hybrid of influences, sounding not unlike when the prog bands of the era went pop. Rodgers' solo is somewhat laboured and Sheila, bless her, sounds completely bewildered.

Although it is not all cartoon imagery: 'Charge Plates and Credit Cards' is one of Rodgers and Edwards most underrated pieces of work. 'It's funny; I felt like a science fiction writer,' Rodgers continues. 'Because when I wrote that, no-one in France knew what a Visa card was. Sheila had a big problem with that. She kept saying to me, "Why can't we say Carte Blanche?" I replied that Visa was going to be the cool thing. I asked her to trust me. I now go to France and there is no other credit card!'

'We were told about *Sheyla* as they call her – she's a model, a star and actress, and I kept thinking in the Chic tradition of writing about real stuff. From a supermodel or an actress's point of view, what's their biggest problem? Overspending, trying to keep up their image. She walks down the street and she is offered all the best things that she has to buy. So we thought that paying her credit cards make her life hard.'

At times, the album feels like an elaborate jape: especially on the song 'Misery', where a heavily treated Sheila grapples with the lines:

'Misery is a part of me …
It's hard to continue when all's on the menu is misery …
End it all, it's so inviting'

against a swaggering, high-speed pop. As if to underline the joke, the record fades out and is quickly brought back into focus by a clattering, discordant guitar blast. It was a perfect example of Chic writing to order, and then not actually being that bothered: As Brian Chin argues, 'then again, what they gave her was tailored to what they thought of France.'

Tony Thompson remembered the album in 1985: 'That was a great jam. But it didn't do squat in the States. And there was some good stuff on the album. But when she came in the studio…wow! There were some looks when she opened her mouth to sing. She was terrible! I couldn't believe my ears. "Spacer" should have come out as Chic. It was too good.'

Although Sheila's reedy voice lets the album down, *King Of The World* was an album of contrast: 'Don't Go', 'Spacer' and 'Your Love Is Good' bear the trademark Chic sound. On the latter, the strings and Rodgers' jazzy riffing mark it out as a missing number from *C'est Chic*. But records like 'Mayday', 'Misery' and the title track almost set the template for mid-80s synth rock. 'The King Of The World' is ripe for re-discovery. Sounding not unlike the more synth-driven end of The Cars catalogue, it is ladled in Rodgers dirty lead. In fact, at times it sounds like a demo for Stevie Ray Vaughan's guitar parts on David Bowie's *Let's Dance*.

On the album's American release in June 1980, *Billboard* commented that, 'Steering a course close to dance-orientated rock, the masterminds of Chic have produced a very European-sounding album, as befits French singer Sheila. Sample the Kraftwerk influence on "Mayday" and the blistering guitar work on "Cover Girls"; it's Rodgers and Edwards as you've not heard them before. But the album's high spot is unquestionably "Charge Plates and Credit Cards", a tribute to life with plastics which rocks into a sparse and spacious rhythmic groove which never lets up.'

So, Sheila and the B Devotion was an incredible one-album diversion for Rodgers and Edwards: as fabled UK columnist Julie Burchill decried in *The Face* magazine: Sheila was an 'Old Trojan warhorse slipping into the disco citadel via the Chic Organization and maybe the year's most ecstatic three minutes – "Spacer". What a silk purse Chic made out of a Frog ignoramus.'

Julie Burchill continued about the prolific nature of Chic's work. 'The Chic Organization is established as deevy, dynamic deities in the weak minds of the wishful; but of course they are mortals, and their talent is as finite as yours and mine. One must admire Rodgers and Edwards though for being the only disco band not to wear sequined spacesuits and for knocking them out so quickly. While hardly in the black-hack-and-a-half class of Marley, Chic certainly beat Barbara Cartland when it comes to being prolific. Of course there is the point that all of her output is trash and only half of Chic's is.'

Now it was time for Chic to prove themselves as a group again: It had been a year since the last new album. A time in which disco had begun to suck. Their productions were well-known, yet their commercial success in terms of chart positions was beginning to decline. As Raymond Jones says, 'Disco became a dirty word' and after ages denying he was part of the disco movement, with wilful perversity, Nile Rodgers began to embrace it. 'Now, we wanted to be disco because we were so pissed off that people could diss an entire movement and lump it all together.'

'I think we were viewed as a novelty act and weren't taken seriously,' Alfa Anderson suggests. 'Particularly in the beginning, it was a source of frustration for Nile and Bernard and they worked hard to try and overcome that.' *Real People* was the opportunity to make a big, grown up album.

Released in July 1980, *Real People* was, in a great deal of respects, Chic by numbers. It coincided with Chic becoming an enormous touring band, with the commensurate level of hangers-on. Rodgers had his people, Edwards had his. 'It was like everyone around us was fake,' Rodgers recalled to Marc Taylor. 'The problem was that we couldn't see it. We didn't know who was real. That was the beginning of the end for Chic. Bernard and I broke our promise to each other. We now started to do records that were overtly about what we were thinking and were political. And we messed up. We didn't need to say "I need to live my life with some real people," all we had to do was call up each other and laugh about it. It was so distant.'

'When success comes in, it gets very confusing – there starts to be a lot of other people around that can be telling one person one thing and the other person the other thing,' Fonzi Thornton recalls. 'Those guys were best friends – they had different things that they wanted to do. Nile would try one thing and Bernard would want to try something else. Both of them were so talented they both had things that they wanted to do.'

The album, the only original not to feature Rob Sabino, who was away on Simms Brothers duties, is, however, a strong selection. Compared to its predecessors though, it does leave something to be desired. An album that sounds as if it were recorded in a vacuum with only a 'How To Be Chic' manual for guidance, it feels strangely distant. Nevertheless, from the opening notes of 'Open Up', it is clear that *Real People* is a very smart album. Bright, shiny, sophisticated and occasionally smug, it acts almost as a desperate reassertion of the elegance and sophistication that those in the know knew they possessed anyway.

The title track was possibly one of the most pinched and bitter tracks that had been heard from the Organization. Although double meanings had been rife throughout all of the material, here was a track that laid squarely on the line their disdain for the machinations of the business that had so helped them. Lyrics like:

'Spread out give me some elbow room,
And some place where I can disappear
I'm so tired of hypocrisy
And why these folks even bother me,
Please, just let me be'

'I'm doggone gonna be with real people';

and

'They received you readily
And will deceive you dreadfully
Oh yeah, it's a reality'

could not display their dissatisfaction more clearly.

Rodgers picked up the thread with Marc Taylor: 'We became our worst enemies. We had always claimed that we weren't a disco group and then when people started saying that they hate disco, we wanted to fly that flag. We were so pissed off because it felt like racism and I couldn't stand by and watch it without saying something.'

The album is certainly not without its moments. The guitar breakdown at the end of 'Rebels Are We' is arguably one of the finest ever performed by Rodgers – and the final coda is perfect jazz funk. Alfa Anderson delivers a remarkable performance on the ballad 'I Loved You More'. 'Chip Off The Old Block' is the final 'Chic' track as we know it and 'You Can't Do It Alone' finally spotlights Fonzi Thornton's fantastically emotive vocals. His lead here supports one of the best songs in Chic's catalogue. With its coda and Nile's incredible Spanish guitar solo, it is one of the most mature pieces that Chic released. With its glib humour, '26', which received a great deal of radio play in the UK, was quite superb. Tapping into the zeitgeist with references to the then white-hot 'rating system' from Blake Edwards' mid-life crisis film, *10*, the record's lopingly infectious rhythm was one of the album highlights.

'If certain things had happened,' Rodgers argues. 'If journalists had said, "it's not embarrassing to say that you like Chic. These guys are poets, the sound of New York, The Funk Brothers, a great rhythm section; it's OK to like these guys who know how to make you dance," it would have put us in a position that when people started to say that "disco sucks", we could have continued and been above it. But we listened too hard to the criticism. We tried too hard with *Real People*, and made a reactionary record. When we wrote "Good Times", we didn't care what anybody was saying, we wrote it from our hearts. When we wrote "Real People", we did it to convince people we were artists; we were *trying* to be intellectual – that is the kiss of death. What I write comes right from my heart; when there's no pressure, my mind is a stream of consciousness.'

Real People had all the hallmarks of the bitterness of on-the-road albums such as *De La Soul Is Dead*: 'It was a combination of factors working against us,' Edwards recalled to *Zigzag's* Kris Needs in 1981. 'The attitude people have to you. Previous to our success everyone was rooting for us. Then all of a sudden, when we made it, they turn against you. Nile and I were hurt and angry. It's hypocritical, but there's very little you can do about it. You can decide if you're going to write about it or not. We decided to write about it.' It also found them recycling their by now instantly-identifiable sound to the point of parody.

'Suddenly, we dropped the fantasy vibe,' Rodgers told *Details* in 1992. 'That was so unlike the philosophy of Chic. I remember a shopgirl coming up to us and saying "where are you coming from? How can you stop writing about love and dancing?" We looked at her like "Damn, can't you grow up?" But in retrospect, she hit the nail on the head.'

'Things weren't rosy internally,' Luci Martin recalls. 'When problems started to happen in the group, it came out onstage and on record. I don't think that the decrease in our success came because of not having the talent, or only being an overnight kind of thing; it was because we were so honest in our music, putting our feelings into what we were doing. In the beginning, the happiness and excitement came through, but towards the end, so did any anger or dissension. You can feel it. We were going through some very severe growth changes.'

Real People was simply too knotty and complex for the mainstream. It also was a classic damned-if-they-do, damned-if-they-don't moment, for if Chic had simply made an album of discredited disco, it would have equally been ignored. 'There's never been one suggestion from the record company or others around us that we ever took seriously, until we got to *Real People*,' Rodgers recalls. 'That's when our lives changed drastically. Oh god, that was the beginning of the end. For  the first time we didn't sell and we thought that somebody knew something we didn't know. Everybody hates you guys now, so what you got to do is this – we should have done our own thing. If everybody hates us, then let them hate us.' Stephen Holden was spot on in his review in *Rolling Stone*: 'The group's blasé irony has turned rancid. "I Got Protection", which compares love to VD, and "26" a send up of the Bo Derek rating system, manage to be snide without being catchy.'

The album reached No. 30 in America and failed to chart in Britain. 'Real People' and 'Rebels Are We' were the single releases, reaching No. 79 and No.

61 in the US respectively. The days up in the giddy heights of the Top 10s seemed to be over for Chic.

Around this time, almost too late, Chic gained an official fan club. Based out of Radio City Station in New York, you could be kept up to date with the activities of the not-quite-so-fabulous fivesome. The timing in some ways though could not have been worse.

Nonetheless, the tour to support the album was not without its highlights, including, on 1st September, playing the Miss America contest in Atlantic City. As millions of Americans tuned in to see Cheryl Prewitt of Ackerman, Mississippi claim the 59th Miss America crown, Chic became the first African-American group to play the contest, a clear sign that Chic had been absorbed into the American mainstream. Alfa Anderson remembers the significance of the contest with affection. 'We actually ushered in an era where musicians of colour

Fan club biography cover

were treated differently. In lots of different areas, we broke though the colour line. I can't remember racism towards us. We experienced almost the opposite. We weren't part of the chitlin circuit that had to go in back doors and not stay at the best hotels, or go into restaurants.' Luci Martin recalls the concert for different reasons: 'That was fun. I loved my outfit; beaded with rhinestones and loads of crinoline underneath it. It had a short, puffy skirt with a camisole type top and some beading around the neckline, with a white fox-fur – *you couldn't tell me anything.'*

Generally, however, attendances were down: 'We went up to Portland, Maine and played a basketball stadium that had maybe 3000 people there,' Karen Milne recalls. 'We all knew the end was coming. We played in a college out in New Jersey and there was hardly anybody there. We were waiting for Nile and Bernard to call us and get rid of us. We played at Farleigh Dickenson University – after that they called us to the office and dismissed us.' In the first week of September 1980, the Chic Strings were disbanded and received their final paycheck.

17.
TAKE IT OFF

'So what happened to Chic? Well, cultural attitudes may have had
something to do with their slide from their commercial pinnacle.
The brevity of their hit span was not uncommon for artists tattooed
with the ghettoising ID, "disco act."'
KEN BARNES, The Best Of Chic II

BY THE END OF Jimmy Carter's presidency, with the failure in dealing with
the Iranian hostages, the 'crisis of confidence' in America, the second oil
crisis, double-digit inflation, 20% interest rates and 8% unemployment, the
liberal hope was all but extinguished. It was time for major change. In
November 1980, Ronald Reagan was elected. The 'me' decade was truly
beginning. Personal politics, greed and selfishness were now to become the
order of the day. There also seemed to be an almost instant revisionism.

In Britain in 1980, the *Virgin Rock Yearbook* trumpeted that 'disco smelt
increasingly fishy over the past 12 months, but the mouths that sing it have
never looked better. It's the only corny glamour magnet left in entertainment,
like films were in the 50s, fashion in the 60s, white rock in the 70s.' None
seemed more glamorous than the life Chic was leading and the company they
were keeping.

For Chic, although the Diana Ross album had demonstrated their ongoing
commercial potency, *Real People* had caused some confusion. It became clear
that now the day-trippers had moved on, Chic themselves didn't actually
possess an enormous fan-base. Not that that overtly troubled Rodgers and
Edwards. As producers and joint writers of all they had released, they were
two of the richest young men in the world. Which was why there were few
immediate problems when the hits began to dry up in 1981. 'They had good
enough deals with Atlantic and Warner publishing and the pipeline money
was deep,' Raymond Jones recalls.

'By that time, so many people wanted a little piece of Chic fairy dust on
their product that you got the impression that they were beginning to spread
themselves very, very thinly, very quickly,' veteran critic Geoff Brown argues.

'It was not necessarily a kind of feeling that the pop market had lost interest in them, but it was partly perhaps due to the fact that they didn't want to turn any projects down. It was probably the gigging musician instinct in them. They wanted to maximise their potential as quickly as possible.'

Meanwhile, the differences between the two personalities became more marked: Rodgers became a party animal and Edwards would be there in the background. 'Bernard was getting his share of the parties too, but Nile *really really* liked being the centre of attention,' Raymond Jones recalled. Rodgers, by his own confession, at this point was a 'crazy, out-of-control drug addict'. Edwards, on the other hand, remained rooted. 'Bernard was the big warm fuzzy teddy bear of a guy – he would always cut through the bullshit,' Rob Sabino adds. 'He was super-responsible and there was a phase we went through when Nile was not being as responsible as he should. He was not taking care of his health. Bernard had to cover for the many missed sessions and late sessions. All of us have succumbed to that lifestyle, however when the boss is doing that, it's tough.'

Tony Thompson, meanwhile, was, according to James Truman in 1979, 'the only member of the band who seems to be in the confidence of its controllers.' However, things began to change, subtly. "The band stuff started to go away," Rob Sabino recalls. "It was definitely Nile and Bernard. It was always them for the vision, but Nile had definitely started becoming more of a production company."

As 1981 dawned, there was little sign of the workload flagging. There were often short-notice calls placed to the players to come and record. 'We kind of knew beforehand if we were going to be doing a single or an album, with Johnny Mathis or Sister Sledge,' Raymond Jones remembers. 'We did 10 albums, played on a 100 songs in such a remarkably short space of time – a glut, you could say.'

There were also two aborted projects around this time that have passed into Chic's history. One, the Johnny Mathis album, *I Love My Lady*, happened. The other, a proposed album with Aretha Franklin, most certainly did not.

'I know that there were several stages when Aretha's career was not going as well as she liked and she was thinking of changing producers,' Ahmet Ertegun recalls. The turn of the 80s was one of them. As Chic were white-hot, they were considered to oversee a change in direction for the Queen Of Soul.

'We never wrote anything for her,' Rodgers remembered. 'We had one meeting with her and we were so turned off, we couldn't believe that Aretha wanted to do disco. Bernard and I were sitting in the Queen Of Soul's house, this beautiful mansion in Los Angeles and she was singing, "I'm going to be the only star tonight down at the disco." And Bernard and I were looking at each other in disbelief, thinking "holy shit! We're with Aretha Franklin and she's telling us she's going to be the only star in the disco tonight.... Is she nuts?" We were stunned and dumbfounded. We were sitting at the piano with her and we couldn't say anything. If we told her that was great, she would say "are you kidding me, you want me to sing some shit like this?" We didn't know if it's a joke.'

It did not take them long to decide against the venture. 'We were not going to go down in history as the producers of Aretha Franklin's disco record! In the end, she went with Van McCoy – we were shocked he would do it – but then, he did write "Do The Hustle" which IS a disco record. I thought of her history and we certainly weren't going to produce her. That was the only time that we ever met her.'

However, the Johnny Mathis project, recorded at The Power Station in February 1981, remains one of the great lost Chic moments. In 1980, his management contacted Rodgers and Edwards to produce what was to become *I Love My Lady*.

Johnny Mathis was a serious player. Since he made his recording debut in 1955, only Elvis Presley and Frank Sinatra have had more hit albums in America; he has performed for presidents and dignitaries the world over. In 1958, his fourth album, *Johnny's Greatest Hits,* became the first record ever to be called 'Greatest Hits' and spent an unbroken 49 weeks on the American chart. He began to take off in Britain, too. He enjoyed his first Top 10 hit in September 1956 with 'A Certain Smile', quickly followed by the enchanting 'Someone', which reached No. 6 the following summer. 'Misty', for many his signature tune, was a transatlantic hit in 1959.

By the 70s, Mathis had become known as much for his golfing as for his music. Looking to the success of Thom Bell and Linda Creed's work with The Stylistics, Mathis covered this material and found the soft soul vibe most suitable for his audience. His version of 'I'm Stone In Love With You', a Top 10 hit for The Stylistics in 1972, took him back to the higher reaches of the UK charts in January 1975. However, Mathis wanted to take a new turn; he wanted to move in a more soulful R&B direction. Duetting with former Stevie Wonder vocalist and 'Free' hit maker Denise Williams gave Mathis his greatest US success since 1963: 'Too Much, Too Little, Too Late' hit the No. 1 spot in both the pop and the R&B charts in April 1978. It was the first duet either singer had recorded. It climbed to the UK Top 3 as well, and led to a Top 20 album, *That's What Friends Are For.*

Being impressed with the success of the Diana Ross album, Rodgers and Edwards seemed a natural choice to bring some of their magic to Mathis' mix. 'We completed an album with Johnny that was actually great,' Rodgers recalls. 'He had been this big superstar, and then his light dimmed a little, and then he came back after that massive record with Denise Williams. His popularity rekindled, he went on this reckless tear – partying and hanging out; it really frightened the people who were closest to him. When we did this record, it was totally exciting and youth-oriented. All his people went "oh my god". At the time I was offended but, in retrospect, I can see that they did a good thing. It'll never see the light of day, it's buried somewhere in the Sony archive.' Columbia (who were to become Sony) felt that whereas it was possible to move Diana Ross down toward the street, Mathis was still too identified with his predominately white, middle-aged audience. It was important that the African-American was not brought out in him. Chic had identified this 'reckless tear' in him, and by using their powers of observational writing, emphasised it.

Fonzi Thornton did the guide vocals for the album, which was to contain eight tracks; 'I Love My Lady', 'I Want To Fall In Love', 'It's All Right To Love Me', 'Judy', 'Love And Be Loved', 'Sing', 'Take Me' and 'Go With The Flow'. It contained all of the key players of the Organization, and it was to be the last time that they were together on record. Mathis himself was an eager participatant in the sessions.

'It was a serious album and it's on the shelf,' Tony Thompson said in 1985. 'I think that Columbia, his record label, thought it would alienate his audience. So they didn't want to release it and it was such a good album. You never heard Johnny Mathis sing like this. No-one has. He grooves to death with this album. We did like a Brazilian type funk-samba on it; oh, incredible. Sang his ass off. Phut. No-one's ever gonna hear it. I hate that. We spent time on this. It was a real good album.'

Rob Sabino concurs: 'The Mathis album was really good – but I have no idea where I could find it! There was some wonderful stuff on it.' It was a classic example of cold feet by an artist faced with commercial change. In the place of *I Love My Lady*, out came the Jack Gold-produced *Different Kinda Different*, which paid lip service to the times with versions of 'I Will Survive' and 'With You I'm Born Again', but to underline the record company's concern that he not alienate his market, the album was somewhat schizophrenic, as it included versions of 'Deep Purple' and 'Temptation'. Mathis was then to return to older, more familiar waters in 1983 with the incredibly successful *Unforgettable* album, a collection of Nat King Cole standards sung with Cole's daughter, Natalie.

'The Johnny Mathis record to me sounded like Al Jarreau meets Chic. It didn't sound like Johnny Mathis to me – it was a little more edgy than I'd ever heard him,' Rodgers recalls. 'That's why it was pulled. His audience at the time was like middle-aged women who would go out to Vegas, and this was pushing his envelope. His big hits were like "Too Much, Too Little, Too Late" – these were not that. I remember this incredible song called "Love And Be Loved". I actually found one of the tracks, "Go With The Flow", the other day. I gave it to a few DJs and the response is extremely good. It shows the level of our groove in those days; it's totally unique and happening – but we didn't think it was good enough at the time. It smokes!'

I Love My Lady remains, at the time of writing, in the Sony vaults. Johnny Mathis respectfully declined to be interviewed for the project. Twice.

The most anticipated Chic-related project of 1981 was the summer release of *Koo Koo*, the first solo album by the enigmatic lead vocalist of Blondie, Debbie Harry. Those with only a passing interest in late 70s pop would have been aware of Blondie. With her smouldering peroxide looks and, for pop, advancing years (she was 33 when the group broke in 1978), ex-Playboy bunny Harry had created this wonderful, strident, knowing pop persona. Supported by a crack team of players including her boyfriend, guitarist, Chris Stein, Blondie had earned their spurs on the New York live circuit since forming in 1974. The band was able to blend art, dance, punk and power pop and had become enormous. By early 1981, they had enjoyed three American and UK No.1s. Their most recent single, 'Rapture' was a note-for-note homage to 'Good Times' which featured Harry rapping; the first white artist of note to cotton on to the style. She had also, as if to affirm her status, been a guest on *The Muppet Show*.

However, tension within Blondie had grown and it was decided that some time apart was essential; Harry and Stein wished to pursue an artier groove that combined their love of new wave with disco. It was time for her to go solo. She was stretching out – she had just made a film noir called *Union City*. She was soon to work with David Cronenberg. It seemed natural that Chic and Harry would gravitate towards each other, both being sophisticates at the centre of the New York sound. It should have been a marriage made in heaven.

Although they had been aware of each other from Max's Kansas City days, Stein and Harry had first met Rogers and Edwards at The Power Station in 1979, when Blondie were recording their *Eat To The Beat* album. Stein had suggested that Rodgers and Edwards produce their next album, *AutoAmerican*, but the task eventually fell to the producer of their previous three albums, UK pop guru Mike Chapman. The four became reacquainted after meeting on *The Glenn O'Brien Show*.

Understandably, there was intense media interest in Harry; and when it was announced that she was to team up with The Chic Organization, everyone was waiting in happy anticipation. The initial meeting went well and recording began at the Power Station in late spring of 1981, taking five weeks in total. There was

little rehearsal; they went in and created. 'While we were recording, they told a lot of race jokes and tried to make us feel inferior for being white, but it was just in fun,' Harry wrote in 1982. 'The secret of being a good producer is being over-the-top crazy in the studio. Nile and Bernard definitely are. They're also very superior type of people; if you hang around with them, they'll start putting you down anyway.' Sessions were punctuated by Rodgers taking the players out in his newly-acquired speedboat on the East River, moving so fast that Tony Thompson and Debbie Harry were hanging on for dear life.

The album was divided between composers, with Edwards and Rodgers, and Stein and Harry composing four songs each and the remaining two tracks were four-way collaborations. It's clear that Rodgers and Edwards wanted to be Devo (Spud and Pud from the group sang backing on the album) *and* they wanted to be Blondie; they wanted to be anything but Chic. As a result, it's the album the phrase 'hotchpotch' was invented for. It's all a little like the soundtrack to a school play. Which is a shame, because on paper, it was one of the most potent combinations of the early 80s.

To compound the misunderstanding of the album, the sleeve was designed by Swiss artist H.R Giger, who had just achieved world-wide recognition for designing Ridley Scott's groundbreaking science fiction film, *Alien*. Accustomed to seeing her peroxide blond in a mini-dress, her fans were treated to a picture of her (taken by Brain Aris, adapted by Giger) as her natural brunette, hair scraped back on her head, a circuit-board head-band and four skewers rammed through her skull.

On completion, Harry felt proud of the album: 'We felt we had really accomplished something in making a successful fusion of rock and R&B, which hadn't really been done on that level before.' However, reaction was mixed to say the least. The cover image stunned her fan base and led to the sleeve being banned in certain countries and the promotional videos she shot with Giger in Switzerland being left unbroadcast.

The Face magazine, at that point the only magazine writing about style and music for a Britain emerging from its own depression, suggested that the album was full of 'slim variations on the, by now, well passé 'rap' sub-genre; all rambling kindergarten lyrics, non-melodies and a thin-thin-thin production that leaves La Harry's every flat note painfully naked. The closing "Oasis" is kebab-house disco of the sort Bowie did much better on 'Lodger.' *Rolling Stone* suggested it 'never quite got off the ground,' while, although *Trouser Press* suggested she was out of her depth, 'trying to insert herself into Chic's musical format.' It also noted that 'the controversial pairing with the Chicmen stands as an example of the prescient and adventurous trailblazing that had typified Harry and Stein within Blondie.'

The lead single 'Backfired', a cross between Chic and 'Rapture', all staccato riffs and uneasy choruses, led the way, becoming a minor hit on both sides of the Atlantic. Elsewhere on the album, Rob Sabino's circling keyboards at the start of 'Jump Jump' informed virtually all of Trevor Horn's productions. It also has a sly nod to Queen's 'Another One Bites The Dust'. 'The Jam Was Moving' certainly penetrated the psyche of Larry Blackmon, as 'Word Up' can at best be described as an affectionate tribute to it (at worst ... well, you get the picture). Where it does really lose out is on material like the quite awful

'Inner City Spillover', where Harry's English accent acts as a perfect precursor for Madonna and 'Military Rap' is simply confused. The languid ballad, 'Now I Know You Know' is possibly the album's best moment, but Harry's plaintive voice makes you wish for Anderson and Martin.

Geoff Brown remembers the album's release all too well: 'The Debbie Harry thing was just laughable when it came out. That they could have been involved in making a record that poor, her too, come to that. It was lame and trite. What were they thinking of?' Even Rodgers, normally ebullient about his recordings, was unsure: he stated in 1982, that, 'We felt we could have played it better. It was a little unclear what the concept was, what Debbie really wanted to say with the thing. As far as the songwriting goes and my guitar playing went I felt it was one of the best things I've ever done. I just wish I'd made more money out of it.' It wasn't one of the best things Rodgers had done; but it was, at that point the most different and again underlined his need to escape the straight-jacket he now felt he was in with Chic.

Kris Needs interviewed Chic for *Zig Zag* magazine in 1981 and asked what the session had been like: 'The recording wasn't difficult,' Edwards recalled. 'Me and Nile used to work with three or four people in a band all the time. This record was going back to that kind of thing. We had a ball. We got real close to each other. There was great communication once we got in there.'

'We learned a lot from that. It was a very good experience. When we did that album, everyone was expecting a combination of Blondie and Chic,' Rodgers continued. 'They thought it would be the ultimate commercial venture, with the best elements of both. But we didn't do that. I know it's not gonna sell, but I had to play it like that.

'There's a lot of good stuff on that record. "I Surrender" that's one of the hippest guitar solos I ever played! The trouble is there's nothing traditional you could put your finger on. Everyone expected it to be the ultimate commercial seller, but instead of that we tried to make it more of an artistic endeavour communication thing. Once you get to a certain point in your

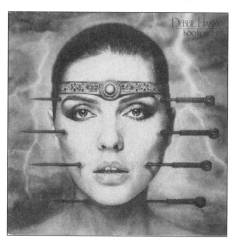

career it's important to make that kind of album, where you want to say something else.'

'When I go back and hear *Koo Koo*, it's an uncomfortable thing to listen to, very angular and peculiar,' Rodgers states today. 'There are a couple of things on it that's cool but it's a little too rough around the edges. That record is what I call "survivor guilt" – you're doing really well and you don't understand why and you feel bad for people who aren't doing as well, and you try to move them forward. I did this cool thing with so and so – If I do it with someone else, that will be cool too – it doesn't always work like that.'

Raymond Jones recalls that although not commercially well received, making *Koo Koo* was great fun, of which pictures taken in the recording studio testify. 'Debbie Harry was great; Chris Stein was great. People would say *Koo Koo* was not successful, but it did go gold. For me, an album's success is that you can make enough money to do another one.' The problem was simply one of what was expected in marrying two of the great New York musical forces. 'But they had invested so much money and had so much hope in it. I don't know what they expected,' Jones concludes.

Koo Koo was just too eagerly awaited, and ultimately collapsed under the weight of its own expectation. Released in summer 1981, it is often thought of as being an enormous flop. The album reached No. 25 on the US charts and made No. 6 in Great Britain in August 1981. It can be filed under the bracket of 'noble failure'; the intentions were there, it just failed to ignite.

'Both Debbie Harry and Chic put a brick wall in front of *Koo Koo*; it had all the aura of winning removed from it,' Brian Chin recalls. 'In the record industry if you've had two bad ones in a row you're in a real fucking deep hole, you're gonna have to come back with something death-defying. Otherwise, funds are gonna stop.' For Rodgers and Edwards, after the less than satisfying *Real People* album, it seemed that the halcyon days were over.

The three Chic albums released between 1981 and 1983 – *Take It Off*, *Tongue In Chic* and *Believer* – have always received a rough time by the critics. Garry Mulholland has called them 'grim and formulaic.' However, that is to do them a disservice. In some respects, where could you go after *C'est Chic* and *Risqué*?

But by now, the Chic brand seemed dated, and, for the first time, out of step. Their autumn 1981 release, *Take It Off* was the opportunity to right the wrongs, and reassert the importance of the group, who less than 24 months before had been the biggest in America. Edwards and Rodgers took the decision, that in order to move the music forward, they would depart from their trademark sound.

Mainstream disco was finally over. Steve Rubell and Ian Schrager were found guilty of fraud and imprisoned and Studio 54 finally closed its doors on 28th February 1980. Raymond Jones recalled 'I was trying to put together a band with a friend, and this guy, Gary, had got himself in a little trouble. He had got himself into a Federal institution in Alabama. I wanted him in the band, so I went to speak at his parole hearing. He introduced me to his room-mate, who was none other than Steve Rubell from Studio 54. He was so humble. I kept thinking how far they fall. This was Mr Cocaine, and here he was surrounded by his family at an air force base in Montgomery.'

Although never meaning to have written the music for *Saturday Night*

Fever or 'going disco', after their 1979 album, *Spirits Having Flown*, The Bee Gees got the full strength of the disco backlash and tumbled into a hit wilderness. Although selling in excess of 25 million copies, you were hard-pressed to find anybody who actually owned a copy of *Saturday Night Fever*. If recession and the new conservatism of the Reagan era slowed down the party, 'the big disease with a little name,' AIDS, was to act as the final pulling across of the velvet rope. It began to ravage what was left of the disco community. As gay clubs like the Saint in New York took disco in through hi-nrg, the hedonism of the lifestyle began to take its toll.

To the ears waiting for the next Chic album, the music had to be as far away as possible from that which they had become so identified. 'We talked it over for a while,' Rodgers told *The New York Times* in 1981. 'We knew that on the next Chic album we were going to have to come up with something really different.'

Rob Sabino (who was known as 'the special guest star') returned to the recording studio after missing *Real People* through Simms Brothers commitments, and found, that whatever the pressures, when the group settled down to play, the old magic was still there: 'It wasn't a shared creative vision – it was definitely Nile and Bernard's,' Sabino recalls. 'But we would all support them in their ideas. I did solo type stuff in other bands, but I was aware they wanted texture stuff, so I'd put a couple of little riffs down here and there – and decided which was the best instrument to support their vision. We were successful.

'They would both give me a lot of latitude and knew that I loved attention to detail and explored different ways of doing things and knew that I would like to do outlandish things. They would maybe have a time limit on me – "OK, we're gonna let Rob go" – I would say something wild. They would give me my head and say yeah or nay afterwards.' However, there was never any question whose vision it was: 'It was obvious that this was not a democracy' Jones adds. 'You might have an opinion and Nile and Bernard may appreciate a comment now and again, but this is what you do. We were just hired guns, hired musicians, so we just had to deal with it.'

With its Tony Wright-designed street-cartoon sleeve, *Take It Off*, shorn of Gene Orloff and the Chic Strings, is a more melodic sister of *Koo Koo*, complete with a large and persistent horn section, featuring the Brecker Brothers and Lenny Pickett. Rodgers was trying to emulate the then-hottest thing on the block, Talking Heads, who had also successfully been able to fuse rock and disco into one cohesive stew. They did, of course, have the distinct advantage of being white and cerebral. As an attempt to relocate Chic back on the street, *Take It Off* was brave.

Although Rodgers upbringing was 'dirt poor', the group simply had wafted in with the aroma of money surrounding them. Couple this with the anonymity of the group and it certainly seemed the case that Chic simply didn't exist on the street – they should have been away in their apartment or country manor. 'We started to second-guess everything. Nothing was making sense. Hip-hop was growing, so everything was growing from soft and sophisticated to hard and street,' Rodgers told Marc Taylor.

Jocelyn Brown was added into the Chic choir, while pianist Andy Schwartz had departed to make his name as a Billy Joel type performer. Sabino was working head to head with Raymond Jones: 'Ray Jones was my buddy. I love him,' says Sabino. 'I look up to him as a person of integrity. I had been in enough hippie bands and African-American bands and the only true hippie I ever met was Ray! All of us used to go out for Ribs and Ray would be grazing on macrobiotic food – he was a gentle, well-read, wonderful pianist. We got along really well. It was perfect harmony as to who was doing what, depending on feel. It was very easy to do. Parts would be shared, but there wasn't too much of a plan.'

Stalwart percussionist Sammy Figueroa was also around: 'Sammy is certainly a character, he's a sweetheart,' Jones recalls. 'Percussionists and drummers have a lot of fidgety energy and Sammy is no exception to that rule. He's a sweet guy. He seemed a party kind of boy.' The mood was optimistic when they returned to The Power Station. The recording also marked the debut of engineer Jason Corsaro, who would work with Rodgers and Edwards for the best part of the next decade.

The album contains some fine material: 'Flash Back' seems like a plea to regain the spark in Chic's commercial fortunes. Edwards growls the love song, which also serves to remind the fast-deserting audience just how much Chic had been loved. Bass-led, the track features Rodgers' recorded tribute to Pink Floyd's David Gilmour; the rangy, almost sloppy solo shows how far the group were prepared to dismantle their signature sound.

> *'I've been thinking about*
> *The good times we shared,*
> *Just getting high from the memory*
> *You were always there, so willing to care*
> *Now you're gone, I'm so alone.'*

and the chorus of:

> *'Make love and dance was all we'd do'*

add an air of melancholy over the whole proceedings.

The crispness of 'Your Love Is Cancelled' – Rodgers' lead vocal debut – is frequently angular funk. 'Burn Hard,' is a fantastic funky tribute to Edwards' bass playing ('slap your bass, burn hard, burn hard'), and 'Baby Doll' is the sort of jazzy instrumental that took them back to 'Sao Paolo' territory. There wasn't a great deal of melody on the album. Martin and Edwards sparred on the title track, itself another plea to strip things away and get back to basics. '*Take It Off* was an evolution,' Raymond Jones states. 'But it wasn't a quantum leap at the time. It was more of the same but with additional growth. I really like that record.'

'While the complex, knotty funk of *Take It Off* holds up to repeated listening,' as *Rolling Stone* was to comment, 'only a contortionist could dance to it. No wonder the hit parade stopped cold.' Glenn O'Brien said in *Interview* magazine of *Take It Off*: 'They rock, they bop, they do the jazz and the funky Chic one, they make jungle music for Park Avenue and cool jazz for the jungle and everything good in between. A winner and still champ.' However it was too late. O'Brien

continues, '"Flash Back" is a wonderful dub ballad most sensitively and soulfully sung by Bernard over a spare track that's mainly his perfect lovequake bass, with some very grand piano touches and a lovely soul-powered Luci and Alfa chorus. Nile is out for a smoke until the end when he appears in time for a great low-key delicately rocking, quietly funking, elegantly jazzing solo. This great song shows you what a great bass can do almost alone and how great a low male voice can be with solo bass accompaniment. Bernard may give Barry White heart failure with this one.'

Billboard said of *Take It Off* in November 1981, that the group were taking chances. 'Several of the cuts have a harder instrumental edge, leaning more toward rock than R&B at times. Songs like "So Fine" and "Just Out Of Reach" are looser and more expansive than Chic's usual ultra-tight approach. And "Baby Doll," the closing track, is a hot instrumental with a tenor sax solo worthy of Jr Walker. Now if only rock stations will ease up on their restrictive programming, this can get the across-the-board exposure it deserves.'

The New York Times featured Chic in December 1981, over an extended review of the album entitled 'Chic Discovers Life After Disco'. Critic Robert Palmer suggested that '*Take It Off* was more lyrical than most funk, sparer and harder than disco, more complex rhythmically than soul, more heavily groove-oriented than rock. Like much of the best popular music, it resists easy categorization. But it's certainly the freshest, most satisfying album of dance music this listener has heard in a long time.'

Despite the great coverage the album received, it only managed to reach No. 124 on the US album charts and failed to register in the UK. Chic's perceived fall from the summit of disco was seized upon by the bourgeoning English style press. *The Face* writer James Truman wrote in a perceptive piece entitled *A New Realism: Is All Well In The House Of Chic?* that 'for a couple of years Chic held the franchise on moments of grand obsession, and they had a subliminal gift for expanding them into three, four, five-minute pop songs. Then they didn't. Over-prolific, over-imitated, over-exposed, they seemed to let it all slip away.'

'*Take It Off* is a great album. But then again at that time, even more Italians were making Chic-style records that were just stroking the listener a little more,' Brian Chin argues. 'All these records were taking an obvious formula. I don't feel too sorry for them, because they could always go and produce another record for someone else.'

'Sometimes it's really hard to grow in the public eye – people like what you're doing and they want you to continue that,' Alfa Anderson states. 'You can't write the same song, you can't do the same thing. Sometimes growth can be painful; but people don't always give you the opportunity to depart from what you've done before – *Take It Off* was something of a departure, but it was an opportunity to see other ways we could grow.'

When "Good Times" came out, it was the very start of the next stage of the groove. Now, as 1982 dawned, Chic were following rather than leading.

Although attendances were smaller, Chic still smouldered on the road. Rob Sabino finally got out on tour with them. 'It was like a Big Apple Band reunion. The group was going down, but we were really good live. People would be waiting for this disco band and we would knock 'em sideways. With Tony on drums and our sensibilities about how rock had influenced disco and R&B music, it was very impressive live – we were a very heavy band.'

One particular show from this era that remained in Rodgers mind was when they played with The Clash at Bond's Nightclub on Broadway in June 1981. 'When The Clash did the residency, we played Bonds – Blondie, The Clash and us,' Rodgers recalls. 'It was one of the best nights in music history – and we ripped that shit. At the end of the night, we went out on stage – after we finished, we played "Rapture" and brought up every rapper in New York City to rap over it – and it was one of the most exciting nights ever. We just kept playing the riff, and then we'd break off into "Good Times", then we'd break off into "Another One Bites The Dust", then we'd break off into "Radio Clash" – It was like a live version of "The Adventures Of Grandmaster Flash On The Wheels Of Steel!" We just kept going off into these things – Fab Five Freddy, Futura 2000. I still remember one of Fab Five's raps – "See the girl in the red with the scarf around her head, see the girl in the yellow with a faggot for a fellow."'

Yet few people recorded Chic's triumph. The world had turned and they were seen as old hat. 'I thought how come the writers aren't writing about this shit? It was like the community wanted to separate us in a weird way. Maybe it was the beginning of the corporatisation of our culture, or it was like when we write about rock, we are powerful and we know all those people. But, with dance and black music, we don't know any of those people. I don't know what it was. I really wish we had the key. I always think if two or three things had been reported accurately, my life would have been very different. If they had reported about that show at Bond's in the cultural way that it felt in that room; how punk and Chic came together and were the same. You talk to guys in The Clash, they're our boys. You talk to Blondie, you talk to Duran. The press didn't advance what the musicians were actually thinking. When I looked at the coverage in *Rolling Stone,* it was all about Blondie and The Clash – Chic was sort of mentioned in passing. The journalists loved us, but it was almost like that's not the job, this is not what this paper talks about.'

To maintain their level of commitments, there was an immense amount of the drug around that seemed perfectly to accompany this fast-paced lifestyle. Cocaine. The rise in popularity of the drug in the late 70s and its hefty price tag meant that very many of the music industry succumbed to its dubious pleasures. Many would argue there was now no difference between corporate executives and rock stars. Rodgers has made no secret of his dalliances. 'Cocaine is not an aid to creativity. Cocaine was just cocaine,' Rodgers told Clark Collis in 2003. 'It was the same thing as drinking or the same thing as acid, when I was younger, or the same thing as sniffing glue when I first started. Cocaine was just part of what you were doing.' Still, it was becoming an increasingly integral part for both principals. 'And on it, judgements get a little blurry.'

'It makes you very insular and isolates you and was contributory to Nile taking on more and more stuff, feeling that he could do it all himself,' Rob Sabino adds. 'Not maliciously or consciously saying he didn't want anybody else; but then the posse he had around him, saying everything he did was fantastic. That plus some coke and you think you're on top of the world. People tell you that no matter what you did, it was great. You succumb to that when it's a party time. Bernard was also involved, but he was a little more responsible. He didn't let it affect his work as much.'

'In terms of their ego, they might have been perplexed that they weren't having hits,' Raymond Jones comments. 'But then, I wasn't up in the mix as they would like to say. I believe they were having problems. Cocaine was in the studio, but it wasn't prevalent. It was recreational, but as I was a 20-year old vegetarian, I was a little: "I don't want anything to do with that." As a sideman, I couldn't afford much recreational stuff. My view was how long is this going to last?'

Quietly in 1981, the deal with MK, Mark Kreiner and Tom Cossie reached its natural conclusion. 'Tom Cossie and Mark Kreiner left them after the fourth album,' Jerry Greenberg recalls. 'It was a production deal – they got the override on Chic – they were signed to their production company and their production company made a deal with Atlantic. Eventually they left.'

From now on it would simply be Rodgers and Edwards.

Tony Thompson never quite reconciled himself to the fact that there was just the two of them; no matter how much they flagged themselves as The Chic Organization Ltd., 'It was never just Nile and Bernard or Nile by himself,' Thompson recalls. 'It was me, Nile and Bernard. They were my mentors, man.' Resentment grew as he was not treated equally to them. 'I was too naïve and I wasn't taken care of like I should have been in terms of everything, because I had so much trust in them. I can honestly say, looking back, that they broke my heart like you have no idea. But, they also made me happy in a lot of ways, too. There are some things that Nile and Bernard did for me, that no-one else has. There was this bond and love we had for each other, besides creating music and watching the fruits of our labour grow.'

☆ ☆ ☆

The band continued its session work. Fonzi Thornton received a call to work with Roxy Music on what was to become *Avalon*, partially a wistful chronicle of New York. Bob Clearmountain had suggested that he would make a good foil for Bryan Ferry's voice. 'It was a great combination,' Ferry recalls. 'The pair of us worked well together. He's very cool – he often wore a pork-pie hat. His voice is amazing, rich and warm; it was much bigger than my voice and he would ghost some lines that would add an aura around mine.'

'I can imagine Nile saying that Chic were influenced by Roxy,' Thornton says. 'Bryan Ferry has got to be the coolest man in rock history – the way he moves, the way he uses his voice, the big, deep, atmosphere he creates. That big, deep dark atmosphere that Roxy had is very akin to what Chic had. I adore Bryan.'

Avalon, recorded mainly in 1981 with Rhett Davies and Bob Clearmountain – was so refined that it became responsible for The Blue Nile, George Michael's solo melancholy and Sade. Much has been made of the album's mellow flow. Music creeps in and out; fragile tunes appear like magic eye pictures from warm washes of instruments and Ferry is at his most succinct and poignant. But through all the lushness, an inherent bleakness remains. The whole project courses with a melancholia that is at times only lifted by the sweetness of the music; it's the record Joy Division would have made if they'd been coffee table stylists. Although critics sniped at the time at Ferry's ennui and how they had taken a decade to go from the cutting edge to the furthest reaches, *Avalon* is cool; its release meant that the high, bright spring of 1982 was kissed with the gentlest caress Roxy ever left. 'To Turn You On', a left-over from *Flesh + Blood* is still the most successful track, an upbeat rumination on love. The last track proper, 'True To Life', simply drifts away, with Ferry's suggestion 'I'll soon be home' signalling closure. Its weariness and mention of the New York nightlife seems to bring a distant conclusion to the whole era.

During the 36 months from autumn 1978 to autumn 1981, The Chic Organization Ltd. played, wrote, sung and produced eight albums, as well as touring and promoting their work. It was a phenomenal work-rate. The big chart numbers may have been over for Chic per se as the 80s dawned, but the American Hot 100 was still displaying liberal doses of Chic cheer. Diana Ross's 'Upside Down' enjoyed three weeks at No. 1 in September, to be replaced by Queen's 'Another One Bites The Dust', a song so obviously a skeletal re-write of 'Good Times' that Grandmaster Flash had little option than to mix them together on 'The Adventures Of Grandmaster Flash On The Wheels Of Steel' in 1981.

Chic had made their mark; but with every passing release they seemed to be undermining their achievements. With the tension between the two main protagonists and the pincer effect of Rodgers' love of new technology, the band's increasing reliance on cocaine and huge numbers of advisors; it became apparent that the group could not exist for much longer.

18.
WHY DOES MY HEART HURT SO MUCH?

'We were going so fast and making so much money – two brothers
from New York generating millions – and we did it to ourselves …
we got separated.'
NILE RODGERS

THE IRANIAN HOSTAGES WERE RELEASED after 14 months in captivity on
January 20th, 1981, the day Ronald Reagan was elected as president. Reagan
was all broad strategy and show, while detail would be taken care of by his
surrounding team. America suddenly became all about getting ahead. The
conservative backlash of the early Reagan years meant that money had to be
made, and wealth had to be displayed. Considering less than 15 years had
passed since our story began in earnest, by 1982, it was questionable
sometimes whether the 60s had ever actually happened at all.

'We have a twenty-year plan,' Bernard Edwards told Robin Katz of *Smash
Hits* in November 1979. 'We give it another five years or so as Chic. And then
eventually, we want to have our own production and publishing company.
Then we can help call the shots for younger and less experienced artists.' By
1982, Edwards' statement was looking sage-like. Rodgers and Edwards were
in pole position to capitalise on prudent investments and an enormous
publishing catalogue which meant that although commercially their star was
in the descendant, their catalogue was extremely bankable. The productions
of the past years had strengthened their hands, yet it was undeniable that they
were pulling apart. Thompson and Rodgers had formed into an intense party-
going outfit, while Edwards and his family, which numbered five children by
this point – Bernard Jr., Portia, Michael, Mark and David, preferred to
disappear from the limelight.

It had all been a whirlwind. With a frenetic gigging, writing and recording
schedule, the pressure began to take its toll. There was an increasing use of
substances to fuel the workload, and often lines would become blurred:
Edwards commented to *Melody Maker* in 1981 that 'I'm standing on stage
playing "Good Times" and I'm thinking about "Upside Down" or something,

y'know.'

However, the duo were feeling somewhat under appreciated. They had seen disco come and go and now, their smooth, urban dance music was finding it hard to locate within the mainstream radio formats. Perhaps it was because they had made money: a considerable amount: 'The other thing that burns me is the idea that a person can't make good music if he's finally made some good money,' Edwards told *Smash Hits* in late 1979. 'My money (Edwards and Rodgers are both millionaires now) doesn't impress me. Nile and I are the same two crazy hams we have always been. We still have a ball making music. We still got a lot of dreams and projects up our sleeves.'

At that time, people simply did not put the importance on producers that they do today: 'Back in the day the producers did not get any light. No matter whether my father and Nile were artists and they were in the limelight, as producers you were totally in the backseat,' ruminates Bernard Jr. 'Even if you had written the song, everyone looked at the artist ... it was a glamorous time. People wanted to see it – and it's a very visual thing – you can't see a producer make a track, so nowadays the producer can be everything – it doesn't matter – everybody is a star now.'

'I thought after *Real People* it was over,' Rob Sabino suggests. 'But I still called us Chic. I knew we were going to play together as a unit.' Before their solo production ventures got fully underway, there was still some unfinished Chic business. It was a time for tying up loose ends before branching out. Nominally, the Chic brand was still very much in existence, but it was not the same. 'The toughest thing in your life is when you're accustomed to putting out hits, and that stops happening,' Rodgers told *The Observer* in 2003. 'There came a time when I would go to the office and it would be like, oh man, not another platinum record. Then the whole "disco sucks" movement came along and the party ended. Once people said our music sucked before they'd even heard it, we didn't have a chance.' With confusion and egos flying sporadically out of hand, it was a wonder there were any Chic records made at all after *Real People*.

One of the first projects was to record an album with Fonzi Thornton. It was time for Thornton, their loyal backing vocalist, to receive a piece of the action: 'They recorded an album of eight or nine songs with me and we shopped the deal around,' Thornton recalls. 'When they shopped my demo around, nobody picked it up. Robert Wright, A&R at RCA, told me how much he loved it, but it simply had too huge a price tag and they weren't prepared to pay that amount of money!' The album was never released. None of the songs, apart from 'I Work For A Living' appeared anywhere. Thornton was disappointed, but remained sanguine. It wasn't that he was short of offers, and ten years into his career as a sought-after member of New York's musical support team, he knew that a solo deal would one day materialise. Thornton, fresh from the success of working with Roxy Music on *Avalon* went out on tour with them between August 1982 and March 1983, taking Michelle Cobbs with him.

Around this time, a very successful, if overlooked, moment in the Chic canon came with Rodgers, Edwards and Sabino's playing – complete with the concert mastering of Gene Orloff – on the track 'Together' on New York disco ensemble Odyssey's *Happy Together* album. Although a Linn drum is supplying the beat, Lillian Lopez' vocal is warm, intimate and passionate; similar to the way Kathy Sledge brought out the emotion in 'We Are Family', so does Lopez. Rodgers' Beatle-esque figures complete with Edwards' slippery-fingered bottom make for one of the most satisfying moments from the desultory early 80s.

✫✫✫

Faced with dwindling commercial success, Rodgers was increasingly defiant. 'I took the view that if everybody hates us, then just let them hate us. Just listen to those records at the end there. It wasn't as if they weren't inspired, it's not as if there are not pearls and gems in the middle of them. We wrote "Why" for Carly Simon amid all that chaos and we wrote "Soup For One."'

Chic had been approached to score a film project, written and directed by Jonathan Kaufer, who had written for the TV series *Holmes And Yo Yo*. *Soup For One* set out to be a contemporary adult rom-com set in Manhattan in the 80s, starring Saul Rubinek as Allen and Marcia Strassman as Maria. The slender plot involved a nice Jewish boy travelling to the Catskills with a friend in search of the perfect woman to marry. It even featured former Harold Melvin and the Bluenotes frontman, Teddy Pendergrass as a nightclub singer. With the tagline 'When you're looking for love, you find yourself doing some very funny things,' the film barely made a ripple at the box office. Veteran composer Johnny Mandel scored additional music for the film. Chic themselves made a cameo appearance in the film's nightclub sequence.

The contribution that Edwards and Rodgers made to the *Soup For One* soundtrack was artistically successful. It acted as a round-up of some of the odds and ends within their recent catalogue. 'Let's Go On Vacation' from the second Sister Sledge album, *Love Somebody Today*; Debbie Harry's 'Jump Jump' and 'I Want Your Love' were included. 'Dream Girl', which was written especially for Teddy Pendergrass was a fine approximation of early 80s Philly. 'I Work For A Living', from the aborted Fonzi Thornton album was included, which gave Thornton no end of pleasure: 'When that album came out, it had all of these stars on it, plus me!' The brief instrumental, a duo between Rodgers and Rob Sabino, 'Tavern On The Green', was deft and richly evocative of Led Zeppelin's pastoral side.

There were two significant new tracks on the album, which acted as the perfect commercial coda for Chic. They enjoyed a final slice of US chart action with the title track. 'Soup For One' reached No. 80 on the pop charts and No. 14 on the R&B charts. It was a somewhat jagged slice of funk that was to provide the basis for one of Europe's biggest chart successes of 2001, 'Lady' by French group, Modjo. 'Bernard ended up singing that one,' Rodgers told Barry Alfonso in 1999. 'The film was nothing like Chic. They were trying to mix styles, and we were there just because we were big. And I think at that point, we were too out of touch – we couldn't look at the film objectively and write for it. It has to be the Chic way or no way. But I'm actually glad we wrote that song – it's one of my favourites.'

Soup For One also gave them the chance to work with Carly Simon. The New York chanteuse was enjoying her tenth year as a top flight singer-songwriter. 'Why', with Edwards' bass at once stilted and fluid and its pop-reggae groove, actually showed the Chic sound developing, allowing Simon's childlike refrain of 'la di da di da' full space to breath. Lines like: 'You said our love was sacred, but you left me alone to make it' make 'Why' the last truly great Chic Organization production. The

session was full of laughs and showed the core team of Thompson, Rodgers, Edwards, Jones and Sabino working eye to eye. Ironically, the song never actually made it to the movie, and it flopped on release in the US. The response in Britain was much more positive, giving Simon her first UK Top 10 hit for five years, and remaining on the chart for 13 weeks.

The *Soup For One* project came to a close in Spring 1982; As Maxim Jakubowski stated in *The Rock Album*, it 'mixes both old material and newer stuff by the likes of Carly Simon, Fonzi Thornton and Teddy Pendergrass. All benefit from the Chic connection, while existing songs by Sister Sledge, Debbie Harry and Chic themselves polish off an attractive collection.' Atlantic turned the album down, unthinkable just two years previously. Jerry Greenberg, recently departed from the company stepped in to help. 'I had started my own label, Mirage,' Greenberg recalls. 'The Chic Organization had relocated and we shared an office in Connecticut for four years. Atlantic didn't want the *Soup For One* record, so I paid for that and put it out.' However, Greenberg's intervention was not to be as successful as it was in 1977. The album reached No. 168 on the US pop charts and No. 42 on the R&B chart.

In the late summer of 1982, Nile Rodgers had two meetings that were to change the course of the decade for him. He met, by chance, David Bowie at The Continental Nightclub in New York and he also encountered Duran Duran backstage at the final gig of their American tour in New Jersey supporting Blondie and David Johansson.

Birmingham-based Duran Duran had been major Chic fans from day one and had spent a considerable amount of time on their first American tour dropping their name in interviews. In fact, John Taylor, the group's bassist, saw Duran Duran from the beginning as a combination of Chic and The Sex Pistols. 'I was in a pub in 1979 and The Sex Pistols and Chic came on back to back on the jukebox. I remember saying "I love both of these records, why can't we fuse the two?", instead of them being so removed from each other. There was tremendous power and energy in both their records; power was almost exclusively synonymous with out-of-tune guitar players and fast drummers. Chic had tremendous energy and power but with refinement and sophistication. It was around the time I started playing bass. To that point I'd had no interest in playing bass – they were the quiet ones. I'd always been attracted to guitar players, they were like the sex symbols of the band. I thought I could be a guitar player, but everybody wanted to do that. Nile and Bernard were the model for us.'

Three years later, the groups met. 'Nile and Tony were there,' John Taylor recalls. 'They had worked with Debbie Harry by that point. Tony was the first guy we shook hands with – he introduced me to Nile. Within 20 minutes we were bonding in the bathroom over a line of Charlie. I was so excited to meet them, and they were pretty excited to meet us. In America at that point we were like a cool underground English band. Everywhere we had been we dropped their name, and they were aware of that. There was definitely an opposites attract thing. We went into Manhattan clubbing with the two of them. How great to be there with those two.' The two parties both registered the possibility to work together if the moment were to arise.

The remainder of 1982 found Chic gigging, Rodgers and Edwards working separately on material, and putting the finishing touches to that year's Chic record, *Tongue In Chic*. Between the album being recorded and its release, Chic began to dribble to a close. Raymond Jones became the next keyboard player to depart. In between Chic sessions and tours, he had begun working with Nona Hendryx, who had been singing in the recently-expanded 'T-Funk' line-up of Talking Heads. 'I heard that Bernie Worrell was leaving the group and they needed someone to replace him on a summer tour. David Byrne was hanging out with Peter Gabriel and they both came to see me gig with Nona,' Jones recalls. 'David decided he wanted me in their summer tour. I had called to let Nile and Bernard know I'd got myself this gig – I was concerned how it might reflect on our relationship.' Jones was reassured that this would be no problem, and that he would be reinstated to the payroll when the tour finished. 'When I got back, that wasn't what happened: I was told that they didn't need my services any more. It came as a complete and utter shock to me. I was not amused, because as a musician you have to forward plan how you are going to pay for things. And at that point I had a place; I think the car was paid for, but that was about it.'

Although he had shared many good times over the previous five years as their first-call live keyboardist, Jones was well aware of his situation: 'As much as I loved working with Chic, I knew I was a sideman. I knew my place; I'm not going to build a career being a side person in that sort of organisation – because there was definitely a glass ceiling. They were going to write everything, they were going to produce everything,' he adds. But there was little animosity. 'I learned how to write and produce through watching them. They were great instructors, not so much by sitting you down and teaching you, but letting you hang out and see what was going on and how to deal with artists like Ms Ross. How Bernard was with the singers with Luci and Alfa – which really helped me when I worked with Norma Jean later on.'

By the time of *Tongue In Chic*, released in November 1982, with its bright Day-Glo sleeve, the game for The Chic Organization Ltd. was almost over. Recorded at The Power Station throughout the year, it was mixed by Scott Litt, one of the new breed of Power Station engineers, who later would go on to make a name for himself with R.E.M. Jocelyn Brown once again added vocal support to all the regulars, as well as Dolette McDonald, who had recently sung with Talking Heads.

Tongue In Chic is the most successful late period Chic album and their best since *Risqué*. The Bernard-sung 'I Feel Your Love Coming On', with its synth-bass and drum machine is close to the sound James Williams was achieving with D-Train, complete with the gospel choir introduction. Edwards' voice, never the strongest, is clear and assured. Alfa Anderson's showcase 'When You Love Someone', is a two-in-one classic, a ballad that sweeps into an up-tempo dance chugger half way through.

'Chic (Everybody Say)' features the recently-departed Raymond Jones, rapping about the glory of Chic. 'When Robert Mugabe was running for office,' Rodgers laughs, 'he used to play that song from the campaign truck over the loudspeakers. There's a lyric that goes "everybody down in Zimbabwe talking bout president Moe-ga-be and Chic". This came right from his niece Sharon Mugabe!'. With the crowd noise, the record is an effective update of 'Chic Cheer'. It marked the return of the string section and a scorching guitar solo from Rodgers. Whatever was going on within the group, this is a full-on tribute to its early sound, complete with the rap, 'Luci, Alfa, Tony, Bernard and Nile, these are the five that are doing it in style, Chic'. 'Sharing Love' at a little under three minutes could do with being at least double the length; it's a sweet, tentative tune with vocals by Edwards, a hidden gem. 'City Lights' is a good example of urban groove from the early 80s.

The lead single from the album, 'Hangin'', was a bone fide classic. The intro rap between Thompson and Rodgers, although a little forced and clumsy, is a classic. It reinforces the social rapport the pair had; 'Tony's party pal was Nile,' John Taylor recalls. 'I love that beginning of "Hangin'" – "yo slick!, wassup" that's the two of them; It's fucking great! They must have had a lot of good times together.' The song, according to Ken Barnes, is 'hard edged, strip-mined funk.' Fronted by Edwards, it is full of the bounce and brio that only Chic could produce. The group were clearly out to gain a little of hip-hop's credibility. In the accompanying video – their first for the new MTV generation – Rodgers locates himself behind the wheels of steel, they all appear borderline farcical. This is simply not how Chic should behave. The single belatedly made the UK chart in March 1983, where it reached No. 64 for one week. It reached No. 48 on the US Black chart.

Doing the project few favours either was the garish oh-so-1982 sleeve. Because of the effects of the world recession, it seemed to become *de rigeur* for fashion to return to bright rainbow colours for everything. The front cover was an amusing critique on the rise of feminism in the early 80s, an issue that was always close to Rodgers and Edwards' hearts. A pink-tighted mini-skirted voluptuous female builder is sitting astride a bright orange girder. Wearing a hard hat, she is clearly making an innuendo to a passing Tony Thompson below. Thompson's laughing surprise is shown, as is his pink jacket, v-neck vest and slim tie. It's odd and not a little unsettling. But nothing quite prepares you for the reverse. The last time the world had seen a picture of Chic, it was on the cover of *Real People* in 1980, at the very apogee of their dinner-suited elegance.

The back sleeve of *Tongue In Chic* reveals the five dressed in a garish boiler/flying suit combination. Although entirely in context with its time, it smacked a little of desperation. And Rodgers' fixed, almost maniacal grin could not have been in greater contrast to the understated beauty of *Risqué* from less than three years previously. Moreover, both Martin and Anderson weren't the willow-slim girls of the early years, making the group from *C'est Chic* look almost unrecognisable; and in the middle of the picture, in his brown boiler suit, Bernard Edwards looks tired and otherworldly.

Tongue in Chic received slightly better reportage than *Take It Off*. Maxim Jakubowski stated in *The Rock Album* that the album was, 'Partly a return to form, but never fully recaptures the polished magic of a few years back. Impeccably arranged disco rhythms, with one sure fire classic, "Hangin'", with all the tantalising joy of past successes but the rest of the songs appear to be going through the motions. But what groovy motions!'

Billboard suggested that 'Chic's latest is far short of past creative and commercial peaks. Problem may lie with the apparent reluctance of Rodgers and Edwards to showcase the talents of vocalists Alfa Anderson and Luci Martin, except on "Hey Fool," a catchy, melodic tune that's the best cut on display, and "When You Love Someone," a mellow ballad. Instrumentation is faultless, of course, but the spark is missing, even on the first single, "Hangin.'" The Chic reputation will probably ensure reasonable sales activity, however.' But sales didn't follow; the album missed out on the UK charts entirely. It reached No. 173 on the US charts, a full 169 places lower than the peak of *C'est Chic* in 1979. 'Although they had a deeper effect on black music, in the pop music context, they sputtered out like a rocket, up there in the firmament,' Geoff Brown argues.

The problem within Chic, according to Rob Sabino, had become one of Rodgers' thirst for being at the cutting edge. 'The musicians, engineers and equipment merely became tools for Nile to work with,' he recalls. 'Nile has so many talents and he is a real nice guy, but he dropped the ball a little bit when he started taking on just a bit too much. Being the writer, the arranger, booking the musicians, doing all the production stuff and then playing all the stuff.' It was one thing taking all of this on, but when you have one of the most talented bands in the world at your disposal, it was somewhat worrying.

Sabino continues, 'He got a Synclavier and started having people programming drum machines instead of using Tony. In the end, it became like all that was wrong with disco, a producer's medium. He started interfering. Between 57 and 96th streets, there are 20 better pianists than I. I always need to think about what is best for the song. Nile had some not well-thought out plans.' The period became a muted and low-key end to the glories of the past four years. Thompson told Ian McCann in *Echoes* in 1985 that, 'Bernard didn't want to use drum machines, he wanted to stick to the old formula, and then Nile was kinda like going off, he had different ideas, and I'm in the middle of this sucker, and all this is going on. I could see it was all gonna blow up and fall apart. Unfortunately.'

'When some of the material was dying towards the end of Chic, that's because the time wasn't spent on it like it was on the first couple of albums,'

he continued. 'Nile and Bernard were writing separately, they never used to do that. I was seeing the break-up happen. They wouldn't write together at all. Nile's songs began to sound like his, Bernard had his own … it was a drag.'

Ahmet Ertegun, founder and chairman of Atlantic Records saw Edwards and Rodgers' potential as producers, together and apart. 'They were great producers. Nile is a great producer, and a terrific musician. They've certainly got incredible groove. They are among the great R&B producers of all time. The records they made have that timeless quality; they survive all changes in style. I think that they are the kind of records that people will be listening and dancing to 50 years from now. At the time they came out they were so on, so hip; they were right at the cutting edge, ahead of everything – unbelievable records. It's wonderful that the great records, the great music, every time you play it after a certain time elapses, it brings back the same excitement that it did on first hearing. That's only true of the great records that have special magic. Their records had that.'

Hip-hop, which had been moulded in the furnace of the partnership's bass lines, was now occupying a key space in people's minds. *Koo Koo* had been too angular, too strange, *Soup For One* had been too marginal. When Chic's popularity waned initially, they still had the strength of the Organization to hide behind; now joint production work had lost its appeal. The very facelessness of Chic did not translate to the new MTV Generation. The two needed a professional break.

19.
ADVENTURES IN THE SERIOUS MOONLIGHT

'When there's dissension between mom and dad and they are ready to divorce, the children in the family pretty much don't have a choice.'
LUCI MARTIN 2004

As 1982 progressed, both Rodgers and Edwards worked on solo albums. Immediately after recording *Tongue In Chic*, Edwards started *Glad To Be Here* and Rodgers began work on what was to become *Adventures in the Land of the Good Groove*. While recording the latter, Rodgers bumped in to one of his heroes.

David Bowie, who, after a decade, had established himself as the world's foremost art-pop superstar met Nile Rodgers completely by chance for the first time during the autumn of 1982 at an after-hours bar in New York called The Continental. Bowie had been dividing his time between New York and Switzerland since the late 70s. 'It was fast becoming my first choice city to live in,' Bowie recalls. 'I found it then, and still do, the most persuasive argument for polyculturalism. Though still pretty scary at night, it had so many rewards if you pushed the door open. Some instructive, some dangerous.' At the time, by his own admission, Rodgers was the 'completely wild, out-of-control drug addict who just loved the life and music, amazed that he's in the game.' Bowie, following his Berlin triptych and *Scary Monsters* art-noise attack, wanted to return to simpler times: he had been impressed by Chic's glacial disco noir and he felt that it was time once again to dust down his dancing shoes. Rodgers was also an ex-hippie who had been a major Bowie fan since *Hunky Dory*. Rodgers had even played with mutual friend Iggy Pop way back in February 1970, when New World Rising supported The Stooges at Unganos. What really impressed Bowie though, was that Rodgers had played on the recent album by Bill Laswell's avant-funk outfit, Material, 'I was very aware of Nile's work,' Bowie states, 'but ironically, it was the guitar playing and his involvement with Material that hooked me right into the idea of working with him. His willingness to work with what was considered an 'out there' outfit made me terribly enthusiastic to work with him.'

'We talked and then he sought me out for some time after that. We decided to meet in a neutral place, The Carlisle Hotel.' They discussed working together on what would become the most commercially significant calling card of Nile Rodgers' career; its success would sound the death-knell for Chic. Bowie wanted Rodgers to produce him and said 'Nile, I really want you to make hits.' Bowie had absorbed the New York sound and emerged with *Let's Dance*. In some respects, it was inevitable that Rodgers and Bowie would work together. The pair's obsession with the now has lead them down many paths and dead-ends over the years, but when it has struck gold, my has it struck. Pure and unadulterated.

What clinched the deal for Bowie was Rodgers' own recorded work, especially his first newly-finished solo album; 'I think that must have come from him meeting me that first night. Him feeling my spirit and energy – and then I played my solo record for him, which is what sealed the deal. I played him *Adventures In The Land Of The Good Groove*. I'll never forget it, he was in my apartment and he said to me after it had finished playing, "if you do for me a record half as good as that, I will be very happy." I was so blown away – it was like – *he thinks this shit is good?'*

Let's Dance was recorded at The Power Station in the first three weeks of December 1982. Although the material was slight, it delighted Bowie and its simple, pared-down, straightforward groove alerted Rodgers to the possibilities of the world outside Chic.

This meant that Bowie's old friend and producer for his last four albums, Tony Visconti, was off the case. 'I was shocked. I was meant to take a flight from London to New York to do what was to become *Let's Dance*,' he recalls. 'There was a kind of a silence from the Bowie camp. Someone eventually called my secretary and said that David was already in the studio with Nile. I was hurt on two levels – one, that I was cancelled at the very last minute by my good buddy – and he never did phone me and speak to me directly and the other thing was I had quickly to fill a two month period, which I set aside for him. There is nothing etched in stone that you always have to work with the same producer. It hurt that he didn't cancel me himself. Nile was so big in those days, he's had those big songs, a big success story and I think David must have been slightly in awe of him and feeling very privileged to work with him. To work with David Bowie, it liberated Nile; it gave him an opportunity to stretch out, too.' Bowie was too busy constructing his new American dream to care.

Given that disco was, by now, supposed to suck big time, Bowie was asking a black man heavily associated with the movement to produce him. Whereas today a second thought would not be given to such issues, in 1982 it was a very big deal. 'There was an underlying tone of racism,' Rodgers believes. 'David told me how many times people said to him *"you mean you are going to do an album with a disco producer?"* To me "disco" is another word for black or lesbian or Martian or something. So, I thought it was cool because Ziggy was a spider from Mars.'

'When we sat around talking about the people of the past, David's list of people he loves are almost unanimously R&B people,' continues Rodgers. 'And English musicians of a certain age group grew up with the blues and Little Richard. There are a lot of black American artists who don't even know who Little Richard is.' Bowie would need a new team to make this recording possible; his usual studio band, like Visconti, were out.

Whereas Bowie had originally hoped that the Philadelphia International Records house band, MFSB, would be his players on 1975's *Young Americans*, this time he successfully ensnared the remnants of the 80s equivalent – Chic. Rodgers was joined by Rob Sabino and, guesting on 'Without You', Edwards on the bass. Although Omar Hakim was the first call drummer for the sessions, Tony Thompson was drafted in later in the project: 'I used Tony on "Cat People" as it needed a whole different thing,' Rodgers recalls. 'When he played it, he was hitting the snare so loud; the volume in the studio was making the lights dim with every hit. And David said "wow, why didn't you call him before?" David is like anybody else, he responded to the showbusiness of it all. I'd never seen it before, but it was certainly theatrical.'

The song that clinched the whole project was the swaggering groove of the title track. Bowie presented it to Rodgers as an acoustic number: 'It wasn't a ballad, but it didn't have a groove,' Rodgers recalls. 'If I play a folk song, it's going to be a folk song; you can tell by the way I play it. When he played it for me, I didn't think of it as a dance record. And I certainly didn't think of it as an R&B record. Because he gave me the latitude and freedom and respect to interpret what he played for me, which was what was fantastic and that's when I really shine.' Bowie also updated 'China Girl' which he had written with Iggy Pop back in Berlin, and 'Modern Love' was a tremendous hark-back to Bowie's R&B roots.

Rodgers is still impressed by the freedom Bowie gave him. 'This is a guy who took his own money, went out and found a producer, let the producer hire the band and basically sort of do what a film director does – hire all the people, have them read the script, then do the shot blocking, the location scouting; I did everything – I said, "hey, we are going to record at this studio, with these people, this engineer": they were all complete strangers to him. His ideas – such as bringing in guitarist Stevie Ray Vaughan – were phenomenal. It was like the moment when Bernard and I finished "Dance Dance Dance" and he said "man, it's almost happening, something is missing" and I went "Yowsah, Yowsah, Yowsah." There you go – record done. Bowie added so much to the mix. Which shows a lot about him – I mean, wow, how do you trust this new guy?' Bowie recalls with great affection Rodgers' reaction to the Texan guitar maverick: 'I'll never forget the expression on Nile's face when I brought Stevie Ray in as our guitar player, and then his look of disbelief changing through one hundred expressions to ecstasy when Stevie started playing.'

There was also no doubting how important the American market was to him, certainly as Bowie was now freed from his restrictive MainMan deal with former manager Tony deFries and the RCA contract. And the first thing he would deliver to his new company was exactly what he'd denied his old company, RCA, for so long – a soulful album like *Young Americans*. On 21st January 1983, the deal with EMI America was signed, a five year contract for five albums, for a reported $10 million. With a shimmering pop-dance album in the bag, some obvious singles, two films (*The Hunger* and *Merry Christmas, Mr Lawrence*) and a world tour, David Bowie was about to become bigger than ever. It fitted in perfectly with his new lifestyle: an album in 19 days, films taking a bit longer.

The single, 'Let's Dance', was released in March, with the album following on 9th April in the UK. With its shadow-boxing cover but no perceived search for the truth in the groove, it was a very smart album. The robust title track was an instant classic and was on every turntable that spring. At a time when most sides sounded like the demo button of a Casio in an electrical retailer, this was old-fashioned, wide-screen R&B.

Bowie later explained to Visconti that he had wanted that 'economical New York sound'. 'Nile would use few instruments, but make them sound really important. If you listen to Chic records, the drums and bass were great and he had the funky guitar and the backing vocals and there was little else. David wanted that kind of sparse economical sound that Nile could do which was really opposite to the way David and I work, so he was absolutely right to choose Nile for that because I most likely wouldn't have done that.'

It has been said that Bowie wanted to relax on the sofa while Rodgers made the album. This is true to a point, but Bowie was certainly involved in every aspect of the record. 'What that felt like to me was not that he wasn't interested in his record or anything like that; it was an extreme feeling of comfort and confidence,' Rodgers states. 'He wanted me to do the record with my people, what I do. Maybe he knew that if he was sitting in that room, he might start sticking his nose in where he shouldn't. That could just be incredible self-awareness.' Simplicity was the order of the day. 'I could have played a lot more on *Let's Dance*,' Rob Sabino adds, 'but I talked Bowie out of it. He was a lovely guy.'

Bowie's actions were a triumph for commerce. The music scene, which Bowie had been a part of in the 60s had graduated to be the music business in the late 70s and became the music industry in the 80s. Instead of churning out new product to generate revenue, existing material could be fully exploited. Why record new material and incur further studio costs when one album could have as many as six singles taken off it. It wasn't the first time his albums had been filleted for singles, but then again, as *Let's Dance* only contained eight tracks, to have five tracks out as singles only left 'Criminal World', 'Ricochet' and 'Without You' to entice fans to buy the album.

With some extremely cold records behind him, Bowie's hot albums always split the audience; *Let's Dance* was loved by the public, viewed with disdain by the literati. *The Face* was immediately dismissive of the work: 'None of the icy, sour, sidelong glances at his own career that characterised 1980's *Scary Monsters*. The sarcasm of 'Fashion' and the bitter taste of 'Ashes To Ashes' have come round to *Let's Dance*, a shrug and a grimace.' Nile Rodgers dismisses the critics: 'If politically it were seen at the time the same way people were experiencing it in their hearts – everybody's career would be different – after Chic couldn't get arrested, I fundamentally could do the same type of music with someone else. I could do it with a white artist; I could do *Let's Dance* with David Bowie. Some people consider that album as blasphemous when compared to David's career; they don't think of it in the same way as *Scary Monsters* or even *Young Americans* which was a precursor to what we did. Why do they look at *Young Americans* in a more artistic way than *Let's Dance* which is viewed as a commercial sell-out?

'But put the two records together and listen to them artistically, pound for pound – *Let's Dance* is fucking avant-garde for a pop record. If you just take the track "Let's Dance" – the 12" with the whole duel, the trading of fours between the pocket trumpet and the saxophone – that ultimately became a pop record. If you listen to that and compare it to the Go-Gos, it's like, what planet are you on? To me, that is high art! That's taking something that was meant for very sophisticated ears and being able to give it to the consumer. It's like taking a person who normally wouldn't eat foie gras and make a dish that would be so tasteful to them that only afterwards could they say – you're kidding – that was foie gras? Instead of it being looked upon as something really amazing, it was like "sell out". Listen to "Ricochet" – that record is no joke. People treat it like "Funky Town."' However, it introduced Bowie to a whole new audience. 'Most people never bought a David Bowie record before or since they bought *Let's Dance*, because he was this weird drag artist,' Rodgers continues. 'This was able to sell Bowie to people who would *never* buy his records.'

'Rodgers did make Bowie appeal to a whole new audience,' American Studies professor Dr Mary Ellison explains. 'I remember loads of people who'd never loved Bowie, who then went back and investigated his previous work because Rodgers made him palatable to a massive group of new listeners.' The album became a statistician's dream, topping charts the world over. As in Britain before it, On May 21st 1983, David Bowie reached No. 1 in America with the single, 'Let's Dance'. The last time he'd been there, it was with 'Fame'. From *Young Americans*.

The attendant tour was even more successful – the year was cleared for performance and perform he did: The Serious Moonlight Tour ran from 18th May to 8th December 1983: 98 concerts; 2.5 million fans; four continents. Within 24 hours of the UK dates being announced – London's Wembley Arena (June 2-4) and Birmingham NEC (5-6) – over 120,000 applications had been received, and that in itself is a record.

Rob Sabino was asked to be in the touring band: 'I was offered to tour with him and at the same time I got an offer from Simon and Garfunkel. And they paid four times as much – it was an easy decision.' One person who really wanted the gig was Tony Thompson. Although his friend and long-term Chic associate Hakim had played on the majority of the album, Thompson needed to fill the void left by the winding-down of Chic. 'I remember like it was yesterday, hearing David say that he hadn't chosen a drummer,' Karen Milne stated. 'I remember feeling angry, but not surprised, that Nile did not immediately tell David that Tony would be perfect for the gig. Tony was reluctant to approach Bowie. Then Tony, completely nervous on the inside, but confident on the outside, said, "I'm available if you're looking for a drummer … completely available." I vaguely remember David saying that he thought Tony would be involved with other projects. There were other projects, but nothing more important to Tony than touring with Bowie.' Thompson was in. The band also included long term Chic ally Carmine Rojas on bass, Carlos Alomar on guitar and from Sabino's old band, Frank and George Simms on backing vocals.

The shows presented all the classics, in an audience-friendly singalong, complete with a huge inflatable moon that showered stars at the crowd during the climactic version of 'Modern Love'. With his hair piled high and his braces and tie, Bowie resembled a 1930s haberdasher. In the same way Tony Blair and George Bush now make a point of taking their jackets off to mean business, Bowie looked like he'd come out of a boardroom where he'd just clinched the deal. It was a pure spectacle, part soul review, part rock out. In America, *Let's Dance* went platinum in 1983. To give it context, it was the same year that 1973's *Aladdin Sane* finally went gold. Momentarily, Bowie had both artistic success and commercial credibility, playing a very particular sort of David Bowie for the world's mainstream.

One year of work had made Bowie finally *really* rich. All the books, articles and updates that were written at this time of unparalleled activity painted *Let's Dance* as a glorious comeback, payback and grand finale. Rodgers, a life-long fan states, 'I look at the world of rock and roll as before *Let's Dance* and after *Let's Dance*. Two different worlds: the ripple effect it had on the world rock community was phenomenal.'

However, Rodgers still felt somewhat marginalised by the white art-rock community by whom he so wished to be accepted: 'I've never felt more like a producer and appreciated than I was on David Bowie's *Let's Dance*, but I was really pissed off when it came out,' Rodgers states. 'It's still the most commercially successful album of David Bowie's career – and when it came out, he did this huge interview with *Time* Magazine and all he could talk about was Brian Eno, Iggy Pop and all these rock people. He was almost embarrassed to talk about the "disco producer". He gets tremendous success from this dance guy – and he just wants everyone to know how rock he is, how important he is, how precious and arty he is. That really broke my heart – I though *I* was precious and arty. He asked me to do the big pop record.

He could say "I got Nile, who's really precious and arty to do this dance record because I wanted a pop hit." But if David Bowie does a pop record, it is *still* seen as precious and arty. He's such a charismatic, powerful artist, that when he says something, we all take notice and he could have been the ambassador for Nile Rodgers to the world. Nowadays he will say that's a Nile record with David thrown in, but when I needed him to mention it – he didn't.'

Although it has subsequently been dismissed by critics and Bowie alike, *Let's Dance* and Bowie's new persona at that time felt like the simplest, happiest rush there had ever been in wide screen, superstar pop; it was a bright sunrise after the long shadow cast by John Lennon's death. Even Bowie's hairdo screamed sunlight at you. One of the most famous slogans to emerge in the post-punk era was 'Fuck Art ... Let's Dance.' Bowie appeared to have taken this advice to heart. 'There was the ultimate excitement of realising we were creating a new vital form', Bowie recalls. 'No-one had hybridised the blues, British art rock and dance the way we were doing it.'

The straightforward grace of the album and its R&B influences harked back to a simpler time. And Nile Rodgers had helped mastermind it all.

While the world continued to turn at high speed for Rodgers, Edwards, who was feeling somewhat left out, continued work on the only project which bore his sole name: *Glad To Be Here*, which trickled out on Atlantic in 1983. Although Rodgers is featured on several of the album's tracks, Edwards called up one of his oldest musical friends, Eddie Martinez to be his principal guitarist. 'I really worked with Bernard in earnest on his first solo album, *Glad To Be Here*,' Martinez says. 'I 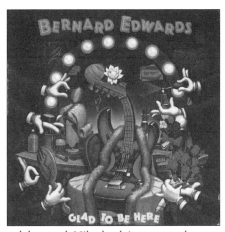 remember going down to the studio and he and Nile had just parted ways and they were both working on their own things. I worked with Bernard and one track became several.' From this moment on, Martinez, Rodgers' oldest musical friend, was to be Edwards first call guitarist. 'Bernard was remarkable – I worked with him on many records,' Martinez continues. 'He had such huge ears. His approach to the bass was so genius in terms of feel, vibe and technique, but most importantly, his pocket, in terms of where he sat in the track. It was great.'

The album contains 'Don't Do Me Wrong', arguably one of the greatest Chic ballads, showcasing the emotive tones of Jocelyn Brown over Martin and

Anderson's choral intonations. The duet with Brown and Edwards on 'You Really Got A Hold On Me', against an arrangement by Luther Vandross, marks his first appearance on a Chic-related album since *We Are Family*. There are banks of vocalists throughout – as well as Alfa, Luci, Fonzi, Michelle and Dolette; upcoming session players Curtis King, Philip Ballou and Brenda Joy Nelson, all compensate for Edwards' frail voice.

'There was nothing on there to grab and hold as far as the mainstream was concerned,' Bernard Edwards Jr recalls. 'It was really my dad doing my dad – you know "Glad To Be Here" and "You Really Got A Hold On Me" – that was a great cover tune. Not a lot of people looked at dad as a singer. I love it when people say he was one of the greatest bass players in the world – that's an honour – but when you do something like that and you are stuck in that niche – people don't look at the other things that you can do.'

In a sleeve designed by commercial artist Roger Huyssen, *Glad To Be Here* was an untroubling, upbeat affair. Edwards appeared simply still glad to be around and doing his thing. To emphasise his lack of ego, the cartoon sleeve illustrated his bass sitting in the chair, being pampered. Edwards was nowhere to be seen. And when he was seen on the back sleeve, he was looking away, smiling, in his sweater, a direct contrast to Rodgers on the back sleeve of *Adventures In The Land Of The Good Groove*, where he is sitting, smouldering, in a leather jumpsuit, slashed to the waist, looking straight to camera, with his legs as far apart as possible.

Glad To Be Here had an old-school feel, sounding more like a Chic record than Rodgers' all sweeties-out-of-the-box *Adventures In The Land Of The Good Groove*. The two albums perfectly encapsulated the differences between the two men. Rodgers was running as far as possible from the Chic sound, while Edwards was bathing in it. Not in an entirely reactionary manner; there were developments and nuances to the groove. 'Hard Loving Man' has a great swagger to it. In case any of his dwindling audience had forgotten, the album, as the sleeve suggested, was a showcase for the Edwards' bass. On 'You Don't Know Me', it is incredible; popping yet understated. It sounds like FM jazz with balls.

The album was organic. Edwards explained pointedly to Gene Santoro in 1985: "I like playing with *people*. I don't like to sit around and play with machines all day. The human aspect of the music can get lost. Y'know, you look over at the drummer smiling or the piano player: they're just grooving on each other. When you feel that way on tape, people can tell." The difference in the approach of Rodgers and Edwards was now marked. While Rodgers was embracing new technology, Edwards was sticking with the real thing. Edwards continued: "It's one of the problems with all the techno toys: what we're getting is a lot of records that have perfect time, no fluctuations in tempo, everything's perfect because all the machines are locked in. You can't go off tempo a little – it's sterile. What I hear on the radio … is a lot of ways to make money." It was as if Edwards, the younger of the two, was the reactionary parent, while Rodgers was still the experimental teenager, flipping from idea to idea.

Glad To Be Here would be Edwards' only solo record. He was not a man who liked to stand in the spotlight.

'He knew he couldn't sing! ' Bernard Jr says. 'He wanted to try it. He would tell you to your face that he wasn't a singer – but he tried it – it was definitely artistic expression at its best.'

For his first solo album, *Adventures in The Land Of The Good Groove*, Rodgers wrote all the songs at home, playing everything himself. When he got to the studio, his idea was to replicate that sparse, almost minimalist feel. Using different musicians on every cut, including Edwards, Thompson, Sabino and Rachel Sweet, the record was released in February 1983. 'My album was weird – it was the anti-Chic record,' Rodgers said. Whereas Edwards' album came with little

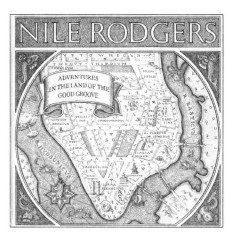

expectation, Rodgers' was loaded with hope.

Rodgers had signed a solo deal with Jerry Greenberg at Mirage. Recorded across 1982, *Adventures In The Land Of The Good Groove* is actually an exceptional album, full of the direction and focus that had been missing from the recent Chic albums. 'My Love Song For You' was a duet with his old crush from Labelle, Sarah Dash. ('When I was younger, I was head over heels in love with her – to me that was god's perfect woman. Sexy and nice.') The result is one of the most poignant and simple ballads on any Chic-associated record; 'It's All In Your Hands' and 'Most Down' are brisk, modern grooves, and the title track with its springy drum box is a triumph.

The lead single in America, 'Yum Yum', an update of the old playground sex song caused consternation and was actually banned by several black stations. The track particularly impressed David Bowie: 'Bowie gave me an award one night,' Rodgers recalls. 'He said this is for Nile Rodgers – the man who wrote "Poon Tang Poon Tang, where you want it, slept all night with my hands on it, give me some of that yum yum before I sleep tonight."' The subject material – about having sex – stirred a debate in *Billboard* magazine in March 1983. The record was blacklisted by Black radio; something that Rodgers felt was inversely racist: 'Can these programmers really deny the existence of black street life? Can they really pretend that most black people in America grow up with a 1950s suburban value system and live in the world of Mary Poppins? Without exception, the white critics and the white press have supported me 100% on this solo album. This is a good record which deserves to be heard. And my question to the programmers who have turned against me is: why am I being betrayed by the very people who should be the first to support me as I have always supported them?'

Rodgers was alarmed by how *Let's Dance*, embraced as a white record, took off while his album, *Adventures In The Land Of The Good Groove*, vanished without trace. Racism was more prevalent than ever in the American music industry, but this was a moment when Rodgers seemed to be unsupported by both African-Americans and whites.

The first two solo efforts by the principals of Chic were, altogether, something of a disappointment. They failed to connect with an audience, yet Rodgers had shown there was still an appetite for the sound he could create. It would just have to be with other artists. 'I was never really convinced by their solo stuff,' states critic Geoff Brown. 'For me, the sum of their parts was much, much greater than their individual efforts.'

With the success of *Let's Dance*, Nile Rodgers' production skills were in great demand. Offers came from Australian group INXS, Southside Johnny And The Asbury Jukes, and Kim Carnes. Rodgers, Edwards and Sabino also did some session work with Paul Simon for his *Hearts and Bones* album. Sabino went to work with Simon permanently.

Just over a decade after Edwards told Rodgers to lose his number, the two men were finally to part. Chic were over. We tend to think of groups splitting along the The Beatles' model – four friends growing apart and then drawing a line and going their separate ways. Because of the studio collective nature of Chic, there was, by this time, no clean break as such. There was nothing really to break from.

'There was friction in the group at the end,' says Rob Sabino, 'because there was a problem with Nile and Bernard and that affected the whole group.'

The resentment between Rodgers and Edwards was exacerbated by the success of *Let's Dance*, even though Edwards played on the album. Over the next year the two would barely speak. Edwards told Gene Santoro in 1985, 'That was the first time our two names were separated. After that people asked me "so what do you do?" "Well, uh, I just play the bass, write the songs, arrange them, produce the records" – but I didn't do Bowie, I'm sorry. In America, you know, the success of Bowie and the success of Chic are two different things. It overshadowed everything we did because Bowie was white. That destroyed the group, basically, because from then on, it wasn't equal anymore, it was this one guy pushed into the spotlight. It changed everything, but it's funny: the reason Bowie was interested in Nile to begin with was the success of Nile, myself and Chic.'

'When success comes in, it gets very confusing – there starts to be a lot of other people around that can be telling one person one thing and the other person the other thing,' suggests Fonzi Thornton. 'Those guys were best friends – maybe they, even musically, had different things that they wanted to do. Nile would try one thing and Bernard would want to try something else. Both of them were so talented. I never saw their friendship get strange, it never happened like that – I think maybe business-wise they needed to move on so ultimately they could come back to each other, which is what they did.'

'I guess they fell out,' Bryan Ferry states. 'Things happen – maybe they'd felt they'd done enough together – they then wanted to work with other people, and then they both went and produced.'

'I think they just got on each other's nerves at one point and they needed a break,' Raymond Jones adds.

So Rodgers and Edwards went their separate ways. Except, they didn't really. Not ever. 'They were like brothers. They loved each other, they loved to hate each other,' Edwards Jr recalls. 'They were competitive. Everything that happens between me and my brother Michael would happen between my father and Nile – that's how close they were. It was all fairly good natured. There was never a time when they hated each other and didn't deal with each other; they were just competitive. When they both started doing their different productions and things they still kept in contact. No matter how they felt – if they were upset with each other, having a little hissy fit, they still knew that together they worked well – that's one of the teachings I learned – just to make the hit – make the timeless song.'

Even though the demise had been on the cards for some time, it came as a shock to the rest of the group. Alfa Anderson is still bemused about why the group finally finished: 'It didn't end well for me,' she says. 'I wish it had. I really don't know what happened between Nile and Bernard. I know that all of a sudden – we all know that it can never be *all* of a sudden – it was over. I was shocked. I was left with emptiness. No matter what had happened between us as a group; I loved making music with them and that was the thing we did extremely well, together. It's the elements of that particular group of personnel that brought so much energy; whatever it was that we brought to the table seemed to work in that mix. When it was no longer there, I was deeply saddened.'

Anderson's sadness was compounded by the manner in which the information was delivered to her: a letter through the post. 'I was never even told why. Not even a conversation or discussion. There has always been that question mark for me. And that was sad. That made me very sad.'

'When there's dissension between mom and dad and they are ready to divorce, the children in the family pretty much don't have a choice,' Luci Martin sighs. 'We were working doing regular things, social events – then, all of a sudden, they say, right that's it, we're splitting up. We were really dumbfounded that Nile and Bernard had got to that point where they didn't even want to speak to each other. It was pretty shocking. We were a family and we were a group, it wasn't Nile's group or Bernard's group – we had invested all of ourselves; everything had been built round making this group work. It was hurtful to receive the news as if you were simply an employee. We were really truly blindsided. People argue and have creative differences, but to go to that point so abruptly without any warning was very shocking.' A letter seemed somehow appropriate for a group who once wore business suits and became an Organization. The management were dissolving the business and issuing the P45s.

The split hit Tony Thompson the hardest. 'As time went on,' he said, 'it was unfortunate to see the change in everybody and then finding out exactly what my place was. I thought we still had a lot of life left, we still had that musical ability to create when we were together, but everyone was thinking different, especially Nile. He didn't want to be in the band anymore; he wanted to be a solo artist – his ego was too large for me.'

'I was out of work. A lot of people kind of thought, "This guy's worth using," and they said, "wish I could've got you for my album,"' Thompson told Ian McCann in 1985. 'I was there, but everyone assumed I was too busy. And I was out of work. I was still on salary, and still with Chic in some capacity. But they weren't doing much, they weren't even talking, I don't think. When Nile and Bernard told me they were going to dissolve the company, this was after the Bowie album. I heard that Bowie was putting the band together; I just asked him if he needed a drummer. It was as simple as that. I got the gig.'

'Tony felt a little frozen out,' Eddie Martinez recalls. 'Between those three guys it was like a love-hate, love-hate type thing. There was an ebb and flow to all of it.' 'It became a case of Nile knowing exactly how everything should sound. It happened to Tony – other drummers would come in or people programming drum machines,' Sabino recalls. 'Tony was upset. I'm not knocking drum machines – Nile should not have depended on them for the creative part. If you wanted something that was drum machine-like, fine, come up with all these ideas and discuss it and then suggest that it should be a drum machine. At least you can have a collaborative creative process. Lennon and McCartney would work things out between them.'

The benefits of the association with the group worked well for certain key players: Fonzi Thornton finally got the deal he had patiently waited for with RCA, where he was to cut a couple of albums. Robert Wright, who Edwards and Rodgers shopped Thornton's unreleased solo album to the previous year, signed Thornton. He benefited from the Chic period, after constantly showcasing him on the final tours, with his solo spot drawing more and more applause, 'Record people were paying more and more attention, so my deal finally came through them,' he says.

Alfa Anderson went on to sing with Luther Vandross on his most commercially successful albums. Luci Martin did session work and then took a nursing qualification. As for Thompson, although work was available, his lack of self-confidence meant he felt cut adrift. 'There was acrimony between Tony and Nile,' John Taylor recalled. 'Tony felt let down; I think Tony missed being in a band where he could be on the cover.' However, John Taylor and Duran Duran had met up again with Thompson at the David Bowie show in Frejus in the South of France in May 1983. They talked about working on a project together. Thompson felt that something would surely come out of that.

There was one last piece of joint business; the final Chic album, *Believer*, which was released in late 1983. Considering it came at the end of such a tumultuous year, which had seen the Bowie album scale the heights, the relative failure of their solo work and their final split, it was actually quite a vibrant record. With its sleeve designed by Japanese illustrator, Pater Sato, it was about as far from the suits of 1977 as possible. Chic had fully embraced the new era of informality.

Although the songs were little more than vocoder-saturated repetitive grooves with Alfa, Luci and Fonzi supported by Brenda White and Curtis King, the record did put the emphasis back on the female leads. With Raymond Jones gone, it was actually the closest the Big Apple Band came to being on record; all music was handled by Edwards, Rodgers, Sabino and Thompson.

'Music was changing, and what people were looking for (in music) started to change,' Thornton recalls. 'I think the last album was a really good record, but the way it was received and the way that it was promoted was poor. There had been a shift in the music and what people were listening to. The fans moved on. Nile and Bernard's opportunity to put their music over changed based on what record companies were doing – and there was a lot of good music on that album.' The album was underpromoted and disappeared under 1983's welter of Chic-related releases.

'There are a lot of real gems on *Believer*,'' Rodgers offers, and, on one level, it's hard not to disagree. Sabino's synths dominate. 'You Are Beautiful' is a fantastic track, repeating the title phrase over and over again. There is an undercurrent of the need for reconciliation in the words –

'Love could be so tender
Don't you know?
Like it was, remember, long ago.
My cards are on the table, at a glance –
Unlike Clark Gable
(Frankly my dear) – I give a damn.'

With the nasally-treated Gable impersonation, we are taken right back to their very first record, where Kenny Lehman pinched his nostrils and intoned 'Yowsah Yowsah Yowsah'.

Still the album felt like an end. The title track was bright, if a little laboured; writ large by the line,

> *'You must go on with the show even when you're running on empty –*
> *That's just how it goes.'*

'Show Me Your Light' was a synthesised masterpiece, with complex, interlocking vocal arrangements and Rodgers' lead chasing the fade; 'You Got Some Love For Me' is anaemic, not unlike a *Sesame Street* ditty – and then 'In Love With Music' is an incredibly mellow follow-up to 'Lost In Music'; Anderson sings passionately about being in love with music and never wanting to lose it. Although the ever-present drum machine is clattering; the fabulous vocal arrangements sing through the reintroduction of Edwards' bass. It evokes the happy brightness of 'Thinking Of You'. If the album had ended there, it would have been fitting closure for the first, classic stage of Chic. Anderson, who was now working as a singer and dancer with Luther Vandross, recalls: 'I actually have great memories of that record. I remember feeling hopeful about the project. I didn't realise that the group was on such shaky ground at that time because I was on tour with Luther. I was just about to really stretch out as a lead vocalist when the bottom fell out. Yes, it was still a group project. But I felt that some of the songs were written with me and my voice in mind. That was gratifying.'

However 'Party Everybody', the final track on the final original Chic record, subtly undermines all the good work done on the rest of the album. The tired rap is not unlike your dad doing his party piece. By now, we were all fully aware that hip-hop had happened. With the drum machine noise that defined every single record of the eighties and a pointless guitar solo, this track more than any other signified that Chic had gone past their sell-by date. What they had that was so fresh, classic and original a few years previously had been spread too thinly; there were bigger fish to fry for some of the participators and boy, did the remaining audience know it. Wheras Chic had created timeless records by instinctively doing what they felt was right, aiming for texture and blankness; by playing every production trick in the book, this record is made to sound obsolete. As, in fact, it did by the time most people heard it in 1984.

It marked the end of the line in this instance for Chic – *Rolling Stone* called it 'slightly wan and over-synthesised'. *Playboy* suggested: 'Now that Nile Rodgers and Bernard Edwards are working day jobs, cutting first-rate solo LPs and producing other artists, their contributions to the mothership are beginning to falter. Try as we may, it's hard to believe in as average a record as *Believer* or in the band's long-term future...' *Believer* failed to chart on either side of the Atlantic.

And so, quietly and somewhat frustratingly, Chic sputtered out. It would take another decade before people began to realise just what it was that they had lost. The last great rhythm section was gone. Although they would work together on one more album, after that they would not play together on record ever again. Chic. The radicalism put through the reactionary filter. Rodgers and Edwards' ying and yang. It had all gone, in the programme of a drum machine, in a cloud of white. Not that it mattered at this point. The band that used to share that sandwich while rehearsing at Brandice High would go on to prove themselves over and over again.

The financial dissolution of the Chic Organization happened quietly and quickly. The Chic Organization liquidated when Chic disbanded in 1983. It was time to pursue life outside. Edwards had some session work lined up, including a project that Rodgers wanted him to work on – the second album by a relatively new artist called Madonna.

20.
ON YOUR LADDER, I'LL BE YOUR PEG

*'In the little piece of time that Chic were not together, Bernard and Nile
were moving into different areas. I was working with Nile on a bunch
of his projects and working with Bernard on a bunch of his projects.
The difference between them was not so much in the way that they heard,
but Nile had such a free spirit about the rock thing – he was always
reaching for that rock-pop success – as was Bernard, but they just
had two different approaches.'*
FONZI THORNTON 2004

EVERYTHING HAD CHANGED. The Reagan era slid back into a temporary
Cold War paranoia. All the talk was of the Strategic Defence Initiative ('Star
Wars') programme: technology that could intercept enemy missiles. With a
popularity rating of around 50%, Reagan made it clear he would be standing
for a second term. A succession of Russian leaders passed and, in Mikhail
Gorbachev, there seemed to be a man with whom the West could do
business. The early cases of AIDS had been diagnosed in 1981. Now more
than 270,000 Americans had died of the disease. The 'Make Love Not War'
message had turned into one of 'Safe Sex'. There seemed to be less fun
around.

Music, too, had changed. Of the artists who shared the disco spotlight with
Chic, many were in a similar predicament. Donna Summer had found
Christianity and was making wholesome pop confections for a dwindling
audience; The Village People seemed like a novelty act from a distant era;
Blondie had long split; Grace Jones had become an increasingly grotesque
caricature. John Travolta was rapidly heading for the 'where are they now?'
file. Against this backdrop, two artists had flourished. Prince, who had
enjoyed his first major success with 'I Wanna Be Your Lover' in 1979, topping
the R&B charts, had developed a Hendrix/funk hybrid and was to exploit his
charisma perfectly in his debut motion picture, *Purple Rain*. Michael Jackson,
who had released *Off The Wall* contemporaneously with Chic's *Risqué* in
1979, was bigger than ever, still milking the *Thriller* album released in late

231

1982, for hit singles. However, another artist was about to reach commercial fruition, successfully synthesising all the music that they had heard growing up in Detroit and New York. This artist took Chic's smart disco; the style and glamour of Studio 54 and the prevailing Reaganomic attitude and put it all through a punk filter. Madonna Louise Ciccone had enjoyed some success with her debut album in 1983. Her second album, produced by Nile Rodgers, was to change the face of pop in the 1980s.

Madonna was to become an iconic American superstar, who, after two decades, is now one of entertainment's untouchables. A metaphor for the American Dream, her actions have frequently become international news. And for one period in the 80s, it was virtually impossible for her to do anything without it being slavishly reported in the world's media. Conflating her personal politics to the global stage, she is the ultimate proof of how hard work, luck and an ear for the now can be commodified and marketed to the widest possible audience. However, when Rodgers was asked to produce her in late 1983, she was another dance artist who had enjoyed moderate success after years on the New York club scene.

Madonna was the end product of the politics of disco; she had absorbed the freedoms that had been granted, and worried later about the meaning. She had taken everything in and begun to mass-market it. Her years of hanging round studios, mixing freely between African-American, Hispanic and gay scenes, dancing and singing, while stealthily pursuing and building her career, meant that she was almost entirely free of the prejudice that had been rife within the music industry. But she did not suffer fools gladly. With a completely focussed drive, she was going to make it. She told American television that her aim was to rule the world, and later told *The Face* magazine in 1985 that she'd been misrepresented. What she really wanted to do was 'stand next to God'.

Madonna's second album was finished in early 1984, with plans for a summer release, when her debut album, released to little fanfare in August 1983, started to explode across the world on the back of singles 'Lucky Star', 'Holiday' and 'Borderline'. Rodgers received a call from Warner Brothers asking him for advice about delaying the album. 'I said, "do you want to know the truth?"' Rodgers remembers. 'I'd release another single, because that shit is happening. We then drop the album after "Borderline" and "Lucky Star" – holy shit – biggest record of my life, biggest record of her life.'

So, delayed until November 1984, *Like A Virgin*, Madonna's second studio album would make her a household name. The Rodgers-produced opus churned out four U.S. top five singles: the title track (No. 1 for six weeks), 'Material Girl' (No. 2), 'Angel' (No. 5) and 'Dress You Up' (No. 5). The album remains her biggest selling studio set in the US with over 10 million units sold. The album spent three weeks atop the Billboard 200 and remained on the chart for over two years.

Released in late 1984 in the states, the lead single, 'Like A Virgin', went to No. 1 just before Christmas; with Rob Sabino's opening synthesiser,

Thompson's huge drum fill, Rodgers' guitar, underpinned by Edwards' bass; it was Chic, back at No.1 in America. Considering that Chic had not had a big single in four years, it proved just how far from fashion they had fallen. But with someone else fronting it; someone white, it was easy. 'It was horrible to us,' Rodgers comments. 'I don't want to make it heavy because it is just music – it's not like being in Tibet or anything, but it is weird one day to be some innovative, creative great thing and the next day you can't get arrested – but you can go and take the exact thing that you do and do it with Madonna and its OK. You go *"that's more disco than what we do"*, but it's not disco because of who they are.'

Rodgers is realistic about his luck with that record. *'Like A Virgin* was a fluke. When I got hired to do that album, her first album had been out a year and had only sold 700,000. That seems cynical – only 700,000. But everybody was concerned. We do *Like A Virgin*, and then out of nowhere, "Borderline" hits, out of the clear blue sky.'

Tony Thompson remembered making the album with affection. He would eat Chinese food with Madonna in a little restaurant around the corner from where they were working. However, Karen Milne, his then partner, who played on the album, was not as welcome. 'I was hanging out,' she remembers. 'I was there when Tony, Bernard and Nile would lay down the rhythm tracks. I don't think Madonna liked having other women around. Tony came home one night and said they didn't want anybody else there. The string sessions, however, went fine – even though she was inexperienced, she was really clear about what she wanted. She was such a business woman. I really respected her a lot; just amazing to watch. She got along great with Nile and Bernard and she liked Tony a lot.'

Edwards however, was struggling somewhat in the shadows of his partner's success and Madonna's taskmaster tendencies were already fully in place: 'One morning Bernard was one hour late,' John Taylor recalls. 'When he arrived, she went off on one, saying that nobody should be late for her sessions. We were gobsmacked when we heard that anyone could do that to Bernard. Where I was coming from, Bernard was a god – to her, he was just the fucking bass player, a hired musician. She had no sense of the history, which was really scary. He's late because he's struggling with his life, but he's one of the greatest talents in the world. She should have been fucking grateful that he was going to contribute two hours to her record. And therein lies the sea change. That was scary – I'm sure James Jamerson had a lot of similar experiences – and he was Bernard's main man.' The occasional tensions were masked by an overall camaraderie, however, and a very strong selection of material.

'At that point, Nile worked with the A-list artists,' Brian Chin argues. 'He helped them make great sounding records. Madonna never did a Chic pastiche – it was because they were digging in on music – what they knew about music was this (*mimes arms moving wide*) but they sometimes made records like this (*small distance*). At that time nobody would have been surprised at their ability to arrange. Today, it's all about getting the right beat and loop. This is a talent, but it's not the same talent.'

'Few people knew that the whole Madonna thing was produced by Nile,' John DeMairo adds. 'Whereas now, the whole business is so producer driven – it's like "oh wow – that's Timbaland" – if it came out now it would be "Madonna produced by Nile Rodgers"; the whole scene, everything has changed so much. They were so far ahead of their game – but it was artist-driven then.'

With Madonna thundering around the world's charts, apart from one session with Mick Jagger, Rodgers and Edwards did not work together again until 1991. Rodgers and Thompson never played together again.

It is difficult to pinpoint exactly what drove Rodgers and Edwards apart. But the drift that had begun before *Real People* now reached its conclusion. However, Rodgers remains quick to suggest that the two were always close: 'Here's the greatest thing about my relationship with Bernard. It doesn't make any difference what he and I were going through, the stuff was in the press, things like "Bernard Edwards says Nile Rodgers can't play guitar". What he would say, what I would say. We were talking major drama here. Any time I could call him on the phone and go "yo 'Nard , wassup, bitch. Do you want to go to a movie?" That's more than friendship, that's complete respect, that's respect on a level you can't put in any contract – or anything like that.'

As for Thompson and Rodgers, the split seemed a culmination of many factors; it has been suggested that their personalities were just too similar for them to remain close. It became a case of self-fulfilling prophesy – Thompson felt hard done by. He felt he should have been cut in on the Chic Organization deal and becoming difficult to work with, alienating Rodgers, who had all of New York's sessioneers and original first-choice drummer Omar Hakim at hand to do his work – and also, as suggested before, technology. 'There was the whole thing with Bowie,' Karen Milne suggests. 'Nile, not then and there, suggesting Tony for the job. Tony would say that he thought Nile was his friend and got bitter about it, and Nile found it easier to work with other people and not have all those personality things going on. I always felt Tony should have been an equal partner with Nile and Bernard from day one – he should have got credit for writing some of those tunes; nobody told him what to play. Bernard or Nile didn't tell him anything apart from "keep it simple". He should have been getting the big bucks like they were. And that ate away at him. He always felt they should have taken care of him. Nile could always take him or leave him, because there's always somebody else.'

Rodgers came under the spell of the Synclavier, an early sampler. He spoke about its glories in 1985: 'I can't play the French horn, but I have some great French horn sounds in my Synclavier. It allows me to interpret the French horn the way I hear it. In the old days when I had Chic, sometimes it was damn frustrating to write out the arrangements and listen to them played poorly all day.' However, as time passed, it became clear that the Synclavier was not the future. Bryan Ferry, who worked with Rodgers at the time, recalls: 'Nile went off the boil when he got into the Synclavier. Everything became "Synclavier this" and "Synclavier that". He would go "THIS IS AMAZING" and it wasn't amazing, really – he got fooled, like a lot of people, me included. I didn't really like the track "Help Me", which we did for *The Fly*. He should have been playing guitar and producing people through the guitar.'

Rodgers raved about ISDNS and stated that with technology, he was 'the most stimulated he had been in his whole life'.

David Bowie had begun making a new album. Nile Rodgers, like Visconti before him, was not to be called back for the new sessions. 'I felt just like Tony had,' Rodgers recalls ruefully. 'David made a statement as powerful as *Let's Dance*. I had just given him a record that's on the same level as *A Love Supreme* or *Bitches Brew* – and I'm standing back as a fan, this is Bowie's record. So it was like you do this great piece of work that is really rock'n'roll history and how do you not say to that guy 'let's do this again'? We're smoking, we're a great team, let's keep this going.' But it was not to be. *Tonight* – which was a poor album by anybody's standards, utilised some of the touring players from the *Serious Moonlight* tour; Carmine Rojas, Sammy Figueroa, Omar Hakim; George Simms, Curtis King. But that was the only connection with the wider Chic circle.

Not that Rodgers was left idling. He did some session work in the spring of 1984 at Atlantic Studios on the project that was to become The Honeydrippers with Robert Plant, Jeff Beck and Jimmy Page, working personally with Ahmet Ertegun. The idea for the album came after Plant had recorded a version of Charlie Rich's 'Philadelphia Baby' at the Sun Records studios in Memphis. Spurred on by the session and encouraged by Ertegun, Plant recorded five R&B/doo-wop staples with Ertegun producing under the pseudonym 'Nugetre and the Fabulous Brill Brothers'. Further recording took place in London with Beck and Page adding solos.

It was a homage to white rock's inspirations. 'I made a record with Robert Plant called The Honeydrippers,' Ertegun recalls. 'Nile plays on some of that, although Jeff Beck had most of the solos. Originally the great rock and rollers were African-Americans like Little Richard and Fats Domino – they were the inspiration of many of their white peers.' The side project was a tremendous success, with the 10" album, *Volume One* reaching the American Top 5, and the single, a spirited cover of Phil Phillips' 'Sea Of Love', going to No. 3 in October 1984.

In 1980, the movement that became known as the New Romantics began sweeping through British youth culture. It emerged as a reaction against recession, inner city violence and the oppressive policies of Conservative Prime Minister Margaret Thatcher. Youths in the major British conurbations, who had grown up with the image of David Bowie from *Top Of The Pops* in their heads, all went and formed bands. It seemed also that the concurrent punk and disco movement started to breed funny little groups with strange names and a reliance on xeroxing Chic. By the early 80s, it was as if Rodgers' guitar sound was being taught to bands across the UK. Stimulin, Funkapolitan, Mark White from ABC, Graham Jones from Haircut 100, all were slavishly and respectfully emulating his sound. But one group, Duran Duran, wore their Chic influence right from the very start. They were a true product of the barriers broken down by disco.

Duran Duran was formed in the late 70s in Birmingham, by Nick Rhodes and John Taylor. By the early 80s, they had a deal with EMI, a producer who had worked with Bowie (Colin Thurston), and a ruck of prejudice from the London-based music press. By 1982, they were hugely popular in the UK. With the advent of MTV, they became darlings of America, as a palatable version of British New Wave. Having met Rodgers and Thompson in 1982, John Taylor had harboured a desire to work with Rodgers.

'We were coming up to finishing *Seven And The Ragged Tiger* in October 1983. I heard "The Original Sin," the INXS production that Nile had done. There was the song on our album; "The Reflex" and we just couldn't get it right. The intro was a conscious homage to the guitar and drum breaks that Tony and Nile had been doing – there was one in "I'm Coming Out" and one in "Believer"; we just couldn't get the feel. The album was finished and delivered, and "Union Of The Snake" was the single. After listening to "The Original Sin", we decided to approach Nile with a view to doing a remix.'

'By the time I did "The Reflex", *Seven And The Ragged Tiger* was over,' Rodgers recalls. 'They asked me if I would do a remix. I said no, that's not what I do, I'm a producer. I said I will do your song as if I'd done it if you'd called me in the first place as a producer.' Duran's people were clear with Rodgers, he could call it what he wanted, but it was going to be known to them as 'a remix' when it was released in summer 1984.

Rodgers quickly realised that the fairly listless song was missing a hook. Identifying the 'tra-la-la' section, buried in the middle, as that very hook, he engineered, with Jason Corsaro, a new introduction to the record. 'I set it up with that bit at the start, and punctuated with 'fle-fle-fle-fle-flex. By the time you hear the hook, you want it back. I made the best record I could. The record company said I made it too black.'

In February 1984, Duran Duran heard their single played down the telephone while were on tour. 'We were listening to this really fucked-up version of the song over the phone,' John Taylor laughs. 'Fl-fl-fl-fl-flex a-ya-ya-ya-ay, all that fucking shit! EMI didn't get it but we felt quite strongly about it – and it was our biggest hit.'

'The Reflex' remains one of Rodgers' favourite productions. However, he came in for some criticism, for working with a group that were perceived as uncool; he reasons it thus: 'Musicians have always made lots of money. Talking about it in a cynical way is what Chic used to do all the time. I can work with anybody with a great sense of humour. Duran are working-class guys, from places like Newcastle and the Midlands. If these guys didn't make it as rock stars, what would they be doing? These are guys who got a break and were crucified for their success. Simon's lyrics are terrific. If I'd never worked with them, I could still appreciate where they are coming from. I liken it to a lot of what Chic was trying to do.'

The group actually worked together with Rodgers on their next single, 'Wild Boys'. 'Nile came and sat in with us. We started playing a drum groove and he liked the way it was going. He steered that song; then he took it away; He was breaking a lot of ground with the Synclavier; him and his engineer Jason Corsaro – he's always had incredible engineering talents.' The group took to working with Rodgers with great ease: 'He was very laid back, full of enthusiasm – he had the expertise to take an idea to completion,' Taylor recalls. 'Being a musician, he'd always pick up the guitar and chip in – being a groovemeister, he always had a sense of where to place the drum overdub.'

To this day, Rodgers cites Duran Duran as the act he enjoys working with the most. 'It's a marriage made in musical heaven,' John Taylor laughs. 'We're musicians and we are what we are. We can never be what Nile can be, but then again, he can never be us. He loves punk rock, Led Zeppelin, Roxy Music; he loves where we're coming from. We all love so much music.'

It was during this period that Rodgers began working with Mick Jagger on his star-studded debut solo album. The album, *She's The Boss*, which was released in 1985, caused great controversy at the time, as it led to The Rolling Stones postponing the recording of their proposed album and fuelled rumours of a split. People assume the Mick Jagger album was a tremendous flop. It wasn't. It went platinum in America. Produced with Jagger and Bill Laswell, it finds Jagger somewhat desperately trying to emulate Bowie's success. In among all the top-line guest stars were Martinez, Thornton, Thompson, Rodgers and Edwards, all present and correct, while Duran Duran dropped in frequently to The Power Station during recording. Lead single, 'Just Another Night', reached No. 12 in the US and the album reached No13.

Nile Rodgers was voted *Billboard*'s 'Rock and Roll Producer of the Year' in 1984. With all this activity and limelight for Rodgers, Bernard Edwards was feeling somewhat left out of the frame. It was time to redress the balance.

21.
WE WANT TO MULTIPLY

'While Nile really jumped into the technology, Bernard did "A View To A Kill" – distinctively different, equally brilliant.'
EDDIE MARTINEZ

BERNARD EDWARDS NEEDED A REST. He too, had burned the candle at both ends for the best part of a decade. But the studio was also his first love and he needed to ensure that people knew he was also out for hire.

After working with Rodgers on various sessions, Edwards produced *The Heat* for Nona Hendryx with Jason Corsaro for RCA. Hendryx had known Edwards for years, right back to when Edwards used to be thrown out of Labelle's rehearsals. Manager Vicki Wickham recalls that Bernard was "super professional, great fun and with a great sense of the big picture." There was only one issue that needled Wickham, just like Madonna the year before – Edwards' timekeeping. "He would come into sessions late – one or two hours or more. But he did come in from Connecticut, so I should have probably been more understanding." He also returned to Diana Ross to produce and play bass on 'Telephone' from 1984's *Swept Away*. But his first major opportunity to stand away from Rodgers came from Duran Duran.

The Power Station was an important project for Bernard and one that provided a degree of parity with the success that Rodgers had enjoyed with Madonna. The project came about as a result of something of a happy accident: John and Andy Taylor were on the run from Duran Duran.

'Andy and I had finished our third album. It was a bitch and we were out there wrestling with our lives,' John Taylor recalls. 'It was like being on a really out-of-control racehorse, whereas we had been used to being on the donkeys at Paignton. We decided we weren't being heard, so we wanted to do a side project as soon as we got the touring done. We didn't quite know what it was going to be. The idea of working with Bernard came about because this idea of working with Tony, first mooted backstage on the Serious Moonlight tour, had gestated.'

The idea was simple: for the Taylors to produce a record for John Taylor's then-girlfriend, Bebe Buell, whom he had started seeing on Duran's US tour. Taylor had T. Rex's 1971 hit, 'Get It On' in mind. As Duran were the hottest thing on EMI at that point, Taylor quickly got the green light. He hooked up with Thompson to play drums. He readily agreed. Buell and Taylor fell out. So, there was a band without a singer – and no producer. 'We were driven by the fact Tony was a star, that his playing had such character, it could be a star vehicle for him,' Taylor recalls. 'Tony was a little bit embittered from his Chic experience – we thought if we could take his sound and put it behind us, it would be fantastic.'

They decided that the project, which was going to be called Big Brother, could feature the three of them and a parade of guest vocalists. The Taylors thought about asking Rodgers to produce. Thompson suggested that they use Edwards instead. "We had no idea what he was like, as he had no public persona," Taylor continues. "We met him at the Parker Meridian Hotel in New York, with Jason Corsaro. He was so mellow, so opposite to Nile – who was the party animal – you rarely saw Bernard without a big grin on his face. He was the sweater guy; he was dad."

Edwards told Gene Santoro in 1985 that, 'I told them if we're going to do this, we're going to do a *record*, something *different*. It's what Nile and I used to do with Chic: we took *chances*. Then all of a sudden you're the fat cat with gold records and attitude, and you're afraid. But when I met those guys, I was no longer afraid to take a chance with success, because there was all this strange energy around them that revived me.'

Having been used to working with Rodgers, Taylor was amazed at Edwards' peaceful, mellow style in the studio. British born vocalist, Robert Palmer, who had partied with Duran Duran, became first choice as vocalist for the project. 'We were in Maison Rouge,' Thompson recalls. 'Bananarama were in there and we were in there – me, John Taylor, Bernard, we were knocking out "Some Like It Hot" and we didn't even have a vocalist. It was John who suggested Robert. Robert loved it so much, he wrote the lyrics on the way over. He was an extremely talented cat.'

It was one of those things that just fell into place. They sent Palmer an instrumental demo for a new song, which was to become 'Some Like It Hot'. 'They'd gone to goof off in the studio. They'd come up with four minutes in G minor and then asked me if I'd write a melody for it,' Palmer told me in 2001. 'I loved the groove, so I wrote the lyrics and melody for it on the plane to New York.' According to Taylor, 'Robert came in, wrote a lyric, sang this song, and asked what else we had, and quickly we did "Bang A Gong."' Palmer's urbane, controlled, yet powerful delivery, honed with blues bands in his native Yorkshire and then taken out to the world stage through Vinegar Joe and a ten-year solo career at Island, was ideal to front this heavy-hitting stew that Thompson, Edwards and the Taylors were cooking up. The guest vocalist idea was quickly abandoned. Palmer was now the frontman for the project.

In the middle of recording what was to become The Power Station album, Duran Duran, who by now were on the verge of splitting, had to honour their commitment to record the theme to the 14th official James Bond film, *A View To A Kill*. For any artist, singing a Bond theme has always been one of those rare accolades few have bestowed on them. It suggests a certain acceptance on the widest level. Duran Duran were about to join a cast of singers and players that included Paul McCartney, Shirley Bassey, Carly Simon, Tom Jones and Nancy Sinatra. Although the Bond movies by this point had become flabby parodies, with little of their original cold war brio, they were still enormous at the box office.

The recording sessions in late 1984 at Maison Rouge in Fulham were tense. 'We'd just started with Bernard, so he came in and produced it. That was one of Bernard's greatest production achievements – because we weren't really talking to each other,' Taylor recalls. 'We were really split down the middle – you couldn't get all the band in the studio at the same time.' On top of that, veteran Bond composer and arranger, John Barry, who was writing the score for the film, worked with them all on the track simultaneously. 'He hated most of us and most of us hated him,' Taylor laughs. 'It was a real show of fucking egos. Bernard just came in, and eked out some amazing work from us. He got a great bass line out of me; and he took it away; then he worked with John, getting the score, getting the orchestration down, all on to that three-minute song. That was a mega fucking production job. It was almost "River Deep Mountain High" – you've got the band, you've got the sound effects and then you've got the orchestra – it's a big little record.' Edwards and Corsaro did indeed do an amazing job on what is a slight and eminently forgettable theme. Somehow, however, combined with Duran's popularity and the economy of the song, it has become one of the most loved Bond themes, dwarfing the film's aged plot and actors and becoming one of the biggest selling Bond records of all time, and the only one to date to reach the top of the charts in America.

It was to be Bernard Edwards' first solo production No. 1.

Meanwhile, the Big Brother project at The Power Station was not only gathering speed, but also a name. 'A journalist saw John and I going in to the studio,' Palmer recalled. 'They then wrote a piece "John Taylor and Robert Palmer in The Power Station". So we had a name.' *Rolling Stone* reported at the time that, 'After settling on Palmer, The Power Station spent the next several months playing intercontinental hopscotch. The project was assembled in pieces: basic tracks were done in London; overdubs and embellishments at the Power Station in New York and most of the vocals in Nassau, where Palmer lives. Palmer wrote lyrics to fit the existing music, sometimes while jetting to the studio. Rarely were all four in the same studio at the same time.' It was a complex and involved process that seemed to bring out the best in the four performers, to the obvious enjoyment of their producer.

It was a troubling time, however, for Taylor, playing with his hero Edwards on a daily basis. 'I was so fucked up at the time, I would suggest that he played it,' Taylor says. 'He would say "get the fuck outta here – you're the fucking bass player, you play it." He would always say you got to keep playing, you got to keep playing, don't ever stop playing. There were a couple of things he would do. If you listen to his playing in "Bang A Gong", he had an amazing way of getting underneath the groove.'

Overall, it was a very cheerful time. Bernard Edwards Jr recalls happy barbeques with the group and learning a lot at the studios with them. 'Jason Corsaro, Andy Taylor, Robert, John and Tony were like family to me.' Palmer added that, 'It was a non-stop party in the studio at the time – Mick Jagger, Herbie Hancock were always dropping by. It was always 'catch the vibe' with Bernard around.' After the tension of the final Chic and the current Duran Duran situation, it felt like a relief. 'We moved to New York and mixed it. We were kings of the world, notwithstanding the huge hangovers,' Taylor laughed. 'We were 23 and we were playing with the big boys at The Power Station.' And of course, there were a few old faces at hand to help out. 'Curtis King and I sang on the Power Station album,' Fonzi Thornton recalls. 'It was a new type of rock thing and Bernard was bringing that soul, R&B bass stuff to that whole movement. I remember John Taylor saying that he had learned to play bass by listening to Bernard.'

Edwards was a stern taskmaster to the Taylors. 'There were times when I had to beat 'em up in the studio,' Edwards recalled in 1985. 'Stay on their behinds, and they *loved* it, they responded. Here are these famous guys and girls are screaming outside and Bernard's inside whippin' them to death.'

To highlight the madness at the time, the group invited Roger Taylor, Duran Duran's drummer, to fly over from Paris to play on one track. 'We wanted him to play timbales; we fly him in on Concorde, with his roadie,' Taylor says. 'Put them up in a hotel for a week; they waited in a hotel for five days before they got the call to come over and play on it. Everybody thought it was a good idea; Bernard in particular didn't want to break up Duran Duran. That was never part of the plan. Bernard was very sensible. When we would insult the others, he was all "It goes up and down, you guys are great and you'll work it out". He was a great stabilising influence on me. He would listen.'

Given that they were estranged at this juncture, there was little obvious ill feeling between Edwards and his former band. 'Nile and Bernard would always refer lovingly to each other,' John Taylor says. 'There was no sense of disappointment or disillusion – it was all about what was happening right there and right then. It had all had its time, and each individual was evolving to its full potential.' Taylor also saw how Tony Thompson related to his two former bandmates. 'Nile was his pal, but Tony had a hard time making music without Bernard. He always needed Bernard to keep him anchored, but Tony's party pal was Nile. The next day in the studio, Tony would be guided by Bernard, he could sail Tony through the toughest courses. And lest we forget, most of Nile's great productions are with Tony on drums and Bernard on bass.'

The Power Station was a huge American hit on release. Although *Rolling Stone* called it 'the technofunk equivalent of Hungarian goulash: throw in a little bit of everything and stir,' it works. More surprisingly than you would think. Edwards drew out a cast-iron bass performance from Taylor. Edwards said to Palmer after the take for 'Some Like It Hot,' 'Robert, my moustache just fell out!' The album reached No. 6 in America, and the two principal singles, 'Bang A Gong' and 'Some Like It Hot' both reached the Top 10.

It certainly caught the ear of old Chic players: 'I used to tease Tony about how The Power Station record was the loudest on the radio – those drums!' Raymond Jones recalled. But the sound that the record cooked up in many ways was to define the remainder of the 80s: At the studio, they took close mic'ing to the max, placing mics all over the floor. They used elevator shafts as echo chambers to create huge, natural, reverb rooms. They reverbed, gated and delayed all the drums. 'If you're going to work with noise like that, you've got to know what you're doing,' Taylor remembered. 'There were some fucking major moments on that record. Andy was on the top of his game; Tony was on the top of his game. Bernard would then arrange these fucking horn parts, bring in characters like Lenny Pickett. There are incredible baritone sax parts on that record. Who could make those kind of records these days? These were guys playing live. It didn't take forever. It was kitchen sink, but done quickly. They'd done it all. When they created the Chic sound, it was a big sound but it never sounded overwrought. They innovated in the use of string synthesisers, because they had been using real orchestras. But they used them in a way that they never sounded more than texture.'

1985 is known for being the year of Live Aid, both the high-watermark for 80s music and arguably, the beginning of its slow commercial death. The concert, which was organised by ex-journalist and musician Bob Geldof to help the Ethiopian famine, demonstrated how central to people's lives commodified music had become. With global TV tie-ins, over a billion people tuned in world-wide to see a concert which involved virtually every top-line act then currently active in the world. Of disco's Diaspora, only Kool and the Gang, Ashford and Simpson, and Teddy Pendergrass sang, but then they had all been active long prior to disco. Although not playing as a unit, Chic alumni were present on both sides of the Atlantic for the event.

Rodgers played with Madonna and The Thompson Twins; Rob Sabino played with The Thompson Twins. Over in England, Fonzi Thornton sang with Bryan Ferry. But it was Tony Thompson who was actually a band member on the day, as The Power Station took to the Philadelphia stage. But that wasn't his only task. Alongside Phil Collins, he filled in for his hero John Bonham with the reformed Led Zeppelin.

The Zeppelin connection was reinforced further when Thompson began to rehearse with Robert Plant, Jimmy Page and John Paul Jones in Bath early the following year.

The Chic family were now all spread out across the recording industry. Rob Sabino went touring with Simon and Garfunkel; worked extensively with Paul Simon, Todd Rundgren and Ace Frehley. Thornton and Anderson were much sought-after as sessioneers, and Raymond Jones found work with Jeffrey Osborne. 'After I was jettisoned from Chic, I called around – fortunately I heard about a tour with some guy who had just left his group, L.T.D., Jeffery Osbourne. I had no idea who he was – that was one of the best things I did. I wrote "Stay With Me Tonight" and tried to get Jeffery to sing like David Byrne. It was a blend of Talking Heads and "Give Up" from the *diana* album.'

Rodgers and Edwards were always listening to each other, looking out for what the other one was up to. Rodgers even found time to release a second solo album, which he had commenced working on in May 1984. Although the press release suggested that the album was a 'stunning piece of musical mastery that is certain to do for 80s music what his work for Chic did a decade earlier,' *B-Movie Matinee* was so understated that it was almost entirely overlooked when it was released in June 1985. An affectionate homage to all the Cold War science fiction films that burgeoned in the 50s and early 60s, Rodgers attempted to take a visual approach to music. Unfortunately, apart from the ripple caused by the album's lead single, 'Let's Go Out Tonight' (No. 88 in the US chart), no-one was listening, which perplexed Rodgers. Although his credentials were there for all to see as a backroom boy, he still craved the limelight. Again, it demonstrated how far Rodgers was prepared to use technology. He played guitar, bass, Juno 60, and Synclavier while Rob Sabino played Juno 60. Alfa Anderson and The Simms Brothers returned for vocal work. The album became known more in the UK for its gimmicky, 3-D cover. Davitt Sigerson, writing in *Rolling Stone* suggested that, 'Let's just say it's not one of the moments for which he'll be remembered.' There was a co-producer credit on the album, for Tommy 'Rock' Jymi. It was Rodgers' alter-ego. He told *The Wall Street Journal*, the pseudonym 'could shift some responsibility whenever I want to do something weird.'

Edwards had proved himself as a producer. Robert Palmer had never met or even heard of Edwards before The Power Station. However, he was so impressed with his playing and producing skills, he enlisted Edwards to produce the album Palmer had began working on when he interrupted his schedule to make the Duran-Chic fusion album.

Possibly the most remarkable product of this purple patch was Edwards' production of 'Addicted To Love' from Robert Palmer's *Riptide* album. It reunited The Power Station minus John Taylor, put Edwards on bass and long-term friend and associate Eddie Martinez on guitar alongside Andy Taylor. Edwards' bass part is quite something else. 'If you listen to 'Addicted to Love', Bernard had this way of moving underneath a straight bass and drum, kick snare part,' John Taylor enthuses. The whole package, combined with its legendary Terence Donovan-directed video and Fonzi Thornton providing support on backing vocals, proved irresistible and took Palmer to the No. 1 spot in America.

The album, *Riptide* was a remarkably robust piece of work, especially the follow-up single, 'I Didn't Mean To Turn You On'. It transformed the Cherelle track, written and produced by Jimmy Jam and Terry Lewis into a sleek, urban hymn. The tale of a young girl giving her boyfriend the wrong impression was translated to Palmer's urbane middle-aged man. As a showcase for Thompson's drumming and Edwards' bass, it's unstoppable.

Edwards had two No.1s. He was finally being talked of again as Rodgers' equal. In 1986, Rodgers gave a long, four-page interview to *New York* magazine. It did not mention Edwards once.

It was Rodgers' turn to work with Duran Duran again. The group had lost both Andy and Roger Taylor after they had worked on their solo projects, and vocalist Simon Le Bon had gained a level of notoriety for capsizing Drum, the boat in which he was due to sail round the world. '*Notorious* was a tough album for us to make,' John Taylor remembers. 'Nile had to refashion us. I'd met drummer Steve Ferrone at the Power Station. He had a lot of what Tony had, but he was more consistent. Nile came in as guitar player and really fashioned a world for us to live in as we'd lost Andy and Roger, two key sound stylists. We had to create a sound for ourselves. It's really successful on "Skin Trade" and "Notorious". Perhaps there are other parts that needed to be darker, or whiter.'

This period of intense productivity coincided with 'very, very serious drug and alcohol problems' for Rodgers. *The Guardian* noted in 1999 that *Notorious* was produced from the floor of the studio as Rodgers was 'so smashed out of my mind'. Rodgers added that, 'I come from the 60s. It was OK to be high all the time because of our extreme pressure and our extreme success. We believed we deserved extreme rewards.' Today, Rodgers simply states: 'I can't remember all those songs, I was so high in that period – I think wow! How much coke did I do that day?'

In January 1986, Jimmy Page and Robert Plant invited Thompson to a secret rehearsal at a village hall near Peter Gabriel's Bath studio. Along with John Paul Jones, the four attempted to rehearse new material for a possible Led Zeppelin reunion, seeing the band pursuing a David Byrne/Husker Du direction. Page was not in good shape and the sessions ground to a halt within days. Thompson went out one night to party. The taxi he was travelling in left the road and he ended up in hospital. Allegedly, Plant had a call at 5 am from Bath Royal Infirmary informing him, 'We have your Mr Thompson here. He states Mr Plant as next of kin'. Plant replied, 'but he can't do that, he's black!' The remaining members carried on for a couple of days with a roadie drumming, but it never really went anywhere and Zeppelin abandoned the idea of a reunion.

Thompson fought for his life and recovered, but he was never exactly the same again. On recovering, he quit the flat he shared with Milne, and moved to California. 'The accident was severe,' Milne recalls. 'I knew then that our lives would never be the same, and I know Tony eventually realised that the accident was a turning point in his life and a major blow to his psyche and career. He had such an ego when he went to California. He had some problems when he was working with Rod Stewart; he didn't feel he needed to go to rehearsal. Bowie toured again in 1987 and used the same band but didn't use Tony. Tony had his share of problems; financial, personal, getting involved with the wrong people. He resisted coming back to New York – I don't think he could face the people here. I think he burnt his bridges too much.'

Bernard Edwards divorced his wife, Alexis, in the mid-80s. Although more content to rest in his new-found California lifestyle with his new fiancée, Bambi, Edwards was to take up the offer to work with another long-term admirer, Martin Fry, to cut three tracks for a forthcoming ABC project in October 1986.

Fry had formed ABC in 1980, as an attempt to inject some glamour into his adopted home town of Sheffield. He linked up with Stephen Singleton and Mark White, who were in an electro-noise outfit, Vice Versa. Chic were an early reference point. 'We were obsessed with trying to play with the same sort of precision that you'd hear on those records,' says Fry. 'You just knew that the drummer in Chic was streets ahead of the drummer in Eater. Chic looked immaculate. It was almost as if they had stepped straight out of a movie. They just weren't sweaty. It was at the time when people were dismantling rock and roll and rejecting it, and Chic came along. They were as extreme as Kraftwerk in their own way. They seemed to filter everything. Nile's playing, Tony's drumming, the bass, the vocals, the strings. It's not really disco. It's in its own tradition. They always credited Roxy, but they were a different machine, it was like the difference between a Rolls Royce and a

Bentley. They were their own orchestra.'

By 1985, ABC had released three albums and their third, *How To Be A Zillionaire* had broken big in America. Mercury wanted the group – by now Fry and Mark White – to go back to the studio and make another record working with a producer. 'We'd had some success, we'd created a number of blueprints, but we wanted to consolidate and go back to what we knew best,' Fry recalls. 'We wanted to do a really sophisticated record. Mark White wanted Bernard Edwards because he wanted to, not so much chase the sound he'd done on *The Power Station*, but the stuff he'd done on *Riptide* with Robert Palmer, the string stuff.' When Edwards accepted, ABC were delighted. 'We were really confident. It was time to meet somebody we really idolised.'

Edwards and Bambi flew over to London on Concorde and began work on three tracks, 'When Smokey Sings', '24 Carat Plastic' and 'The Night You Murdered Love'. Edwards brought his bass of the day, Big Red with him, but it remained resolutely in its case. It was not an ideal time. Fry, suffering from Hodgkin's Disease, had been near death and recently undergone chemotherapy and radiotherapy. Amid this, Fry had got married and White's father had just died.

'Somehow we kept going,' Fry states. 'We cut our tunes. Bernard just sat there and he just liked it – it was because Mark and I were really trying to show off to Bernard. I went in and sang my heart out. I went into see him and he said, "yeah, it's great". I thought I was going to be singing seven more times, but he said – "no, that's it". I thought this is the guy who's responsible for a whole back catalogue of incredible music, so he must know what he's talking about. He was very laid back at the time. He suggested we brought in bass players – so we had a few very strange scenarios where Brad Lang came in and played in front of Bernard Edwards – it was like Pavarotti doing vocal coaching.'

Fry was an eager pupil, but at least wanted to know some secrets, but he found Edwards reticent to discuss past glories with Chic. 'I kept asking him how he produced those records, and 'Nard would say – "no, it sucks, that's gone". I was flabbergasted, as was Mark. We were shocked he would say this about his own work. He was on the back of big rock records, and the thing with Nile meant he'd erased a lot of stuff out of his memory, really. He was a man who didn't want to talk about the past. He played the bass on "Good Times", for heavens sake, and I was talking to him. He was very disparaging.'

Edwards seemed to be in a different place. 'He and Bambi went up to Scotland in the middle weekend we were recording,' Fry recalls. 'I went home and played Sister Sledge. I wanted him to open up a box of tricks and say, "right, these are the charts – this is how you make four violins sound like the Chic Orchestra". It was mystifying, but it was to be. We were really intense – and he seemed just so laid back. That was his experience talking.'

This was at the height of Rodgers and Edwards' separation. While working with ABC, on 31st October 1986, Edwards' 34th birthday, Nile Rodgers phoned up to wish him happy birthday. 'It was a period when they were just not speaking. It was nice. He said you'll never guess who that was on the phone – that was the last person I expected to hear from.' The session ended in early November. 'Once I'd nagged him to play his bass,' Fry laughs. 'As soon as we finished recording, he picked it up and then, boy, did he start to play! It was freaky.'

Although Edwards ended up producing only two of the tracks on their 1987 album, *Alphabet City*, 'When Smokey Sings' became ABC's biggest hit in America, reaching No. 5, and returned them to the UK Top 20 for the first time in four years. 'He was very pleased the records were hits,' Fry recalls. 'We met, cut the tracks and we moved on. We cut a B-side at PWL, and we put on a new bass line – I think we might have sampled Chic!'

Rodgers continued to work at a breakneck pace, and also found time to form a group with keyboard player Philip Saisse, The Outloud. The Outloud album was Rodgers' opportunity, like Edwards with The Power Station, to create a new band with a new sound. It also marked the first time Rodgers worked without anybody who had been directly associated with the Chic Organization.

He had also, since 1985, worked with Laurie Anderson; with Sabino on Jeff Beck's *Flash*; with Sheena Easton; finally hooked up with Grace Jones on *Inside Story*; worked on a reunion with Sister Sledge on the album *Where The Boys Meet The Girls*, which yielded the UK No. 1, 'Frankie'. Other clients included The Thompson Twins and Philip Bailey. In September 1985, Rodgers played guitar on 'In Your Eyes' on Peter Gabriel's *So*. He also produced old cohort Al Jarreau's *L Is For Lover*, played guitar with Howard Jones, Cyndi Lauper; Terri Gonzalez; the list went on.

One of the greatest moments was when Rodgers met and worked with Bryan Ferry, the man who had so inspired him all those years previously: 'Nile playing on my records was a great treat for me,' Ferry recalls. 'I started working with Nile through Bob Clearmountain, because Bob had worked with them. I was in his flat one night, early 80s, when I first met him. He was constantly playing records and walking round with a guitar strapped on.'

Rodgers played on 1985's *Boys And Girls* album, and then worked on *The Fly* Soundtrack with Ferry. 'We already had the tracks cut, and he would just come in and do overdubs,' Ferry recalls. 'You could throw song after song at him – he'd be banging up against the console, playing away. Really exciting and very quick. He would have so many ideas rushing into his head at once. His head's leaping all over the place from one idea to another, like a mad person. He brought such a lot to the tracks we worked on. "Cool" is a very big word with Nile. He's incredibly articulate – he can talk about anything convincingly. He has amazing yarns – all sorts of yarns.'

As the decade that Chic had entered on a high and then helped redefine musically, drew to a close, Edwards found lucrative work producing part of Jody Watley's platinum-selling solo debut and Rod Stewart's *Out Of Order* album. Both albums saw him working with the post-Power Station unit of Eddie Martinez and Tony Thompson; he also worked on Stewart's *Vagabond Heart*; as well as with the Hunter-Ronson Band. Thompson and Martinez formed The Distance, a melodic metal outfit with Edwards and Jeff Bova, who'd played guitar with Robert Palmer, and Robert Hart on lead vocals. Their sole LP, *Under The One Sky,* was released by Reprise in 1989. "The Distance was Tony's favourite project of all them – Eddie Martinez is such a dear friend", Thompson's widow, Patrice Jennings-Thompson recalls.

After an increasingly desolate late 80s, relations between Rodgers and Edwards began to get easier. Ronald Reagan's Vice President, George Bush became President in late 1988, ensuring continuity in the right-wing government that had prevailed in America since 1981. On top of that, recession had hit again with the stock market crash of 1987. Dance music had undergone another revolution with the advent of cheap technology that put sampling within everyone's reach. Perhaps the conditions were right to reheat the Good Times again. The key question would be how would Chic's music stand up in this new climate?

22.
CRISP CLICHÉS AND WITTY WORDS

'By Chic-ism, *they were as thick as thieves again.'*
FONZI THORNTON 2004

THE WORLD WAS CHANGING. By the 1990s, communism was resigned to history; the détente favoured between Mikhail Gorbachev and Ronald Reagan in the 80s, had succeeded ostensibly in making the world a safer place. The Berlin Wall had fallen in 1989. Reagan's successor, George Bush, had reacted against the Iraqi invasion of Kuwait in August 1990, by sending in Allied Forces to recapture the country in January 1991.

Chic were by now, a heady, quickly disposed of and compartmentalised memory; like disco itself; what it stood for, what it had meant seemed distant. The whole era seemed redundant, remote. Of course, disco really didn't die. It quietly returned to its roots. Through clubs such as Paradise Garage and The Warehouse, DJs such as Larry Levan and Frankie Knuckles would define whole new musics. House music, which swept through the charts from the later 80s was disco in all but name. Its greatest hit, 'Ride On Time' by Black Box was simply a rework of Lolleata Holloway's 'Love Sensation'. Minor disco tracks that had so enthralled producers when they were young were being replicated, sampled and re-presented. In Britain, a record by DJ Mark Moore, 'Theme From S-Express' became a No.1. It was based around an enormous sample of 'Is It Love You're After' by Rose Royce. Artists such as Jocelyn Brown, who had sung on the later Chic albums and had an enormous UK hit with 'Somebody Else's Guy' in 1984, had relocated to Britain to find work on an increasing number of productions that would give endless credibility to the pasty faced white boys who made them in their bedrooms.

Hip-hop too, had proved that it was no gimmick. Ten years since The Sugar Hill Gang appropriated 'Good Times' as 'Rapper's Delight', there was now old-school and new-school rap. Gangsta rapping was all the rage, with Niggaz With Attitude, Ice-T, et al; while to counterbalance this aggression, there was the Daisy Age/Native Tongues school, with hippie philosophy and non-aggression, acts such as De La Soul, The Jungle Brothers and A Tribe Called

Quest. And The Beastie Boys, three middle class Jewish white boys from New York, became the Elvis Presleys of the genre by marketing the African-American phenomenon to the widest audience possible. Although Debbie Harry brought white rapping to the masses in 1981 with 'Rapture', by the late 80s it was simply *de rigueur* for virtually every record, black or white, to have a rap interlude.

By 1988, with the proliferation of cheap MDMA, Ecstasy, once an elite designer drug at the tail end of the Studio 54 years, had seen, in Britain at least, the second summer of love, where repetitive, machine-driven beats would enliven a crowd, already high on this new drug. Whereas cocaine had always been for the privileged, and speed's connotations made it too pikey for the masses, E was a cheap and inclusive way to unite in euphoria.

In this new dance climate, Chic saw action in the UK charts with the wholly execrable 'Jack Le Freak' mixes, which reached the UK Top 20 in 1987. This is not snobbery in any way – turds can indeed be polished and frequently are by remixers and some silverware can be buffed up a treat, too (witness DJ Paul Oakenfold's Perfecto Mixes of U2's material). But Chic; when there was such understated perfection before, why ruin it with swathes of overproduction when the whole trick of the production in the first place was to leave so much space?

However, it demonstrated that there was still a market for the group.

Although they had not produced together since 1983, Nile Rodgers and Bernard Edwards remained in contact. It may not have been everyday communications, but each checked up on the other. In some respects, it was difficult not to: just opening up the pages of *Billboard* would indicate where their latest records had got to. The size and the scope of the dance explosion that emanated out of the house movement, the explosion of cheap technology and the music industry's annual decampment to Ibiza gave Rodgers the idea to reunite with Edwards professionally. Eventually, it would become impossible for the two not to work together again.

The producing and remixing work continued apace for both of them. Rodgers had had more success by producing half of The B-52s enormous album, *Cosmic Thing*, which had yielded the hit single, 'Roam'. In 1990 alone, Rodgers produced Paul Young, The B-52s and Philip Bailey. In the same year, Edwards worked with Cathy Dennis, The Triplets and The Hunter-Ronson Band.

Edwards had relocated to California and restarted his life. 'I lost weight, got into health foods, spent a lot of time on my own and finally had the chance to know myself again and do my own thing,' he told *Blues & Soul* in 1992. His eldest son, Bernard Jr, also moved to California, with the intention of getting involved in music. Edwards was having none of it. 'My father didn't want me to do music,' Edwards Jr states. 'I was the hard-headed one in the family because I definitely had to experience it before someone told me not to do it. So, I knew I wanted to be a musician since second grade. He didn't want me to do it. I've seen him go through the lows and the highs. The lows were really low…. I have the natural love for the music just like he did, so it was not a money-driven thing – I was simply into the music. So, he would let me go to the studio and see and learn but it never was a case of this is what I want you to do.' Edwards seemed adamant that music was not the correct career approach to take: 'He wanted me to go to college and get a regular 9 to 5. My father's goal was to work so much and do so many songs that none of us would ever have to work again in our lives.'

Edwards seemed bruised and outside the music industry. The Distance, the project with Eddie Martinez and Tony Thompson had proved moderately successful, but he was tired. Like Martin Fry, Martinez found it especially difficult to get Edwards' reminiscing. 'Once in a while he would talk about the old days,' Martinez sighs, 'he was so economical, but the words spoke volumes.'

The band actually played together one more time, at Rodgers 36th birthday party in 1990, 'We played at the China Club,' Fonzi Thornton recalls. 'Me, Luci, Alfa, Nile and Bernard – Omar Hakim was on drums as Tony was off in California.' After the show, Edwards and Rodgers got talking, and plans tentatively begin to hatch. 'It was the first time we had played together in six years,' Edwards said at the time. 'The magic was still there.'

One of the biggest indications that there could still be a market for Chic was in the success of Robert Clivillés and David Cole. They had been producing together and apart since the early 80s, but by the end of the decade their remixing skills and studio ensemble they had put together, The C&C Music Factory, with rapper Freedom Williams, had made them the hottest producers on the block, and comparisons were frequently being drawn between them and The Chic Organization at their height. Perhaps this was the appropriate time for Rodgers and Edwards to return and bask in the acclaim that had been denied them at the end of the first stage of the band.

Rodgers told Fonzi Thornton that for Chic to exist in the 90s, he wanted to establish a new band. Norma Jean Wright couldn't, as she was signed to Sony with Raymond Jones as State Of Art, which would have meant that even if asked, she would only have been able to provide support vocals. 'Raymond and I continued to collaborate way after Chic,' Norma Jean recalls. 'He is also one of my best friends. It was very easy for Raymond and I to do the State Of Art project because we are so in tune musically.' They released an album on Sony in 1992.

Jones, who had been working with incendiary African-American film director Spike Lee for several years, actually did get the call: 'I wasn't available. But they wanted to rehearse, I didn't need that.' However, their other long-serving keyboard player, Rob Sabino didn't. 'I was out of sight out of mind,' he recalls. 'All the hangers around meant there were more than enough people to fit the bill and also there wasn't much money as they weren't very successful then. I was told they had somebody local, so I didn't bother.'

Alfa Anderson was not asked. Nor was she available. In 1988, she had returned to her original vocation of teaching. 'I left showbusiness because I was backstage once in my home town and a little girl came up and said, "Oh you were so great, I love you. I want to be just like you when I grow up, you're my hero",' Anderson recounts. 'Her eyes were so clear and so bright, they served as a mirror for me. I saw my face reflected in this little girl's eyes as it was almost as if I could see my soul. She looked at me with these worshipful eyes that only a child can have. I looked at her and said, "but sweetheart, your heroes are the people that nurture you, that mentor you and work with you every day. I'm here for one night and then I'm gone. What about your teachers and your scout leaders and the people that are with you in church and your communities?" It was at that instant that I thought I wanted to go back into education, because I felt that I could have more of an impact on young people's lives by working with them day to day. It's been hard at times. Regular people don't get their nails done at Elizabeth Arden on Fifth Avenue!!! It was a real lifestyle change for me.' Anderson returned to college and got a second Masters in supervision and administration. She is currently the Principal of a New York high school. 'I enjoy it and it's very much a political act,' she states.

Luci Martin would certainly have appreciated the call. 'Not to be asked for the reunion was hurtful to me,' she sighs. 'It was as hurtful as when we received the letter saying that the group no longer exists. Regardless of what had gone on in the past, a reunion should always be just that. It just didn't make sense to me. I'm not even sure I would have done it, but I wasn't given the opportunity to choose.'

However, there was one person whom everybody had expected to be in the line-up. Tony Thompson. Edwards was publicly disappointed that Thompson wasn't with them in the reunited line-up. 'Yeah, it would have been great to have Tony with us,' he told *Blues & Soul* in 1992. 'I mean he was one of the guys and we were really tight. He had the option to be a part of what we were doing but he's got his own deal with a band in California and he wanted to focus on that.' Although he *was* busy with studio projects in California, Tony Thompson never received the call. He presumed that he wasn't invited

because of the bad feeling over credits toward the end of Chic's career: 'They were just watching out for themselves,' he said in 2003. 'They couldn't care less about me or my contribution to the band. That broke my heart and it still does. I have bad thoughts about how much I used to love them and how things turned out and how things are now between me and Nile.'

'The whole situation with him and Nile was not good,' Patrice Jennings-Thompson recalls. 'Bernard and Nile had fallen out at one point and Tony and Bernard stayed close, but then Nile didn't. Nile and Bernard rekindled their friendship, but Tony remained estranged. Tony just got disillusioned and disappointed that they were making a ton of money off of Chic and he was making nothing. He felt he had been as much a part of it as anybody. Tony was not asked by Nile to rejoin. Tony wouldn't have done it either way – his motto was always "No going back, but he would have loved to have been asked".' Sonny Emory and Sterling Campbell were to play drums on *Chic-ism*, the first new Chic record in nine years.

New personnel, then, would be needed to support Rodgers and Edwards. The duo auditioned over 70 singers, looking for, as the *Chic-ism* press release stated, 'the exact combination of voice, visuals and sheer style.' In Sylver Logan Sharp, they found a truly talented vocalist. Sharp and her friend Jenn Thomas had relocated from South Carolina to Washington DC and sung in an ensemble called Brown's Creation, providing live support to artists such as Jean Carne. She auditioned for the Chic and was immediately hired. 'When you've been in the business as long as Bernard and I,' Rodgers said at the time, 'You get to know what you're looking for. We found it with Sylver.' Edwards was delighted at the prospect of working with her: 'Sylver is gorgeous looking, 5ft 10'. When we saw her, we thought "oh oh – if she can sing there's gonna be trouble. Then when she opened her mouth, we knew straight away she was the one!"'

Fonzi Thornton was impressed with their choice of lead vocalist. 'I was actually there the day they met Sylver. I went in the studio with her and gave her directions. From the day she came in, she really gave the group a powerhouse singer – a soulful, stretchy alto voice. We bonded right away.' After auditioning a further 25 vocalists for the support vocalist role, Sharp suggested that they try her friend, Jenn Thomas, from up in DC. Edwards was convinced when he heard the two of them together that not only was it a magic combination, but moreover, it 'was pure Chic.'

A great deal had changed by the time Chic took to the studio again. The whole experience of live performance for funk and soul acts had been replaced by the notion of one man and his sampler. Hip-hop and rap had made things go smaller. It was a reflection of the simple socio-economics of the music business. Touring cost could be halved, and a moody promo clip would suffice. The politics of disco had shifted yet again.

Recorded at The Power Station and Skyline Studios in New York, in the down time between Rodgers and Edwards' hectic schedules, *Chic-ism* was a bold attempt to update the Chic formula. It was necessary to move forward. The sound was more soulful than before with new vocalists Sharp and Thomas providing a richness and emotion to the grooves. The only other old faces present were the ever-calming presence of Fonzi Thornton, Michelle Cobbs and Brenda White-King on vocals with Gene Orloff again providing concertmaster duties. 'Your Love' sounds like a mixture of 'Ride On Time' with 'Ladies Night' and 'Out Come The Freaks'. The lead single, 'Chic Mystique' had a terribly dating 'hit it' sample introducing it, reducing the credibility of the tune. The clunking early 90s drum machine and raps date the record far more than the sides cut 15 years earlier. 'High', the song that Rodgers and Edwards, both reformed users, wrote about getting their highs from music again, is wholly successful, and could have fitted in on previous Chic albums, utilising Thornton and Edwards full vocal support for Sharp and Thomas. 'Chic-ism' updated the 'Chic Cheer'/'Strike Up The Band' template, a viable piece of self-mythologizing, including the lines

> *'Crisp clichés and witty words*
> *Vocalists that chirp like birds*
> *Rhymes topped with sweet harmonies*
> *Magic fingers on the keys*
> *There's more to us than meets the eye.'*

The one utter standout is 'Take My Love', a showcase for Thomas' beautifully soulful vocal. The ballad is so strong that it could comfortably sit alongside 'At Last I'm Free' and 'Will You Cry (When You Hear This Song)'. The album also suffered from that early 90s affliction of being recorded for CD, meaning that at over an hour, it was the longest ever Chic album (compare with the 42 minutes of *C'est Chic* and 36 minutes of *Risqué*). There wasn't enough quality material to go round. It also, in the shape of ex-Bingo Boys rapper Princesa, had the obligatory early 90s rapper on several songs.

Of course, this new group could never really recapture the glory of the golden era of Chic. Like they had been post-*Risqué*, Chic were no longer setting the musical agenda. They were following. And *Chic-ism* was one part of Edwards and Rodgers' busy other lives, instead of being the sole focus.

Chic-ism was released in February 1992. The critics could not get enough of it. Tied in also was the reissue on Atlantic of *Dance Dance Dance, Chic's Greatest Hits*, a souped (for one) up *Les Plus Grandes Succèses* for CD, which meant that they were competing against themselves, the press the reunion got was amazing – it provided, if anything, an opportunity for the balance of opinion to be redressed. *Entertainment Weekly* suggested that, 'songs like the elegant club hit "Chic Mystique" revive the nightlife vibe, complete with real live orchestration and make it funkier for the 90s.' *Rolling Stone* said it was 'a luscious mix of sophisticated soul and haunting street beats.' *Spin* claimed that it was 'refreshingly sophisticated … musically complete, with ballads better than Whitney, house hipper than C&C Music Factory, and funk fatter than the Brand New Heavies.' The praise simply didn't stop. *Q* suggested that it 'sounds like they never went away at all' and long-term supporters *Billboard* reported that, 'It's as if the good times never left, as founding fathers Edwards and Rodgers (with new female vocalists Sylver Logan Sharp and Jenn Thomas in tow) assert some retrofunkification on the reunion set. Grooves may sound anachronistic to some, but those who recall the late-70s/early-80s hits of the original Chic alignment will probably eat it up. Self-mythologizing "Chic Mystique" and ballad "My Love's For Real" stand out in the pack.'

Rodgers and Edwards went all out to promote the album, including a visit to Britain. Nick Coleman interviewed them for *Time Out* magazine in the dressing room for the *Jonathan Ross Show* in 1992. 'We were terrified we'd destroy the whole Chic thing by doing this,' Edwards said. 'All of it, all the way back to the 70s. Thought maybe we should leave it alone,' Rodgers continued. 'Maybe people in the 90s don't wanna hear a live band, playing so-called dance music. Nowadays, of course, you got people listening to modern techno, dance music and most of 'em haven't had the luxury of hearing a band play dance music, the excitement of a drummer working things up. And that's why we decided to do this project. For the fun, for the pleasure of it.'

Coleman, like so many British writers, had the opportunity to wax lyrical about the glory of Chic: 'open speculation raged in hip circles about what Chic *meant*. Here was an ethos that acted like a disco group that looked like uptown dinner guests who wore sharp shoes and read books. And they sounded odd too. Kind of sophisticated but hard; mathematical yet musical; superficial yet trenchant.' Stuart Maconie, writing in *NME*, continued this theme. He wrote in terms of a history lesson coupled with unadulterated praise. 'Edwards' bass was the pulse of the big city, Rodgers' guitar the clinking of ice in a highball martini and the strings the discreet purr of a rolled hundred dollar bill over a line of the finest Bolivian.'

Although loved, the comeback could not work. The world had simply turned too far. In the post-Gulf War era, Chic seemed anachronistic, competing with the world of super DJs and dance ensembles likes Clivillés and Cole, both of whom clearly worshipped at the font of the Organization. *Chic-ism*'s adaptation of motorik beats and house samples found them doing what could never be done in the late 70s, but it simply sounded a little contrived. If anything, the reformation was a little early. 'There had been so many disappointing revivals of various groups by that time,' Geoff Brown recalls. 'I wasn't expecting too much and I wasn't disappointed. It was unfortunate, but I did think a band like that – no matter how good they were as producers and sessioners – once the collective energy that they had, had been dissipated by time, there wasn't a lot they could do to get it back together again, and I don't think they did to be quite honest. It differs from the way the Stones stick together; Bernard and Nile had grown apart. Coming up with new material in a different musical culture by then was actually a little bit beyond them.'

Although the press loved the album, few people bought it. Hopes were high for the first single release, 'Chic Mystique' – with a video and the full weight of Warners behind it – it only made No. 48 in the UK charts in February 1992. Although the single reached No. 1 in the *Billboard* Hot Dance Music/Club Play Chart, it failed to make the Hot 100 and the album, which didn't chart in Britain, only went to No. 39 on the US Top R&B/Hip-Hop albums. 'When they did the comeback, no one cared', adds Brian Chin. Timing was everything. 'They needed to stay away until they were really missed. Although there was a definite appetite for old artists in the early 90s, sometimes you're just not at the right time.' Nile Rodgers agrees: 'I recently heard stuff from *Chic-ism* – man, there are some cool songs on there. I realise now that it just wasn't our time.' There was not enough support and interest for the band to tour. Quietly, Rodgers and Edwards went their separate ways again.

Chic-ism was not the success that any involved expected. It was not for want of trying. Although loved, a new Chic simply were not relevant at that precise moment. And then, just like 10 years previously, a call came through to Rodgers from David Bowie. After milking the commercial phase that *Let's Dance* heralded to its nadir with 1987's *Never Let Me Down*, Bowie had spent a period in a commercial backwater, leading his pet project Tin Machine and exorcising his past with the *Sound + Vision* tour. Rodgers put two and two together and figured that Bowie would want another *Let's Dance*. Another full commercial onslaught that could restore both of their careers to the spotlight.

On 29th April 1992, four white police officers were acquitted in Los Angeles of the videotaped assault on African-American Rodney King. It was proof, if it were needed, that institutionalised racism was still as endemic as ever in America. The worst rioting since the 60s followed, with around 50 deaths and thousands of injuries.

The recording sessions for what was to become *Black Tie, White Noise*, began while *Chic-ism* was still being recorded. Rodgers produced Bowie for the 'Real Cool World' single from the film *Cool World*. Bowie was ready to return to the commercial world, and he wanted Rodgers back with him. Bowie had recently married supermodel Iman Abdulmajid, and had been living in Los Angeles at the time of the riots. He wanted the album to be a soulful diatribe on the situation.

'It's a very different artistic and spiritual place to *Let's Dance*,' Rodgers states. 'By the time we did *Black Tie, White Noise*, I was ready to show the world that David Bowie and Nile Rodgers were a mega combination and we could easily equal if not beat *Let's Dance*. I was driven by that concept.'

Unfortunately, Bowie had different ideas, suggesting that Rodgers should put all thoughts of *Let's Dance* behind him. 'I was going "how could we forget *Let's Dance*, it's just too huge – you and I together, let's top it, let's make that record. We don't stop until we've done it."' Bowie, however, saw the album as a nexus of the various styles he had used over the years.

'I know *Black Tie, White Noise* has real moments of brilliance', Rodgers adds. 'I listened to it about a year ago and was shocked just how much I liked it – but I didn't like it artistically as much as I liked a record like *Let's Dance*. But there were moments of genius. When I played that guitar solo on "Miracle Goodnight", David told me to act as if the 50s never existed, saying that he didn't want to hear a single blue note in this whole solo, and I did it like the old Les Paul solo, it was really clever.'

The album, recorded between Mountain Studios in Montreux and The Hit Factory in New York, with all of Rodgers' current supporting crew, was certainly Bowie's best since *Let's Dance*. It was a passing hit on its release in spring 1993, reaching No.1 in Britain, but only No. 39 in America. It combined all elements of his career to date, but was not bursting with anything approaching irresistible hits. Mick Ronson, who had recently worked with Edwards, was reunited with Bowie; and when the album swings, as on Bowie's cover of The Walker Brothers' 'Nite Flights' and Cream's 'I Feel Free'; it is up there with his finest performances. However, it's just all a bit hollow. Bowie seemed caught by being unsure as whether to deliver the commercial success the showbiz side of his character craved, or something altogether more arty. Caught between the politics of art and commerce, he ended up making a ragged work. Its possible that he too thought initially of cutting *Let's Dance 2*, but then furiously back-peddled once Rodgers was on board.

'I was so driven by trying to outdo *Let's Dance*, and I never really got over it. I thought I had a huge opportunity to come back big,' Rodgers sighs. But Bowie didn't even really champion the finished work. 'With *Black Tie, White Noise*, I didn't have the powerful artist to speak my piece. I usually have powerful artists fighting for me. When I finished *Let's Dance*, I knew that David was going to be in there fighting for me. When I finished *Like A Virgin*, Madonna was pitching for me. I was accustomed to reluctance on the part of record companies. I was not accustomed to reluctance on the part of artists. That really threw me'.

The album did provide the commercial fillip that Rodgers craved. He retreated and produced David Lee Roth's experimental *Your Filthy Little Mouth* album, and worked for the first time in 20 years with his old Village cohort, Robbie Dupree, on his *Walking On Water* album.

However, there was two areas where Chic were to flourish beyond Rodgers' and Edwards' wildest dreams – and they didn't have to lift a finger. Nostalgia and sampling provided the basis for an upswing in the group's fortunes. Although it had been present since the mid-80s, sampling really took off. Suddenly, everybody could make a hit record, by using records of the past. As Nelson George stated, 'In the post-soul era, shards of the black past exist in the present at odd and often uncomfortable angles to each other.' You didn't need a new Chic when you had the old one.

Hip-hop especially became the playground for this to happen, like Rodgers had catalogued riffs he remembered and phrases he had heard and previously turned them into hits, now people no longer needed to be able to play anything to recreate: the records were there already for them. George continued, 'It's post-modern art in that it shamelessly raids older forms of pop culture – kung fu movies, chitlin' circuit comedy, 70s funk, and other equally disparate sources – and reshapes the material to fit the personality of an individual artist and the taste of the times.' The sparseness of Chic's groove allowed many a rapper to project their image right there, just above the Thompson-Rodgers-Edwards triangle. What Sugar Hill started in 1979 was continued through the following 20 years.

In Britain, especially, nostalgia for the 70s began to swing into full view. Records like 'Step Back In Time' by Kylie Minogue had opened the floodgates for this disco nostalgia. Compilations littered the charts. Clubs such as Bus Stop and Starsky And Hutch became hooked on the iconography of the mirrorball and the beige suit. The commodified and easily reductive disco was returning and Chic and its productions could be heard everywhere. And, although they were miles apart at the time, to new ears, 'Le Freak' was the same as 'D.I.S.C.O.' or 'Y.M.C.A.'. In the way people hear collections which feature Mozart and Beethoven and their myriad differences and eras blur into a category named 'classical', so Chic became part of this mythical past where everybody hung out and had good times. The rose-tinted glasses of revisionism were placed on the politics of disco.

Bernard Edwards also returned to the scene of former glories, hooking up in a reformed Power Station again with Tony Thompson, who had been playing with Trent Reznor's experimental Nine Inch Nails. Like Rodgers returning to Bowie, it was just not the same. Robert Palmer came back on board, after he had been replaced by Michael Des Barres for the 1985 tour.

The idea of cutting a new Power Station record stemmed from John Taylor, who was battling the collapse of his marriage and serious drink and drug addictions. 'I was very frustrated with Duran again,' he comments. 'Some reunions work and some don't. I don't know what made me think that it would be a good idea. We started working in Los Angeles and we wrote some songs. It's always hard when you try to define a band for a new age.' The

Power Station had made one of the most defining statements of 1985. Ten years later, it was somewhat difficult to redefine themselves in the age of Rage Against The Machine, L7 and Nirvana. 'I thought it could be done. We all did. We were all on the top of our game in 1985. This time, we weren't,' Taylor suggested ruefully. 'I got halfway into it and we started hitting walls and I couldn't hack it. We did a lot of recording. It didn't feel good. I couldn't keep it together. I think I split after New York. I realised I couldn't tour it.'

As John Taylor left the project, the remaining members of The Power Station decamped to the beautiful Italian island of Capri to finish recording the album, and Edwards overdubbed all of Taylor's bass parts.

While Edwards was recording the second Power Station album, *Living In Fear*, Rodgers was asked by Japan Tobacco to go to Tokyo to be honoured with their Super Producers Award. Rodgers phoned Edwards and asked him to play with him. It would be the first time that Chic would take a public stage since Rodgers' birthday in 1990. Although not feeling at the peak of his game, Edwards agreed.

23.
NOW THAT YOU'RE GONE

'We wish to express deep sorrow on the occasion of Bernard Edwards'
passing away and it is our heartfelt wish that he will rest in peace.'
JAPAN TOBACCO

'I just want to give respect to Bernard Edwards – he was a genius; he really
was. He was one of the best bass players on the planet – and today everybody
copies his style…He was such a vibe. Pure talent. I'm sure it was really hard
for Nile. They really locked together well.'
DEBBIE SLEDGE

NILE RODGERS WAS CELEBRATING his success in cleaning up his act. After
Black Tie, White Noise, he had had a relatively low-key period. He had been
drink and drug free for the best part of two years by this point. He and
Edwards had recorded an album called *Chic Freak And More Treats* in 1995
for release in Japan, which consisted of re-records of a lot of Chic tracks. It
had sold 50,000 copies there. There was an eager market for Nile Rodgers and
Chic.

The band that went to Tokyo to celebrate the success of Nile Rodgers
included Sylver Logan Sharp, ex-Prince protégé Jill Jones (who had replaced
Jenn Thomas), and Christopher Max on vocals; Bill Holloman on saxophone;
Mac Gollehon on trumpet; Ex-Outloud member Philip Saisse and Richard
Hilton on keyboards and long-term cohort Omar Hakim on drums. Gerardo
Velez, who Rodgers had seen performing with Jimi Hendrix at Woodstock,
was also present, on percussion. The special guest was, of course, Bernard
Edwards, who had curtailed his Power Station activities to play live with
Rodgers for the first time since 1990. The roadshow included several special
guests: Simon Le Bon, Slash, Stevie Winwood and the Kathy-less Sister Sledge.
The three concerts had been a great success.

As we all sadly know, by the end of the tour, Bernard Edwards was dead,
alone in a room at the Hotel New Otani. He left six children; Bernard Jr,
Portia, Michael, Mark and David from his marriage to Alexis, and Leah from

his union with Bambi. The man who put the groove into Chic, who contained and complimented Rodgers' artistic exuberance, who marshalled the troops, teased out performances and acted as an anchor, had gone.

'It was my honour to be able to take care of him in death,' Rodgers told Geoff Brown in 2003. 'To deal with the police and immigration. They had put Bernard in a white kimono, a white coffin with a glass front and built an altar in the police station and I thought, well, they're not doing this because I'm in Chic. This is what they do. And they said, "be with your friend". And I was in there and I could say goodbye and thank him for giving me this wonderful life and sharing it with me.'

'Nile was the only one that knew,' Joni Sledge recalled. 'He didn't tell any of us until we got home. It was so shocking. He was upstairs in his room. He was trying to spare all of us because we'd had such a great time with Bernard and we're all a part of this big team – it wasn't until we got back to the States that he called us and told all of us.'

Bernard's silent solemnity was respected and missed by the remainder of the group. 'I used to speak to Bernard over the years,' Raymond Jones remembered. 'The thing I learned from him was how to be a bandleader. When I was on the road later, I used to tell him that I understood why he did what he did with us, and call him and tell him some craziness and thank him. He always had something cool to say.'

The news was broken in America by David Millman, an independent PR who had just established his own company. His brief association with Bernard has been with him ever since: 'After working for record companies for many years, I started my own PR company in the spring of 1996,' Millman states. 'One of my first clients was a company that was managing Bernard's career as a producer. We were working on a press release about something completely unrelated when I got a panicked phone call that Bernard had suddenly died in Japan and that we needed to issue a statement. *The New York Times* ended up mentioning me as the spokesperson, though I'd never met or spoken with the man himself (I'm a big fan though!). For weeks afterward, I got calls and notes from industry friends saying they'd read about me. I'd say, "You mean, in *The New York Times* obituaries?" It's a weird world. I still get called today.'

Everyone in the Chic community, past and present, was devastated. Edwards had always kept his feet firmly on the ground, no matter how many flights of fancy his partner was having.

'One thing I can say about Bernard at that time, was that he was at peace,' Debbie Sledge recalled. 'He had a lot of peace around him. He was a gentleman; there was no stress. He was fighting a cold; he was very respectful of us – any question we had he was making sure we were happy. I appreciated that.'

The news spread quickly. 'I was surprised. Andy called me,' John Taylor recounted. 'I was at my parents. When you look back you think, maybe the guy had his undercarriage down, he was on his way out. It's easy to think that in hindsight. It seemed just so mysterious how he had passed.'

'I thought it was a terribly sad way to go,' Taylor continued. 'They'd made the Chic record, so they'd done that, got back out there to a degree, without Tony, which was a mistake, and then Nile had taken The Nile Show to Japan. Simon was there doing "Let's Dance". Bernard had so many people, family and friends; I guess it's the fate of a lot of musicians to die on the road in some hotel room. It must have been reasonably peaceful. He'd been working. You can only cover up a certain amount of pain.'

'I heard about Bernard's passing on the radio,' says Norma Jean Wright. 'It was such a shock to me because I never even knew he was sick. Bernard was really like the father figure in Chic, and he was another really funny guy, back then between Luther and him, we were surrounded with laughter.'

Alfa Anderson still talks always of 'Nile and Bernard' in the present before correcting herself: 'Even today I run the names together.' Tony Thompson described Edwards as 'my best friend, my mentor, and one of the greatest people I've ever known.' 'I thought he had it all together,' Rob Sabino suggests. 'He was trim and healthy. He'd lost a lot of weight. I never thought he should have done that, he was always a bigger guy. He got in shape and very thin – I think it put a lot of pressure on his heart.'

'I was devastated. Bernard and I were always in touch. He would come over,' Fonzi Thornton sighs. 'They decided they wanted to put together a new band – and when he went over to Tokyo, I never really realised he was ill. I had been at Bernard's wedding, when he married his second wife, Bambi. I had been to his daughter, Portia's wedding. We were really close. It was a shock. I still miss him terribly. He had such a great sense of humour and he was a solid guy. He always had your back. There was one time; Luther was looking for a manager, so he called Bernard, because he knew he would know. Bernard gave us the 411 on this manager – he was saying you don't want to deal with that so and so. He was a very straight up, no-nonsense kind of guy, but a lot of fun. A good, good cat.'

'It was interesting working with him – he was great with vocalists,' Eddie Martinez said. 'So much of making records is all about feel. How does it feel and how does it sound – there is a nexus between the two – he made people feel at home and looking at the best that everything could be. No matter how much technology would precede things, he could never really lose sight of his roots, making things feel good from a live standpoint. The actual spontaneity between musicians – there was always that element – what does it feel like at the end of the day.'

'There had been whispers that he wasn't well', John Taylor suggested. 'By the time of the second Power Station album, 'he smoked a little pot, drank a little beer, but very mellow. We'd all changed, but he was very sweet, just mellow. It was if he'd had some of the life knocked out of him. Andy had a great relationship with him – they'd done Rod Stewart together.'

'It's all a bit of a mystery,' Andy Taylor told Adrian Deevoy in 1996, 'he had pneumonia. I believe he knew there was something wrong with him. He'd been through it all. He did Betty Ford and he used to do a lot of coke. The Bernard I knew went to the gym, drank moderately, had the occasional blow on the reefer but nothing excessive. People called me and said, did he die of an overdose? Of course he didn't. I slammed the phone down.'

'The guy dropped dead from an acute pneumonia attack that ground up his whole respiratory system,' Robert Palmer added. 'He died in his sleep, what a weird ass thing to happen. The phone just rang and I was told his nibs had popped his clogs. He wasn't very well; he was always a bit of a moaner. The last time I saw him he had a mild bout of food poisoning but I'm not going to consider, in retrospect, that he knew he was ill.'

Nile Rodgers felt the passing acutely. He was distraught. 'Bernard is closer to me than any family member and any one-on-one relationship that I've ever had on this earth,' Rodgers sighs. 'Regardless of fights, innuendo, lies and bullshit, I will go to my grave feeling an incredible sense of guilt because the love between he and I was so strong we robbed people around us from having full relationships. He was just my boy. Our whole relationship – we could cut to the crux of a problem with a couple of lines of cynicism. One lawyer would be going on, and Bernard would go *"are you finished?"*

'The love between us is absolutely extraordinary from the first moment he and I hooked up to the moment I walked in to that room and found him on that couch. I miss Bernard in my life. It was a life relationship – it wasn't just about music. There were only two Chic members. Bernard and Nile. It was always about Bernard and me. It was laughable how people criticised us. People approached Chic like it was studio work. We played live. People who work on our music don't understand it. We write and produce – people would show up and play what they had to play. People who work on our records had no idea how it was going to turn out. That's the truth – that's how it always was. We painted a picture that we are a collective – we are an extended family, but artistic decisions were always up to two people – and now that other person has gone, Bernard left it up to me to carry the torch. My relationship with him is so pure – that anybody around it has to respect from whence it comes; it's magical, man. I've seen famous partners in the music business, Keef'n'Mick, Simon and Garfunkel. Maybe it's exactly the same as what we had, I don't know. But Edwards and Rodgers is a real thing. Even now he's passed away.'

All members of Chic past and present rushed to be at Bernard's funeral in Stamford, Connecticut. 'Tony and I were on a plane as quickly as possible,' Raymond Jones recalls. 'We got through it the best we could – there was an enormous outpouring of love.'

'There were several hundred people there. Alexis was amazing ... she brought me in and re-introduced me to the kids who had grown so much since I had seen them last,' Karen Milne, who was temporarily reunited with Thompson for the funeral, recalls. 'I just couldn't go to the burial site, as I felt it was a "family" thing. Alexis wanted me to stay, saying there would be a gathering after, with lots of food. It was amazing, what a crowd. Probably everybody who ever worked on a Chic album was there. It was very emotional.' Rodgers delivered the eulogy at the ceremony.

In pondering Edwards' legacy, long-time friend Frankie Crocker, programme director at WBLS New York, summed it up simply as 'a life so young, a talent so large, and a goodbye too soon. The loss is immeasurable.' 'Bernard was definitely a great bass player,' Robert Bell recalls. 'I was so very sorry to hear about Bernard's passing. He lived near my brother. I used to see Bernard up there from time to time. We hung out. He played in the pocket – he didn't play a whole lot of stuff, but he was right there with the drummer.' Critic Dave Marsh suggested that Bernard Edwards was 'one of the half dozen most inventive electric bassists ever, the true successor of James Jamerson and Duck Dunn.'

'I do have the Musicman bass he recorded "Good Times" on,' John Taylor sighs. 'I don't remember why the fuck he gave it to me. I remember I gave him a silver disc for "Is There Something I Should Know" in return! It was just a very sweet thing to do. It's come to mean so much to me. It didn't mean that much to me at the time, but now. There were times I kept it under lock and key. I now use it all the time – that's the way he would want it.'

Edwards' death brought a close to the golden era of Chic. His passing left Rodgers listless. For the first time since 1972, he had no-one to compete with personally and professionally. Although he had worked with a myriad of performers, Rodgers' best work involved Edwards, or was done as a reaction to him. They were akin to the disco Burton and Taylor, couldn't be together, but couldn't be apart.

However, the Chic legacy received an enormous boost as the 20th Century drew to a close, as nostalgia for the disco era became widespread, and through the kitsch and retro, an understanding began that this was actually revolutionary music, which carried deeper messages. Rodgers suddenly became an in-demand interviewee: intelligent, eloquent and always ready with a neat sound-bite.

However, most of the layers that had built Chic were not mentioned. It had just become 'Nile and Bernard'. Undeniably, the lion's share of the credit should be theirs but other members of the extended collective were not thrilled, especially Tony Thompson. The public image of the group will always be two girls and three guys.

Within a period of months, MC Lyte took 'Upside Down' and converted it into 'Cold Rock A Party'; The Notorious B.I.G. took 'I'm Coming Out' and made it 'Mo' Money, Mo' Problems', Will Smith took 'He's The Greatest Dancer' and made it 'Gettin' Jiggy With It' and Faith Evans converted 'Chic Cheer' into 'Be Faithful'. The Spice Girls, who, lest we forget, in 1998 were a global phenomenon, covered 'We Are Family' in concert...

Nile talked to *The New York Times* in 1998 about the proliferation of sampling. 'When I listen to Biggie's "Mo' Money Mo' Problems," I say to myself when an artist starts with a song like that, they're starting with Chic as the band. Tony Thompson, Bernard Edwards, Nile Rodgers, Rob Sabino: that's who's playing in your band. Then you have Diana Ross as your background vocalist, and you have it recorded in a great room on a magical day with Bob Clearmountain as your engineer. That's what you're starting with. If you can't write a hit from that, then you are weak.' Just as The Sugar Hill team had identified 20 years previously, Chic's cast-iron rhythms were an ideal cornerstone with which to launch or boost a career. 'I hope he gets paid for some of the sampling done of him,' Ahmet Ertegun laughs. 'He gets used quite a lot – which is understandable.'

Rodgers continued, nursing the flame, carrying on with myriad productions, defending Chic's legacy. It appeared that Chic were finally to be put to bed in 1998. After performing again in Tokyo in 1997, of which Rodgers later commented to Ed Condran of the *Philadelphia City Paper*: 'It was hard to do Chic again because Bernard isn't here anymore,' he explained. 'But I thought we could do it one more time in Japan.' Respected session bassist Jerry Barnes stepped into Edwards' shoes. The core of the touring band remained the same as the Budokan line-up, with Logan Sharp leading from the front. She has now been the lead vocalist for 13 years, at least eight more than Luci Martin, Norma Jean Wright or Alfa Anderson.

The gig at Tramps in New York on 3rd April 1998 was to be the final Chic show. 'It will be a full set of nothing but the classics,' Rodgers said. 'The songs still hold up. You can see why these songs still move people... you know New York is going to go insane. We can put this thing to bed after this show.'

Chic are still performing in 2004. The potency of the name, the magic of the brand, the demand for disco, the need for everybody to dance; all of this remains.

Unfortunately, more key players from the golden era of Chic have passed away in recent years: Alexis Edwards, so supportive to her then-husband in the early days, passed away on 16th August 2001 of heart failure. 'It wasn't anything she let us know about,' Edwards Jr sighs. 'She was probably more private than my father. She was walking around with a bunch of pain and we didn't even know it.'

Fortunately, one of the other key players has hung on in there: Luther Vandross, by the turn of the 21st century, a megastar in his own right, with a history of weight fluctuation, survived a massive stroke in April 2003 and is slowly on the road to recovery.

Tony Thompson slipped under the radar in the 90s. A sensitive man, he was slowing down by the time he reunited with The Power Station in the middle of the decade. His adopted brother, Alan, died of AIDS in 1994, which laid him low, and his father had died at the start of the decade. He played with Nine Inch Nails, but he receded into Californian living. As the 90s became the 21st century, he got happily married and played locally with a group of friends he named Non-Toxic. When his wife-to-be, actress Patrice Jennings, met him, he didn't actually mention he'd been in Chic, The Power Station or, however briefly, Led Zeppelin.

'We met in February 2000 and married five months later on July 22nd,' Jennings-Thompson smiles. 'Everyone was pretty shocked when he decided to marry me.' The two had met after a Grammy party. Jennings had absolutely no idea who he was. 'We just hit it off. We ended up talking for five hours. He didn't mention he was a musician, but he talked of starting an advertising business with a colleague in New York. We'd dated several times before I found out who he was. He had mentioned he'd been a musician at some point, but in LA, *everyone* has been a musician at some point, so I took it with a grain of salt! We talked more about his mother being ill, and I knew he'd lived around the world, but I never put two and two together. We mostly talked about family things.'

Jennings had two children from a previous marriage, and certainly wasn't looking to get remarried. It was after five dates, that someone came up to her at a party and told her exactly who Thompson was. 'He said that guy is like the god of drums, he's like on every album under the sun,' Jennings-Thompson laughs. 'Tony just didn't talk about it. Then he told me who he'd played with. Being 12 years younger than him, all I remembered was The Power Station. He was a real simple guy – I had to pull teeth to get it out of him,' she continues. 'When it was in the past, he didn't revisit it. He agreed he should be playing. We finally put a band together called Non-Toxic – they recorded a three-song demo. He had just got a new vocalist and then he fell very ill. I knew a very mellow guy. I couldn't believe it when I heard him hit those drums.'

He had little contact with other members of Chic, but he kept in touch with Ray Jones, Luci Martin and Norma Jean Wright. A chance meeting with Bernard Edwards Jr shook him to the core. 'I saw Tony last year in a gas station in California,' Bernard Jr said in 2003. 'We hugged. That's when he first found out that my mother had passed away – I think it shook him up a lot. He just got in the car and drove away – he just didn't know what to say'.

Robert Palmer – another person who had been close to Chic's inner circle – passed away aged 54 in September 2003. His death played on Thompson's mind a great deal. It certainly made him aware of his own mortality. 'Robert liked to party,' Jennings-Thompson stated. 'Tony never did any drugs when he was with me. Ninety-nine per cent of the time he would have Coca-Cola. He said that Palmer lived a very fast life. It didn't surprise him that he would have a heart-attack.'

'Pretty sad – he was a talented cat,' Thompson said. 'I knew something bad was going to happen to him in terms of his lifestyle – he smoked like a chimney, he drank. I used to have problems, because we would do interviews at nine o'clock in the morning. All the journalists were in one room – he'd come in with Martinis and this was the morning. He was as clean as a whistle, he always carried himself great, but ... When I first met Robert in the 80s, and Andy and the whole bunch of them, it was a time when partying was cool and new and great, doing drugs, whatever. But when I had to do the second album, he was pretty much doing the same thing. I'd gotten older. Robert was a very different guy – he was constantly involved in music. There wasn't a time when he wasn't thinking or singing or trying to come up with something musical. He was a great guy to work with, an extremely talented cat.'

Thompson's final years, although unwell, were especially happy. He loved caring for his adopted children and found happiness with Patrice, after years of itinerant relationships following the split with Karen Milne in 1986. But soon, his health began to deteriorate. 'He was definitely bruised,' Jennings-Thompson suggests, 'and then I realised he was sick all the time. The symptoms were never consistent. He had the same doctor for 15 years and he should have known.' Thompson was rushed into hospital in summer 2003 and had a 7lb tumour removed. Renal Cell Cancer was slowly spreading all over his body.

Tony Thompson died on 15th November 2003. His passing was tragic. It came at a time, as with a lot of the original team in Chic, that he could feel reconciled with the work they had done back in the 70s and 80s, and maybe even enjoy some of it again.

John Taylor told Jennings-Thompson that if, 'Tony had been a singer or a lead guitar player he would be one of the most famous in the world. He had such a presence and was such a nice man. Because he was a drummer he didn't get it. He should have been a billionaire for all the grooves he put in. People asked for him because he had such a groove. His whole story is very tragic.'

'Tony and I were always really tight,' Fonzi Thornton recalls. 'We had a lot of admiration for each other. We were never really close, but we had a great respect. We would hang out on the road together – we would be on the bus, talking, laughing and playing cards – I would always lose. Tony was a really cool guy, very reserved.'

'Tony and I were an outfit,' Sabino recalls. 'We used to go up to Irish bars in the Bronx after a session – it was wild. Nile went to all the upscale places.'

'Tony was such an explosive drummer,' recalls Eddie Martinez. 'Out of the three guys Tony was the most insecure. I don't think he realised his brilliance. Nile and Bernard had a sense of confidence about what they had done, but Tony was like an enigma – he was such a powerful, distinctive drummer, I don't think he understood his contribution to a degree. Bernard and Nile were a bit more comfortable with their status.'

'Tony played with a sort of recklessness that's very exciting to guys with rock backgrounds,' Rodgers said. 'His recklessness worked fantastically with the organisational skills of me and Bernard. What we did was organise confusion, which is what I love to do, which is what we all loved to do'.

I spoke with Thompson three times for this project. He was excited by the prospect of being included and delighted that he had been tracked down. He felt that over the years, his role had been written out of the Chic legend. "Nile and Bernard did all the writing – but they never told me what to play," he told me in October 2003. 'Anything that I played was an integral part of their songwriting. No one ever gave me a chart and told me what to play. This was all my ability, the way that I wrote. Evidentially, that was not recognised and the business – you had to play a melodic instrument or you were not recognised as a songwriter. The problem I had was that that was how I created and I did not get my due. It was a lot my fault too for assuming that I would be taken care of with these guys, and they would recognise my contribution. I recognised that, but it came back and it bit me in the ass. Nile's just a very different person now. But Bernard broke my heart too, because I found out later on that those guys never really watched out for me in the slightest. They would come up with a chord – I would do what I did to it, Bernard would do what he did to it – and that's how all of those damn songs were made. And if you look at it, that is my contribution. That should have been at least acknowledged, but it never was – it was taken for granted.'

When I interviewed Rodgers in June 2003 for this book, he was very vague on the subject of Tony Thompson. On being asked what Thompson may have been up to, Rodgers replied: 'I have no clue. The last time I saw him he was this gigantic body-builder living out in California. When I was in the UK at the *In The City* conference, there was a girl there who told me he was selling seats and busses out to Mecca to wealthy Arabs.'

Thompson was mournful when discussing Rodgers, because he clearly missed Rodgers' contact, love and support. For some reason, the pair just couldn't maintain a relationship. Their contact was intermittent, practically non-existent. It could be argued that Rodgers' focus on the present often excludes him dwelling on the past. His ambition and drive made, destroyed and rebuilt Chic. Rodgers and Thompson were united by telephone in the days before Thompson passed away.

'When Nile called, they put the past behind them,' Patrice Jennings-Thompson recalls. 'Nile was very sweet in trying to get hold of other doctors and specialists, offering his help in every way. He still calls and asks how I'm doing. I take him how he treats me and I can't judge him by anything else. But I do know that Tony had been very very hurt. He was devastated when their friendship ended.'

And so, of the trio that shared the same sandwich out at Brandice High School, only one remained. Nile Rodgers.

24.
MY FEET KEEP DANCING

*'I loved those guys. Being around them was some of the best times
I ever had.'*
TONY THOMPSON 2003

'You haven't heard me for a while, but…couldn't I have another shot?'
NILE RODGERS

JANUARY 29TH, 2003: As America, under George W. Bush mobilised its
forces once again to move forward another questionable foreign policy
decision, Chic celebrated their silver jubilee at the China Club in New York.

A Diana Ross tribute film was shown, and shortly thereafter, the current line
up of Chic began their show with a medley of 'I'm Comin' Out'/ 'Upside
Down'. The show was an enormous self-tribute: 'Ain't No Mountain High
Enough' was played with Rodgers' early collaborators Nikolas Ashford &
Valerie Simpson, 'Roam' with Kate Pierson of the B52s, and 'God Bless The
Child' and 'Lady Marmalade' with key influence Patti LaBelle, in addition to
the usual collection of Chic material.

Appearing on stage at various points were Fonzi Thornton, Wyclef Jean,
Miss Piggy, and some of the Village People. 'Although it's a completely new
band now,' Thornton recalled, 'Sylver introduced me as an original member
of Chic, which meant a lot.' It had been an extremely eventful 25 years since
Kenny Lehman hooked up with Rodgers and Edwards and asked them to
write a B-side for a record in praise of New York.

For one, the disco revival is now locked in a full, perma-swing from which
we may never be able to escape. It is now simply part of the millennial
musical buffet, to be sampled alongside a nibble of grunge or a sliver of
house. And of course, this is how canons are formed – the 20 records that are
popularly seen as 'disco' leave little room for imagination or flair – they've
been devalued simply because of their familiarity – you are, as I've said
before, listening to them without hearing them. 'Le Freak' is in there, possibly
'Good Times' and certainly 'We Are Family'; but so too is 'Staying Alive', 'I

Will Survive' and 'YMCA' – these recycled tunes, that are guaranteed to fill a dance floor, stifle the originality and inventiveness of a great deal of the other music of that era. Disco has been broken and bruised and is now on the way back, receiving its credibility through house and the realisation that the discrediting of disco was merely down to a handful – of albeit absolutely massive – popular tunes.

Crate-digging DJ specialists such as Dave Lee, Dimitri From Paris or Bob Sinclar have ensured that the other side of disco is portrayed, taking a wilfully obscure approach to unearthing old gems, in a manner not dissimilar from the ring-fencing of the groove by Northern Soul elitists. Lee himself, under his Joey Negro moniker revived the first Chic Organization Ltd. production, Norma Jean's forever exuberant 'Saturday' for a Top 20 UK hit in 1998.

What is clear is that Chic still manage to find a place in both camps – they can unite the chinstrokers and the dancers. Chic were as radical to late 70s pop as were groups working more visibly in the avant-garde. They were as out there as Pere Ubu, or any of the Ze roster that took the lead from Rodgers' chicken-scratch or Edwards' elasticity. Chic obviously did it in far better suits. Chic were able to cut through the politics of disco, and briefly control it, with their ironic symphonies blasting out across the world. The great thing was simply, as Rodgers has said, that you didn't need to know about hidden meanings, because you had the rhythmic drive to pull your forward.

That Chic were the ultimate victims of the 'disco sucks' campaign is richly ironic, as their rock backgrounds actually located them as being whiter than many of their peers. Their form and structure was complex, knotty and repetitious – but all people saw was the bass line. This double-edged sword of their very craving of anonymity made them in many respects, one of the anti-disco campaign's obvious targets, as their bio was sketchy, and with their two female lead singers, who most obviously seemed to be living the high life on all their television appearances made them look, to the untrained eye, almost vacuous. There seemed to be little to separate them from any other routine disco team.

Nile Rodgers still retains the idealism of his Village period. He remains politicised and is a most welcome member of the many boards and think tanks that he presides over. 'I get pissed off when people say the Ku Klux Klan shouldn't exist or that the state of whatever should change their flag as it's offensive to black people. Well, hey, I'm a black person and it doesn't offend me. I don't care what you wear and what you say, just don't hurt me. I feel very comfortable with a white supremacist or anyone who has a different point of view, because I'm an open-minded person and I want to hear what you have to say – I believe my opinion can be changed and I think that's a healthy way to be. I grew up believing that dogmatic people were exactly what I didn't want to be, so I have an open mind. You might be able to convince me that a black person's inferior; I'm ready to listen to your story. I have the ability to change.'

While this openness and ability to change can produce fantastic results, it can also lead to musical errors of judgement. That is almost inevitable, with being prolific and multi-tasking, like Prince, for every triumph there can be something that doesn't quite work. Musically, there is an element of Rodgers' personality that simply cannot leave things alone – whatever the latest trend is in dance music, he is willing to experiment. Of course, that is what propelled him to success in the mid 70s by using disco as the method of carriage for his material. He said to *Rolling Stone* in 1979: 'I'll tell you, if Country & Western was the next big thing, I'd be right out there with a cowboy hat on. That is the way of the world.' The problem with the modern technology is the exceedingly transient nature of its sound. So, a record with 'Jack' on it in 1987, to the questionable *Re:Chic* Japanese mixes from 2001 show errors in judgement. It's only natural that Rodgers would want to keep his music in the clubs, but the originals continue to do just fine. They are timeless. It's as bad as someone wanting to make an ambient mix of Pink Floyd. It doesn't need it – the records are blank enough on which to project your own modernism.

Today, Rodgers is like an elder statesman, turning his and Edwards' legacy into something lasting. His post 9/11 charity work, culminating in the *We Are Family* Foundation creates hope for millions of children. He has Bill Clinton's personal numbers in his office Rolodex. Rodgers is in constant demand not just as a writer and producer, but also as a music distribution company owner, a high-class hotel proprietor and a ready and willing talking head for Chic and the era that his group presided over. He is pretty close to being a living legend. He enjoyed two brief years at the very zenith of popular music, then almost 26 years as one of the most in-demand producers in the world. *Rolling Stone* magazine has called him 'the best pop-jazz guitarist since Wes Montgomery, the best producer of pop grooves since Willie Mitchell, maybe the best writer of dance anthems ever.' He may be all this, but he is not famous. Famous in the way David Bowie is famous; the way Madonna is famous.

The frequency with which Rodgers is at pains to stress he is not bitter suggests he protests too much. The desire for anonymity that was Rodgers and Edwards' watchword has led to a degree of obscurity that seems to gnaw away at Rodgers. He clearly adores the fact that Chic continue to get their underground respect, and comments such as this *Guardian* review from 1999 warm his heart: 'labelling Chic "disco" was like mistaking Dom Perignon for Babycham, with Chic's "hint of menace or a tremor of anxiety beneath their sleek commercial veneer', but he is adamant that the wider stage still owes him a living. He still would like more high-profile production gigs, and maybe his time will come again, but as Ahmet Ertegun states, 'You know what happens in our business, don't you, with producers? Time changes so quickly. Very few survive. New techniques come in'.

'No one really knows who I am,' Rodgers laughs. 'We did our job too well. Dick Clark said this is the biggest song about a dance that nobody knows how to do – that was almost prophetic – he was almost saying you guys are huge and we don't know who the hell you are. The biggest selling record in Warners' history is still "Le Freak" and no one will touch it – who is going to sell six million singles in America again?'

'History has dealt us different cards and we're not sitting at the table with Sting or Bowie, Eric Clapton, Billy Joel and all of those guys who were around us at the same time,' Rodgers sighs. 'How musicians feel about us, and people write about us are two different things. I'm not complaining and I'm trying not to protest, but it's not fair if I don't. There's a certain political correctness – when people ask me what my favourite albums and songs are, I'm not above doing that old bullshit – do I give my honest answer or what I'd say to make me look cool? My favourite records are quite cool, but sometimes, I wish they were naff so I could go to the grave defending my position.'

'I make a lot of money, I run a lot of great businesses; I have a very exciting, active life. I just wish the cards were dealt a little differently. One day Eric Clapton and I were having a conversation and Eric said to me "I'm the happiest man in the world, because for the rest of my life I can play the music that I love – the blues." I had to hold back tears and I thought "why the fuck can't I play the music that I love for the rest of my life; dance music, disco?" How come if walk out on stage and play Kool & The Gang's "Hollywood Swinging", that seems weird to people, but Eric can play any number of classic songs written by others and it feels artistic and spiritual. Why is the spiritual and political acceptance not the same for music that is essentially the same? It's only history that has changed what blues and black music is, because when Bernard and I were writing about the depression and slavery, we grew up playing the blues. We took something around us that was happening and made something else – we took jazz and rock and R&B and created a primal experience for those people who wanted to move. We can wrap that in intellectualism, but it's culturally, spiritually and artistically the same. There is no difference between Sylvester talking about "(You Make Me Feel) Mighty Real", or Muddy Waters singing "I'm A Man"; this is a gay dude in a super homophobic world who's talking about his trials and tribulations in a way that makes us lose ourselves. Forget whether we hate homosexuals or not; forget if we hate black people; same thing that happened when the hardcore racists hear the old fashioned blues. Music is that great communicator – it changes the way we see each other.'

Although Rodgers will always have an uphill struggle for mass acceptance, the warmth towards the sound that Chic created at the epicentre of a changing time remains strong.

'The voice of that band was so nondescript that anyone could go on top,'

John Taylor states. 'They were the last great human dance machine before the computers took over. What was the last great dance record made by humans? – they are few and far between.'

'I saw a Nubian guy once in Morocco playing an oud and if I closed my eyes, I thought he really reminded me of Nile,' states Bryan Ferry. 'There was the same groove thing going on there – the root of all the music we love, comes from Africa but is filtered through this amazing country called America. And all the things that happened to black people in America conditioned all that. I think there is a kind of longing, and a yearning in that early black American music that you still can hear ringing today. But the rhythmic side of it, which is Nile's speciality, is really interesting. There's the emotional thing – the blues, but then the movement side of it, the rhythm thing, such a physical kind of music – he just taps into something which is very ancient, I think and really beautiful. I think Chic are very important – they made some incredible records. I'm a big fan, and I'm always going to think they are some of the key people. It was an incredible partnership.'

'I was a very proud recipient of the favours bestowed upon us by Chic,' Ahmet Ertegun concludes. 'I still think of Nile Rodgers as a great friend – and I would like the world to know he is a person who has a great talent and great insight into the music they made.'

Chic were simply different: 'They were this incredibly musicianly group, who played as well as anything you'd ever heard in your life,' Geoff Brown recalls. 'Over and above that, the kind of songs they were writing were slyly witty, erudite and referential – they referred not only to the history of black music, but to what was happening at that time. I think they probably were the most influential writers/producers of that particular period. There had been the theory, put about by white rock musicians who didn't really know the time of day by that time that all black music was coming out on a conveyor belt by faceless musicians. We all knew how good the Motown house band had been, Philly's MFSB had been, and here was the New York contingent, incredibly bright, who could play any white musicians off the face of the earth.'

'Every group has a point where they crest,' Eddie Martinez concludes. 'It was just the ebb and flow of their pop world. You look back on those tracks, they still stand up. When you think about what Nile has done in his contribution to the guitar, he set the template for pop-funk.'

'They were bringing together a lot of elements from the past, while being forward looking,' Brian Chin adds. 'Because there was more concept in them, it wasn't just a band that got together – there was obviously more of an intellectual process. Given the visuals and the concept of the group, they were perfect for MTV but I think they were all better off producing Robert Palmer and Madonna. I think that was bigger fish to fry than Chic. Maybe they could have developed some other concept, that could have been their pet – but after the exhaustion of trying and failing with Chic, to get all these gold and platinum records from producing other artists.'

'The hip-hop generation listen to Chic,' Martin Fry states. 'Nile lives in the present. He seems really zenned out, relaxed, quite beatific. It's like Scorsese talking about the next film. The whole spirit still lives.'

'I think Chic played a very important role in the development of dance music as a mainstream phenomenon,' dance historian David Nathan states. 'Their cleverly crafted songs, the production values – most especially with the effective use of strings and vocal harmonies – and the Chic "sound" was different, innovative and exciting. There was a certain quality to their music: when I think of specific songs like "I Want Your Love" and "My Forbidden Lover", I think of the high society days of the 30s and 40s. It's hard to explain exactly what elements of their music evoked thoughts of those bygone days but there was just something about the melody lines, the lead vocals and overall sound – even with a massive hit like "Good Times" – that could evoke another era. In some ways, it was like Chic took over where Dr Buzzard's Original Savannah Band left off with songs like "Cherchez La Femme."'

'Nile didn't come from nowhere – people only think of him as a disco man,' original singer from New World Rising, Robbie Dupree recalls. 'I stood toe to toe with him in these joints. Disco was fantastic and a ticket to the future for him – but he's a thoroughbred, he comes from a deep R&B rock'n'roll background – that's why his career is so varied. It wasn't a black thing. Nile was all about music. Politically he may have been a radical but he was very very cool with all people. All kinds of music, all kinds of people – he was definitely an inspiration in that way.'

Dupree went on to be a soft-rock superstar in America. 'Nile is very much on the scene – he's at the parties, he's into the politics of disco. He as a person, as a musician and an artist had a tremendous effect on me. People say I was influenced by Muddy Waters and The Beatles. Well, of course I was, but the biggest influences are the people that you love and hung out with, first generation relationships. He was one of those guys that set a standard for me that I thought was really important.'

Today, in between Rodgers' myriad business commitments, Chic tour constantly, often as part of disco retrospective packages. October 2004 will be the third time Chic has been to Britain as part of 'The Best Disco In Town' package, leading Ahmet Ertegun to posit the question, "Does Nile do these packages because he needs the money?"'

The answer is simply no, Rodgers does it because that is what he knows and loves. 'Because I have a certain amount of talent, I will always have the chance to do it again. Even if I'm against the most hardcore record executive – you haven't heard me for a while, but … couldn't I have another shot? If Alfred Hitchcock walked in the door, you might just want to give him another shot. You may just have him writing *Porky's IV*, but …' Rodgers is undoubtedly a very busy man. He still plans to make a new Chic album: 'Go

With The Flow', from the Johnny Mathis sessions will be present.

'I've been writing a new Chic album for a couple of years now,' Rodgers adds. 'But I think my next record should be all Chic songs that didn't see the light of day – and rewritten for other people. I want my next record to have Bernard Edwards on it – right now Chic sounds better than ever. Even Bernard Jr says that. I would like my next record to say bass: Bernard Edwards – and then I think once I get that out of my system, then I can move on to the new songs. I want to take one of the Johnny Mathis tracks and do it.'

Bernard Edwards Jr is quick to praise his father's old partner: 'Nile's a feeling cat – if it feels good, that's it. You can take lessons from both of them – it's not about the particulars. It was great to watch them both work.'

Rob Drake, the man who so helped them in their earliest days, is still in touch: 'I must say that the new Chic that I heard within the last year blows my mind. I get a feeling when listening to them live that I never got before. It's the feeling I get when I hear some jazz greats in performance. The musicianship, singing arrangements and charisma is superb.' The group's performance at the Montreux Jazz Festival in summer 2004 raised the roof, causing one very seasoned UK-based writer to phone me and rave for ten minutes about how fabulous they were.

© LEON CARR

At the Montreux Jazz Festival

Not every one shares the enthusiasm: 'The reformed Chic, it's almost like what is the point?' Raymond Jones states. 'I've met Sylver – very talented, very nice. I almost wish Nile was able to let Chic rest and he do something else. That's my personal feeling. At one point Nile worked with all the intelligentsia – if you want to make arty records, go do that.'

'With Nile, it's always about exploring something,' argues Brian Chin. 'It's time for him stop trying to rebrand Chic and bring the market back around and be much happier going to make great records for great artists without trying to solve the problem that won't ever get solved.'

It's a question of where Chic goes. With their stable line-up of virtuoso players, Rodgers is looking for the next step to take. He eyes the Abba model with awe. Abba, long broken-up and discredited, by the mid-90s were a cultural phenomenon again. 'In our circles, you would never hear an Abba record – even when they were huge – there was no club in New York City that would play those records,' Rodgers states. 'Ever. They were not the same as Donna Summer, Silver Convention, Bimbo Jet, Village People – that's the shit you'd hear in a club I went to. Now when I think of how Abba are embraced, being so popular with their musical, I go wow – but people don't think of Chic that way. I'm pretty sure "We Are Family" is bigger than "Dancing Queen". I don't know how to re-brand Chic as important to people, as part of a person's spirit. We were close at one point to doing a musical – perhaps we should do the West End thing.'

The 'West End thing' is a phenomenon that in the past five years has seen artists as diverse as Abba, Queen, Madness, Culture Club, Pet Shop Boys, Rod Stewart and Cliff Richard be immortalised in plays which showcase their songs with a wafer-thin plot linking the numbers. On Broadway, this has happened with Billy Joel's work, choreographed by Twyla Tharp, no less. It is not beyond the realms of possibility to imagine Chic's music incorporated in to one of these showcases. A stage transfer of *Saturday Night Fever* has been one of the more popular shows. As the past gets jumbled and specifics get confused, a disco play, smoothing out the hardship and recession, the politics and the grief, could make entertaining viewing.

☆☆☆

The survivors of the original group look back on the time with a mixture of affection, pride and a deep mourning for both Edwards and Thompson.

Alfa Anderson relishes her community work, yet has not ruled out a return to singing: 'I've been trying to reconcile my current position as high school principal with my previous life. I've got through my hang-ups about it. I work with young people who were not even thought at that time and they know my music. They come in and ask for autographs. Two years ago, the graduating class decided that they were not going to march in to "Pomp And Circumstance", and marched instead to "Good Times". Another year it was "I'm Coming Out".' The politics of youth seem to be all encompassing in the 21st century. When Chic's music is heard, it is loved, as it appeals strongly to the young.

The speed with which it all happened and the passage of time, sometimes makes Anderson wonder if she really knew her band-mates at all; 'I found something with Bernard's handwriting on it and I think, did I really, really get to know these people that I made history with? I don't think any of us really talked. It all happened at breakneck speed and we were all trying to catch up. It was a phenomenon. I don't think any of us were prepared. You sit and you dream about this kind of stuff, but the reality is very different from the dream. It happens quickly in a short space of time – you don't have time to reflect. I regret that. We never really sat down and had any substantive conversations about philosophies of life, about where we were and what led us to where we happened to be and where we saw ourselves. You are not in touch with your mortality at that time – and now two of us are gone ...'

'Even though the records were selling really well,' Thornton recalls, 'people did not like giving them the props as the musical geniuses that they were. You hear the records on the radio today and they stand up really well – the way all the component parts work together, the strings, the horns, the vocals. It was totally innovative. I thought we were making more orchestral funk, but it just got lobbed in with disco at that point. Chic made some of the most serious music of the time. The thing I shared with Nile, Bernard and Luther was that although we came out of the communities, we had an opportunity to travel and realise that there was a world outside of our back yard.'

'We all shared something, like a *Big Chill*,' Kathy Sledge recalls. 'Something happens in life, that you will never be able to recreate, it was that special – nor should you try to. Terry Lewis told Bernard Edwards about how much he and Jimmy Jam had learned from Nile and Bernard. Bernard told me how much they had learned from Gamble and Huff. History repeats itself – that's what we do. The next person learns from the one in front. I have endless respect for them. Not only did they have a plan, but we were included in that plan and it changed our lives.'

'I'm eternally grateful to them,' recalls Rob Sabino. 'They were very supportive to me and I wouldn't have been given the opportunities I have been were it not for them. Some of the debauchery that went on was horrible, but sometimes it was fun.'

The political aspect of the group is becoming stronger for the ex-members in retrospect. 'I knew that the material always felt good to my spirit,' Alfa Anderson recalls. 'I never sang anything that I felt was demeaning or did not elevate and lift people. I grew up in the segregated south, which meant that social class was a fundamental part of my existence. I watched and saw the power of music tearing down barriers, and crossing into areas that it hadn't done before. At the time I was not consciously thinking of it as a political act. It was Modern classicism; we were what Count Basie and Duke Ellington were to their day, but in a pop context.'

'In retrospect and maturity, I understand that people are in our lives for – to use a cliché – a reason and for a season,' Anderson continues. 'And if that be true, then we had quite a season and a wonderful reason for being together – in that it was complete. There are groups that have been together much longer but have never reached the pinnacle of success and find they neither touched people in the way that Chic did or defined an era in the way that the music did nor brought people together in the way that Chic did. So I guess the length of time is not important – what the group did was important and therein lies the perfection. And then the rest of us went on and continued to do what we do best in this world, and continue to share our time and our best in other venues, no matter where they are.'

Luci Martin, who splits her time between nursing and performing and producing, states: 'I'm very proud of what we did; and that it keeps going on. Despite all the ups and downs and all the Hollywood stories you hear, I can say there aren't any regrets, which is a lovely thing to be able to say in your life. I had an absolute ball and it's also affording me to continue doing something that I love. The best memories will always be the ones on the bus. Laughing and joking – that's what I remember and miss the most, that camaraderie. And shopping wasn't bad, either!'

'In retrospect, it ended right when it was supposed to,' states Raymond Jones. 'I didn't know it at the time, but I see what it was supposed to be. I look back fondly; I don't have any misgivings or any anger. Not many people get to go around the world and hear themselves on the radio. The impact that unit has made on music, I'm very thankful for that. It's flattering.'

Karen Milne, who, as one of the most sought-after violinists in New York, always looks back on those times with tremendous affection: 'As a professional violinist here in New York, I regularly play recording sessions at the studio that was once called the "Power Station". When I am in the "big room", Studio A, I remember playing the original string charts for the first record I recorded with Chic, after I had joined the band. I can hear Bernard thumping out a bass line in the hallway. I can feel Tony playing in the booth, his monstrous kit taking up the entire space and the second floor quaking each time he hit the drums. I see Bernard coaching Diana Ross and Johnny Mathis. I hear Luther laughing, cracking jokes with Norma Jean and Bernard, wondering where dinner was. I see a very young Madonna leaning over the board asking questions about the mix. I hear David Bowie laughing with Nile and Tony. And, each time before I walk down the steps after a session, I see Tony sitting there in the window, as he often did, looking down on 53rd Street, watching the kids in the school playground across the street, using the windowsill as his drum pad.'

'No-one's really heard my side about one of my favourite times in my life,' Tony Thompson said in the weeks before his passing in 2003, 'and it's an honour to talk about it – because it was special, there was nothing quite like it, and playing with Nile and Bernard, at that time, was heaven for a musician. Musicians would die to have what I had at that time in terms of playing with great players. All the session musicians would come in and their ability was *ridiculous*. The musicianship that was going on there!'

★ ★ ★

Chic were the definite article, and no matter what else the players did and however they defined and redefined themselves, they will always be seen as being part of the disco movement. It's unlikely that Chic will ever get the accolades that their white rock peers have been given by the mainstream. Yet Rodgers and Edwards were two of the great dance producers, and, if they had appeared some years later, as more journalists than ever are around to catalogue rock's every shape-shift, they would be seen as being at the very genesis of the dance producer as the star of the record. But now, as then, the vagaries of the business and the relentless pursuit of the 'now' throw up many problems as currency moves elsewhere.

But, the dance will always go on. 'We sing and dance through our struggles, and we sing and dance to celebrate our successes and the ability to do that is so powerful,' Alfa Anderson concludes. 'Dance has always been a way for people to express themselves. I saw my young people dancing and I wished that they will always be able to keep dancing through life. Whatever life brings, dance through it. I love the phrase "My Feet Keep Dancing". It reminds me of a time in school. There was a young guy in my class – he just got up and left. I called his name a couple of times, but he just kept on going. I asked where he went. He told me that he heard me with his ears; his mind knew he should stay; his heart knew it was the wrong thing to do, but his feet just walked him right out of that room.'

Chic's appeal will live on in the timelessness of their music. In their heyday, they didn't rush to use the latest technology, so their recordings haven't dated as much as their peers have: no matter how much you love Anita Ward's 'Ring My Bell', with its Syndrum and production, it will always be 1979. The simple repetition and sparseness of their grooves, as detailed elsewhere, made them ripe for at first imitating, and then, simply, sampling. Ken Barnes wrote in *Billboard,* 'when it comes to sampling, borrowing or outright robbery, Rodgers and Edwards rank with James Brown and George Clinton in the source-material elite. Swarms of dance acts borrowed the basic Chic sound. Change based a five year hit career on Rodgers/Edwards variations. Inner City's techno-dance landmark "Good Life" is a direct descendant of "Good Times". Latter-day Kool & the Gang hits, such as "Fresh" are indebted to Chic riffs, and Odyssey, Indeep, Young & Company and Narada Michael Walden all made withdrawals from the Chic sound banks.' Of recent years, 'Rock Your Body' by Justin Timberlake is possibly the most affectionate Chic tribute heard for a considerable period – thanks to The Neptunes – Pharell Williams and Chad Hugo, the hottest producers *au courant* in the dance world.

As long as there remains a need for hedonistic reaction to the struggles of society, there will be the need for the all-purpose placebo that will forever be labelled 'disco'. 'History repeats itself – now they want to go back to the club and they want to dance,' Bernard Edwards Jr laughs. 'What's better to reincarnate than the glam aspects of disco? I love to hear the resurgence of dad's songs; it's in movies; it's on commercials; it's everywhere.'

'With disco, all of a sudden there was this musical form that allowed us to be everything,' Rodgers states. 'When you think about it from my point of view – the greatest thing that has ever happened to me as a result of Chic was that great jazz musicians like Herbie Hancock and Miles Davis saw me on the street and told me how much they loved "Everybody Dance"! I remember going to a jazz club and Harold Mayburn was sitting there and played "I Want Your Love". If you took away Chic and heard the chord changes, it was McCoy Tyner, who was my idol. To think that I could have a post-modernist interpretation of McCoy Tyner's piano style and put it in a pop song and have musicians get it – if the record didn't sell a single copy, that night when Harold sat at the piano and played it, I was like – *that's the shit to me.* That I could touch a musician's intellectual soul and sell a couple of million records – it's unbelievable. And then I got paid!'

Disco was the soundtrack to not only Rodgers', but the world's liberation, no matter how limited history has revealed those advances to be. 'Disco played an important and key role in the music of the 70s,' dance historian David Nathan suggests. 'It was vibrant, exciting, energizing and became more than just a music form but a cultural statement.' Through the increasing availability and affordability of methods of carriage, the power of music, and its universal themes offered the opportunity of freedom to millions. Mocked though it may be – and certainly there is no shortage of bilge sheltering under its gaudy umbrella – disco was about far more than just good times.

And everything about 'Good Times'.

CITY AND ISLINGTON
SIXTH FORM COLLEGE
283 - 309 GOSWELL ROAD
LONDON
EC1
TEL 020 7520 0652

AFTERWORD
LOST IN MUSIC

'You know music will never be appreciated until there is some dust on it.'
RAYMOND JONES

'I don't care how many people put us down, the fact that millions of people have bought our records and found pleasure in them is enough. We come from a generation that had to be into politics, because when we left school it looked then like we were going to be sent to Vietnam. And that political frame of mind continued after the war. The real intelligent people at least had a choice, either to go wholeheartedly into politics or to realise just how ineffective they were as an instrument of change. For most people even that choice didn't exist. Disco was less of a political thing than a social thing, I guess. People wanted a place where everyone could be equal, and discos provided that away from the different factions and styles of rock.'
NILE RODGERS

FABRIC. LONDON. 1.45 A.M., Saturday 18th August 2001. Ultra-cool Austrian DJs Peter Kruder and Richard Dorfmeister are playing one of their extremely rare British performances. Approaching the climax of their set, an unmistakable bass and guitar figure strikes up amid the deep house, smoked-out dub and downtempo of their performance. It's taken from 'Le Freak'. The crowd goes spare, throwing shapes, feeling the rhythm and catching the vibe. Not for the first time in their careers, Chic are located on the underground, cutting edge of dance music.

Hotel Riu Masapalomas. Gran Canaria. 11.24 p.m., Thursday, 17th October 2002. Centennial, the in-house cabaret band, all 'taches, tinsel and Tom Jones, play in the middle of a desultory 'Brown Girl In The Ring'-heavy set, the very same song that delighted the hip Londoners. The effect is exactly the same. Although a far older, more sedate and almost totally benign audience, the crowd goes spare, throwing shapes, feeling the rhythm and catching the vibe.

Dalston. East London. 3.30 a.m., 1st January 2003. As we hurtled through the streets clinging on in an unmarked cab after a New Years Eve extravaganza, the pirate station favoured by the cabbie blared out 'Dance, Dance, Dance (Yowsah, Yowsah, Yowsah)'. It's almost exactly 25 years since the moment when Rodgers and Edwards were barred from Grace Jones' party at Studio 54, an event that led to the pair writing 'Le Freak'.

In 2004, Chic's influence is insidiously everywhere: BBC Radio 2, once that bastion of middle-of-the-road, now frequently plays 'Le Freak'; Rodgers has recently narrated a documentary on Civil Rights, *Walking With The Wind*, for the station. Presenter/author Stuart Maconie has written a memoir, *Cider With Roadies*, complete with a witty recollection of when he, a long term fan, met Rodgers and Edwards in 1992. The advert with cows on the telly at the moment uses 'We Are Family', as does the one for snack product Nik Naks, which encourages the consumer to locate their inner freak, while playing guess what? – 'Le Freak'. Blockbuster *Shrek 2* also has 'Le Freak' playing at a key moment. British superstar Paul Weller has covered 'Thinking Of You'; Sister Sledge themselves received a standing ovation when they played at 2004's Glastonbury Festival; The Michael Douglas film, *The In-Laws*, heavily features 'Good Times'. Within weeks of each other in June, *Rolling Stone* has listed Rodgers and Edwards being turned away from Studio 54 as one of the most influential moments in rock, while in Britain, *Q* Magazine has ranked them the 25th most influential band of all time. The Beastie Boys post 9/11 tribute album *To The Five Boroughs* samples Rodgers and Edwards. Cult New York No-Wave disco revivalists, !!!, pronounce their name 'Chk Chk Chk' ...

The music that Bernard Edwards and Nile Rodgers wrote is never going to go away. A handful of their songs will forever be out there for different generations to enjoy. As Bernard Edwards said to Nile Rodgers just before his tragic passing, 'This thing is bigger than both of us.'

How true he was.

APPENDIX 1:
TONY THOMPSON

*'He was an earthbound angel. He popped in for a little while
and then he left.'*

I was exceptionally fortunate to be able to speak with Tony Thompson in the month before he died. Although he was gravely ill, Thompson joked about his recently-departed friend and 'talented cat', Robert Palmer, and was keen to discuss his input to the group that deserve more than the footnote they are assigned in pop history. His on-off relationship with Rodgers gave him some cause for resentment, but his overall tone was one of resigned calm. It was clear that he found happiness with his wife, Patrice, and had been enjoying working locally in California with his friends in Non-Toxic.

In conversations with Patrice subsequently, she talked of the happiness that Thompson brought her. She talked candidly about being with him in his final moments. He had been immobile in a coma for six hours, when Patrice could bear it no longer; she jumped on the bed and hugged him.

'He opened his eyes and told me he loved me. He had not responded for six hours. My daughter said "daddy, you're the best daddy in the whole world" and he acknowledged her. And that was it. I laid him back on the bed and he never said another word. My girlfriends were going wild – it was like something out of a movie. Three hours later, he died. He was surrounded by total love.

'He did not want a typical funeral. We went back to the house where I first met him. He died three days after my birthday on the 9th November – and his birthday was on the 15th. We still gave him a birthday party. We hired a tent and catered it with all of his favourite foods. We had about 60 guests. We sang "Happy Birthday" and we let 60 balloons go. All the balloons flew up in the air, apart from one, which hovered over the pool and then flew towards me and then went up in the sky.

'When he was in the coma, I told him that every time I heard thunder, I would think of him and the way he played. One of the guys suggested that I might want to choose another state to live in as it hardly ever thunders in

California. The whole day he died, it thundered. I got calls from people all over saying "did you hear the thunder? It was Tony" and these were people who weren't even in the room when I said it. There were rainbows over my house all day. We all think he's around.

'He was so funny. He was a simple guy who loved to go shopping. We joked in our wedding vows we should have added a promise that we couldn't go to CostCo without each other. He loved to eat. Life revolved around eating. He was like a little kid – he had eyes like a child. He looked at the world in a very naïve way. But then, all he did was play music. He never had a proper job. He only knew drumming. He didn't do much else and didn't have a lot of other interests.

'He really was a lovely man. He was so kind, generous and humble. One of my girlfriend's mothers said when he passed away that he was an earthbound angel. He popped in for a little while and then he left. That's how I look at him – he was my little chocolate angel.'

A percentage of profits from this book will be donated to
THE TONY THOMPSON FUND
www.tonythompsonfund.com

APPENDIX II:
UK DISCOGRAPHY

Original UK singles

Atlantic K 11038
DANCE, DANCE, DANCE (YOWSAH YOWSAH YOWSAH) / SAO PAOLO (11/77, No. 6)
Atlantic K 11097
EVERYBODY DANCE / YOU CAN GET BY (4/78, No. 9)
Atlantic K11209
LE FREAK / SAVOIR FAIRE (11/78, No. 7)
Atlantic LV 16
I WANT YOUR LOVE / FUNNY BONE (2/79, No. 4)
Atlantic K 11310
GOOD TIMES / A WARM SUMMER NIGHT (6/79, No. 5)
Atlantic K11385
MY FORBIDDEN LOVER / WHAT ABOUT ME (10/79, No. 15)
Atlantic K 11415
MY FEET KEEP DANCING / WILL YOU CRY (WHEN YOU HEAR THIS SONG) (12/79, No. 21)
Atlantic K 11617
REBELS ARE WE / OPEN UP (7/80)
Atlantic K 11617
26 / CHIP OFF THE OLD BLOCK (9/80)
Atlantic A 9898
HANGIN' / CITY LIGHTS (3/83, No. 64)
Atlantic A 9198
JACK LE FREAK / SAVIOR FAIRE (9/87, No. 19)
East West A 7949
MEGACHIC – CHIC MEDLEY / LE FREAK (7/90, No. 58)
Warner Bros. W 0083
CHIC MYSTIQUE / LOVELY MIX (2/92, No. 48)
Warner Bros. W 0089
YOUR LOVE / YOUR LOVE (MIX) (5/92)

CHIC
Original UK ALBUMS

CHIC
ATLANTIC K 50441, 2/78

Dance, Dance, Dance (Yowsah, Yowsah, Yowsah) / Sao Paolo / You Can Get By / Everybody Dance / Est-ce Que C'est Chic / Falling In Love With You / Strike Up The Band

C'EST CHIC
ATLANTIC K 50565, 12/78, No. 2
Chic Cheer / Le Freak / Savoir Faire / Happy Man / I Want Your Love / At Last I Am Free / Sometime You Win / (Funny) Bone

TRES CHIC (original UK release of C'est Chic)
ATLANTIC K50565, 12/78, No.2
Chic Cheer / Le Freak / I Want Your Love / Happy Man / Dance Dance Dance (Yowsah Yowsah Yowsah) / Savoir Faire / At Last I Am Free / Sometime You Win / (Funny) Bone / Everybody Dance

RISQUÉ
ATLANTIC K 50634, 8/79, No. 29
Good Times / A Warm Summer Night / My Feet Keep Dancing / My Forbidden Lover / Can't Stand To Love You / Will You Cry (When You Hear This Song) / What About Me

LES PLUS GRANDS SUCCESSES DE CHIC – GREATEST HITS
ATLANTIC K 50686, 12 / 79, No. 30
Le Freak / I Want Your Love / Dance, Dance, Dance (Yowsah, Yowsah, Yowsah) / Everybody Dance / My Forbidden Lover / Good Times / My Feet Keep Dancing

REAL PEOPLE
ATLANTIC K 50711, 7/80
Open Up / Real People / I Loved You More / I Got Protection / Rebels Are We / Chip Off The Old Block / 26 / You Can't Do It Alone

TAKE IT OFF
ATLANTIC K 50845, 11/81
Flash Back / Take It Off / Just Out Of Reach /
Telling Lies / Stage Fright / So Fine / Baby Doll
/ Your Love Is Cancelled / Burn Hard / Would
You Be My Baby

TONGUE IN CHIC
ATLANTIC 780 031-1, 11/82
Hangin' / I Feel Your Love Comin' On / When
You Love Someone / Chic (Everybody Say) /
Hey Fool / Sharing Love / City Lights

BELIEVER
ATLANTIC 780 107-1, 12/83
Believer / You Are Beautiful / Take A Closer
Look / Give Me The Lovin' / Show Me Your
Light / You Got Some Love For Me / In Love
With Music / Party Everybody

CHIC-ISM
WARNER BROS. 7599 26394-2, 2/92
Chic Mystique / Your Love / Jusagroove /
Something You Can Feel / One And Only One /
Doin' That Thing To Me / Chicism / In It To
Win It / My Love's For Real / Take My Love /
High / M.M.F.T.C.F / Chic Mystique (Reprise)

CHIC FREAK AND MORE TREATS
VIDEOARTS MUSIC (Japan), VACM-102, 1996
Everybody Dance/ Dance, Dance, Dance /
Let's Dance / Le Freak / Upside Down / Do
That Dance / He's The Greatest Dancer /
Good Times / I Want Your Love / Music Is My
House / We Are Family / Do That Dance
(Dancehall/Rap Remix) / Just One World

LIVE AT THE BUDOKAN
SUMTHING ELSE MUSIC WORKS SE 1003, 2/99
Bernard Introduction / Band Introduction / Le Freak
/ Dance Dance Dance / I Want Your Love / He's
The Greatest Dancer / We Are Family / Do That
Dance / Good Times / Rapper's Delight / Stone
Free / Chic Cheer / Backstage / Bernard #2

NOTABLE COMPILATIONS

THE BEST OF CHIC: DANCE DANCE DANCE
ATLANTIC 7 82333-2, 10/91
Dance Dance Dance (Yowsah, Yowsah, Yowsah)
/ Everybody Dance (12" mix) / Strike Up The
Band / Chic Cheer / Le Freak / I Want Your Love
/ Good Times / My Feet Keep Dancing / My
Forbidden Lover / Soup For One / Savoir Faire

THE BEST OF CHIC VOLUME 2
RHINO/ATLANTIC 8122-71086-2, 11/92
Rebels Are We / What About Me / 26 / Will You
Cry (When You Hear This Song) / Stage Fright /
Real People / Hangin' / Give Me The Lovin' / At
Last I Am Free / Just Out Of reach / When You
Love Someone / Your Love Is Cancelled /
Believer / You Are Beautiful / Flash Back / You
Can't Do It Alone / Tavern On The Green

CHIC ORGANIZATION LTD. PRODUCTIONS

DEBBIE HARRY
KOO KOO
CHRYSALIS CHR 1347, 9/81, No. 6
Jump Jump / The Jam Was Moving / Chrome /
Under Arrest / Inner City Spillover / Surrender
/ Backfired / Now I Know (You Know) / Military
Rap / Oasis

JOHNNY MATHIS
I LOVE MY LADY
COLUMBIA, 1981, UNRELEASED
I Love My Lady / I Want To Fall In Love / It's
All Right To Love Me / Judy / Love And Be
Loved / Sing / Take Me /Go With The Flow

DIANA ROSS
diana
MOTOWN STMA 8033, 6/80, No. 12
Upside Down / Tenderness / Friend To Friend /
I'm Coming Out / Have Fun (Again) / My Old
Piano / Now That You're Gone / Give Up

SHEILA and B. DEVOTION
KING OF THE WORLD
CARRERE RECORDS 630 13657-2, 5/80
Spacer / Mayday / Charge Plates And Credit
Cards / Misery / King Of The World / Cover
Girls / Your Love Is Good / Don't Go

SISTER SLEDGE
WE ARE FAMILY
ATLANTIC / COTILLION K 50587, 5/79, No. 15
He's The Greatest Dancer / Lost In Music /
Somebody Loves Me / Thinking Of You / We
Are Family / Easier To Love / You're A Friend
To Me / One More Time

LOVE SOMEBODY TODAY
ATLANTIC / COTILLION K 16012, 2/80
Got To Love Somebody / You Fooled Around /
I'm A Good Girl / Easy Street / Reach Your
Peak / Pretty Baby / How To Love / Let's Go
On Vacation

NORMA JEAN WRIGHT
NORMA JEAN
BEARSVILLE BRK 6983, 7/78
Saturday / Having A Party / I Believe In You /
Sorcerer / So I Get Hurt Again / This Is The
Love / I Like Love

ORIGINAL SOUNDTRACK
SOUP FOR ONE
MIRAGE 99 236, 6/82
Soup For One (Chic) / Why (Carly Simon) /
Dream Girl (Teddy Pendergrass)/ I Work For A
Livin' (Fonzi Thornton) / I Want Your Love
(Chic) / Let's Go On Vacation (Sister Sledge) /
Tavern On The Green (Chic) / Jump, Jump
(Deborah Harry)

BERNARD EDWARDS

GLAD TO BE HERE
WEA 7800 099 1, 6/83
Your Love Is Good To Me / Don't Do Me
Wrong / You Don't Know Me / Joy Of Life /
You've Really Got A Hold On Me / Hard Loving
Man / Glad To Be Here

NILE RODGERS

ADVENTURES IN THE LAND OF THE GOOD GROOVE
MIRAGE B 0073, 2/83
The Land Of The Good Groove / Yum-Yum / Beet
/ Get Her Crazy / It's All In Your Hands / Rock
Bottom / My Love Song For You / Most Down

B-MOVIE MATINEE
WARNERS 925 290-1, 6/85
Groove Master / Let's Go Out Tonight / Same
Wavelength / Plan Number 9 / State Your
Mind / Face In The Window / Doll Squad

THE OUTLOUD
WARNERS 925632-1, 1987
Out Loud / It's Love This Time /Am I On Your
Mind / Square Business / KAK / Feeling Good
/ Camouflage / Good Together / Fundamental /
Circle Of Love/Music Lover

TONY THOMPSON

THE POWER STATION
THE POWER STATION
PARLOPHONE CDP 7 46127 2, 4/85
Some Like It Hot / Murderers / Lonely Tonight /
Communication / Get It On (Bang A Gong) /
Go To Zero / Harvest For The World / Still In
Your Heart

THE POWER STATION
LIVING IN FEAR
CHRYSALIS 7243 8 53984 2 1, 10/96
Notoriety / Scared / She Can Rock It / Let's
Get It On / Life Forces / Fancy That / Living in
Fear / Shut Up / Dope / Love Conquers All /
Taxman

THE DISTANCE
UNDER THE ONE SKY
REPRISE 2-26014, 2/89
No Way Out / Leave It Up To You / Speech Of
Angels / As You Turn Away / Give It Up / Under
The One Sky / Rescue Me / Looking Over Your
Shoulder / Every Time I Stand Up / Softly
Speak / Stand Up / I Hear You

SIGNIFICANT NILE RODGERS PRODUCTIONS and APPEARANCES

Stacy Lattisaw
Let Me Be Your Angel
1980
Guitar

Revelation
Feel It from Revelation
1980
Guitar

Linx
Tinseltown from Go Ahead
1981
Guitar

Material
I'm The One from Come Down 12"
1982
Guitar

Odyssey
Together from *Happy Together*
1982
Composer, Guitar

David Bowie
Let's Dance
1983
Producer, Guitar, Arranger

Michael Gregory
Situation X
1983
Producer, Guitar

Fonzi Thornton
The Leader
1983
Guitar

Will Powers
Kissing With Confidence & Smile from
Dancing For Mental Health
1983
Composer

Kim Carnes
Invisible Hands from *Invitation To Dance*
1983
Producer

Southside Johnny & The Asbury Jukes
Trash It Up
1983
Producer, Guitar

Paul Simon
Hearts And Bones
1983
Guitar

INXS
The Original Sin from *The Swing*
1984
Producer

Gordon Deppe
Listen To The City (Soundtrack)
1984
Producer

Diana Ross
Telephone from *Swept Away*
1984
Guitar

Madonna
Like A Virgin
1984
Producer, Guitar, Synclavier

Duran Duran
The Reflex
1984
Mixer

Laurie Anderson
Mister Heartbreak
1984
Guitar

The Honeydrippers
Sea Of Love from *The Honeydrippers Vol. One*
1984
Guitar

Duran Duran
Wild Boys from *Arena*
1984
Producer

Jeff Beck
Flash
1985
Producer

Sheena Easton
Do You
1985
Producer, Composer

Bryan Ferry
Boys And Girls
1985
Guitar

Sister Sledge
When The Boys Meet The Girls
1985
Producer, Guitar, Composer

Mick Jagger
She's The Boss
1985
Producer, Guitar

Duran Duran
Notorious
1986
Producer

Philip Bailey
Inside Out
1986
Producer, Guitar, Keyboards, Vocals

Grace Jones
Inside Story
1986
Producer, Bass, Guitar, Arranger, Vocals

Peter Gabriel
So
1986
Guitar

Al Jarreau
L Is For Lover
1986
Producer, Guitar, Keyboards, Vocals

Arcadia
The Flame (12")
1986
Remixer

Howard Jones
One To One
1986
Guitar

Cyndi Lauper
True Colors
1986
Guitar

Laurie Anderson
Home Of The Brave (Soundtrack)
1986
Producer, Synthesizer, Guitar, Keyboards,
Sound Effects, Synclavier

Terri Gonzalez
Is There Rockin' In This House
1987
Producer, Bass, Guitar, Keyboards, Vocals,
Composer

Claude Nougaro
Nougayork
1987
Guitar

Al Jarreau
Moonlighting Theme
1987
Producer

The Missing Links
Groovin'
1988
Guitar

Toshiki Kadomatsu
Lost My Heart In The Dark from *Before The Daylight*
1988
Guitar

The B52's
Cosmic Thing
1989
Producer, Guitar, Remixing

Dan Reed Network
Slam
1989
Producer

Eddie Murphy
So Happy
1989
Producer, Guitar, Vocals, Composer

Carole Davis
Heart Of Gold
1989
Producer, Guitar, Composer

Diana Ross
Workin' Overtime
1989
Producer, Guitar, Composer

Mariah Carey
Mariah Carey
1990
Guitar

Ole Ole
(3 singles) Soldados Del Amor, Puerta, Te Dare Todo
1990
Producer

Cathy Dennis
Move To This
1990
Producer, Guitar

Mica Paris
Contribution
1990
Guitar

Ambitious Lovers
Lust
1991
Guitar

Dan Reed Network
The Heat
1991
Producer

The B52's
Good Stuff
1992
Producer, Guitar

David Bowie
Real Cool World (single)
1992
Producer

David Bowie
Black Tie White Noise
1993
Producer, Guitar

Robbie Dupree
Walking On Water
1993
Guitar

Cyndi Lauper
Hat Full of Stars
1993
Guitar

Bryan Ferry
Mamouna
1994
Guitar

David Lee Roth
Your Filthy Little Mouth
1994
Producer

Michael Jackson
HIStory
1995
Guitar

Toshinobu Kubota
Bumpin' Voyage
1995
Guitar

Toshi Kubuta
Funk It Up from *Sunshine, Moonlight*
1995
Guitar

David Bowie
Little Wonder
1997
Producer

Samantha Cole
Samantha Cole
1997
Producer, Guitar, Composer

All-4-One
On And On
1998
Producer

Various Artists
Public Enemy Soundtrack
1999
Producer, Composer, Guitar

Marta Sanchez
One Step Closer
2000
Producer, Guitar

Tina Arena
Just Me
2001
Producer, Guitar, Electric Sitar

Jimmy Sommers
360 Urban Groove
2001
Guitar

Cheb Mami
Dellali
2001
Producer, Guitar, Vocals

Groove Armada
Drifted from *Goodbye Country (Hello Nightclub)*
2001
Guitar

Nile Rodgers All Stars
We Are Family (foundation single)
2001
Producer, Guitar, Composer, Vocals

Michael Bolton
Only A Woman Like You
2002
Producer

VfromA
Zombie Part Two from *Red Hot & Riot: The Music And Spirit Of Fela Kuti*
2002
Guitar

Cerrone
The Only One & Got To Have Lovin' from *Hysteria*
2003
Guitar

What For
L'amour n'a pas de loi from *L'Album des Popstars*
2003
Guitar

David Lee Roth
Ice Cream Man from *Diamond Dave*
2003
Guitar

Toby Lightman
Little Things
2004
Guitar

SIGNIFICANT BERNARD EDWARDS PRODUCTIONS and APPEARNACES

Roundtree
Roller Disco
1978
Bass

E.P.M.
No Lies
1979
Producer, Bass, Arranger

Stacy Lattisaw
Let Me Be Your Angel
1980
Bass

Odyssey
Together from *Happy Together*
1982
Composer, Bass

David Bowie
Let's Dance
1983
Bass

Fonzi Thornton
The Leader
1983
Bass, Rhythm Arranger

Michael Gregory
Situation X
1983
Bass

Paul Simon
Hearts And Bones
1983
Bass

Nile Rodgers
Adventures In The Land Of The Good Groove
1983
Bass, Vocals

Madonna
Like A Virgin
1984
Bass

Diana Ross
Swept Away
1984
Producer, Composer, Bass

Duran Duran
A View To A Kill 7"
1985
Producer

Belouis Some
Some People
1985
Bass

Jerry Goldsmith
Explorers Soundtrack
1985
Producer

Nona Hendryx
Heat
1985
Producer

Mick Jagger
She's The Boss
1985
Bass

Robert Palmer
Riptide
1985
Producer, Bass

Various Artists
Rocky IV Soundtrack
1985
Producer

Joe Cocker
Cocker
1986
Producer, Bass

Missing Persons
Color In Your Life
1986
Producer, Mixer

Air Supply
Hearts In Motion
1986
Producer

Various Artists
Pretty In Pink Soundtrack
1986
Producer

ABC
Alphabet City
1987
Producer

Hollywood Beyond
If
1987
Producer, Vocals

Platinum Blond
Contact
1987
Producer, Bass

Various Artists
Burglar Soundtrack
1987
Producer

Jody Watley
Jody Watley
1987
Producer, Bass

Rod Stewart
Out Of Order
1988
Producer, Bass, Mixer

Distance
Under The One Sky
1989
Producer, Bass

Cathy Dennis
Move To This
1990
Bass

Ian Hunter/The Hunter Ronson Band
YUI Orta
1990
Producer, Bass

The Triplets
Break The Silence
1990
Producer, Bass

Rod Stewart
Vagabond Heart
1991
Producer, Bass, Mixer

Various Artists
Thelma & Louise Soundtrack
1991
Producer
Various Artists
Wayne's World 2 Soundtrack
1993
Producer

Rod Stewart
Spanner In The Works
1995
Bass
Various Artists
Feeling Minnesota Soundtrack
1996
Bass

APPENDIX III:
BIBLIOGRAPHY

General Music

Brewster, Bill and Frank Broughton. *Last Night A DJ Saved My Life: The History Of The Disc Jockey.* Headline, London, 1999.

Bronson, Fred. *The Billboard Book Of Number 1 Hits: Updated and Expanded 5th Edition.* Billboard Books, New York, 2003.

Clarke, Donald. *The Penguin Encyclopaedia Of Popular Music*. Viking-Penguin, London, 1989.

DeCurtis Anthony and James Henke with Holly George-Warren. *The Rolling Stone Album Guide*. Virgin Books, London, 1992.

Fox, Ted. *In The Groove.* St. Martin's Press, New York, 1986.

Guillory, Monique and Richard C. Green. Eds. *Soul: Black Power, Politics and Pleasure.* New York University Press, New York, 1998.

Gross, Michael and Maxim Jakubowski. *The Rock Yearbook 1981*. Virgin Books, London, 1980.

Haden-Guest, Anthony. *The Last Party: Studio 54, Disco, And The Culture Of The Night*. William Morrow and Co., New York, 1997.

Harry, Debbie, Chris Stein and Victor Bockris. *Making Tracks: The Rise Of Blondie*. Elm Tree, London, 1982.

Hardy, Phil and Dave Laing. *The Faber Companion To 20th Century Music*. Faber & Faber, London, 1990.

Jakubowski, Maxim. *The Rock Album*. Frederick Muller Limited, London, 1983.

Jones, Alan and Jussi Kantonen. *Saturday Night Forever – The Story Of Disco*. Mainstream Publishing, Edinburgh, London, 1999.

Knobler, Peter and Greg Mitchell. Editors. *Very Seventies. A Cultural History Of The 1970s, From The Pages Of Crawdaddy*. Simon & Schuster, New York, 1995.

Marcus, Greil. Editor. *Lester Bangs: Psychotic Reactions And Carburetor Dung*. Serpent's Tail, London, 1997.

Marsh, Dave: *The Heart Of Rock And Soul: The 1001 Greatest Singles Ever Made*. Penguin, London, 1989.

Mulholland, Gerry: *This Is Uncool: The 500 Greatest Singles Since Punk & Disco*. Cassell, London, 2002.

Robbins, Ira A. (Ed). *The New Trouser Press Record Guide*. Collier Books, New York, 1989.

Santoro, Gene. *Stir It Up: Musical Mixes From Roots To Jazz*. Oxford University Press, New York, 1997.

Shaar Murray, Charles. *Shots From The Hip*. Penguin, London, 1991.

Shapiro, Peter. *Soul: 100 Essential CDs – The Rough Guide*. Rough Guides, London, 2000.

Southall, Brian. *The A-Z Of Record Labels. Second Edition*. Sanctuary Publishing, London 2003.

Strong, Martin C. *The Great Rock Discography, Fifth Edition* Mojo Books, Edinburgh, 2000.

Taraborrelli, J Randy, with Darryl Minger and Reginald Wilson. *Diana: The Life & Career Of Diana Ross*. Comet Publishing, London, 1985.

Taraborrelli, J Randy. *Call Her Miss Ross: The Unauthorized Biography Of Diana Ross*. Sidgwick & Jackson, London, 1989.

Taylor, Marc. *A Touch Of Classic Soul 2: The Late 1970s.* Alive Publishing Co, New York, 2001.

Ward, Brian: *Just My Soul Responding – Rhythm and Blues, Black Consciousness and Race Relations*. UCL Press, London, 1998.

Werner, Craig. *A Change Is Gonna Come: Music, Race and the Soul Of America*. Payback Press, Edinburgh, 2000.

White, Adam and Fred Bronson. *The Billboard Book Of Number One Rhythm & Blues Hits*. Billboard Books, New York, 1993.

American Culture and Socio-Politics

Ali, Tariq and Susan Watkins. *1968: Marching In The Streets.* Bloomsbury Publishing, London, 1998.

Borgenicht, David. *Sesame Street Unpaved: Scripts, Stories, Secrets, and Songs*. Aurum Press, London, 1998.

Boyer, Paul S., Clifford E. Clark Jr., Joseph F. Kett, Neal Salisbury, Harvard Sitkoff and Nancy Woloch (Eds.). *The Enduring Vision: A History Of The American People*. DC Heath, Lexington, Toronto, 1996.

Cleaver, Eldridge. *Soul On Ice*. Jonathan Cape, London, 1965.

Dennis, Denise. *Black History For Beginners*. Writers And Readers, New York, 1995.

Dickson, Paul. *From Elvis To E-Mail: Trends Events And Trivia From The Postwar Era To The End Of The Century*. Federal Street Press, Springfield, MA, 1999.

Haden-Guest, Anthony and Niels Kummer. *Studio 54: The Legend*. te Neues Publishing, New York, 1997.

Isaacs, Jeremy and Taylor Downing. *Cold War*. Bantam, London, 1998.

Articles

All The Way Off
by Glenn O'Brien, *Interview Magazine*, February 1982, p.72.

A New Realism: Is All Well In The House Of Chic?
by James Truman, *The Face*, February 1982, p.51.

The Art Of Being CHIC
by David Nathan, *Blues & Soul*, October 9-22 1979, p. 6-7.

Behind The Scenes With One Of Pop's Hottest Hitmakers: Nile Rodgers
by Pam Lambert, *The Wall Street Journal*, 4 June 1985.

Bernard Edwards 1952-1996
by Carol Cooper, *Village Voice*, 7 May 1996.

Bernard Edwards, Groovemaster
by Gene Santoro, *Pulse!,* June 1985, p.53.

The Blues Aesthetic and the Black Aesthetic.
by Amiri Baraki, *Black Music Research Journal*, Fall 1991, volume 11, no. 10, p.107.

The Black Side Of Censorship
by Nile Rodgers, *Billboard* Vol. 95 No. 15, 9 April 1983, p.8.

Chic Discovers Life After Disco
by Robert Palmer, New York Times, 23 December 1981, p.12.
Chic: Hammersmith Odeon 1979
by Barney Hoskyns,
www.rocksbackpages.com,
www.rocksbackpages.com/article.html?ArticleI D=1250.

Chic: Keep It In The Family
by Adam Sweeting, *Melody Maker*, 17th August, 1981.

Chic: Let The Good Times Roll
by JL, *Blues & Soul* 604, 1992, p. 12-15.

Chic: Risqué
by Danny Baker, *NME*, 4 August 1979.

Come Together
by Jeff Giles, *Newsweek*, Vol. CXXVI, No. 17, 23rd October 1995, p.37.

Can You Feel It?
by Geoff Brown, *MOJO* Magazine, No. 122, January 2004.

Chic Is Less Than Meets The Ear
by James Farber, *Rolling Stone*, No. 289,
19 April, 1979.

Discotheque Rock '72: Paaaaarty!
by Vince Aletti, *Rolling Stone*, 13 September,
1973.

The Disco Band That Never Left
by Neil Strauss, *New York Times*, 2/4/1998.

Discotech II: The Producer Is The Star
by Crispin Cioe, *High Fidelity*, September
1979, p: 136-39.

*'Disco Was The Only Time We Were Equal. No
One Cared If You Were Black Or White': Nile
Rodgers*
by Imogen O'Rorke, *The Guardian*,
13th December 1999.

How Woodstock Happened
by Elliot Tiber, *The Times Herald-Record*.

*Jewel Of A Nile: Mr Rodgers Creates The
Sound Of The Eighties*
by Anthony Haden-Guest, *New York
Magazine*, 24th February 1986

Keeping The Power On
by Linnet Evans, *Black Echoes*, 20th October
1979, p. 12-13.

Madonna: The Glamorous Life
by Jeffrey Ferry. *The Face*, February 1985,
p 34-39.

Nicking Nile
by Ken Barnes, *Billboard*, February 2000.

Nile Rodgers Of Chic
by Nelson George. *Musician,* 1980.

*Nile Rodgers: Rock's Hottest Producer Is
Doin' It For Himself*
by Gene Santoro, *Pulse*, July 1985.

*Perfection In Planning Or Wolves in Chics'
Clothing?
by Robin Katz, Smash Hits*,
15-28th November 1979.

Rollerskating On Wall Street
by James Truman, *Melody Maker*,
13th October 1979.

Qui Sont Ces Gens? C'est Chic
by Geoff Brown, *Blues & Soul*, 1979.

Sauce Of The Nile

by Stuart Maconie, *New Musical Express*,
22 February 1992, p.18-19.

Simply Resistable: The Power Station
by Adrian Deevoy, *The Sunday Times
Magazine*, 1986.

*Tales From The Groove: THE RETURN OF
CHIC*
by Nick Coleman*, Time Out*, No. 1123,
26 Feb-4 Mar 1992.

This Much I Know: Nile Rodgers
by Clark Collis, *The Observer*, 20 July, 2003.

Too Legit To Quit
by Mark Coleman. *Details*, April 1992.

*Tony Thompson: The Man Who Put The
Backbone In CHIC.*
by Ian McCann. *Echoes,* 16th March 1985.

Websites

Chic Tribute: www.chictribute.com

All Things Deep:
www.allthingsdeep.com/dge/chic.htm

Bronx Historical Society:
www.bronxhistoricalsociety.org

Disco-disco.com: www.disco-
disco.com/tributes/chic.html

Disco Savvy:
www.discotheque.narod.ru/chic.html

Dick's Diana Ross Page:
www.community-2.webtv.net/rossfan/
DICKSDIANAROSS

Disco Music Was Gay Music:
www.brumm.com/gaylib/disco/

Frenchy, So Chic: www.c-chic.com

The Savoy: www.savoyplaque.org

Sesame Street:
www.tvtome.com/tvtome/servlet/ShowMainSer
vlet/showid-887/

New interviews conducted for this book

Nile Rodgers 22/08/01, 7/06/03, 24/08/03,
2/06/04
Robert Parlmer 9/02

Robbie Dupree 7/08/03
Bernard Edwards Jr 3/08/03
Joe Jackson 27/01/03
Gil Scott Heron 4/02/03
Robert 'Kool' Bell 14/05/03
Joni Sledge 15/07/03
Debbie Sledge 15/07/03
Ahmet Ertegun 6/06/03
David Nathan 18/08/03
Brian Chin 6/06/03
John De Mairo 5/06/03
Raymond Jones 28/08/03
David Millman 1/09/03
Vicki Wickham 2/09/03
Tony Thompson 29/09/03, 30/09/03,
24/10/03
Tony Visconti 27/09/03
Robert Sabino 14/01/04
Nik Cohn 17/01/04
Jerry Greenberg 21/01/04

Martin Fry 4/02/04
David Lasley 7/02/04
Patrice Jennings-Thompson 10/02/04
Fonzi Thornton 11/02/04
Robert Drake 21/02/04
Valerie Simpson 4/03/04
Norma Jean Wright 7/04/04
Kenny Lehman 11/03/04
Rodger Bell 11/03/04
Dr Mary Ellison 11/03/04
Eddie Martinez 15/03/04
Kathy Sledge 15/03/04
Bryan Ferry 24/03/04
Alfa Anderson 20/04/04, 04/05/04
Geoff Brown 6/05/04
John Taylor 07/05/04
Karen Milne 10/05/04
Luci Martin 30/05/04
David Bowie 21/06/04

APPENDIX VI:
1978-1979

A YEAR OR SO OF CHIC'S TOURING SCHEDULE
From Karen Milne's diary

March 27, 1978: rehearsal
3/28/78: rehearsal
3/29/78: rehearsal
April 4: leave for Cleveland
April 6: leave for Kansas City

April 11: 12-3 rehearsal at Bill's (52nd St)
4/13: 12-3 rehearsal at Bill's
4/14: Atlantic City
4/15: Albany
4/19: Cherry Hill, NJ
4/20: Springfield, MA
4/21: Providence, RI
4/22: NYC (Felt Forum)
4/23: Hampton Rhodes, VA
4/26: Leave for LA
4/27: The Roxy, LA
4/29: LA to Bakersfield
4/30: San Francisco
5/1: Travel to LA
5/2-5/4: LA
5/5: San Diego
5/6: San Bernardino
5/7: Palladium, LA
5/8: LA
5/11: leave for Atlanta
5/12: Atlanta
5/13: Florida
5/14: NYC
5/19: Great Adventures (New Jersey)
5/20; Newark, NJ
5/24: Travel
5/25: North Carolina
5/26: Raleigh,VA
5/27: Richmond, VA
5/28: travel
5/29: Memphis

5/30-31: Travel
6/1: St. Louis
6/2: St. Louis
6/3-5: Chicago
6/6: Leave Chicago
6/9: Arlington, Texas
6/10: Jackson, Mississippi
6/12: NYC Home
6/15: Travel
6/16: Boston
6/17: Washington, DC
6/18: Myrtle Beach, South Carolina
6/21: Mobile, Alabama
6/22: Greenville, SC
6/23: NYC
6/24: Worchester, MA
6/25: Jersey City

7/6: leave NYC
7/7: Detroit
7/9: Indianapolis

7/10: leave for LA
7/11: LA thru 7/20
7/21: San Diego
7/23: Albequerque, New Mexico
7/24: NYC

8/21: to Boston for TV show
8/22: Boston

1979:

Jan 4 Brussels
1/5: Amsterdam
1/6-12: London
1/13: Spain
1/15; Paris
1/17: Italy thru 1/19
1/20: Brussels

1/22: off

break to do some recording

April 21: Atlanta
4/22: Tampa, Fl

another break

5/2: Louisville, KY
5/3: Durham, NC
5/4: Atlanta, GA
5/5 Charlotte, NC
5/7: Zane, Ohio
5/8; Pittsburgh
5/9: Uniontown, PA
5/10: Detroit
5/11: Cincinatti, OH
5/12; Nashville
5/13: Knoxville, TN
5/14: Home
5/18: Jackson, NJ
5/19: Richmond, VA
5/20: North Carolina
5/21-23: Las Vegas (TV show)
5/24: Sacramento
5/25: Davis, CA
5/26: Monterey, CA
5/27-30: Oakland, CA (Kool Jazz Festival)
5/31: Oregon
6/1: Portland
6/2: Seattle
6/3: Vancouver
6/4: travel to LA
6/6: Santa Barbera
6/7-6/8: LA
6/9: San Diego
6/10: Santa Monica
6/11-6/12: LA
6/13-6/14: Travel
6/16: Houston TX
6/22: St. Louis
6/23: Kansas City, MO
6/24: to NYC
6/25: NYC: Newport Jazz
6/27: Portland, ME
6/28: Connecticut
6/29: Kool Jazz/ Hampton Rhodes
6/30: Atlanta
7/1 Milwaukee, WI
7/2: Chicago
7/3: travel
7/4: Washington DC
7/5: NYC
7/21: Cincinnati, OH
7/27: Delaware

7/28 Gary, IN
7/30/31: Toronto
8/3: Bear Lake (?)
8/4 New Orleans
8/10: Philadelphia
8/11: meadowlands, NJ
8/15: Springfield, IL
8/16: Des Moines, Ia
8/24: Kansas City
8/28: Kentucky
8/29: Detroit
8/31: Cleveland
9/1: Allentown
Another big break

9/24 Amsterdam concerts and TV shows
9/26: Antwerp/TV
9/27: Brussels /TV
9/28: Paris
9/29: Paris/TV
9/30: Sheffield, England
9/31 Glasgow
10/3: Liverpool
10/4: Manchester
10/5: Bournemouth
10/6 travel
10/7: Brighton
10/8: London thru 10/11
10/12: Birmingham
10/14-15: Rome/TV shows
10/17-18: Bremen, German TV shows
10/19: Home
Another break
Nov 25 – Dec 9: Los Angeles

Other key dates:

8/23/80: Kool Jazz/Meadowlands, NJ

Monday, Sept. 1, 1980: Miss America
Pageant

"Last Chic pay check...." for the week ending
September 7, 1980.

Fonzi session on October 23, 1980 at Power
Station

Debbie Harry party, Feb 14, 1981
Start Debbie Harry recordings Feb 23, 1981.

Johnny Mathis session Tuesday, Feb 24.
1981.

Then more Debbie Harry after that, on 25 &
26.

INDEX

Other Titles available from Helter Skelter

Bob Dylan: Like The Night (Revisited)
by CP Lee

Fully revised and updated edition of the hugely acclaimed document of Dylan's pivotal 1966 show at the Manchester Free Trade Hall where fans called him Judas for turning his back on folk music in favour of rock 'n' roll. The album of the concert was released in the same year as the book's first outing and has since become a definitive source.

"A terrific tome that gets up close to its subject and breathes new life into it... For any fan of Dylan this is quite simply essential." *Time Out*

"Putting it all vividly in the context of the time, he writes expertly about that one electrifying, widely-bootlegged night." *Mojo*

"CP Lee's book flushed 'Judas' out into the open." *The Independent*

"An atmospheric and enjoyable account." *Uncut* (Top 10 of the year)
ISBN 1-900924-33-1 198mm X 129mm 224pp
UK £9.99   US $17.95

Suede: An Armchair Guide
by Dave Thompson

The first biography of one of the most important British Rock Groups of the 90s who paved the way for Blur, Oasis et al. Mixing glam and post-punk influences, fronted by androgynous Bret Anderson, Suede thrust indie-rock into the charts with a string of classic singles in the process catalysing the Brit-pop revolution. Suede's first album was the then fastest selling debut of all time and they remain one of THE live draws on the UK rock circuit, retaining a fiercely loyal cult following.
ISBN 1-900924-60-9 256pp £14.00

This Is a Modern Life
by Enamel Verguren

Lavishly illustrated guide to the mod revival that was sparked by the 1979 release of *Quadrophenia*. *This Is a Modern Life* concentrates on the 1980s, but takes in 20 years of a Mod life in London and throughout the world, from 1979 to 1999, with interviews of people directly involved, loads of flyers and posters and a considerable amount of great photos
Paperback   ISBN 1900924773 224pp
264mm X 180mm, photos throughout
UK £14.99   US $19.95

Smashing Pumpkins: Tales of A
Scorched Earth
by Amy Hanson

Initially contemporaries of Nirvana, Billy Corgan's Smashing Pumpkins outgrew and outlived the grunge scene and with hugely acclaimed commercial triumphs like *Siamese Dream* and *Mellon Collie and The Infinite Sadness*. Though drugs and other problems led to the band's final demise, Corgan's recent return with Zwan is a reminder of how awesome the Pumpkins were in their prime. Seattle-based Hanson has followed the band for years and this is the first in-depth biography of their rise and fall.
Paperback   ISBN 1900924684   256pp
234mm X 156mm, 8pp b/w photos
UK £12.99   US $18.95

Be Glad: An Incredible String Band
Compendium
Edited by Adrian Whittaker

The ISB pioneered 'world music' on '60s albums like *The Hangman's Beautiful Daughter* – Paul McCartney's favourite album of 1967! – experimented with theatre, film and lifestyle and inspired Led Zeppelin. 'Be Glad' features interviews with all the ISB key players, as well as a wealth of background information, reminiscence, critical evaluations and arcane trivia, this is a book that will delight any reader with more than a passing interest in the ISB.
ISBN 1-900924-64-1   288pp   £14.99

Waiting for the Man: The Story of
Drugs and Popular Music
by Harry Shapiro

From Marijuana and Jazz, through acid-rock and speed-fuelled punk, to crack-driven rap and Ecstasy and the Dance Generation, this is the definitive history of drugs and pop. It also features in-depth portraits of music's most famous drug addicts: from Charlie Parker to Sid Vicious and from Jim Morrison to Kurt Cobain. Chosen by the BBC as one of the Top Twenty Music Books of All Time. "Wise and witty." *The Guardian*
ISBN 1-900924-58-7   320pp   £12.99

The Clash: Return of the Last Gang in
Town
by Marcus Gray

Exhaustively researched definitive biography of the last great rock band that traces their progress from pubs and punk clubs to US stadiums and the Top Ten. This edition is further updated to cover the band's induction into the Rock 'n' Roll Hall of Fame and the tragic death of iconic frontman Joe Strummer.

"A must-have for Clash fans [and] a valuable document for anyone interested in the punk era." *Billboard*

"It's important you read this book." *Record Collector*
ISBN 1-900924-62-5   448pp   £14.99

Steve Marriott: All Too Beautiful
by Paolo Hewitt and John Hellier

Marriott was the prime mover behind 60s chart-toppers The Small Faces. Longing to be treated as a serious musician he formed Humble Pie with Peter Frampton, where his blistering rock 'n' blues guitar playing soon saw him take centre stage in the US live favourites. After years in seclusion, Marriott's plans for a comeback in 1991 were tragically cut short when he died in a housefire. He continues to be a key influence for generations of musicians from Paul Weller to Oasis and Blur.

Love: Behind The Scenes
by Michael Stuart-Ware

LOVE were one of the legendary bands of the late 60s US West Coast scene. Their masterpiece *Forever Changes* still regularly appears in critics' polls of top albums, while a new-line up of the band has recently toured to mass acclaim. Michael Stuart-Ware was LOVE's drummer during their heyday and shares his inside perspective on the band's recording and performing career and tells how drugs and egos thwarted the potential of one of the great groups of the burgeoning psychedelic era.
ISBN 1-900924-59-5   256pp   £14.00

A Secret Liverpool: In Search of the La's
by MW Macefield

With timeless single "There She Goes", Lee Mavers' La's overtook The Stone Roses and paved the way for Britpop. However, since 1991, The La's have been silent, while rumours of studio-perfectionism, madness and drug addiction have abounded. The author sets out to discover the truth behind Mavers' lost decade and eventually gains a revelatory audience with Mavers himself.
ISBN 1-900924-63-3   192pp   £11.00

The Fall: A User's Guide
by Dave Thompson

Amelodic, cacophonic and magnificent, The Fall remain the most enduring and prolific of the late-'70s punk and post-punk iconoclasts. *A User's Guide* chronicles the historical and musical background to more than 70 different LPs (plus reissues) and as many singles. The band's history is also documented year-by-year, filling in the gaps between the record releases.
ISBN 1-900924-57-9   256pp   £12.99

Pink Floyd: A Saucerful of Secrets
by Nicholas Schaffner £14.99

Long overdue reissue of the authoritative and detailed account of one of the most important and popular bands in rock history. From the psychedelic explorations of the Syd Barrett-era to 70s superstardom with *Dark Side of the Moon*, and on to triumph of *The Wall*, before internecine strife tore the group apart. Schaffner's definitive history also covers the improbable return of Pink Floyd without Roger Waters, and the hugely successful *Momentary Lapse of Reason* album and tour.

The Big Wheel
by Bruce Thomas £10.99

Thomas was bassist with Elvis Costello at the height of his success. Though names are never named, *The Big Wheel* paints a vivid and hilarious picture of life touring with Costello and co, sharing your life 24-7 with a moody egotistical singer, a crazed drummer and a host of hangers-on. Costello sacked Thomas on its initial publication.

"A top notch anecdotalist who can time a twist to make you laugh out loud." *Q*

Hit Men: Powerbrokers and Fast Money Inside The Music Business
by Fredric Dannen £14.99

Hit Men exposes the seamy and sleazy dealings of America's glitziest record companies: payola, corruption, drugs, Mafia involvement, and excess.

"So heavily awash with cocaine, corruption and unethical behaviour that it makes the occasional examples of chart-rigging and playlist tampering in Britain during the same period seem charmingly inept." *The Guardian*.

I'm With The Band: Confessions of A Groupie
by Pamela Des Barres £14.99

Frank and engaging memoir of affairs with Keith Moon, Noel Redding and Jim Morrison, travels with Led Zeppelin as Jimmy Page's girlfriend, and friendships with Robert Plant, Gram Parsons, and Frank Zappa.

"Miss Pamela, the most beautiful and famous of the groupies. Her memoir of her life with rock stars is funny, bittersweet, and tender-hearted." Stephen Davis, author of *Hammer of the Gods*

Psychedelic Furs: Beautiful Chaos
by Dave Thompson £12.99

Psychedelic Furs were the ultimate post-punk band – combining the chaos and vocal rasp of the Sex Pistols with a Bowie-esque glamour. The Furs hit the big time when John Hughes wrote a movie based on their early single "Pretty in Pink". Poised to join U2 and Simple Minds in the premier league, they withdrew behind their shades, remaining a cult act, but one with a hugely devoted following.

Marillion: Separated Out
by Jon Collins £14.99

From the chart hit days of Fish and "Kayleigh" to the Steve Hogarth incarnation, Marillion have continued to make groundbreaking rock music. Collins tells the full story, drawing on interviews with band members, associates, and the experiences of some of the band's most dedicated fans.

Rainbow Rising
by Roy Davies £14.99

The full story of guitar legend Ritchie Blackmore's post-Purple progress with one of the great 70s rock bands. After quitting Deep Purple at the height of their success, Blackmore combined with Ronnie James Dio to make epic rock albums like *Rising* and *Long Live Rock 'n' Roll* before streamlining the sound and enjoying hit singles like "Since You've Been Gone" and "All Night Long." Rainbow were less celebrated than Deep Purple, but they feature much of Blackmore's finest writing and playing, and were one of the best live acts of the era. They are much missed.

Back to the Beach: A Brian Wilson and the Beach Boys Reader REVISED EDITION
Ed Kingsley Abbott £14.00

Revised and expanded edition of the Beach Boys compendium *Mojo* magazine deemed an "essential purchase." This collection includes all of the best articles, interviews and reviews from the Beach Boys' four decades of music, including definitive pieces by Timothy White, Nick Kent and David Leaf. New material reflects on the tragic death of Carl Wilson and documents the rejuvenated Brian's return to the boards. "Rivetting!" **** *Q* "An essential purchase." *Mojo*

Harmony in My Head
The Original Buzzcock Steve Diggle's
Rock 'n' Roll Odyssey
by Steve Diggle and Terry Rawlings £14.99

First-hand account of the punk wars from guitarist and one half of the songwriting duo that gave the world three chord punk-pop classics like "Ever Fallen In Love" and "Promises". Diggle dishes the dirt on punk contemporaries like The Sex Pistols, The Clash and The Jam, as well as sharing poignant memories of his friendship with Kurt Cobain, on whose last ever tour, The Buzzcocks were support act.

Serge Gainsbourg: A Fistful of Gitanes
by Sylvie Simmons £9.99

Rock press legend Simmons' hugely acclaimed biography of the French genius.

"I would recommend *A Fistful of Gitanes* [as summer reading] which is a highly entertaining biography of the French singer-songwriter and all-round scallywag"- JG Ballard

"A wonderful introduction to one of the most overlooked songwriters of the 20th century" (Number 3, top music books of 2001) *The Times*

"The most intriguing music-biz biography of the year" *The Independent*

"Wonderful. Serge would have been so happy" – Jane Birkin

Blues: The British Connection
by Bob Brunning £14.99

Former Fleetwood Mac member Bob Brunning's classic account of the impact of Blues in Britain, from its beginnings as the underground music of 50s teenagers like Mick Jagger, Keith Richards and Eric Clapton, to the explosion in the 60s, right through to the vibrant scene of the present day.

'An invaluable reference book and an engaging personal memoir' – Charles Shaar Murray

On The Road With Bob Dylan
by Larry Sloman £12.99

In 1975, as Bob Dylan emerged from 8 years of seclusion, he dreamed of putting together a travelling music show that would trek across the country like a psychedelic carnival. The dream became a reality, and *On The Road With Bob Dylan* is the ultimate behind-the-scenes look at what happened. When Dylan and the Rolling Thunder Revue took to the streets of America, Larry "Ratso" Sloman was with them every step of the way.

"*The War and Peace* of Rock and Roll." – Bob Dylan

Gram Parsons: God's Own Singer
by Jason Walker £12.99

Brand new biography of the man who pushed The Byrds into country-rock territory on *Sweethearts of The Rodeo*, and quit to form the Flying Burrito Brothers. Gram lived hard, drank hard, took every drug going and somehow invented country rock, paving the way for Crosby, Stills & Nash, The Eagles and Neil Young. Parsons' second solo LP, *Grievous Angel*, is a haunting masterpiece of country soul. By the time it was released, he had been dead for 4 months. He was 26 years old.

"Walker has done an admirable job in taking us as close to the heart and soul of Gram Parsons as any author could." **** *Uncut* book of the month

Ashley Hutchings: The Guvnor and the Rise of Folk Rock – Fairport Convention, Steeleye Span and the Albion Band
by Geoff Wall and Brian Hinton £14.99

As founder of Fairport Convention and Steeleye Span, Ashley Hutchings is the pivotal figure in the history of folk rock. This book draws on hundreds of hours of interviews with Hutchings and other folk-rock artists and paints a vivid picture of the scene that also produced Sandy Denny, Richard Thompson, Nick Drake, John Martyn and Al Stewart.

The Beach Boys' *Pet Sounds*: The Greatest Album of the Twentieth Century
by Kingsley Abbott £11.95

Pet Sounds is the 1966 album that saw The Beach Boys graduate from lightweight pop like "Surfin' USA", et al, into a vehicle for the mature compositional genius of Brian Wilson. The album was hugely influential, not least on The Beatles. This the full story of the album's background, its composition and recording, its contemporary reception and its enduring legacy.

King Crimson: In The Court of King Crimson
by Sid Smith £14.99

King Crimson's 1969 masterpiece *In The Court Of The Crimson King*, was a huge U.S. chart hit. The band followed it with 40 further albums of consistently challenging, distinctive and innovative music. Drawing on hours of new interviews, and encouraged by Crimson supremo Robert Fripp, the author traces the band's turbulent history year by year, track by track.

A Journey Through America with the Rolling Stones
by Robert Greenfield UK Price £9.99
Featuring a new foreword by Ian Rankin

This is the definitive account of their legendary '72 tour.

"Filled with finely-rendered detail ... a fascinating tale of times we shall never see again" *Mojo*

The Sharper Word: A Mod Reader
Ed Paolo Hewitt

Hewitt's hugely readable collection documents the clothes, the music, the clubs, the drugs and the faces behind one of the most misunderstood and enduring cultural movements and includes hard to find pieces by Tom Wolfe, bestselling novelist Tony Parsons, poet laureate Andrew Motion, disgraced Tory grandee Jonathan Aitken, Nik Cohn, Colin MacInnes, Mary Quant, and Irish Jack.

"An unparalleled view of the world-conquering British youth cult." *The Guardian*

"An excellent account of the sharpest-dressed subculture." *Loaded*, Book of the Month
ISBN 1-900924-34-X
192pp   £9.99

www.helterskelterbooks.com

All Helter Skelter, Firefly and SAF titles are available by mail order from
www.helterskelterbooks.com
Or from our office:
Helter Skelter Publishing Limited
Southbank House
Black Prince Road
London SE1 7SJ

Telephone: +44 (0) 20 7463 2204 or Fax: +44 (0)20 7463 2295
Mail order office hours: Mon-Fri 10:00am – 1:30pm,
By post, enclose a cheque [must be drawn on a British bank],
International Money Order, or credit card number and expiry date.
Postage prices per book worldwide are as follows:

UK & Channel Islands	£1.50
Europe & Eire (air)	£2.95
USA, Canada (air)	£7.50
Australasia, Far East (air)	£9.00

Email: info@helterskelterbooks.com